Organizing to Win

Organizing to Win

New Research on Union Strategies

Edited by

Kate Bronfenbrenner

Sheldon Friedman

Richard W. Hurd

Rudolph A. Oswald

Ronald L. Seeber

ILR Press

an imprint of CORNELL UNIVERSITY PRESS

ITHACA AND LONDON

First published 1998 by Cornell University Press
First printing, Cornell Paperbacks, 1998

Printed in the United States of America

Library of Congress Cataloging-in-Publication Data

Organizing to win : new research on union strategies/ edited by Kate
    Bronfenbrenner...[et al.].
        p.   cm.
    Includes bibliographical references (p.   ) and index.
    ISBN 0-8014-8446-4 (pbk : alk. paper)
    1. Trade-unions—Organizing—United States. I. Bronfenbrenner,
    Kate, 1954– .
HD6490.O72U66D 1997
331.89'12—dc21   97-28827

Cornell University Press strives to use environmentally responsible
suppliers and materials to the fullest extent possible in the publishing of
its books. Such materials include vegetable-based, low-VOC inks and
acid-free papers that are recycled, totally chlorine-free, or partly composed of nonwood fibers. Books that bear the logo of the FSC (Forest
Stewardship Council) use paper taken from forests that have been
inspected and certified as meeting the highest standards for environmental and social responsibility. For further information, visit our website at
www.cornellpress.cornell.edu.

Paperback printing   10 9 8 7 6 5 4 3

*This book is dedicated to the workers whose story it tells,
who toil in factories and schools, on highways and at construction
sites, in hospitals and office buildings—and to all workers
everywhere who are fighting for the better life and better world
that unionism can bring—to all those organizing to win!*

Contents

Acknowledgments

Preparing and producing a volume such as this one requires the dedication and assistance of many people. The editors wish to acknowledge those who played a special role in the conference where the papers that became the chapters in this volume were first presented and in preparing the final manuscript for publication. We would especially like to thank John Sweeney, president of the AFL-CIO, for setting the stage for the conference with his inspiring keynote address, "AFL-CIO Organizing Initiatives." Special thanks also need to be given to Vincent O'Brien of the AFL-CIO for his work in publicizing the conference within the labor community, recruiting union organizers to serve as discussants, and coordinating the rank-and-file panel that was a highlight of the conference.

We also thank the other featured speakers from the AFL-CIO: Marilyn Sneiderman, director of field mobilization; Richard Bensinger, director of organizing; and Andy Levin, assistant director of organizing for cooperative campaigns. In addition, the discussion of the future of organizing research was framed by two panels featuring Martie Voland, UNITE; William Cooke, Wayne State University; Stephen Lerner, AFL-CIO organizing department; Daniel Cornfield, Vanderbilt University; and Tom Juravich, University of Massachusetts, Amherst, who also deserves special appreciation for his rousing performance of labor songs.

Several others at the AFL-CIO and at Cornell University also played important roles in the conference. Teresa Shutters and Christine Shingleton of the AFL-CIO handled conference arrangements in Washington, D.C., coordinating with Robin Burke of Cornell. Katie Briggs from Cornell assisted with conference registration and, with Theresa Woodhouse from Cornell, helped prepare the final manuscript.

Special thanks are extended to the more than sixty academics and trade unionists who presented papers at the conference and who served as session chairs and discussants. We also thank the labor studies students and other volunteers who served as recorders at all the conference sessions, including Jay Armstrong (University of Massachusetts, Amherst); Tanya Boone, Jason

Coulter, and Amy Foerster (Cornell); Michael Eisenscher (University of Massachusetts, Boston); Iain Gold and Helen Jorgensen (AFL-CIO research assistants); John Logan (University of California); and Jennifer Senick-Goldstein (University of California, Los Angeles).

We also express our appreciation for the support and contributions of Fran Benson of Cornell University Press/ILR Press, her staff, and the outside readers she enlisted to do the hard work of reviewing all of the papers in the book.

Finally, and most significant, we acknowledge the contributions of the panel of rank-and-file trade union organizers who participated in the conference: Dee Dee Roberts, UNITE; Kaye Jaeger, SEIU; Yanira Merino and Amelia Estrada, LIUNA; and Anthony Montoya, AFSCME. Their inspirational stories of their organizing victories gave meaning to the research that was presented at the conference and that is summarized in this book.

The Editors

Organizing to Win

Introduction

Kate Bronfenbrenner, Sheldon Friedman, Richard W. Hurd, Rudolph A. Oswald, and Ronald L. Seeber

The American labor movement is at a watershed. For the first time since the early years of industrial unionism sixty years ago, there is near-universal agreement among union leaders that the future of the movement depends on massive new organizing. In October 1995, John Sweeney, Richard Trumka, and Linda Chavez-Thompson were swept into the top offices of the AFL-CIO, following a campaign that promised organizing "at an unprecedented pace and scale." Since taking office, the new AFL-CIO leadership team has created a separate organizing department and has committed $20 million to support coordinated large-scale industry-based organizing drives. In addition, in the summer of 1996, the AFL-CIO launched the "Union Summer" program, which placed more than a thousand college students and young workers in organizing campaigns across the country.

The events at the AFL-CIO are not happening in a vacuum. Simultaneously, some of the nation's other large unions, including the International Brotherhood of Teamsters (IBT), the Service Employees International Union (SEIU), the Communications Workers of America (CWA), the International Brotherhood of Electrical Workers (IBEW), and the newly merged Union of Needle Trades, Industrial, and Textile Employees (UNITE), have made significant structural adjustments at local and national levels to shift resources into organizing. Other unions, such as the Laborers' International Union of North America (LIUNA), the Oil, Chemical, and Atomic Workers (OCAW), and the United Paperworkers International Union (UPIU), have filled voids by establishing national organizing departments, reflecting newfound commitment to organizing from the top leadership of these unions. Many other unions, at both national and local levels, have increased their organizing activities significantly.

This influx of resources and commitment comes at a time when union density levels are at their lowest point since the 1930s and many scholars and pundits have been prepared to write off American unions as relics of a bygone industrial era, important in their time but no longer relevant for the new workplace of the 1990s. Yet recently the familiar litany of union failures and defeats in the nation's media has also given way to coverage of the labor movement's heightened sense of purpose and organizing victories. Whether SEIU's organizing gains among thousands of home health aides on the West Coast, UNITE's string of victories in manufacturing plants in the South, or LIUNA's recent successful campaign with asbestos workers in New York City, some unions are winning and winning big, despite employer opposition and despite an adverse organizing climate.

Individually, each of the efforts we have cited would have been striking for its aggressiveness even a few years ago. They have yet to translate into significant improvements either in union win rates or in the number of workers being organized, but, in combination, these developments reflect a significant strategic shift in focus on the part of American labor. At the core of these union efforts is one overriding goal—to reverse several trends: the decline in membership, stagnation in the organizing effort, and steadily shrinking bargaining and political power. For today's labor leaders, the question is no longer whether they need to make organizing on a massive scale the number-one priority but how that can best be achieved.

Unfortunately, until recently, very little research examined the effectiveness of union organizing strategies and tactics. With this in mind, the AFL-CIO and Cornell University's School of Industrial and Labor Relations jointly sponsored a conference in April 1996 aimed at generating new research on the conditions contributing to union success in organizing the unorganized. The twenty papers in this volume, which were presented at that conference, represent a major leap forward in the body of research available to those scholars, practitioners, and members of the general public who want to develop a better understanding of the organizing strategies and issues currently being debated in the labor movement.

Labor's Challenge

The recent stirrings in the labor movement come at a time when private-sector union density levels have reached their lowest point since the early 1930s. A combination of aggressive organizing, economic expansion, and a favorable political, legal, and social climate allowed for unprecedented growth in union organizing and power in the United States in the 1930s and 1940s, culminating in 1946, when the union share of the workforce peaked at 37 percent. Although membership continued to grow in absolute terms through the 1970s, unions failed to keep pace with the rapidly expanding workforce. After 1946, the percentage of the labor force belonging to unions dropped slowly but steadily to 21 percent by 1980. Thereafter, the decline continued, and membership dipped below 15 percent in 1995 (U.S. Department of Labor, Bureau of Labor Statistics [BLS] 1940–80; Bureau of National Affairs [BNA] 1996:D19).

With only 11 percent of the private-sector labor force now organized, the labor movement stands at a critical juncture. More than 300,000 new members must be recruited each year merely to keep up with the growth of the labor force and compensate for the thousands of union jobs lost each year as a result of layoffs and plant closings. Clearly, millions more must be organized if the labor movement is ever going to recover the membership base it enjoyed in the decade following World War II.

There has been extensive debate in both the labor and academic community over the reasons for the decline in union density.[1] Several explanations have been highlighted, including the changing economic and political climate, growing opposition to unions from employers, deficiencies in the law, and declining effort on the part of unions.

Most labor activists and scholars agree that several gradual but dramatic shifts in the economy have contributed to the challenges unions face today. The rise of global competition, capital flight to low-wage countries and the nonunion Sun Belt, and the transition from a manufacturing economy to a service economy all are interrelated changes and have resulted in significant job loss in unionized industries. These broader economic changes have been coupled with equally dramatic technological changes and changes in work organization that have resulted in both significant losses of union jobs and an increasing reliance on a more flexible and more transitory contingent workforce of part-time, temporary, and contract employees. These pressures have been reinforced by government economic policies, especially trade liberalization and deregulation.

In spite of the importance of these changes, they offer only a partial explanation for the decline in unionization. In their comprehensive article reviewing research on factors contributing to union growth and decline, Gary N. Chaison and Joseph B. Rose (1991) conclude that although the changes in the economic environment have been important, they are responsible for less than one-third of union decline in the United States.

One thing is clear—the contraction in union density does not stem from a lack of interest by America's workers. Many millions of unorganized workers desire the benefits of union representation. Recent polls consistently show that more than one-third of all nonunionized workers would vote in favor of union representation today if given the chance to do so in

---

1. See Chaison and Rose 1991, Lawler 1990, Freeman 1985, Block and Premack 1983, and Fiorito and Greer 1982 for summaries of research on union decline.

their workplaces. The percentages are even higher for women workers, people of color, and younger workers (Lipset 1986; Freeman and Rogers 1994; Hart Associates and the Mellman Group 1996).

Polls also show that millions of additional workers would vote for union representation were it not for employer opposition. After all, in the public sector, where aggressive employer opposition to unionization is extremely rare, union win rates and victory margins are well over 85 percent (Bronfenbrenner and Juravich 1995a). After reviewing evidence on the relationship between public attitudes toward unions and density rates, Chaison and Rose dismiss claims that "[worker] hostility towards unions may influence the ability of unions to recruit new members" (1991:30). They point instead to industrial relations policy and employer opposition as the most important explanations for union decline.

It is no accident that union density peaked in 1946, the year before enactment of the Taft-Hartley amendments to the Wagner Act. The amendments codified into law the decisions of an increasingly conservative National Labor Relations Board (NLRB) and federal judiciary, as the national political climate shifted from the New Deal toward a more business-friendly orientation. Taft-Hartley included strict limits on union organizing and mutual aid tactics while granting employers greater latitude in opposing unionization. In the postwar years, employers became more aggressive in their efforts to contain unionization to already organized industries (Harris 1982). The labor movement failed to respond effectively to this attack. Instead of redoubling their organizing efforts, most unions concentrated energy and resources on servicing their current members.

Although expansion in union density halted after Taft-Hartley, the full force of the changes in the legal climate for organizing was not felt immediately because unions were at their peak of economic power. In the 1970s and 1980s, however, with union membership declining absolutely in the private sector, employers became more aggressive and union-avoidance strategies more sophisticated. In addition, open violations of the laws increased. As Richard Freeman found in his 1985 study of employer behavior in union organizing campaigns: "From 1960 to 1980 the number of all employer unfair labor practice charges rose fourfold; the number of charges involving a firing for union activity rose threefold; and the number of workers awarded back pay or reinstated into their jobs rose fivefold (53)."

In the 1970s and 1980s, this antiunion offensive spawned an entire industry of management consultants who advised corporate America on how best to remain "union free." Employers and their consultants were emboldened in their union-busting efforts by a perception that they had support from the highest levels of government, especially after Ronald Reagan's 1981 discharge and replacement of the striking workers in the Professional

Air Traffic Controllers Organization (PATCO). Today, aggressive employer opposition to unions has become even more pervasive in the private sector. Workers who wish to form unions routinely encounter legal delays, intimidation, harassment, and discrimination. A recent study conducted by the labor ministries of the United States, Canada, and Mexico found that in the period 1992–95, more than one-third of U.S. employers faced with NLRB representation elections discharged workers for union activity, more than half threatened a full or partial shutdown of the company if the union succeeded in organizing the facility, and between 15 and 40 percent made illegal changes in wages, benefits, and working conditions, gave bribes or special favors to those who opposed the union, or used electronic surveillance of union activists during organizing campaigns (Commission for Labor Cooperation 1997).[2]

Even when an organizing campaign succeeds, employer opposition continues. Through a combination of legal and illegal bargaining strategies and management practices, including the discharges, threats, and intimidation so common in organizing campaigns, employers have succeeded in holding down the first contract rate to approximately two-thirds of all certification election wins (Cooke 1985; Bronfenbrenner 1994; Pavy and Smith 1996; Hurd 1996). In short, employer opposition and weak and poorly enforced labor laws have emerged as primary explanations for the decline of unions.

The right to form and join a union is a fundamental human and civil right. Its exercise should not require extraordinary personal heroism or subject workers to employer harassment and retribution. As the framers of the Wagner Act intended, the decision to form or join a union should be up to the workers, not their employers. Major overhaul of U.S. labor law and practice would be required to enforce this right.

At the same time, unions cannot simply look toward deficiencies in the law and other external conditions to explain their flagging fortunes. Unions themselves bear significant responsibility for the decline in unionization. In the decades after World War II, during a period when unions had both resources and bargaining power to launch massive organizing efforts, few unions organized aggressively. In 1970, unions organized 0.5 percent of the private-sector workforce through NLRB elections, compared with 1.5 percent in 1950. By 1980, this share had fallen to 0.25 and by 1985 to 0.10 percent (Freeman and Rebick 1989:31). Whole sectors of the economy, particularly low-wage service and light manufacturing firms employing large numbers of women and people of color, were left nearly untouched by union activity. Nor were the growing ranks of professional, technical, and

---

2. For a thorough discussion of the range of practices by employers during organizing campaigns, see the four chapters in "Part II: Organizing and the Law," in Friedman et al. 1994.

white-collar employees, except for those in the public sector, targeted for organizing.

In the 1970s and 1980s, there was a burst of new organizing among health-care and clerical workers, dominated by such unions as SEIU, District 65 of the United Automobile Workers (UAW), and Local 1199 of the Retail, Wholesale and Department Store Union (RWDSU). Coupled with the rapid growth in public-sector organizing, these new initiatives brought thousands of women and people of color into the labor movement. During the last two decades, however, most unions have continued to run fairly low-intensity traditional campaigns that relied on gate leafleting, mass mailings, and a few large meetings. Although those tactics may have been enough to organize workers in the more friendly organizing climate of the 1940s, they are clearly inadequate to overcome the ever-more sophisticated and more aggressive employer opposition workers routinely face in attempting to organize in the private sector today (Hurd 1997; Bronfenbrenner and Juravich 1995c; Bronfenbrenner 1997).

By the mid-1980s, unions were running fewer and fewer organizing campaigns in smaller and smaller units. At the same time, the nation's largest industrial unions had lost hundreds of thousands of members as unionized companies shut down, "automated," or drastically reduced production. By 1990, as win rates continued to hover below 50 percent, many unions began to recognize that they seriously needed to reevaluate both the resources they were committing to organizing and the intensity and quality of their organizing campaigns. They understood that they could not wait for a less hostile climate but instead needed to focus their efforts on the one element of the organizing process that was within their control—their organizing strategies and tactics. As the new officers of the AFL-CIO have put it, "The most critical challenge facing unions today is organizing. . . . We must first organize despite the law if we are ever going to organize with the law" (Sweeney, Trumka, and Chavez-Thompson 1995:5).

Why Organizing Matters

The outcome of organized labor's revitalization efforts will have influence well beyond national union offices and local union halls. The economic impact of the decline in union bargaining power has been felt throughout the workforce. Although not the only factor, this decline is closely tied to the rising economic polarization in American society. As a vast academic literature attests, unions raise wages. Unions also reduce wage inequality, increase equity (through the principle of "equal pay for equal work"), reduce gender- and race-related pay differentials, and tend to reduce age- and tenure-related pay differentials (Freeman 1992; Spalter-Roth, Hartmann, and Collins 1994). In a nation in which the constitutional right of free speech does not extend to the private-sector workplace, unions are also the only true vehicles for workplace democracy and the only means through which workers gain an independent voice regarding their daily working conditions.

According to the 1995 *Economic Report of the President,* a "significant portion of the increase in wage inequality during the last fifteen years" is due to the decline in unionization (President's Council of Economic Advisors 1995:182). Falling real wages, growing disparities in wealth, economic insecurity, and the erosion of the middle class are all tied in some way to the diminished presence of union representation. Even though unions most directly benefit those covered by collective bargaining agreements, the spillover to nonunion workers from a strong labor movement is substantial.

As union density declined in the 1970s and 1980s, the influence of the union sector on the wages and working conditions of nonunion workers diminished. Paradoxically, this decline occurred while productivity was rising. Since 1979, productivity has increased by 21 percent. Over the same period, the average weekly earnings of America's production and nonsupervisory workers has fallen by 12 percent after adjusting for inflation (AFL-CIO Department of Economic Research 1996; President's Council of Economic Advisors 1996:330, 332). Without strong unions, workers have been unable to capitalize on those gains in productivity and turn them into wage and benefit improvements. Meanwhile, without the restraining power of unions, corporate leaders have been emboldened to expropriate an ever-larger share of profits for themselves. Fifty years ago, executives were paid forty times the earnings of average workers; today, executives' salaries are more than two hundred times those of workers (Jost 1996). Since 1979, 97 percent of the aggregate increase in income has gone to the richest 20 percent of households (AFL-CIO Department of Economic Research 1996; U.S. Department of Commerce 1995).

Lower levels of unionization have also led to a loss in political power. The labor movement has been able to contribute to the enactment of legislation that benefits workers generally, such as civil rights laws, wage and hour regulations, plant-closing legislation, family and medical leave provisions, and occupational safety and health laws. In the last fifty years, however, even during periods of relative strength, unions have not been able to press successfully for "pro-union" legislation, such as labor law reform or a ban on hiring replacements for strikers. Today, with union density at its lowest point in over sixty years, even the protective laws are under attack as never before. At federal and state levels, conservative legislators are attempting to roll back long-standing protections, such as the Occupational Safety and Health Act (OSHA), the Davis Bacon Act, state workers' compensation, and the National Labor Relation Act's ban on company unions.

Labor's declining political power became starkly evident when the much-heralded Dunlop Commission, established by President Bill Clinton in 1993, failed to recommend the kind of substantive labor law reforms necessary to guarantee workers and unions their rights to organize and bargain collectively with their employers.[3] In the aftermath of the commission's recommendations, American labor leaders were faced with the grim reality that substantive labor law reform, no matter how badly it was needed or how well it was justified, could not be achieved without first significantly expanding labor's political power through massive new organizing of unorganized workers.

Research on Organizing

Given the prominence of the issue, it is surprising how little is known about the strategy, tactics, and process by which groups of workers form and join unions. Although there has been considerable macro-level research documenting the magnitude of labor's decline, there has been much less micro-level research that looks intensively at the organizing process itself, particularly the role played by union strategies and tactics. Furthermore, much of the academic research suffers because the samples are small, the databases are limited, and the researchers lack an understanding of how the union organizing process actually works. Most industrial relations research on private-sector organizing continues to focus primarily on the election, unit, and employer variables easily accessible from NLRB data. From this research we have learned much about the influence of environmental factors, the National Labor Relations Board, and worker attitudes toward unions. Despite the great volume of research, however, few studies examine the actual process of union organizing campaigns and the importance of union characteristics and strategies in determining election outcomes.

There are several different streams of quantitative research on organizing: studies of workers' and the public's attitudes toward unions, individual voter decision studies, bargaining unit-level studies, organizational-level studies, and time-series research. Complementing the quantitative research is a small body of qualitative case study literature.

The attitudinal research on organizing focuses primarily on the relationship between workers' attitudes toward unions and organizing success. This research includes studies that compare differences in attitudes and characteristics between union members and nonmembers and between unorganized workers "with a propensity to organize" and those who do not see any benefit in bringing a union into their workplace. Several of these studies, such as the 1977 Quality of Employment Survey conducted by the Univer-

---

3. For a summary of the problems facing the commission, see Friedman et al. 1994.

sity of Michigan, have relied on national surveys (Kochan 1979; Farber 1983; Jarley and Fiorito 1991) or on Gallup and Harris Poll data on workers' changing attitudes toward work and the labor movement (Bok and Dunlop 1970; Lipset 1986). This body of research can be helpful in determining which groups of workers have the most positive attitudes toward unions and which variables contribute most in determining their attitudes toward unions. Since these studies measure attitudes and not actual union votes, however, they do not necessarily tell us which workers would be most likely to vote for a union in an actual campaign. To date, none of this research has examined the role played by union organizing strategies in influencing and changing workers' attitudes toward unions.

Individual voter studies examine the factors affecting individual workers' decisions to vote for or against a union in a specific certification election. The primary factors analyzed in these studies include job satisfaction, attitudes toward unions, individual characteristics, campaign characteristics, and the organizing climate (Getman, Goldberg, and Herman 1976; LeLouarn 1980; Schriesheim 1978; Wheeler and McClendon 1991). Although these studies better reflect the propensity of workers to organize than do surveys of workers' attitudes, they suffer from serious methodological limitations. Particularly problematic is their limited scope and generalizability, since most involve small samples of workers employed at a single work site.

The largest body of quantitative research on organizing includes bargaining unit-level studies of NLRB certification elections (e.g., Cooke 1983; Seeber 1983; Lawler 1984; Reed 1989; Maranto and Fiorito 1987; Hurd and McElwain 1988). This research tends to focus on the effect that external economic and political factors, combined with union and employer characteristics and tactics, have on certification election outcomes or the percentage of votes for unionization. Most of this research has been based on NLRB election tapes, thereby limiting the data to such variables as unit size, election type, number of days between petition and election, industry, unit, and unfair labor practices. Researchers have supplemented these data with employer and organizing climate data collected from other sources for variables such as unemployment rates, firm versus industry wage differentials, corporate structure, and regional demographic and political variables. The NLRB data have given researchers easy access to comprehensive and representative samples. But, in return for the large sample, these studies sacrifice important insights into the organizing process because there is no way to acquire more than minimal information from the NLRB on bargaining unit demographics, employer tactics, and union characteristics and tactics.

A small number of studies have focused on the variance in organizing trends among specific unions, employers, or industries (e.g., Craft and Extejt 1983; Reed 1992). Although this research has the potential to provide important insights into the relationships among union characteristics, tactics, organizing resources, and organizing success rates, to date these studies are few in number and limited in scope.

The final category of quantitative research includes time-series studies that focus on factors contributing to changes in union density, percentage union votes, or union election win rates over a specific period of time (e.g., Ashenfelter and Pencavel 1969; Bain and Elsheikh 1976; Dickens and Leonard 1985; Rose and Chaison 1990). These factors include economic, political, and legal variables as well as changes in workforce demographics and employer and union structure and tactics. Although time-series research may give us a better understanding of the impact of a changing environment, it provides little concrete information that can aid unions currently attempting to revitalize their organizing strategies, since there are no data on organizing strategies that would enable us to track changes in strategy and tactics over time.

In combination, the quantitative research on organizing has taught us a great deal about the influence of environmental factors, the National Labor Relations Board, and workers' attitudes toward unions. More recently, a great many studies have focused on employers' behavior during certification elections and on the effectiveness of employer strategies in thwarting union organizing efforts. With the exception of recent research by Kate Bronfenbrenner (1997), Bronfenbrenner and Tom Juravich (1995b), and Richard B. Peterson, Thomas Lee, and Barbara Finnegan (1992), most of these studies fail to address the critical role played by union strategies in the organizing process.

When union strategies are included in certification election models along with organizing climate, bargaining unit demographics, and employer tactics and characteristics, union strategies have been found to play a greater role in explaining election outcomes than any other group of variables. As recent work by Bronfenbrenner has shown, in a climate of intense and pervasive employer opposition, union success in NLRB elections depends most on the quality and intensity of union organizing campaigns (1995b, 1997).

Although the role of union strategies in the organizing process has been largely ignored in the quantitative research, since the mid-1980s a small body of qualitative case study research has been developing that closely examines union campaigns (e.g., Green and Tilly 1987; Hurd 1989; Fetonte and Braden 1990; Lynn and Brister 1989). These studies typically contain descriptive analyses of one or more union drives, based primarily on interviews with organizers, bargaining unit members, and employers. Supplementing these sources are union and management campaign material,

NLRB records, BNA reports, and newspaper articles. Unlike other academic research, case studies rarely include statistical analysis and are often written by labor educators and union staff members rather than by industrial relations researchers. In fact, many of the authors of these studies are involved in the campaigns as participant observers. Because the authors are much more likely to have organizing experience or familiarity with organizing campaigns, these studies often do a much better job of capturing the reality of the organizing process, particularly the complex interaction of employer and union characteristics and tactics, than many quantitative studies.

There are some major weaknesses associated with case study research, however. Without random sampling, the cases selected are often unrepresentative of the typical campaign. Many focus on major union victories, large and nationally known white-collar bargaining units, which are not representative of the majority of union organizing campaigns. Further, by focusing on one or two campaigns, the researchers may be unable to determine how much of what occurred was simply specific to the conditions prevailing in those campaigns. Too many of these studies lack critical analysis, neglecting or avoiding the weaknesses of the union campaign. Nonetheless, despite these limitations, case studies can play a very important role in clarifying the organizing process and in filling in the gaping holes in the quantitative research.

Origins of This Book

Despite the value of this organizing research, with few exceptions it has not contributed in a practical way to union efforts to confront the organizing challenge. What is missing from most of the studies is the critical role of union strategies and tactics in the organizing process and how those strategies interact with broader environmental factors, bargaining unit demographics, and employer tactics and characteristics to determine outcomes. The editors of this volume believe that the labor movement could clearly benefit from sound research that addresses these issues.

It was in this spirit that the AFL-CIO Department of Economic Research and the School of Industrial and Labor Relations at Cornell University jointly set up the conference that led to the development of the research and papers on union organizing that has resulted in this book. In setting up the conference, we sought to encourage the presentation of both case studies and quantitative research on innovative union organizing strategies across all industries and sectors of the economy. In addition, we sought to encourage joint union and academic interaction on research projects. Often unions have information and data of great interest to academics but have neither the time nor interest necessary to analyze the information. Academics have the necessary research tools but often lack access to concrete data and information. We sought to bring together these two groups to produce research that would provide fresh insights into the current state of union organizing in both the public and private sectors and to make that research accessible to both trade unionists and academics.

In our call for conference papers, we also sought to encourage research in previously neglected aspects of the union organizing process, particularly non-NLRB and community-based campaigns, industry-based studies, and both qualitative and quantitative studies that focused on innovative union organizing strategies and the relationship between those strategies and employer behavior, bargaining unit demographics, and workers' and the public's attitudes toward unions. We received more than sixty proposals for papers for our conference, reflecting the renewed interest and commitment to organizing in both the labor and academic communities.

The conference, which was held from March 31 to April 2, 1996, brought together more than two hundred trade unionists and academics from a wide range of disciplines who support workers' rights to organize and was opened by AFL-CIO president John Sweeney, who outlined his administration's agenda for organizing. Nearly forty papers were presented, all of which offered new and original research on factors contributing to union success or failure in organizing campaigns. In addition to generating new research that greatly expanded our knowledge and understanding of the organizing process, the conference provided a rare and valuable opportunity for dialogue between union organizers on the front lines and academics whose research has been dedicated to the study of organizing.

Outline of the Volume

This volume contains a selection of the papers from the Cornell University–AFL-CIO conference. We have grouped the papers into five parts, reflecting common themes. Part I, "Strategic Initiatives in Union Organizing," sets the stage for the volume by focusing on broad questions of strategy. Part II, "Overcoming Barriers to Worker Support for Unions," offers insight and a variety of tactical suggestions on the relationship of the labor movement to unorganized workers. Part III, "Community-Based Organizing," presents a series of case studies that share the common focus of union organizing rooted in a broader community-based strategy. Part IV, "Building Membership and Public Support for Organizing," contains case studies that analyze membership involvement and the development of alliances with clergy and other community groups. Finally, part V, "Organizing Initiatives by Industry and Sector," includes industry-based essays that analyze experiences from the coal mining, construction, and steel industries and from the public sector.

The essays we have included represent a diversity of both qualitative and quantitative research methods. In combination, they make a significant contribution to filling the void in research on union organizing strategies and to addressing some of the methodological weaknesses permeating so much of the previous research in this area.[4] The quantitative studies are representative of four of the major research streams, including studies on workers' attitudes toward unions, individual voter studies, bargaining unit-level election outcome studies, and organizational research. Yet, unlike so much of the earlier research, the essays in this volume provide a much richer portrait of the organizing process and the critical role played by union strategies. The essays by Jack Fiorito and Angela Young and by Dan Cornfield and his coauthors use population survey data to examine the potential role union strategies can play in influencing workers' attitudes toward unions before and during organizing campaigns in an atmosphere of anti-union employer tactics or when combined with community involvement, respectively. Similarly, the essays by Larry Cohen and Richard Hurd and by Roger D. Weikle, Hoyt N. Wheeler, and John A. McClendon examine the effect of employer opposition on workers' propensity to vote for a union but, unlike earlier individual voter studies, go on to examine the implications of their findings for union organizing strategies. The bargaining unit-level studies, including James Rundle's and the two essays by Kate Bronfenbrenner and Tom Juravich, build on Bronfenbrenner's earlier work on union strategies by focusing on new areas (Rundle's work on employee involvement) and new sectors (Juravich and Bronfenbrenner's public-sector study) and by tracking changes in employer and union behavior over time (Bronfenbrenner and Juravich). Organizational studies by Immanuel Ness and by Fernando Gapasin and Howard Wial lay the groundwork for future quantitative research on non-NLRB organizing strategies and the role of central labor councils, respectively, in the organizing process.

The qualitative research included in this volume also makes an important contribution by addressing some of the methodological and analytical weaknesses so prevalent in earlier case study research. These include the seminal essay by Roger Waldinger and his coauthors in which a group of scholars from a wide range of social science disciplines provide an in-depth critical analysis of the Los Angeles Justice for Janitors campaign; Gregor Murray's comparative analysis of the disparate organizing strategies of two districts of Steelworkers in Canada; Katherine Sciacchitano's comprehensive analysis of the United Electrical Workers' organizing and first contract vic-

4. The papers were chosen based on the quality of the research and analysis and the contribution they make to our understanding of successful union organizing strategies. The views and recommendations of the authors are not necessarily fully shared by the editors, the AFL-CIO, or Cornell University.

tory among African American workers at the Steeltech plant in inner-city Milwaukee; and Bill Fletcher, Jr., and Richard Hurd's important analytical work on the implications of the servicing and organizing models of unionism for union organizing success. Going well beyond the somewhat superficial pieces that constitute so much of case study research, these essays do an excellent job of expanding the framework of analysis beyond an individual union in an individual campaign to address critically the broader social, economic, and strategic issues that affect organizing success.

Other case studies follow a more traditional model by telling the story of one or more campaigns, but once again they greatly expand our knowledge and understanding of the importance of union strategies by focusing on new areas neglected in previous research. Included in this group are essays on the role of clergy in organizing, by Ronald Peters and Theresa Merrill; on rank-and-file participation in organizing, by Lowell Turner and by Bruce Nissen; on community-based organizing, by Ruth Needleman; and on organizing in specific industries such as coal, by Adrienne M. Birecree, and construction, by Janet Lewis and Bill Mirand and by Brian Condit and his coauthors.

Conclusion

The reemphasis in the labor movement on organizing presents a unique opportunity to conduct a critical analysis of which organizing strategies are most effective in rapidly and dramatically reversing labor's declining membership and power. Until now, there was a paucity of academic research that unions could use to aid them in their efforts. By significantly expanding this body of research and by encouraging research of a higher standard in both method and relevance, this volume provides union leaders with information and analysis to aid them in their current organizing efforts and, at the same time, lays the foundation for future research.

This volume is only a beginning, however. As the labor movement rapidly expands its organizing efforts and initiatives, there is a great need for continued research on effective strategies and tactics. It is our hope that this book will spawn more extensive research on areas first addressed here, such as non-NLRB organizing, industry- and community-based campaigns, and the role of central labor councils, community groups, and volunteer organizers. We also hope that this work generates research in critical aspects of organizing that are not addressed here, such as the role of race and gender in organizing, strategic targeting, training and recruitment of organizers, union commitment of financial resources, and large-scale multiunion campaigns. There is clearly a great deal of work to be done and many critical questions that still need to be answered.

Will the AFL-CIO and individual unions be able to help large numbers of unorganized workers attain union representation without labor law reform? Will unions be able to shift the necessary resources to organizing so as to overcome a hostile employer community and weak and poorly enforced labor laws? Will wider use of the best available organizing tactics and strategies help unions surmount their daunting challenges? Will these organizing initiatives play a significant role in reversing the deteriorating economic and social conditions of most American workers? These are among the questions that this volume leaves with the reader and the questions that face everyone who values and supports a strong and independent labor movement. The answers will be significant in shaping the labor movement, our system of industrial relations, and the fate of American workers for a generation to come.

Building a Framework
for Sustainable Organizing

Achieving consensus on the importance of organizing and allocating significant resources to the task do not ensure success. The chapters in part I deal with the challenges unions face as they attempt to build a framework for sustainable organizing. The first hurdle, implementation of organizing strategies and tactics that lead to victory, is addressed by Bronfenbrenner and Juravich, who build on their pioneering work on this subject. The second hurdle is to institutionalize organizing at all levels of the labor movement; the other two essays in part I report on structural innovations that respond to this challenge. Fletcher and Hurd analyze efforts in the Service Employees International Union (SEIU) to transform local unions to ensure that organizing is a continuing priority. Gapasin and Wial report on initiatives by central labor councils to support organizing by affiliated unions.

Chapter 1, Bronfenbrenner and Juravich's study, presents a revealing analysis of the modest progress unions have made in adapting organizing strategies to fit the difficult contemporary environment. They estimate that in 1994 only 15 percent of American unions were running the aggressive grassroots campaigns that Bronfenbrenner's earlier research had shown are essential to overcoming employer opposition to unionization. The authors argue that the relative weakness of union campaigns in a climate of increased employer opposition helps explain why recent organizing initiatives have produced only modest results. They also conclude, however, that when unions do run comprehensive rank-and-file campaigns, win rates improve considerably. These findings build a strong case that unions can win despite the current economic and political climate.

Chapter 2, by Fletcher and Hurd, is based on an analysis of twelve local unions of SEIU with active organizing agendas. Their research is potentially extremely important because local unions control 70 percent of the financial resources of the labor movement, so that their direct involvement in organizing is essential. Fletcher and Hurd find that internal mobilization that does not also focus on the recruitment of new members through external organizing will not be sufficient to revitalize the labor movement. Indeed, they uncover real limitations of such a focus, including staff burnout and difficulty in sustaining rank-and-file involvement and commitment. Concentration on external organizing creates other problems, but they can be surmounted and rank-and-file acceptance can be won when external organizing is integrated into all the work of the local union. Fletcher and Hurd commend this strategy for providing hope that union organizing can be revitalized at the local level.

Gapasin and Wial round out part I with a unique view of central labor councils (CLCs), a small but growing number of which have become active in their support of union organizing. Gapasin and Wial find considerable variation in the role of CLCs in organizing, rooted in differences in the orientation of the leaders. The authors divide leadership styles into two broad orientations—conventional and transformative. Conventional leaders view the CLC as a self-contained provider of services to affiliated unions, while leaders with a transformative orientation see the CLC as part of a larger network of groups advancing a pro-worker agenda. Gapasin and Wial conclude that transformative leaders tend to conduct a broader range of organizing activities and are more deeply involved in the process. By training volunteer rank-and-file organizers, coordinating multiunion campaigns, creating associate membership programs, and forging alliances with nonlabor community groups, these leaders succeed in building support for organizing.

Chapter 1

It Takes More Than House Calls: Organizing to Win with a Comprehensive Union-Building Strategy

Kate Bronfenbrenner and Tom Juravich

Until recently, some national and local union leaders still argued that labor should circle the wagons and take care of existing members rather than spend scarce resources on organizing nonunion workers. Today those voices have largely been silenced by the hard numbers of labor's dramatic decline. As expressed in the platform of the new AFL-CIO leadership slate, the American labor movement must "organize at an unprecedented pace and scale." The question unions face today is no longer whether to make organizing a priority but how that can best be achieved.

Yet it is important to recognize that organizing has become increasingly difficult. Under the crushing weight of weak and poorly enforced labor laws, rabidly antiunion employers, and an increasingly hostile political and economic climate, it is no wonder that so few American workers overcome the threats, fears, and delays and go on to actually organize a union and bargain a first agreement. Matters are only made worse when labor leaders are told time and again by their supposed friends in government and academia that American workers are no longer interested in unions but see a more viable and less threatening alternative in management-proffered participation programs.

Faced with an increasingly hostile environment, the labor movement has begun to focus its energy on the one element of the organizing process that it controls—union strategies and tactics. For some organizers, this has meant organizing outside the traditional NLRB process through broader community-based and industry-based organizing campaigns. For others, this has meant critically analyzing union organizing strategies used during the NLRB election process, from targeting to winning elections to bargaining first agreements.

Unfortunately, although considerable macro-level research documents the magnitude of labor's decline, surprisingly little micro-level research looks intensively at the organizing process itself, particularly the importance of union strategies and tactics. In part, this is because many industrial relations researchers are not convinced that union tactics play a significant role in determining election outcomes. Some researchers, such as William T. Dickens (1983), believe that union tactics are entirely reactive, determined solely by management tactics. Other researchers may believe that union tactics matter but are unable to include them in their research models because they either have a limited understanding of the range of union organizing tactics or lack access to union campaign data. Thus, most industrial relations research on private-sector organizing continues to focus primarily on the election, unit, and employer variables easily accessible in NLRB databases.[1]

Bronfenbrenner's study of private-sector NLRB certification election and first-contract campaigns that took place in 1986 and 1987 provided the first comprehensive analysis of the most effective union organizing strategies (Bronfenbrenner 1993 and 1997). The findings suggest that union success in certification election and first-contract campaigns depends on using an aggressive grassroots rank-and-file strategy focused on building a union and acting like a union from the very beginning of the campaign. Although the research confirmed the prevalence of egregious employer behavior in the private sector and the effectiveness of that opposition in thwarting union efforts to win elections and bargain first contracts, it also showed that unions can overcome even the most intense opposition when they run aggressive bottom-up campaigns.

In the almost ten years since the elections Bronfenbrenner addressed in her study, dramatic changes have taken place in the organizing arena. Many of the largest unions in the country have shifted resources into organizing and have revamped their training and recruitment programs for organizers, putting more focus into conducting more aggressive and more strategic campaigns. Other unions have turned to the AFL-CIO Organizing Institute for help in screening and recruiting new organizing staff. But despite these efforts, NLRB election win rates remain below 50 percent and fewer than one-third of the more than 300,000 private-sector workers who attempt to organize each year end up being covered under collective bargaining agreements. Clearly it is time to reevaluate union campaigns to determine

---

1. For a detailed review of the literature on union tactics, see Bronfenbrenner 1993 and Lawler 1990.

whether unions have made significant changes in how they organize and, if so, why those changes have not resulted in greater organizing success.

This chapter examines data on 165 NLRB certification election campaigns conducted in 1994 to track the changes that have occurred in union and employer behavior since Bronfenbrenner's study. In so doing we test the hypothesis that unions make significant organizing gains only when they utilize a comprehensive union-building strategy. Simply throwing money and staff at campaigns is not enough to overcome employer resistance and worker fear. Nor does any individual organizing tactic—whether sophisticated media campaigns, stockholder actions, or a blitz house calling of every worker in the unit—guarantee success. House calling, in particular, has in some quarters been offered as the silver bullet, the panacea for all types of organizing campaigns.

But to be successful in today's hostile climate with today's workers, it takes more than just house calls. We suggest that unions will continue to fail in organizing if all they do is graft individual innovative tactics onto more traditional organizing approaches. Further, we hypothesize that these tactics are truly effective only when they are integrated into a comprehensive rank-and-file approach to organizing that focuses on the use of personal contact, leadership development, and a combination of aggressive and creative internal and external pressure tactics.

Private-Sector Organizing in 1986–87

Bronfenbrenner's 1986–87 study (1993 and 1997) was designed to evaluate the influence of several factors that contribute to union success or failure in certification election campaigns. Through a survey of the lead organizers in 261 NLRB campaigns, Bronfenbrenner was able to determine which union tactics had the most positive impact on election outcomes while controlling for the impact of election environment, organizers' background, bargaining unit demographics, and employer characteristics and tactics. A summary of the findings from the original study is presented in the first three columns of table 1.1.

Perhaps the most striking finding of Bronfenbrenner's study was that union tactics as a group play a greater role in explaining election outcome than any other group of variables, including employer characteristics and tactics, bargaining unit demographics, organizers' background, and election environment. This suggests that union strategies not only matter in determining election outcome but that they may matter more than many other factors.

For the labor movement, this means that union strategies and tactics can make a significant difference in whether unions win or lose elections, even

TABLE 1.1 Summary of NLRB Election Campaigns, 1986–87 and 1994

	1986–87 NLRB Elections			1994 NLRB Elections		
	Sample proportion or mean	Proportion or mean for wins	Percentage win rate[a]	Sample proportion or mean	Proportion or mean for wins	Percentage win rate[a]
OUTCOME						
Election outcome	.43	1.00	.43 (.00)	.42	1.00	.42 (.00)
Percentage union vote	.47	.65	NA	.49	.71	NA
First contract outcome	.35	.75	NA	.27	.65	NA
UNIT BACKGROUND						
Sector: Service	.34	.39	.48 (.39)	.28	.46	.70 (.31)
Manufacturing	.66	.61	.39 (.48)	.72	.54	.31 (.70)
Number of eligible voters	138	105	NA	178	141	NA
Percentage women in unit	.46	.54	NA	.39	.43	NA
Unit at least 75% women	.27	.39	.59 (.36)	.19	.28	.61 (.37)
Percentage people of color in unit	.28	.34	NA	.28	.31	NA
Unit at least 75% people of color	.14	.21	.64 (.39)	.12	.13	.45 (.41)
Average wage	6.31	5.72	NA	8.74	8.35	NA
Other units of employer organized	.46	.52	.49 (.38)	.38	.42	.46 (.39)
Unit different than petition	.22	.12	.22 (.47)	.25	.20	.33 (.43)
EMPLOYER TACTICS						
Outside consultant	.71	.67	.40 (.50)	.87	.81	.39 (.62)
Five or more captive-audience meetings	.33	.22	.28 (.49)	.64	.45	.29 (.64)
Five or more company letters	.40	.36	.38 (.45)	.24	.23	.40 (.42)
Supervisor one-on-ones	.79	.79	.43 (.42)	.76	.71	.39 (.51)
Discharges for union activity	.30	.35	.51 (.39)	.28	.27	.40 (.42)
Discharges not reinstated before election	.18	.19	.37 (.44)	.26	.25	.40 (.42)
Employer gave wage increases	.30	.23	.32 (.47)	.24	.26	.45 (.41)
Employer used layoffs	.15	.18	.53 (.41)	.11	.17	.67 (.39)
Unilateral changes in benefits	—	—	—	.29	.28	.40 (.42)
Leaders promoted out of unit	.17	.19	.47 (.42)	—	—	—
Employer ran media campaign	.10	.13	.52 (.41)	.07	.03	.17 (.44)
Employer assisted antiunion committee	.42	.37	.37 (.46)	.50	.33	.28 (.56)

TABLE 1.1 Summary of NLRB Election Campaigns, 1986–87 and 1994 (cont.)

	1986–87 NLRB Elections			1994 NLRB Elections		
	Sample proportion or mean	Proportion or mean for wins	Percentage win rate[a]	Sample proportion or mean	Proportion or mean for wins	Percentage win rate[a]
EMPLOYER TACTICS (cont.)						
Employee-involvement plan in effect	.07	.04	.22 (.44)	.33	.23	.30 (.48)
Employee involvement set up after petition	—	—	—	.09	.04	.20 (.44)
Employer used bribes	—	—	—	.42	.29	.29 (.51)
Management change after petition	.21	.20	.41 (.43)	.38	.31	.33 (.47)
Number of employer tactics used	4.15	3.74	NA	4.87	4.23	NA
Employer used more than five tactics	.21	.15	.32 (.45)	.39	.30	.32 (.48)
UNION TACTICS						
Percentage on committee	.10	.13	NA	.12	.14	NA
Representative committee	.23	.34	.62 (.37)	.44	.57	.54 (.32)
Percent house called	.36	.45	NA	.58	.64	NA
50% or more house called	.28	.41	.61 (.35)	.39	.39	.42 (.42)
Number of small-group meetings	5.26	5.36	NA	11.16	12.99	NA
Ten or more small-group meetings	.22	.20	.39 (.43)	.39	.46	.50 (.37)
Rank-and-file volunteers did house calls	.18	.23	.52 (.40)	—	—	—
Ten or more rank-and-file volunteers	—	—	—	.17	.20	.50 (.40)
70% or more surveyed one-on-one	.53	.57	.46 (.39)	.21	.28	.54 (.38)
Bargaining committee before election	.15	.23	.64 (.39)	—	—	—
Solidarity days used	.12	.15	.53 (.41)	.56	.58	.43 (.40)
Union held rallies	.03	.04	.50 (.42)	.41	.38	.39 (.43)
Union held job actions	.02	.05	.10 (.41)	.13	.19	.62 (.38)
Community-labor coalitions used	.16	.19	.50 (.41)	.30	.30	.43 (.41)
Union used media	.11	.14	.52 (.41)	.12	.16	.58 (.39)
Dignity, fairness primary issues	.27	.36	.56 (.37)	—	—	—
Total number rank-and-file tactics used	2.12	2.69	NA	3.24	3.49	NA
Union used more than five rank-and-file tactics	.03	.06	1.00 (.41)	.15	.30	.67 (.38)

[a] Number in parentheses is the percentage win rate when the tactic or characteristic did not occur.

NA = Not applicable.

in a climate of intense employer opposition, economic decline, and weak public support. It also means that industrial relations research models that exclude union tactics fail to capture one of the most important elements of the organizing process.

The study showed that unions are most likely to win certification elections when they run aggressive and creative campaigns utilizing a grass-roots, rank-and-file-intensive strategy, building a union and acting like a union from the very beginning of the campaign. Thus, campaigns in which the union focused on person-to-person contact, house calls, and small-group meetings to develop leadership and union consciousness and to inoculate workers against the employers' antiunion campaigns were associated with win rates that were 10 to 30 percent higher than traditional campaigns that primarily used gate leafleting, mass meetings, and glossy mailings to contact unorganized workers. These results do not imply that something is inherently wrong with union leaflets and mailings but, rather, that personal contact is necessary to build support for a union and counteract an employer campaign.

Bronfenbrenner's study also found that unions were more successful when they encouraged active rank-and-file participation in and responsibility for the organizing campaign, including developing a large rank-and-file organizing committee representative of the different interest groups in the bargaining unit. The importance of rank-and-file participation extends beyond representation on the committee to involvement in internal and external pressure tactics that build solidarity and commitment to the union and compel the employer to run a less aggressive campaign.

The findings of the 1986–87 study also showed that it is essential that the union develop a long-range campaign strategy that incorporates building for the first contract into the original organizing process. Election win rates were more than 20 percentage points higher in units in which the union conducted bargaining surveys, selected the bargaining committee, and worked with the rank and file to develop proposals before the election rather than waiting until after the election to prepare for the first-contract campaign.

The issues the union focuses on during the campaign also are very important in determining election outcome. Unions that focused on issues such as dignity, justice, discrimination, fairness, or service quality were associated with win rates that were nearly 20 percentage points higher than those that focused on more traditional bread-and-butter issues, such as wages, benefits, and job security.

Finally, unions were also more successful when they developed a culture of organizing that permeated every activity and structure of the union. This included a serious commitment of staff and financial resources to organizing, the involvement of the international in local campaigns, and the training, recruitment, and effective utilization of rank-and-file volunteers from already-organized bargaining units.

Bronfenbrenner found that individual "rank-and-file intensive" tactics were associated with win rates 10 to 30 percentage points higher than win rates in campaigns that did not use these tactics. She also found that when these tactics were included in a regression equation controlling for the influence of employer tactics and characteristics and unit and election environment variables, many were associated with as much as a 3 percent increase in the percentage of votes received by the union and with as much as a 10 percent increase in the probability of winning the election. Given that so many NLRB election campaigns are lost by only a few percentage points, these results strongly suggest that unions organizing in the private sector could significantly improve their win rates if they used all or most of these rank-and-file-intensive tactics.

Unfortunately, the findings also show that in 1986 and 1987 only a very small number of unions were using a comprehensive union-building strategy in their certification election campaigns. As shown in the first column of table 1.1, fewer than one-third of those unions surveyed had representative committees, house called the majority of the members of the unit, held ten or more small-group meetings, or focused on dignity and fairness as the primary issues. Even fewer had solidarity days, established a bargaining committee before the election, or used such tactics as forming community-labor coalitions or holding rallies, job actions, or media campaigns.

Most striking of all, only 3 percent of the unions ran comprehensive campaigns in which they used five or more of the rank-and-file-intensive union-building strategies. In the small number of campaigns in which a more comprehensive strategy was used, however, unions won every election. This compares with a 41 percent win rate in those units in which the unions used fewer than five rank-and-file-intensive tactics. Further, controlling for the influence of employer characteristics and tactics and unit and election environment variables, the probability of the union winning the election increased by 10 percent for each additional rank-and-file-intensive tactic the union used.[2]

1994 Data and Research Methods

As part of his recent study, described in part IV of this volume, on the impact of employee-involvement programs on union organizing campaigns,

2. Tactics included in this variable were whether the union had a representative organizing committee, house called at least 50 percent of the members of the unit, held ten or more small-group meetings, used rank-and-file volunteers from other units to make house calls, had solidarity days, established a bargaining committee before the election, surveyed 70 percent or more of the members of the unit one-on-one about the contract, utilized community-labor coalitions, held rallies, used job actions, and focused on dignity and fairness as primary issues.

James Rundle surveyed a random sample of lead organizers of two hundred single-union NLRB certification election campaigns that took place in 1994 and involved units with fifty or more eligible voters. The 165 campaigns in his final sample represented approximately one-quarter of all the NLRB elections that took place in units of fifty or more eligible voters in 1994. Although the sample contained a slightly higher concentration of blue-collar manufacturing units than the election population and underrepresented units with high concentrations of low-wage women and minority workers, overall the sample was representative across unions, industries, regions, and types of bargaining units.

In addition to collecting data on employer-initiated employee-involvement programs, Rundle asked the lead organizers a series of questions about the demographics of the bargaining units, employer tactics, and union tactics. Although this information is much more limited in scope than the election and unit background data collected in the 1986–87 study, it does provide an important opportunity for comparison.

Descriptive statistics were calculated for each of the variables included in the model to capture the nature and extent of union and employer organizing activities in 1994 and to enable us to make comparisons between those findings and the data obtained for 1986–87. In addition, logit analysis was used to determine whether union tactics variables, both individually and as a group, had a statistically significant impact on certification election outcomes when controlling for the influence of election environment, bargaining unit demographic, and employer tactics variables.

Like Bronfenbrenner's study, this research is based on a theoretical model that sees election outcome as a function of interacting elements, including background variables, union and employer characteristics, and union and employer strategies.[3] It tests the hypothesis that union success in certification elections depends on the utilization of a comprehensive union-building strategy that incorporates personal contact, leadership development, and creative and aggressive internal and external pressure tactics. We hypothesize that although some individual union tactics may have a positive impact on election outcome, significant union gains will depend on a multifaceted, comprehensive campaign that utilizes as many rank-and-file-intensive tactics as possible. Union tactics variables in our model include the following: having a representative rank-and-file committee;[4] house calling of 50 per-

---

3. For a full description of the theoretical model used in the 1986–87 study, see Bronfenbrenner 1993:137–81.

4. A representative committee is defined as a committee that is representative of at least 10 percent of the eligible voters of the unit and that has at least 10 percent women and/or 10 percent people of color for any units with at least 10 percent women and/or 10 percent people of color.

cent or more of the members of the unit; holding ten or more small-group meetings during the campaign; enlisting the help of ten or more rank-and-file volunteers from already organized units during the campaign; holding solidarity days, rallies, and job actions; launching media campaigns; utilizing community-labor coalitions; and conducting a one-on-one contract survey of at least 70 percent of the members of the unit. When combined in a single rank-and-file-intensive union tactics variable, it is hypothesized that the probability of the union winning the election will significantly increase for each additional tactic the union uses.

In addition to the union tactics variables, we were able to control for election environment, employer characteristics, bargaining unit demographics, and employer tactics with the following variables: number of eligible voters, presence of other organized units, board-ordered or stipulated change in the unit from unit for which the union originally petitioned, unit at least 75 percent women,[5] percentage people of color in the unit, average wage in the unit, and number of employer tactics used. The tactics constituting the employer scale variable include whether the employer used an outside consultant, held five or more captive-audience meetings, sent five or more antiunion letters to employees, discharged workers for union activity and did not reinstate them before the election, enlisted supervisors to campaign one-on-one, gave wage increases, made unilateral changes in benefits, laid off workers during the campaign, ran a media campaign, used bribes, assisted the rank-and-file antiunion committee, set up an employee-involvement program after the petition was filed, held social events, and made changes in management structure and personnel.

Results

Table 1.1 summarizes the descriptive statistics for both the 1986–87 and the 1994 studies. What is perhaps most striking is how little the data have changed. In the 1990s, as in 1986–87, the win rate in units with more than fifty employees continues to average about 43 percent. The percentage union vote remains unchanged, and the first contract rate has gone down slightly. Although unions continue to enjoy dramatically higher win rates in service-sector units than in manufacturing units (70 percent versus 31 percent), most election activity is concentrated in the manufacturing sector. Similarly, although win rates have been shown to be significantly higher in

5. Seventy-five percent women was used rather than a simple continuous percentage women variable because previous research by Bronfenbrenner (1993) and by Ruth Milkman (1992) found that gender homogeneity has a significant influence on election outcome. Union win rates are highest when a clear majority of the unit are women but are higher in all-male units than in units with 25 percent to 50 percent women.

units in which women and people of color predominate, less than 20 percent of the units being organized include a significant majority of either women or people of color. The percentage of stipulated versus NLRB- and court-ordered changes in the bargaining unit is unchanged.

The data show that unions are attempting to organize slightly larger units. Thus, in 1986–87, there were no elections in units with more than five hundred eligible voters and the average size of the units in which unions won was only 105, whereas in 1994, 5 percent of the organizing campaigns in the sample were in units with more than five hundred eligible voters and the average number of eligible voters in units in which the union won increased to 148. Such an incremental improvement is hardly sufficient to stem the tide of labor's decline.

Employer campaigns have undergone the greatest change, not so much in the tactics being used but in the overall intensity. Just as they did a decade ago, the overwhelming majority of employers use a broad range of aggressive legal and illegal antiunion tactics, including discharging workers for union activity, giving workers illegal wage increases and imposing unilateral changes in benefits, conducting one-on-one supervisor meetings with employees, offering bribes, supporting antiunion committees, holding captive-audience meetings, establishing employee-involvement programs, holding social events, and mailing letters and distributing leaflets. And, just as in 1986–87, most of these tactics are associated with significantly lower win rates.

Many employers have also increased the use of specific tactics. For example, 87 percent of the employers in the 1994 sample used outside consultants as opposed to 71 percent in 1986–87. Similarly, whereas only 33 percent of employers held five or more captive-audience meetings in 1986–87, 64 percent held them in 1994, and 33 percent had established employee-involvement committees, compared with only 7 percent in 1986–87.

What is most striking about the employer tactics, however, is that whereas only 21 percent of employers used more than five aggressive antiunion tactics in 1986–87, by 1994 that number had jumped to 39 percent. Not surprisingly, win rates were significantly lower in units in which employers used more than five aggressive tactics (32 percent) than in units in which five or fewer such tactics were used (48 percent).

The nature and the intensity of union campaigns have also changed. The percentage of campaigns in which the union had a representative organizing committee increased from 23 to 44 percent, while the percentage of campaigns in which the union conducted house calls of the majority of the members of the unit increased from 28 to 39 percent. Likewise, the average number of small-group meetings the union held during the campaigns went from 5.26 in 1986–87 to 11.16 in 1994, and the percentage of units in which the union held ten or more small-group meetings increased by 17 percent. Unions were also much more likely to have solidarity days (56 percent versus 12 percent), to hold rallies (41 percent versus 3 percent), to utilize community-labor coalitions (30 percent versus 16 percent), and to conduct job actions (13 percent versus 2 percent) in 1994. With the exception of house calling of the majority of the members of the unit and holding rallies, all these tactics were associated with higher win rates than campaigns in which these tactics were not used.

Looking more closely at the intensity of the campaigns, however, we find that the change has not been very significant. Fewer than half the campaigns surveyed had representative committees, ran more than ten small-group meetings, actively used rank-and-file volunteers from already-organized units, or conducted one-on-one surveys. The average number of rank-and-file-intensive tactics the unions used was only 3.24, compared with 2.12 in 1986–87. Contrast this with the number of tactics used by employers, which averaged 4.87 in 1994 and 4.15 in 1986–87.

Most striking of all, in 1994 only 15 percent of the lead organizers surveyed ran comprehensive campaigns that used more than five rank-and-file-intensive tactics. Although this is a fivefold increase from 1986–87, the figure still represents an extremely small portion of NLRB campaigns. In those 15 percent, however, the win rate shoots to 67 percent, versus only 38 percent when the unions used five or fewer tactics.

Clearly, the majority of unions continue to run very traditional campaigns that do not involve personal contact, leadership development, and the internal and external pressure tactics so essential to establishing the rank-and-file commitment and support necessary to overcome increasingly aggressive employer campaigns. Even when they do use such tactics as house calling, small-group meetings, and solidarity days, unions tend to use these tactics in isolation, without benefit of a more comprehensive campaign. The question then becomes, how does house calling, for example, which is meant to be part of a larger grassroots effort aimed at reaching workers one-on-one, work in the absence of other tactics, such as forming a representative committee or using internal pressure tactics or building for the first contract during the organizing campaign?

As we can see from table 1.2, the importance of developing a more comprehensive campaign becomes even more apparent when included in a logit estimation controlling for the influence of election environment, bargaining unit demographics, and employer characteristics and tactics variables. Two models were used to estimate the predicted impact of union tactics on the probability of the union winning the election. The first model, A, includes each individual union tactic. The second model, B, combines the individual union tactics into a rank-and-file-intensive scale variable, adding one unit for each additional tactic used.

As predicted, the number of eligible voters, changes in the composition

TABLE 1.2. Impact of Union and Employer Tactics on Election Outcome, 1994

Independent variable	Hypothesized sign	Mean or percentage of sample	Percentage union win rate	Model A		Model B	
				Coefficient	Predicted impact on probability of union win[a]	Coefficient	Predicted impact on probability of union win[a]
ELECTION BACKGROUND VARIABLES							
Number of eligible voters	−	178	NA	−1.941**	no perceptible impact	−1.568*	no perceptible impact
Other units represented	+	.38	.46	.317	—	.497	—
Unit different than petitioned for	−	.25	.33	−1.779**	−15% if different	−1.852**	−16% if different
Average wage	−	8.74	NA	−1.606*	−2% for $1 increase in average wage	−1.204	—
Unit at least 75% women	+	.19	.61	1.701**	15% if 75% women	2.006**	9% if 75% of women
Percentage minority in the unit	+	.28	NA	1.263	—	1.319*	2% for 10% increase in people of color
Number of employer tactics used[b]	−	4.87	NA	−4.209***	−7% for each additional tactic	−3.897***	−7% for each additional tactic
UNION TACTICS							
Model A							
Union had representative committee	+	.44	.54	2.661***	20% if had representative committee		
Union house called majority	+	.39	.42	−0.011	—		
Union held ten or more small-group meetings	+	.39	.50	1.392*	10% if 10 or more		

TABLE 1.2. Impact of Union and Employer Tactics on Election Outcome, 1994 (*cont.*)

Independent variable	Hypothesized sign	Mean or percentage of sample	Percentage union win rate	Model A Coefficient	Model A Predicted impact on probability of union win[a]	Model B Coefficient	Model B Predicted impact on probability of union win[a]
UNION TACTICS (*cont.*)							
Model A							
Union used at least ten rank-and-file volunteers	+	.19	.50	2.153**	22% if 10 or more		
Union used solidarity days	+	.56	.43	1.233	—		
Union used rallies	+	.41	.39	−1.135	—		
Union used job actions	+	.13	.62	2.228**	24% if job actions used		
Union used media	+	.12	.58	1.836**	22% if media used		
Union used community labor coalitions	+	.30	.43	−0.054	—		
Union used 70% of voters surveyed one-on-one	+	.21	.54	1.390*	12% if surveyed		
Model B							
Number of union tactics used	+	3.24	NA			3.902***	9% for each additional tactic
Total Number of Observations		165	.42				
McFadden's Rho-squared				.253		.17	
2 (log-likelihood)				56.638	.000***	38.23	000***

*Significance levels: * = .10 ** = .05 *** = .01 (one-tailed tests)*

[a] Based on partial derivative for statistically significant variable from logit estimations of election outcome with dependent variable win-lose.

[b] Employer tactics include five or more captive-audience meetings, five or more company letters, supervisor campaigned one-on-one, change in management after the petition, company gave wage increases, unilateral change in benefits, employer held social events, company used media, company used bribes, company assisted antiunion committee, workers discharged and not reinstated before the election, and employer set up employee-involvement program during campaign.

of the unit, and employer tactics were also found to have significant negative impact on election outcome. Employer tactics in particular were found to affect election outcome dramatically. The probability of the union winning the election declined by 7 percent for each aggressive antiunion tactic the employer used when the influence of election environment, bargaining unit demographics, and union tactics were controlled for.

The results also provide support for the argument that unions are more successful in units with a majority of women and/or people of color. As shown in the results for the partial derivatives in model B, the probability of the union winning the election increased by 9 percent in units with at least 75 percent women and by 2 percent for each 10 percent increase in the number of people of color.[6]

The results for the individual union tactics variables included in model A are quite mixed. Although tactics such as having a representative committee, using at least ten rank-and-file volunteers, conducting job actions, and using a media campaign exhibited a strong positive and statistically significant impact on election outcome, other tactics, such as holding ten or more small-group meetings and surveying 70 percent of the unit members one-on-one, exhibited a relatively weak effect (only a 0.10 level of statistical significance). The remaining union tactics, including house calling the majority of the members of the unit, holding solidarity days, having rallies, and forming community-labor coalitions, were not found to have a statistically significant positive effect on certification election outcomes.

Yet when these tactics were combined into a single union tactics variable in model B, adding one unit for each rank-and-file-intensive tactic used, the number of tactics was found to have a strong positive impact on election outcome (statistically significant at 0.001 or better). The results from the logit estimation controlling for the influence of election environment, bargaining unit demographics, and employer tactics variables suggest that the probability of the union winning the election increases by as much as 9 percent for each rank-and-file-intensive tactic the union uses.

These results lend strong support to our hypothesis that whether there is a comprehensive union-building campaign that incorporates person-to-person contact, leadership development, escalating internal and external pressure tactics, and building for the first contract is more important in determining election outcome than whether the union uses individual tac-

6. The relatively weak results for the percentage people of color variable (not statistically significant in model A and significant at only a 0.1 level in model B) may be explained by the fact that Rundle's sample underrepresented low-wage manufacturing- and service-sector units, in which people of color dominate. This is particularly true of SEIU hospital and nursing home campaigns and of UNITE's manufacturing campaigns in the Deep South, which were underrepresented because of difficulties in tracking down the organizers in the short time allotted.

tics. The more union-building strategies are used during the organizing campaign, the greater the likelihood that the union will win the election, even in a climate of intense employer opposition. Given that the probability of the union winning the election is reduced by 6 percent for each aggressive antiunion tactic the employer uses and increased by 9 percent for each rank-and-file-intensive tactic the union uses, these findings once again suggest that union tactics as a group matter more than employer tactics in determining union success in NLRB certification election campaigns.

Conclusions

This examination of recent certification elections provides important insights into the state of organizing in the private sector. The findings not only suggest directions for further research but provide guidance for the labor movement in its revitalization efforts. One of the most fundamental findings for both labor activists and scholars is that union tactics and activities are central to the organizing process. Although many academics and trade unionists traditionally looked only to the deteriorating economic and political climate and antiunion campaigns as the determinants of organizing outcomes, this study underscores that union tactics matter as much, if not more, in determining results.

The data from 1994 give credence to many voices from the front lines of the labor movement who report that employers have intensified their antiunion efforts. As we have seen, employers have not necessarily adopted new tactics, or shifted their behavior in favor of some tactics over others. Instead, they have continued to utilize the model honed throughout the 1980s and early 1990s but with greater intensity. Despite recent cries for labor law reform, our data show only too well the outcome of that effort, as workers face greater and greater risks and pay higher and higher costs for simply attempting to exercise their right to organize a union in their workplace.

The data from 1994 provide further support for the finding of the 1986–87 study that despite the intensity of employer opposition, what unions do during organizing campaigns is what matters most. Unions can still win, as demonstrated in UNITE's string of victories in manufacturing plants in the South, SEIU's success in organizing more than two thousand workers at Crouse Irving and Corning Hospitals in upstate New York, or the Teamsters' national campaign against Overnite. And, in support of the original 1986–87 study, we once again have found that the use of a grassroots, rank-and-file-intensive, union-building strategy is fundamental in significantly raising the probability of winning. Overall, these data suggest that the recommitment of the labor movement to organizing is not a futile effort. If unions use the right tactics, they can still win, despite the odds.

This good news is tempered, however, by current union practice in choosing tactics and running organizing campaigns. Despite increased training, staff, and budgets, unions have made only minor improvements in embracing a more rank-and-file-intensive approach to organizing. The 1994 data suggest that the labor movement has been more tied to traditional top-down, plant gate types of organizing than many have assumed.

The current data indicate the willingness of many organizers and unions to experiment with some grassroots union-building tactics. Clearly, these tactics have been discussed and have begun filtering out to front-line organizers. Yet the approach has been largely piecemeal; organizers have used one or two isolated tactics without incorporating them into a more cohesive and consistent strategy. Only a handful of campaigns have fully embraced a union-building approach, and this is reflected in the overall win rate, which continues to hover at about 50 percent.

Although individual tactics, such as having a representative committee, using rank-and-file volunteers, and conducting media campaigns, are important, our data clearly indicate that the use of individual tactics is not enough. The question this piecemeal approach raises is, what does it mean to have a representative committee, for example, in the absence of other grassroots strategies? Having a representative committee is one thing, but if rank-and-file workers are never trained in one-on-one organizing and if they are never given an active leadership role in the campaign, then the very purpose of developing rank-and-file leadership is defeated. Whether they are conducting house calls, organizing job actions, or rallying community support, rank-and-file organizing committees are effective in overcoming employer opposition or in mobilizing worker support only when they, rather than organizing staff, are doing the primary work of building a union in their workplace. Individual tactics are not effective when they are used in isolation from other union-building efforts.

Similarly, the quality of the tactics being used also matters. A campaign in which every worker receives a house call in a weekend blitz by outside organizing staff that is little more than a ten-minute visit to drop off literature will be much less effective than a campaign in which the union sets up small-group meetings with two or three workers at workers' homes, in community centers, or in the workplace and workers have an opportunity to express their concerns and to be inoculated against the employer campaign, to mobilize for solidarity actions, and, most important, to develop leaders for the long haul to come.

Effecting the kind of sea change in organizing that the new leadership of the AFL-CIO has correctly suggested is crucial for survival will take more than house calls, coordinated campaigns, volunteer organizers, or the use of any individual tactic. It will take an unprecedented commitment of staff and resources. It will also take mass industry- and community-based organizing that goes far beyond small-scale hot shop by hot shop campaigns. As our data also clearly show, effecting such a sea change requires a commitment to a comprehensive grassroots rank-and-file-intensive model and all the hard work that entails. Only by making such a commitment will unions become truly successful in organizing.

Given the level of employer opposition, and the likelihood that such opposition will continue to intensify until the labor movement has grown enough to enact real labor law reform, our research indicates that it is not enough to tinker with organizing techniques. To win takes nothing short of truly exceptional effort, including an exceptional organization committed to building a union from the bottom up.

In addition to increasing the win rate in individual elections, the use of a rank-and-file-intensive model for organizing has several important long-term benefits. First, if unions are going to organize on a scale unprecedented since the 1930s, they need more than just professional organizers. Given the recommitment by the labor movement to organizing, discussions have occurred concerning the costs of organizing individual workers and the astronomical budgets that will need to be committed to organize at the pace and scale required. It would be incorrect to suggest that the union-building model of organizing is less expensive than more top-down methods. In fact, in the short run, it may be more costly. Yet the long-term benefit of this grassroots model is that it creates a tremendous capacity for organizing. By fully involving rank-and-file members, however, the potential exists to create an army of experienced and committed rank-and-file organizers. There is no better example of this than UNITE's campaigns in its southern region, where recently organized rank-and-file volunteers have played a crucial role in organizing plants in neighboring communities.

Although investing dollars and people in organizing is fundamental to jump-start and sustain organizing efforts, the use of rank-and-file union-building approaches can create an even larger capacity for organizing and, in turn, a mass movement of workers. At this point the calculus of what organizing will cost changes. From this perspective, the use of a union-building model does much more than increase the likelihood of winning an individual election; it also creates a culture, climate, and capacity for organizing in the future.

But there is more at stake in a grassroots union-building campaign than just getting new members and dues payments. Organizing should also not be viewed as independent of the other activities of unions and their members. Particularly in an antiunion climate, organizing is just the first step in creating a strong and viable bargaining unit and local union. The unit must get a first contract and over time build an organization with real power in the workplace. It not only needs to achieve real dignity, justice, and fairness for its members but it must be ready to stave off the many challenges it will face over time. Thus, not only does the union-building approach allow for victory, it also creates an opportunity for the union to become strong and viable, as workers early in the organizing process gain leadership skills and understand the real power associated with their involvement in the union. There has been much discussion in the labor movement about moving from a servicing to an organizing model; our research suggests that this process should begin during the organizing process itself.

Rank-and-file grassroots organizing strategies are also critical to the development of different kinds of unions. Union efforts during organizing campaigns to create an active and well-informed rank and file are wasted if these workers are squeezed into already existing, service-based organizations in which staff alone negotiate contracts and handle grievances. Particularly for the growing number of women and people of color who are increasingly involved in organizing campaigns, these traditional structures often involve serious obstacles to inclusion.

Newly organized workers need to be seen as more than just members of a special interest group to be accommodated in an existing structure and agenda. Especially given the recent lack of union growth, these new members—their ideas and issues, their dreams, and their desires—represent the future of the labor movement. Their enthusiasm and excitement should not be bridled in a structure that has often been perceived as cliquish and exclusionary. Instead, these newest members must become central to an inclusive and rejuvenated unionism of the 1990s.

Overall, our research demonstrates that there are indeed no silver bullets in organizing. Although some in the labor movement have seen individual tactics such as house calling as panaceas, as we have shown, these tactics are effective only when used in the context of a broader rank-and-file union-building approach. Unquestionably, it will take a great deal of hard work to move away from a reliance on traditional top-down strategies to the use of a more comprehensive grassroots union-building model. Yet, as the history of organizing in places as diverse as Lawrence, Flint, and Memphis have demonstrated, the fruits of this approach are many. More than simply organizing new members, rank-and-file-intensive campaigns will allow for the rebuilding of the labor movement—not simply individual labor organizations but a mass movement poised to regain its rightful place in society.

Chapter 2

Beyond the Organizing Model: The Transformation Process in Local Unions

Bill Fletcher, Jr., and Richard W. Hurd

The ideological foundations of traditional U.S. trade unionism have been called into question by world and domestic events. The post-World War II labor movement, founded on a social truce with capital and the apparent inevitability of a rising living standard, has hit a bulkhead-piercing iceberg of dramatic proportions. The global economy, economic restructuring, deregulation, and privatization have wrought destruction on U.S. unions. In the wake of this devastation, it has become common, even for union leaders, to define unionism in objectively negative terms (e.g., without a union, you have no protection from arbitrary management). As a movement, we have offered little in the way of a comprehensive explanation of what we stand for.

The upheaval has forced new questions and problems to the surface and has set the stage for an internal debate about the future. The dialogue has included little that is fundamentally new. There have always been disagreements over labor strategy and tactics, the relationship of unions to capital, and the appropriate form of organization for the labor movement. This debate has taken on new urgency since the mid-1980s, however, and has concentrated on whether there is a viable alternative to the prevailing form of business unionism, which appears to be leading workers nowhere.

Borrowing from the South African antiapartheid movement, we could say that two camps have formed that we could label TINA and THEMBA. TINA (There Is No Alternative) has included the defenders and practitioners of the bureaucratic insurance agent form of unionism. THEMBA (There Must Be an Alternative, and the Zhosa word for *hope*) has included those who have challenged the status quo and who have spent the last ten years trying to reach consensus on just what the alternative is.

An internal organizing manual published by the AFL-CIO in 1988, *Numbers That Count* (Diamond 1988), provided the nucleus for a new way to conceptualize the debate. A brief section entitled "Servicing Model vs. the Organizing Model" contrasted the "servicing model of local union leadership—trying to help people by solving problems for them"—with the "organizing model—involving members in solutions" (Diamond 1988:6). This contrast was elaborated in an important article by Andy Banks and Jack Metzgar in a 1989 issue of *Labor Research Review*. As Banks and Metzgar portray it, the servicing model is equivalent to stale unionism; there is an overreliance on union staff and the grievance and arbitration process and a concomitant suppression of rank-and-file involvement. By contrast, the organizing model emphasizes the need for member mobilization, collective action, and militancy. A later issue of *Labor Research Review* reinforced this conceptualization through articles and case studies, most notably "Contract Servicing from an Organizing Model" (Conrow 1991).

The organizing model has an irresistible logic. Banks and Metzgar promise that by involving "many more people in [its] daily life, . . . [the union] will be able to take on and solve more problems" (1989:50). Similarly, Teresa Conrow argues that the answer to staff burnout "is to involve more people and expand leadership roles" (1991:54). Banks and Metzgar project that as a result of the mobilization of a militant membership, unions will have a "transformed self image" but only "when organizing becomes the norm, the everyday experience of unionists on the shop floor" (53). Banks and Metzgar's conclusion ultimately caught on and has been articulated by progressives throughout the labor movement: "The fundamental task confronting the labor movement is the challenge to switch from a reliance on the servicing model of unionism to an organizing model" (54).

Although we ascribe to the perspective we have labeled THEMBA, we are concerned that the organizing model has proved to be an insufficient antidote to labor's ills. We have reached this conclusion based on discussions with local leaders and staff in SEIU and several other unions. To explain our emerging anxieties, we will briefly describe SEIU's "local union transformation" initiative and then report on the experiences of SEIU locals that have been experimenting with strategies for moving beyond the insurance agent/servicing model morass.

Local Union Transformation in SEIU

Discussions regarding the organizing model evolved in SEIU over time. Great enthusiasm was expressed for finding new methods to increase membership involvement. This commitment took several forms, including production of the *Contract Campaign Manual,* of which SEIU is justifiably proud. This document presents an approach to bargaining that emphasizes internal organizing, building alliances, and conducting the struggle in a militant fashion.

But even while pushing for implementation of the best elements of the organizing model, there was a growing conviction within SEIU that something else was needed, specifically, a way for local unions to shift greater resources to *external* organizing. (In most of the literature regarding the organizing model, there is little reference to this issue.) Would mobilization of the members for militant action on the shop floor create momentum that would induce bottom-up support for external organizing? Alternatively, could the existing members essentially be ignored while efforts and resources were put into such organizing? Was there a different way to perform representational work that would emphasize the role of existing members rather than that of the staff?

Attempting to grapple with these questions led a work group at SEIU to consider what the characteristics of an organizing local would be. These discussions and the experimentation they encouraged came to be known as local union transformation. Unable to reach agreement as to the features of such a local, except in a general way, the work group decided to look at local union "best practices." The idea was to examine how local unions actually conduct representation, to identify innovative approaches to representation that streamline the process, and to explore the relationship of these efforts to external organizing. It was in this context that Cornell University was engaged to study the best practices of twelve local unions within SEIU.

The locals were selected based on their commitment to external organizing and their implementation of innovative approaches to representational work.[1] Although they were not selected randomly, one objective was to ensure that they were representative of all SEIU locals, by region, size, and industry. Each of the twelve locals was visited for on-site interviews with elected leaders, staff, and rank-and-file activists. The remainder of this chapter reports on the results of the study. Although most of the specific experiences we relate come from these twelve locals, the interpretation is based as well on discussions with leaders of other locals and staff of SEIU and other national unions.

The Organizing Model in Practice

Half the locals in the best-practices project have made an explicit commitment to the organizing model. Two have engaged for ten years in internal

1. Interview schedules and a list of the locals involved may be requested from Mary Ann Collins at SEIU.

practices now associated with this approach. But even among locals committed to the model, there is a lack of clarity regarding what this means in practice. There is a general understanding that some application of organizing principles to representational work is desirable. For some unionists, this implies that internal practices are more democratic; for others, it means there is an emphasis on activities aimed at mobilization and on direct action; and for others (in the public sector and in right-to-work states), the aim is to involve members in actions that attract coworkers who then join the union. Many unionists presume that a direct link exists between the internal implementation of the organizing model and the local's potential ability to organize externally, but very few unionists could clearly articulate the connection.

In spite of the diversity in interpretations, some patterns have surfaced among those locals with the deepest commitment to the organizing model. We have identified three such patterns. The three cases described below are compilations based on information about several of the locals included in the project. Although the details are drawn from actual practice, the cases do not match precisely any specific case.

Local X has made the organizing model its byword; it is the standard against which all the local's work is measured. Staff representatives are referred to as internal organizers. They keep up-to-date charts on each workplace to monitor members' commitment and place top priority on recruiting rank-and-file leaders. Depending on the size of the unit, a specified number of positions need to be filled—unit officers, chief steward, stewards, work site organizers, and political activists. These volunteers are expected to conduct the day-to-day work of the local within their units. Formal training offered by the union combined with informal training by the internal organizers ensure that the volunteers have the tools to perform the roles they have accepted. Stewards handle all grievances through step 3, for example.

The internal organizers focus on identifying issues that can be used to mobilize members, and each internal organizer is expected to schedule a minimum of two major actions each month. In addition to regular actions around workplace issues, a more extensive contract campaign is implemented for each contract negotiation. Political activists are encouraged to become involved in grassroots political action in local and statewide campaigns. Rank-and-file leaders are selected as media spokespersons. In short, Local X does everything with the organizing model in mind and pushes decisions and actions down to the lowest possible level.

More common than the situation just described is the case of Local Y, where, to a person, staff voice commitment to the organizing model but there is only periodic mobilization of members, mainly at the time of contract negotiations. This local negotiates multiple contracts annually and organizes member-driven contract campaigns for each negotiation. New stewards are recruited, a contract committee is created, and the staff representative assigned to the unit trains the activists in campaign principles. A contract survey is developed and distributed using one-on-one techniques. Workplace actions are planned and implemented by the members, the filing of grievances is accelerated, and, where appropriate, OSHA complaints are initiated. There is a high level of energy, members are mobilized, and involvement is maximized.

Between contracts, however, this level of activism is rare unless there is a crisis. In the better units, the day-to-day business of the local is conducted by rank-and-file leaders, some of whom hold the position of unit chair for years and essentially perform as unpaid staff. Some of these units are always ready even if they are not always active. Many other units are more passive and rely heavily on staff during the lulls between contract campaigns.

Local Z represents the third standard interpretation of the organizing model. At the center of Local Z's operating style is an emphasis on communication. The president of the local meets with staff weekly to discuss recent developments and upcoming actions. Stewards councils have been established in most units, and field representatives meet with them monthly. In addition to the face-to-face communications made possible through these channels, the local publishes a monthly newspaper that discusses the direction in which the union is heading and highlights militant campaigns conducted by or supported by the local. In addition, site-specific newsletters are distributed quarterly in all workplaces with three hundred or more members.

At Local Z, all contract negotiations are approached as campaigns to involve the members. In addition to promoting activism at contract time, Local Z has a strong presence in Jobs with Justice and supports the struggles of other unions in the area. Nonetheless, only a small percentage of the members are highly active, creating an image of member involvement that is not matched in reality. The local's creativity in actions and demonstrations is enhanced by what is acknowledged to be a "shell game" or "smoke and mirrors."

Elected leaders and staff in Locals X, Y, and Z voice commitment to similar values and objectives. All three locals seek to involve the members, to promote activism and militancy, and to "move to the highest level of collective struggle." There is a consistent refrain that "people change when they take on the fight." Also present though not as universal is a belief that the role of the union is "to radicalize the members."

Although operating with a common set of values, there are also important differences among Locals X, Y, and Z. Local X attempts to achieve a comprehensive program that fits the organizing model. Member involvement in all the work of the local is paramount, and democratic process is a priority. Stewards handle grievances, members are politically active, and a high degree of mobilization has been achieved. Staff at Local Y are no less zealous in their enthusiasm for the organizing model, but in practice the local has been successful at achieving its objectives only during contract campaigns. Nonetheless, its philosophy is rooted in member activism and the contract campaigns are "bottom-up" events. Local Z has done more than either Local X or Local Y to integrate its work with progressive elements of the broader labor movement, but it has not achieved a comparable level of member involvement. Local Z's activism and militancy are heavily dependent on staff.

Although there are unions like Local X scattered throughout the labor movement, the experiences of Locals Y and Z are more common in practice. But even in this more limited form, organizing model locals have accomplished a great deal and their efforts are laudatory. At the same time, these locals have encountered significant difficulties; it is to these experiences we now turn.

Limitations of the Organizing Model

When a local adopts the organizing model as a way of doing business, it encounters resistance. Staff representatives are experienced in servicing, and most were hired because of their negotiating skills and expertise in the grievance/arbitration process. They are proud of their work, and many oppose the shift to an approach that may leave them behind if they cannot adapt. These concerns are often mirrored in the initial response of members, who have not been expected to take responsibility and are accustomed to being serviced. The typical member is not interested in the activities of the union except at contract time and when there is a problem at work. A worker with a grievance will want to talk to a representative rather than trusting a steward; a common refrain is "That's why I pay dues."

Locals experienced with the organizing model address these problems over time. Staff either change or leave, or in some instances a few representatives specialize in grievance and arbitration work, which frees others to concentrate on internal organizing. Training is offered to stewards, and members learn to trust them with grievances. The demands to be serviced do not go away, however. Even where staff embrace the organizing model, they "have a hard time letting go and letting members run things." Stewards continue to rely on staff for advice and often are reluctant to take independent action. And elected leaders are moved by angry phone calls from members. As one representative expressed it, "Don't say we're going away from the servicing model when we pamper every squeaky wheel." In practice, then, there is a constant tension between the organizing model and the servicing magnet.

A more significant problem is the increased stress on staff in locals that work the hardest to involve members in the work of the union. The staff at Locals X and Y have continual problems with burnout; the staff-driven approach of Local Z creates a similar challenge, but it is less severe. Every staff member interviewed in Locals X and Y agreed that following the organizing model creates more work than sticking to the servicing model. This position was echoed in discussions with experienced leaders of locals in other international unions. It is easier for staff to handle grievances and arbitrations than continually to recruit and train stewards to do this work. It is also easier for staff to plan and run contract campaigns (as Local Z does) than to recruit, train, and support campaign committees.

A few comments reveal the dilemma these locals face. The first are from Local X, where there is strong staff support for the organizing model in spite of the drawbacks: "It is an exciting democratic process—our local is absolutely member driven"; "It's more work for staff, but the rewards are better"; "You get to be in the field, you find out the issues, you offer training —but the workload is the downside."

Other staff at Local X do not temper their concerns. Most simply state the reality: "The organizing model demands an incredible degree of commitment from staff." Some express regret: "We are on a platform of a high level of activity which interferes with family. The local should appreciate the value of breaks and time off." The most committed staff view these concerns with suspicion, lamenting that "some staff don't see this as a religion."

The views of the staff at Local Y are similar. On the positive side, "Power emanates from the members' unity," and "Getting members involved brings in energy." But the concerns qualify the praise for the organizing model: "It is a myth that the organizing model will free staff; you constantly have to train members to do things you could do faster yourself," and "More active units mean more work and less time for external organizing."

Staff burnout is directly linked to members' reactions to the organizing model. The typical member is either timid or disinterested and reluctant to be too active. Some members are dedicated but are willing to take on support functions only. Even those with a more activist bent find it difficult to be involved all the time. People tire of fighting. There is little or no emotional support at work for what these activists do on behalf of their coworkers and their unions. And inevitably there are conflicts because of the loss of personal time. The result is that stewards and other leaders at the grassroots level rotate through these positions.

Recruiting stewards is difficult, and training them is time-consuming. As one longtime rank-and-file activist in Local X sees it: "The organizing model works well with a group of experienced union people in the unit. However, it is intimidating to those without experience. . . . Members really want a combination of servicing and internal organizing."

Staff and leaders in Locals X, Y, and Z agree that it is easier to mobilize workers at contract time and in workplaces where the boss is really bad. Otherwise, there is a "constant tension to come back to servicing." In fact, "members even see mobilization as a staff responsibility." To return to our point, it is more work to solve problems with the organizing model.

These limitations lead to some substantive questions. First, there are strategic concerns. The organizing model works in some settings but not in others. Locals with small units and multiple contracts have more difficulty maintaining high levels of mobilization than locals with large units and few contracts. Similarly, units of workers who face a crisis or arbitrary tyrannical supervisors are easier to mobilize than units in stable situations with more reasonable bosses. Furthermore, many workplaces face occasional crises (such as at contract time) but also experience long periods of relative calm. Does it make sense to pursue an organizing model at all times in all workplaces given these variations?

Second, there are budgetary limitations associated with the organizing model. Considering the demands this approach places on staff, there are clear resource implications that accompany full commitment. A staff member at Local Z summarized the dilemma: "Is mobilization a luxury we can't afford or a necessity we can't live without?" The resource constraint is particularly problematic for locals with an active external organizing program. The leaders of Locals X, Y, and Z are convinced that following the organizing model has helped them activate their members, reinvigorate their unions, and fight their bosses more effectively. When asked whether they are better off than they were five years ago, however, they confess that the *external* environment of economic restructuring and declining union membership has seriously limited potential gains. They are left explaining how adhering to the organizing model has enabled them to hold their own or minimize losses. As one high-ranking staff member at Local X lamented, "We're a stronger union, but without better contracts and increasing membership, what's the point?"

Leaders of other locals (not Local X, Y, or Z) raise concerns about the value of the organizing model as a vehicle for lasting change. In particular, they object that the model fails to elucidate any clear path from internal mobilization to external organizing. Their analysis concentrates on the decline in the power of unions, which they argue can be addressed only through growth. For growth to occur, they say, resources must be reallocated to external organizing. Although they are as critical of the servicing tradition as are proponents of the organizing model, these leaders believe that the focus of the labor movement should be on finding ways to free resources and staff from representational work. As one leader put it: "Start from the premise that organizing is the priority. Next ask yourself, 'How much of our disposable income is allocated to organizing?' *Then* ask, 'How do we service?' "

Concerns with resources and declining power have persuaded some leaders to reject the organizing model explicitly. They believe that it is more important to embrace a comprehensive program of external organizing. A particularly sharp critic explains why: "The organizing model is not about building power. It points unions in the most narrow way. The better job you do with 15 percent of the market, the more it motivates the boss to wipe you out. We have to direct our energy outside."

The next section reviews the experiences of locals that have decided to make external organizing their priority. These locals have not necessarily repudiated the organizing model, but they have decided either to bypass it or to move beyond it.

Organizing Locals

All the locals involved in the best-practices project have active external organizing programs, and about half have dramatically reallocated staff and other resources to support the effort. From among this latter group, we have identified three types of "organizing locals." Again, these are composite sketches drawn from actual practice.

Local A is a public-sector union for which organizing is the top priority. All staff members are referred to as organizers, and the only rank-and-file committee is the organizing committee. For many years Local A attempted to attract members by offering representational services, but membership stagnated. Six years ago the local's leaders concluded that "super-servicing is a recipe for disaster" and decided to become an organizing local. Since then, membership has tripled. Approximately equal shares of the growth have come from newly organized units of the same employer and from increases in membership in existing units.

Local A has freed resources for organizing by dramatically reducing staff time devoted to representational work. All grievances are now handled by stewards and by "grievance technicians," part-time union employees hired out of the unit. Members are required to play an active role in preparing their own grievances, and, as a result, there has been a decline in the number of grievances filed. As one steward describes the new philosophy, "If we don't make each person feel responsible, we won't have a union." Some staff members are a bit less charitable. "The goal is not to make people happy but to build the union," one staff member said. "We believe in tough servicing, which is like tough love," another commented. And, finally, another remarked, "The job of the union is to create power, not protect whiners."

Freed of most servicing responsibilities, organizers spend their time in the field. All new employees are visited personally, and unorganized units are targeted systematically. Organizers are assisted by "lost-timers" out of the shop, members who take leave without pay one day per week (covered by the union). Members of the organizing committee conduct much of the recruiting activities among nonmembers in existing units. Local A's philosophy was summarized succinctly by a steward: "Strength doesn't come from individual grievances but from getting a better contract; better contracts come from organizing more workers."

Local B operates in a different setting and takes a decidedly different approach. The local represents low-skilled workers in a private-sector industry, negotiates multiple contracts, and has a geographic jurisdiction that includes several municipalities. About eight years ago, Local B, faced with a gradual erosion of membership, decided to shift its attention from servicing to organizing. It adopted a long-term objective to organize the entire market in its jurisdiction. The local moved resources from representational work to organizing and facilitated the shift structurally through staff specialization. Standard servicing duties are handled by field representatives, while external organizing is coordinated by a separate organizing staff.

Because of the shift in resources, field representatives have been required to take on much larger routes with a corresponding increase in responsibility. A variety of experiments have been tried to ease the burden. Part-time grievance technicians out of the rank and file assisted the field representatives for a while, but the positions were eliminated because of budgetary concerns. A service center was set up, where a full-time staff member took all phone calls from members and assisted them with their questions, but members and field representatives were uncomfortable with the arrangement. A temporary employee with organizing experience was hired to conduct an internal organizing campaign to mobilize the members but was eventually assigned to the external organizing staff. Currently, one field representative has a reduced route and is handling all arbitrations, while a specialist on loan from the international has assumed some of the local's bargaining load. Although there have been some difficulties in conducting the representational work, Local B has been willing to accept this as a cost it must bear to support the organizing program.

The organizing story is quite different. Local B has pushed an aggressive agenda; demonstrations, civil disobedience, and creative actions have attracted public attention and have helped mobilize workers in the targeted companies. These activities have been supported by some activist members from established units, and some field representatives have assisted. Local B's membership has increased by about one-third as a direct result of the organizing, although no major breakthroughs have occurred recently. Some subdivisions of the local's jurisdiction are fully organized, but the share of the entire market is still less than half.

Local C has an industry jurisdiction that is similar to Local B's but a much larger territory. Local C is a private-sector union with multiple employers operating in related industries. It has concentrated on external organizing for ten years and has gradually adapted its structure. The organizing and representational work of the local are integrated, and all the staff endorse the local's organizing mission and the members support it. Although there are a few full-time organizers, the rest of the staff ("administrative organizers") are assigned geographic territories and are responsible for representational work and some external organizing in their areas.

Local C abandoned an earlier structure in an effort to move its external organizing to a higher level. To free administrative organizers from handling grievances, an educational program was established and a grievance chair was trained for each chapter. To be a grievance chair, one must support the local's organizing program. As one staff member explained it, "We need rank-and-file leaders with political commitment, not bureaucrats." Grievance chairs are expected to handle all step 3 hearings, and administrative organizers are responsible only for arbitrations. In many chapters, the result has been fewer grievances because "our members are telling problem workers, 'Get off it and get on with your life.' "

Perhaps the most exciting characteristic of Local C is the high degree of member involvement in organizing. The local runs an organizing internship program that brings six members out of the shop at a time for five weeks. This program trains about fifty members per year, who go back to their chapters to become chairs of organizing committees. Each chapter organizing committee is expected to identify a target and initiate an organizing campaign. Once a campaign is up and running, an administrative organizer lends assistance, but the members own these campaigns, which supplement the local's central organizing program. Local C has gained member support for organizing by projecting a straightforward message: "Organizing is about building power to protect the members we have." In recent years members have voted a dues increase to support organizing and have voted to commit more than one-third of the local's budget to organizing. Membership has grown steadily by about 10 percent per year.

The organizing locals we have described are all succeeding in increasing their memberships. Their styles are quite different, however. Locals A and

C have integrated organizing into all the work of the union and are healthier as a result. Local B has created an organizing program that is separate from the day-to-day activities of the union and its members.

Unlike the organizing model cases, there is no ideological consistency across these locals. Local A leaders, staff, and activists talk about empowering individual members, while their Local C counterparts voice concern about social and economic justice and the fight over the distribution of wealth. These differences in part reflect the different objective conditions of the members. Local A's members are public-sector workers with stable jobs and decent pay and benefits, while Local C's members are private-sector workers with low wages and bad working conditions. What is important is that the values articulated by the two locals seem to fit the workers they represent. Local B, by contrast, has not reached agreement on a coherent set of values. Organizers and workers involved in organizing are concerned about achieving economic power and "taking it to the streets." Field representatives and members in established units envision a union that protects workers. This ideological dissimilarity reflects underlying discontent that has the potential to undermine the local's commitment to organizing. It is to this and other difficulties that we now turn.

External Organizing, Internal Dissonance

As happens when a local embraces the organizing model, there is resistance when a local decides to shift from having a servicing orientation to being an organizing local. Many experienced staff are uncomfortable with organizing. In Locals A and C, staff either changed or left. In Local B, however, the creation of a separate organizing team was inspired by respect for the experienced servicing staff, and there has been very little turnover. The continued presence of staff who do not fully support the need to make organizing a priority has spawned constant tension with organizers. As one field representative describes the environment, "The organizers have been separate from day one; there is no connection; we don't even talk." Another complains, "The organizers have an attitude because we're not into their actions." The organizers voice similar frustrations. One organizer simply observes, "Servicing and organizing don't mesh; there is no coordination, no bridge." Another is more bitter: "The field reps don't block organizing, they just don't get it. They're scared . . . on a power trip . . . hiding their own failure."

Because organizing locals are attempting to do more with the same resources, "Every talented person is incredibly overworked." But this increased workload does not seem to lead to complaints of burnout as frequently as in organizing model locals. In Local B, the greatest stress is on the field representatives. As the staff director explains the situation, "Servicing is still staff intensive, and people get tired; the problem is that members are very dependent." The extra workload is handled by setting priorities and letting less pressing demands slide: "We are always scrambling to keep up. . . . We usually default to damage control."

The organizers in Local B, who network with other organizers in the area and in other locals of SEIU, have adjusted to the long hours and intense job pressures. As an official from another national union with a full organizing agenda commented, "Burnout is not the result of hard work and long hours but of not feeling part of the movement." This assessment fits the situation in Locals A and C, where organizers talk of feeling fatigue but quickly move on to express great pride in their union's record of growth as an organizing local.

Members of Locals A, B, and C have been affected indirectly by the splits in staff. One union leader believes that "if organizing staff are separate and apart with no integration, there will be no member ownership of the [organizing] program." This has certainly been a problem at Local B, where the organizing director concedes that the local "is not coming together" and recognizes a need to "integrate staff and members into organizing." Field representatives and members of the local are skeptical, however, about organizers' efforts to do this. One representative, who strongly supports making organizing a priority, complains, "External organizers see members and staff as bodies for rallies and marches; members feel tension from being taken for granted." Another is less critical but relates a similar problem: "Members need to be educated about organizing; you ask them to participate in an action and they look at you like you are crazy." A rank-and-file leader assesses the situation this way: "Members rightfully have a 'me-first' attitude—we need to take care of our members before sending people out to organize more." A member of the executive board echoes this view: "Our members see no connection to external organizing in [a city sixty miles away]; we're doing good there, but we need our staff here." With these sentiments, it is no wonder that a proposal for a dues increase was overwhelmingly defeated in 1995, shortly after we heard these comments.

Member apathy is also a problem in Locals A and C, in spite of their more integrated approaches. In Local A, "Getting people involved in organizing is difficult—they have second jobs, other priorities, and they are scared." Similarly, in Local C, "Most of [the] members are passive; you have to get them past their fears to get them to participate in organizing."

Probably more important than the apathy is the outright opposition. Members have difficulty understanding why they should support organizing unless there is a direct link to their own situations. Local A, which initiated an organizing campaign in 1995 in the private sector in response to privatization, has run into resistance from members: "Members don't recognize the need to organize. . . . They ask, 'How can we fight privatization when we're organizing it?' " Although a substantial majority of Local C's members support its external organizing, a large unit of professional workers do not. They find it "difficult to feel a connection" to an organizing program that focuses on low-skilled workers, even though they are from the same industry.

Most organizing locals push some representational work down to unit chairs and stewards to free staff and resources to do external organizing. As an unintended side effect, a cadre of rank-and-file leaders is created who become familiar with and often wedded to servicing. Thus, in Local B, "the most effective leaders in the workplace are problem solvers," and "the most active executive board members focus on grievances." Similarly, in Local A, "Sometimes stewards get into a social worker mold." It is not surprising that this commitment to servicing can turn into opposition to organizing. A chapter president in Local B reflected: "We don't have time to help with organizing because we're too involved in our chapter. We're not too happy that so much of the local's resources are devoted to external rather than internal. . . . We lost our conference room to organizers."

The dissonance around a local's external organizing reflects a failure to achieve consensus. This failure may be caused in part by the local's ineffectiveness in addressing the problems of its current members. The staff director in Local B is concerned that "as well as we do in organizing, we haven't been able to get respect from employers on the job." One staff member mused: "How do you service, get better collective bargaining agreements, and organize? The devil is in the detail." An equally important concern was voiced by the organizing director: "Organizing is not having a lasting impact on the local." The members have not considered organizing victories as their own, which makes deficiencies in the representational realm all the more noticeable.

When Local A decided to shift direction six years ago, the idea was to build a different culture. By collapsing all committees into an organizing committee, the local was making a statement. An intense one-on-one campaign was initiated to reach every member to convey the local's new image. Every educational function and chapter meeting reemphasized the organizing theme. As the local's office manager describes the philosophy, "Part of the organizing approach is education—what it means to be a union, what it means to be an organizing local." In the process of breaking the hold the servicing mentality had on the local, some rank-and-file leaders were alienated and quit. The end result, however, was a clear focus and strong support for organizing. Every organizing victory is a victory for every member.

Over the past ten years, Local C has gone through a similar process. The local's president recalls that "members and staff were perverted by the old ways. We had to struggle with the question 'How do you build political will?' " Diligent attention to the organizing mission accomplished the objective. Every staff meeting and executive board meeting starts with personal reports from participants involved in organizing victories. The local's extensive training program emphasizes the need to organize. Local C's education director explains the message this way: "You have to have conversations with people about power and numbers." Another staff member notes that "enthusiasm for organizing is contagious once it takes off."

Locals A and C have succeeded in building a coherent program supported by staff and members by making clear the link between organizing and the members' self-interest. Local A's focus on organizing other workers with the same employer has made the connection obvious. Not all locals will have this option. Local C has convinced its members of the importance of organizing other workers in the same industry and geographic area. The more widespread the feeling among members that the local's organizing targets are unrelated to or too far removed from their own labor market, the more difficult it will be to elicit members' enthusiasm.

It is extremely important for organizing locals to command the unified support of staff and their executive boards. Divisions at higher levels translate into dissension among the members, an untenable situation for a local that is breaking new ground. For locals in which staff specialization is necessary, attention must be devoted to cultivating and reinforcing political will among those responsible for representational work. The servicing magnet is powerful, but disproportionate commitment to servicing can undermine the commitment to organizing.

Members must identify with external organizing. Mere participation in actions is not enough if the members have not been involved in planning those actions. In both Locals A and C, the members are with the program. Although only the most activist members actually participate, most members understand the need to organize and are proud to be part of an organizing local. Assuming continual attention is paid to maintaining political will, the president of Local C concludes, "We need to build a structure that works, then train people and get out of the way."

Reflections on Building a Movement

In our opening discussion of TINA versus THEMBA, we noted that those who believe that "there must be an alternative" have not yet reached consensus on what the alternative is. We have endeavored to provide practical information from local union experiences that point us toward a workable solution to this conundrum. SEIU's local union transformation initiative is helping to identify the characteristics of a viable form of progressive unionism at the local level and in the process is contributing to the development of a positive program of innovation.

We have reviewed two broad approaches: the organizing model, which relies on internal organizing, and the organizing local, which focuses on external organizing. Locals that follow the organizing model stimulate member involvement, increase the ability to fight the boss on the shop floor, and generate the development of a more cohesive local with improved member commitment. Few locals achieve the ultimate objective of organizing as the everyday norm on the shop floor, however, because workers prefer normalcy and find it hard to take on the fight continuously. As a result, in practice, mobilization is staff driven and leads to stress and burnout.

The evidence from locals committed to the organizing model convinces us that as *the* alternative to the status quo, the organizing model is not realistic and is not good strategy. We believe that the inadequacy is conceptual as well as practical. If the weaker definition of the word *model* were intended ("an example to be emulated"), we would not hesitate to endorse the approach; however, most trade unionists have assumed the stronger definition of *model* ("a schematic description of a system or theory"). Thus, some unionists do not view the organizing model as a step but as the answer. We do not agree with the implication that militant rank-and-file action by itself can build a working-class movement.

The juxtaposition of the organizing model with the servicing model is essentially descriptive rather than analytical, insofar as it tends to address elements of the crisis of labor unionism rather than its source. The prescribed militancy and mobilization around issues of common concern are appropriate tactical steps to breathe life into local unions that have relied too heavily on bureaucratic methods. These tactical improvements do not translate into a comprehensive "model," however. To state this observation another way, that the organizing model has relevance to representational functions does not render it a sufficient antidote to the broader deficiencies of business unionism.

If the organizing model is not a viable alternative to business unionism, then what is? Although we are not prepared to answer that question definitively, we tend to agree with those who argue that attention should be directed toward achieving power in the marketplace and therefore toward external organizing. The experiences of organizing locals are instructive. These locals have been experimenting with different ways to free resources for organizing by reducing the scope and extent of their representational activities. Many of these experiments have involved initiatives parallel to the organizing model idea that more responsibility should be placed in the hands of rank-and-file leaders. The objective, though, is not to organize around grievances but to reduce the emphasis on grievances. These locals have determined that trivial grievances and problem workers should not chew up resources needlessly. These efforts make a lot of sense, and further experimentation in this direction seems warranted.

A key to institutional stability for organizing locals is consensus. In most cases in which consensus has been achieved, the local has emphasized its need for power and has appealed to the self-interest of its members ("organizing is about building power to protect members"). There appear to be two essential components to consensus building: a leader with vision who aggressively promotes organizing as critical in building political will and a comprehensive educational program that offers training in organizing and representational skills *and* that promotes the organizing mission.

In spite of the success of those organizing locals that have achieved consensus, it is difficult to think of local union transformation that is self-perpetuating without going beyond simply organizing for market power. The advantage of the market power approach is that it appeals to self-interest and is consistent with the U.S. tradition of job-based unionism. This approach is self-limiting, however, because once the relevant local labor market is organized, from the perspective of the members the need has been met and the tendency will be to return to servicing. We conclude that organizing locals offer a useful strategic approach for unions to regain market share in the short run, but they cannot serve as the basis for a legitimate alternative to business unionism.

Not addressed directly by either the organizing model or the organizing locals are a series of larger questions about the strategic direction of the entire labor movement. These go to the very ideological basis of U.S. trade unionism. These questions include the following: Who is identified as the constituency of organized labor? What is the mission of the labor movement? What is the relationship of organized labor to corporate America? How do those in the labor movement deal with issues of globalization and international solidarity?

However these questions are answered, a vision needs to be articulated that offers a clear alternative to business unionism, a vision that can touch a large segment of members and be relevant to everyday life. Consistent with the experience of the organizing locals, this vision should encompass principles such as empowerment, social justice, and equitable distribution of wealth. For now, unions such as SEIU can only assist locals in the process of philosophical, practical, and organizational transformation based on the principle of organizing for growth and power. We believe that by learning from the experiences of innovative best-practices locals that are willing to take risks, we will be able to develop a clear picture of what unionism should look like in the twenty-first century. Through this transformation of local unions, we expect to advance toward a new model of unionism based on social and economic justice.

Chapter 3

The Role of Central Labor Councils in Union Organizing in the 1990s

Fernando Gapasin and Howard Wial

We're aiming to create a culture of organizing throughout the union movement . . . and CLCs can and will be the center of that culture.
—Linda Chavez-Thompson, in Rosier 1996

A central labor council (CLC) is a voluntary federation of AFL-CIO locals in a particular U.S. city, county, or region. The local analogue to the national AFL-CIO, a CLC obtains funding and direction from the local unions that choose to affiliate with it. These locals designate some of their members as delegates to the CLC, and these delegates carry out the work of the federation. The national AFL-CIO has only indirect authority over CLCs, via AFL-CIO rules that prevent CLCs from competing with international unions for members. For example, a CLC may have only local unions and not individual union members as affiliates. Regardless of its size, each CLC may send only one delegate to the annual AFL-CIO convention, whereas each international union is represented at the convention in proportion to its membership (Ulman 1966; AFL-CIO 1991).

CLCs represent the oldest federated structure in the U.S. labor movement. They predate national labor federations, including the American Federation of Labor and the Knights of Labor. In the nineteenth century, CLCs played a key role in organizing unorganized workers into local unions (Burke 1968; Foner 1974). After the 1890s, when the American Federation of Labor adopted the rules that prevent CLCs from competing with national and international unions, national and international unions rather than CLCs played the lead roles in organizing.

During most of the post-World War II period, CLCs were active mainly in electoral politics and political lobbying. They played only minor roles in organizing. To the extent that CLCs were involved in organizing at all, they mainly gathered information about unorganized work sites and conveyed this information to international union organizers (Cook and Stanley 1970; Golper and Roberts 1973). In recent years, however, several CLCs have become more actively involved in organizing nonunionized workers.[1]

This chapter explores the recent renaissance in organizing activity among CLCs. We are primarily interested in describing the various organizing activities in which CLCs are engaged and in understanding why different CLCs are involved in different activities. In addition, we seek to discover what, if anything, CLCs contribute to organizing efforts that other actors, such as international unions, are unable to contribute. We also probe the limits that currently exist on the CLCs' organizing activities. Finally, we develop some hypotheses about the potential contributions of CLCs to future organizing efforts.

Sources of Data and Research Method

Our data were obtained from open-ended telephone and personal interviews that we conducted with officials of seventeen CLCs, two community-labor organizations, and one AFL-CIO regional director who worked closely with a CLC in his region. We were interested in describing and understanding the organizing activities of those CLCs that are most active in organizing. We hoped that CLCs other than those in our sample, as well as union organizers and scholars, would find the concepts and activities that we described to be useful in their own practice and in the development of theories about CLCs and organizing. We were not interested in making descriptive generalizations about the organizing activities of CLCs throughout the United States. Thus, the sample we selected was not representative of all CLCs in the nation. Instead, we began our research with a list of CLCs that, according to the AFL-CIO's Department of Organization and Field Services, had organizing committees as of July 1995. We believed that the CLCs on this list would be among those most active in organizing.

We were able to interview officials of nine CLCs on the AFL-CIO's list, and we asked each of our interviewees to suggest other CLCs that he or she believed were "doing good work." Using these referrals, we were able to contact six more CLCs, two community-labor organizations, and one AFL-CIO regional director. We obtained additional data on the involvement of

---

1. According to a recent unpublished AFL-CIO survey of CLCs, about 23 percent of the 572 active CLCs in the United States engage in organizing activities that go beyond support work and transmitting information to international unions.

CLCs in organizing from an unpublished survey of CLCs conducted by the AFL-CIO in the summer of 1996. Finally, we interviewed representatives of some CLCs that were not active in organizing.[2]

In each case, we interviewed the president of the CLC or, if the president was not available, a staff member who was involved with or knowledgeable about the CLC's organizing efforts. Each interview lasted between forty-five minutes and two hours and took place between October 1995 and February 1996.

During our interviews, we asked about the kinds of organizing activities in which the CLC was involved and our interviewees' views on organizing and on the broader role of the CLC. To place these responses in context, we also asked for a great deal of background information about the structure and nonorganizing activities of each CLC. We developed our interview questions on the basis of the experience of one of the authors, who was formerly the secretary-treasurer of a CLC, and with the assistance of one of the CLC leaders we interviewed.

General Features of Organizing Activity

Although this chapter is concerned primarily with the organizing activities of CLCs, it is important to note at the outset that electoral politics and political lobbying, not organizing, are the principal activities of CLCs. Moreover, even those CLCs that are most active in organizing do not often engage in such direct organizing activities as targeting particular groups of nonunion workers for inclusion in bargaining units, obtaining signatures on union authorization cards, petitioning for NLRB elections, or conducting campaigns for voluntary recognition of a union by an employer.[3] All the CLC leaders we interviewed regarded direct organizing as the primary responsibility of local or international unions; the CLCs' main role in organiz-

2. We interviewed leaders of the following CLCs and community organizations: AFL-CIO Region 6 (western United States); Allegheny County (Pittsburgh), Pennsylvania; Atlanta, Georgia; Boston, Massachusetts, Jobs with Justice Campaign; Chicago, Illinois; Cincinnati, Ohio; Fresno, California; Ithaca, New York; Kansas City, Missouri; Los Angeles Manufacturing Action Project (LAMAP); Milwaukee, Wisconsin; Northeast Indiana (Fort Wayne); Northwest Florida (Pensacola); Rochester, New York; St. Louis, Missouri; San Francisco, California; San Mateo, California; South Bay (San Jose), California; and Westmoreland County, Pennsylvania. Additional CLC leaders who were surveyed: Detroit, Michigan; Flint, Michigan; King County (Seattle), Washington; New York, New York; Roanoke, Virginia; San Diego, California; South Central Iowa (Des Moines); South Florida (Miami); and Wichita/Hutchinson, Kansas.

3. AFL-CIO Region 6 coordinates organizing activities in the Los Angeles area in cooperation with the Los Angeles CLC and has initiated its own organizing campaigns, but this is unusual.

ing, according to our interviewees, is to support the organizing efforts of the locals or internationals.

Nonetheless, there is a great deal of variation in the extent and nature of the CLCs' organizing support activities. All our CLCs convey information about unorganized work sites to the appropriate local or international. Some confine themselves to this relatively passive role. Others play more active roles, such as coordinating multiunion organizing campaigns, creating their own associate membership programs, or using their ties with public officials or nonlabor community organizations to pressure nonunion employers into recognizing unions.

A major difference between the more passive and the more active CLCs appears to be the resources that are available for all purposes, including organizing. Those CLCs that are active in organizing have one or more full-time staff members[4] and/or a high degree of involvement in CLC activities by the CLC delegates who represent the affiliated unions. In addition, more active CLCs have leaders who believe that organizing is an important council activity, and at least one affiliated union and a segment of the nonunion community has demonstrated support for union organizing. The CLCs that serve only as information conduits lack any of these resources.[5]

The organizing activities in which CLCs are involved depend largely on the way in which their leaders view the role of CLCs in both the labor movement and the broader community. Our interviews reveal that CLC officials hold two contrasting orientations concerning this role. We label these orientations "conventional" and "transformative." These orientations are ideal types; some CLC leaders clearly subscribe to one of the two orientations, while others reflect a mix of both. The interview responses show, however, that each of our interviewees holds views that are closer to one or the other orientation.

The orientation of its leadership does not determine whether a CLC is active in organizing or whether its organizing efforts are successful. It does, however, influence the organizing activities in which the CLC is involved if it is active in organizing. Having one or the other orientation makes some CLC activities, including organizing activities, seem natural, important, or necessary if the CLC is to play its proper role in the labor movement and the broader community. At the same time, having one or the other orienta-

4. According to the AFL-CIO survey of CLCs, about 30 percent of CLCs have full-time or part-time staff dedicated exclusively to CLC work. (This percentage excludes United Way labor liaisons.) Only about 5 percent of CLCs with an affiliated membership of ten thousand or fewer workers have any staff at all.

5. According to the AFL-CIO survey of CLCs, 17 percent play no role in organizing other than to serve as information conduits and 23 percent play no role in organizing.

tion makes other activities seem unimportant, unnecessary, or inconsistent with the appropriate CLC role.

The Conventional Orientation

CLC leaders who have a conventional orientation believe that the proper roles of the CLC are to provide services, especially political campaign and lobbying services, to affiliates; to implement the AFL-CIO's agenda at the local level; to present a positive image of organized labor to the local community; and to help affiliates work together on matters of common interest. These leaders view the mission of the CLC as substantially constrained by, and perhaps even as reflecting, the CLC's structural position in the labor movement[6]—in other words, as a federation of local AFL-CIO unions[7] that are voluntarily affiliated with it (AFL-CIO 1991).

Two things follow from this perspective. First, the CLC is relatively passive in relation to its affiliates. As a CLC official in a large midwestern city said, "We're a union of unions; we can only do what the locals direct and fund us to do." Second, the CLC is a relatively self-contained federation that has only limited and sporadic ties with other community organizations, such as neighborhood, women's, racial or ethnic, and environmental groups, that have an interest in work and employment issues. Conventionally oriented CLC officials often serve on boards of directors of local charitable organizations, such as the United Way, Boy Scouts, and Girl Scouts, and sometimes work with other community organizations on matters of common interest, especially political campaigns. However, they do not engage in strategy sessions with members of non-AFL-CIO organizations, and they view their interactions with members of those organizations as opportunities to advance the interests of their local affiliates. An official of one conventional CLC in a large midwestern city even expressed a dislike for working with non-AFL-CIO organizations. He believed that the other organizations rather than the unions would receive public recognition and "credit" for any joint accomplishments.

Several leaders of conventional CLCs questioned whether CLCs should play any role in organizing other than referring possible leads to the appropriate affiliates. They believed that the international unions should do the organizing and that if the CLCs played a more active role, the internationals might view such activity as interference.

---

6. Several scholars of the labor movement also hold this view (Ulman 1966; Tomlins 1979; Rathke and Rogers 1996).

7. To our knowledge, two CLCs include non-AFL-CIO unions or organizations as affiliates.

Other conventional CLCs have, over the course of the past decade, adopted innovative practices that support and encourage organizing. Two such CLCs, both in large midwestern cities, have sponsored conferences or seminars on organizing. Speakers have included organizers and organizing directors from international unions and the AFL-CIO, labor educators, and, in one case, a prominent consultant who formerly specialized in advising employers on how to thwart union organizing drives. One CLC in a large midwestern city has formed an interfaith committee of local clergy who use moral suasion to enlist support for organizing efforts and advocate union positions on workplace issues. This CLC also provides its affiliates with advice about what kinds of employers are and are not promising targets for organizing.

Several conventional CLCs help their affiliates resolve disputes when different unions try to organize the same groups of workers. For the most part, the CLCs mediate only if affiliates ask them to do so, but one conventional CLC in a large midwestern city has a cooperative organizing committee that helps unions clear organizing targets on an ad hoc basis.[8] Committee membership is open to any affiliated local that is willing to observe committee guidelines. Representatives of affiliated locals meet quarterly with a CLC staff member and submit a list of their proposed organizing targets to the entire committee for its approval. If more than one member union seeks to organize the same group of workers, the committee attempts to resolve the conflict. If the conflict cannot be resolved, unions that are not parties to the dispute agree not to try to organize the workers whom the quarreling unions have targeted. In one case, the committee helped two locals agree that one of the two would have the first chance to organize a target but that if that local did not succeed within a specified time period, the first local would turn the union authorization cards over to the second local. The second local successfully organized the target.

Some conventional CLCs help organizers meet to exchange strategies and tactics. One CLC simply provides organizers with a meeting place. Another holds a monthly breakfast for local and international union organizers in its region. The latter also helps its affiliates "lend" organizers to other local unions to assist with major organizing campaigns.

Two conventional CLCs have organizing committees that are especially active. The members of one committee in a small southern city assist local unions by making house calls to workers whom the locals are trying to organize. Committee members also arrange space in local hotels for affiliates that wish to hold meetings for unorganized workers. Members of the

---

8. We know of five such co-ops sponsored by the national AFL-CIO. This one operates within the CLC as a working committee (Richardson 1995).

other organizing committee assist affiliates by providing informational picketing and strike support. Both committees do their organizing support work only at the request of an affiliate.

Finally, although initiating or coordinating a multiunion, cooperative organizing campaign is not an activity that fits easily into the conventional orientation, one conventional CLC in a large midwestern city assisted local building trades unions in running a successful cooperative drive to organize a local convention center. The CLC's role was to help the unions talk out their problems during the campaign, not to run the campaign itself.

The organizing activities of conventional CLCs reflect the basic features of the conventional orientation. Activities aimed at directly recruiting new union members are conducted only at the request of affiliated unions that have already initiated organizing campaigns. Support activities that the CLC initiates are limited to such efforts as holding conferences and forming interfaith committees, which do not directly involve CLC personnel in the process of recruiting new union members. Conventional CLCs do not use electoral or lobbying activities as a means of promoting organizing except in the most general sense that electing union-friendly public officials or influencing legislative decisions can be said to promote a political climate that is conducive to organizing. Nor do such CLCs use their ties with nonlabor groups to encourage organizing. When they establish new institutions to facilitate organizing, such as cooperative organizing committees or monthly organizers' breakfasts, they limit participation to members of affiliated unions. Despite these limitations, though, conventional CLCs are capable of being actively involved in organizing and have developed innovative practices that support the effort.

The Transformative Orientation

CLC leaders who have a transformative orientation believe that CLCs can become active participants in the development of grassroots regional economic and political power. These leaders view CLCs as vehicles for social change. They believe that the proper role of the CLC is to bring affiliated unions together with each other and with nonlabor community organizations to advance the interests of workers, especially in the political arena. In keeping with this view, they believe that the CLC should be concerned with advancing the interests of nonunion workers as well as the interests of current union members and the institutional interests of affiliated unions. These officials do not believe that these interests are in fundamental conflict. Unlike conventional CLC leaders, most of the transformative leaders we interviewed see a gap between what they view as the AFL-CIO's "definition" of the CLC's role and their own view of that role. These leaders typically see the AFL-CIO's definition as narrower, more focused on servicing local affiliates and on endorsing political candidates.

Transformative CLCs engage in many of the same organizing activities as conventional CLCs, but they also do much more. Transformative CLCs view themselves and their affiliates as key nodes in a broader network of progressive organizations that are concerned with work and employment issues. It is therefore natural for them to use their ties with other organizations to promote organizing. In a large southern city, the CLC joined forces with neighborhood and African American community organizations and with local unions in an attempt to ensure that union workers and African Americans would be employed in the construction of an athletic stadium. As a result of their efforts, corporate officials, under pressure from the city government, agreed to build the stadium at prevailing union rates, hire local residents (most of whom were African American), and provide training. In a similar situation, a CLC in a large midwestern city helped match the African American community's need for jobs with the building trades unions' interest in having the city's convention center built by union workers. Drawing on coalition partners to build mass pickets, the CLC helped the parties achieve a project agreement that guaranteed that 25 percent of the jobs would go to members of the predominantly African American community and that the workers would be paid the prevailing union rate. The CLC in another large midwestern city helped organize clerical workers at a local university by using both its representative on the university's governing board and a mass demonstration by members of area unions and women's groups as means to pressure the university to recognize the union.

Leaders of transformative CLCs frequently strategize jointly with leaders of community organizations that are involved in a variety of issues. One northeastern CLC even recruits environmental and community activists to be CLC delegates. Transformative CLCs are often characterized by strategic plans that combine demands for jobs with community demands for economic justice and increased political power for both union and nonunion workers. In raising broad-based issues, transformative CLCs often focus their demands on such community-related concerns as the need for safe and humane working conditions, economic and job development, job training, improved industrial technological capabilities, defense industry conversion, and "living wages." In a large midwestern city, the CLC allied with an environmental group in an attempt to support unionization of an employer that was a major polluter. The CLC and the environmental group initially had different goals (unionization for the CLC, pollution control for the environmental group), but they developed a common strategy so that both goals could be accomplished.

The primary source of revenue for most CLCs is the per-capita dues paid by the affiliated locals. Many, but not all, transformative CLCs aggressively seek additional funding through grants from governments, foundations, and charitable organizations. This enables them to hire staff on "soft money." Because many transformative CLCs have positioned themselves at the intersection of labor, community, and local business interests, organizations with concerns about such matters as defense industry conversion, job training, job development, job placement, and the need for collaborative labor-management programs are often predisposed to award funding to CLCs. A transformative CLC in the rural Northeast obtained a city government grant to operate a job rights and job referral center for local residents. Another, in a large midwestern city, uses government and foundation grants to operate both a job placement service for laid-off workers and an occupational health center that includes a walk-in clinic. Using a combination of state and federal grants, a CLC in a medium-sized city in a midwestern right-to-work state has been able to create a center for dislocated workers and a statewide labor institute that employs six workers. These programs serve nonunionized as well as unionized workers. Although CLC leaders do not conduct such activities for the primary purpose of organizing, they believe that CLC-provided employment services can interest nonunionized workers in unionization or provide unions with information about promising targets for organizing. The labor institute in the medium-sized midwestern city helped the CLC make contact with workers who were interested in unionization, and through these contacts the CLC was subsequently able to organize four separate bargaining units in four different industries for three different international unions.

Some transformative CLCs, fearing the "strings" attached to outside money, have chosen an "organizing" style of leadership that has enabled them to extend their resources by using volunteer labor. By visualizing the CLC itself as an organizing tool, some transformative CLCs have been able to tap into networks of labor and community activists. Some have launched extensive labor-to-community outreach programs, such as "Labor to Neighbor." These programs use union member volunteers to increase organized labor's visibility in and integration into the communities in which labor activists live. The programs are aimed at "organizing neighborhoods" around issues that are of concern in the neighborhoods. Thus, organized labor becomes the catalyst for grassroots neighborhood activism. In two large cities, one in the West and the other in the South, CLC-driven labor-to-neighbor programs have been instrumental in the election of prolabor candidates at both city and county levels. More important, these labor-neighborhood coalitions have sometimes resulted in the creation of neighborhood economic development programs and jobs paying union wages for neighborhood residents, as in the case of the athletic stadium and the convention center.

Other transformative CLCs use volunteers to extend their affiliates' organizing resources in more direct ways. In all regions and in both large cities and rural areas, transformative CLCs train volunteer rank-and-file union members to be organizers. These volunteers then become available not only to their own unions but also to other unions in the area during organizing drives. In addition to maintaining lists of activists, creating phone trees, and providing education, transformative CLCs create a climate in which rank-and-file union members expect democratic participation, responsibility, and activism. For these CLCs, activists are not just "hands to staff picket lines, stuff envelopes, or help organize new members" (Bronfenbrenner and Juravich 1994:13). For example, a CLC in a southern right-to-work state included in its mission statement a mandate to have a "Strategic Organizing Response Team to provide an effective and timely response to any employer action that threatens the rights of employees to organize." Rank-and-file activists are expected to mobilize on short notice to provide mass picketing at any job site where employers obstruct union organizing.

In another CLC in a midsize city in a midwestern right-to-work state, the CLC president explained: "They celebrate right to work for less down here. So our job is to stay in their face. We don't take no shit, and we won't take no for an answer." With its core of rank-and-file activists, this CLC picketed the groundbreaking of the "centerpiece" hotel in town and "picketed the hell out of them" until the hotel agreed to recognize the union. The CLC's activists also helped stop local reporters from working as strikebreakers at the *Detroit Free Press* by confronting them personally and convincing them not to work for the newspaper despite Knight-Ridder's offer to double their pay.

Perhaps the most extensive CLC program to encourage rank-and-file activism around organizing is found in a large midwestern city. The CLC there has a program called "Developing Secondary Leadership," which trains rank-and-file members in organizing and leadership and then organizes them into teams that assist local unions in their organizing efforts. Team members not only act as volunteer organizers but also assist local unions with picketing and strike support and work with local church groups to develop strategies for saving jobs.

Transformative CLCs sometimes use associate membership programs to "organize" workers who cannot have or do not currently want collective bargaining. The associate members usually pay dues to the CLC and are eligible for minimal consumer benefits available to union members, such as union credit cards. More important, the associate members often volunteer to assist the CLC or affiliated unions with organizing, political activities, or strike support. In some instances, associate members initiate organizing drives in their own workplaces. AFL-CIO Region 6 created an ethnically based associate membership program, the California Immigrant Workers Association (Lazo 1990), which became essential in two successful organizing drives involving Latino immigrant workers. Another Region 6 associate membership program, the Korean Immigrant Workers Association, supported Latino hotel workers against Korean hotel owners in a demonstration of interethnic worker unity.

Transformative CLCs also use a variety of "direct" unionizing strategies. In addition to supporting traditional single-union and single-employer NLRB strategies, they sometimes coordinate multiunion or regionally based union organizing or (more rarely) organize independently in advance of international unions. Some transformative CLCs have helped affiliated unions that were interested in conducting cooperative multiunion organizing campaigns form joint steering committees or resolve interunion disputes.[9] For example, a CLC in a large western city created an areawide "Downtown Organizing Committee," whose members came from every union that represented workers in any downtown workplace and every union that was interested in organizing workers in the downtown area. The committee also included volunteer organizers who had been trained in one of the volunteer organizing classes that AFL-CIO Region 6 conducted jointly with this CLC. The CLC directed organizing drives, using volunteer organizers to develop strategies and collect signatures through work site visits and house calls. The CLC's efforts resulted in the successful organizing of shuttle drivers, restaurants, and the largest hotel in the area (AFL-CIO n.d.).

Three big-city CLCs, two in the Midwest and one in the West, as well as AFL-CIO Region 6, obtained signatures on union authorization cards for international unions. These efforts resulted in successful unionization through voluntary recognition of the unions by the employers.

In several cases, transformative CLCs have become the community base for multiemployer, multiunion organizing efforts, such as SEIU's Justice for Janitors campaign, and for such joint community-labor organizing efforts as the Campaign for Justice and Jobs with Justice. In the latter cases, workers were organized in both their neighborhoods and their workplaces.

Implications for Organizing

Our interviews suggest that a CLC is likely to go beyond mere information sharing and to be active in organizing under three conditions: the CLC has resources in the form of full-time staff and/or active volunteer delegates; it has CLC leaders who believe that organizing is an important CLC activity;

9. These efforts were important CLC activities earlier in this century (Barbash 1956).

and it has affiliated unions that have some interest in organizing and support for union organizing in the local community. The activities the CLC will undertake will depend on whether the CLC leaders have a conventional or a transformative orientation. Transformative CLCs seem to be more deeply and more broadly involved in the organizing process than conventional CLCs. Coordinating multiunion organizing campaigns, creating associate membership programs that assist or serve as springboards for the organization of bargaining units, participating in labor-community alliances, exerting political pressure on public officials to promote organizing, training rank-and-file organizers, providing employment services to nonmembers, and organizing independently in advance of international unions are among the activities that only transformative CLCs appear to undertake.

The literature on the structure of business organizations (e.g., Eccles and Nohria 1992; Powell 1987) and on social movements (e.g., Tarrow 1994:135–50; Gerlach 1983) suggests that organizations that have extensive "network" ties to other organizations outperform organizations that have rigid boundaries and few ties to outside groups, especially when their external environments are uncertain and rapidly changing. We are unable to assess the relative organizing success of conventional and transformative CLCs; however, transformative CLCs that are networked with nonlabor organizations engage in deeper and more extensive organizing activity than the more self-contained conventional CLCs. In this sense, our findings are broadly consistent with research findings on the advantages of network forms of organization. Yet our analysis also suggests that CLCs will not be able to achieve the advantages of networks simply by creating ties with nonlabor organizations. The development of a network form of organization, at least for CLCs, flows out of the transformative orientation. Transformative leaders view themselves and their CLCs as mobilizers for diverse groups within their geographic communities. Because they hold this view, they can build coalitions among groups, such as white building trades unionists and African American city residents, that do not usually work together.

Where the social structures and cultures of local unions and nonlabor groups make it possible for a CLC to be effective at organizing, the best way to promote deep and extensive organizing activity is to encourage the leaders of the CLC to adopt a transformative orientation or to choose leaders who have such an orientation. But it may not be possible for all CLC leaders to have transformative orientations. In some geographic areas, there may be too few union-friendly nonlabor groups to enable the CLC to become part of a labor-oriented community network. In other regions, potential nonlabor allies (including, on some issues, businesses) may be self-contained, bureaucratic organizations and may therefore not be willing to form a network. In either case, a transformatively oriented CLC leader would be unable to act in accordance with the transformative orientation because the CLC could not become part of the kind of network the leader envisioned. For some CLCs, then, a conventional orientation may be the only possibility.

One of the messages of our research is that, although the transformative orientation is preferable where it is feasible, CLCs with either orientation can participate in organizing activity. To know what organizing work is possible to undertake, CLC leaders need to be aware of both their orientations toward the CLC and the constraints that community structure and culture may place on their activities.

Are there organizing activities in which CLCs can participate that go beyond those in which even the most active CLCs have thus far engaged? Might CLCs organize workers into new unions in occupations or industries in which no existing international union has jurisdiction, as the CIO did in the 1930s when it formed industrywide organizing committees to organize mass production workers? Might CLCs create general unions that, like the federal labor unions of the AFL in the early twentieth century (Hoxie 1923), include workers from several occupations and industries, no one of which has enough workers in the CLC's region to form a viable local? Or might CLCs organize the kinds of geographically localized general unions that, as some industrial relations theorists have suggested (Sabel 1993; Miles 1989), could set wages and employment standards for all occupations and industries in the area, provide training and job referral services, and help workers deal with the growing interdependence of work and family life? The organizing activities of some transformative CLCs, especially the formation of associate membership programs and the provision of job placement services to nonunionized as well as unionized workers, suggest that CLCs might be appropriate vehicles for these new types of organizing.

Without addressing the merits of any of these possible activities, we suggest that CLC leaders will have to develop new orientations toward CLC activity if they are to adopt fundamentally new roles in organizing. Jonathan Tasini (1995) and some CLC leaders have proposed that CLCs be transformed into "community labor councils" that include as members both unions and nonunion groups interested in work issues. A community labor council might well become an umbrella organization that represents workers' interests generally. The community labor council orientation would make organization of local general unions a natural activity of the council.

Another orientation that some CLC leaders might adopt would view the CLC as the principal provider of financial and technical support for its local union affiliates. One transformative CLC leader in a large midwestern city may have foreshadowed the emergence of this view when he said: "The changing world economic and political situation has redefined the role of central labor councils. Decisions that affect the day-to-day lives of workers are becoming more regional and local. Corporate decisions and government decisions are becoming decentralized. There is a dramatic decline in national pattern bargaining, and national worker standards are eroding. There is a vacuum of power that can be filled by central labor councils." A CLC with this orientation would find it natural to organize new local unions that would affiliate directly with the CLC. These unions could be organized on an occupational, industrial, general, or other basis. They might choose to join an international union or to affiliate only with the CLC.

The AFL-CIO's current leadership is changing the federation's stance toward CLCs in ways that seem to support at least the transformative orientation if not some of the more speculative orientations suggested above. In July 1996, the AFL-CIO for the first time held a national conference of CLCs in Denver. One hundred and seventy-five CLC officers attended the conference, which highlighted the efforts of transformative CLCs to build interunion and union-community networks, and conference attendees held workshops on strategies for developing such networks. AFL-CIO president John Sweeney formed a CLC advisory council whose members, officers of CLCs, will set priorities and direction for the councils. Sweeney said at the conference that "the bulk of the resources for reorganizing the American work force and rebuilding the American labor movement must come from international and local unions," but that "the coordination and community support for such efforts must come from our central labor councils" (Rosier 1996:5). AFL-CIO organizing director Richard Bensinger stated that CLCs need to be "cradles of solidarity" that will play key roles in geographically based organizing campaigns.[10] It is too early to tell whether the initiatives discussed at the Denver conference will lead to a major expansion of the role of CLCs in organizing. However, if geographically based, multiunion organizing is to expand, then regional structures must exist that facilitate the growth of an activist base, community coalitions, and bold, new organizing strategies.

10. Bensinger's comment was recorded by one of the authors, who attended the conference.

PART II

Community-Based Organizing outside the NLRB

There are many groups within the changing workplace for whom the standard model of organizing under the National Labor Relations Board simply does not fit. This is especially true for contract labor, contingent workers, and those employed in the underground economy. When the tenuous nature of the employment relationship for these workers is accompanied by a heavily immigrant workforce, the challenge to unions is even more complex. The three chapters in part II report on cases in which unions have chosen to bypass the NLRB and concentrate instead on organizing in the community. Needleman looks at two cases in which alliances with community-based organizations (CBOs) offer promise to unions. Ness describes a UNITE experiment to establish centers in the community for immigrant garment workers. Waldinger and his colleagues at the University of California in Los Angeles (Erickson, Milkman, Mitchell, Valenzuela, Wong, and Zeitlin) analyze the SEIU Justice for Janitors campaign in that city, which combined organizing of immigrant workers, a strong community-based campaign, and economic pressure to win union recognition.

Needleman finds that although there is potential conflict between unions and CBOs, there are also major opportunities for synergy. CBOs may not place the same priority as unions do on achieving employer recognition and collective bargaining rights, but both organizations are committed to improving the status and lives of workers. Unions and CBOs have complementary strengths that are especially important in organizing low-wage women workers. Concluding that unions and CBOs must find a way to work together, Needleman presents ideas about how to turn sometimes shaky coalitions into longer-term partnerships.

For the past three years, UNITE has operated centers for immigrant and minority garment workers in New York, Los Angeles, San Francisco, and Miami. These centers offer associate membership in the union, skills training, English-language instruction, and assistance in dealing with problems with employers. The research by Ness surveys immigrant garment workers in New York to determine whether their participation in UNITE's center in the Fashion District is an effective alternative, or prelude, to traditional NLRB organizing. He finds that the center has produced positive results. It is viewed favorably in the immigrant community, among center members and nonmembers alike, as an agency that defends workers in disputes with abusive employers. Ness's survey also reveals that the center has succeeded in contributing to the development of an interest in unionization among the workers.

The final chapter in part II is a timely and insightful case study of the successful Justice for Janitors campaign in Los Angeles. Driven by economic and demographic changes, by the mid-1980s the once highly unionized building cleaning services industry in Los Angeles had become predominantly nonunion and very low wage. Exploited Latina immigrants made up a large and growing part of the workforce. Building services employment shifted sharply, away from building owner-managers and toward outside cleaning contractors. Rather than capitulate, SEIU fought back with an innovative and militant campaign that bypassed cumbersome and ineffective NLRB election procedures. With the help of vocal support from the immigrant community, SEIU brought pressure on the building owners who held the real levers of economic power. Waldinger and his coauthors conclude that although the future of unionism in the building services industry in Los Angeles remains threatened, it is likely that the gains for low-wage, oppressed workers that have been achieved in recent years by Justice for Janitors in Southern California can be consolidated, maintained, and extended.

Chapter 4

Building Relationships for the Long Haul: Unions and Community-Based Groups Working Together to Organize Low-Wage Workers

Ruth Needleman

Working in poorly lit and crowded sweatshops, Asian immigrant women make up 85 percent of the Bay Area's twenty thousand garment workers. In Los Angeles and New York, the story is similar. Contractors squeeze labor out of women at or below the legal minimum wage, and when profit margins dwindle, they close their doors and pay nothing for work already done. Of this nation's estimated fifty thousand such operations, about one-third operate without licenses, keep no records, pay in cash, pay no over-time, and on a much too regular basis pay nothing at all (Foo, Ho, and Kim 1995; Foo 1994; Henry 1993; Wong 1993).

The garment industry is not alone in amassing profits from the nation's most vulnerable workforce—immigrants and women of color. Millions of working women of color occupy positions beyond visibility at the bottom and at the margins of the U.S. labor market. Whether African American women laboring in the Deep South in poultry or catfish operations, Chi-cana/Mexicana or Latinas in canneries, electronics, and home care, or Asian immigrant women in garment manufacturing, high-tech industries, and res-taurants, their economic status is low and their work experiences are char-acterized by segregation and discrimination. They represent a substantial proportion of the expanding contingent workforce.

Women of color are more concentrated in traditionally female jobs than white women and are crowded into fewer occupational categories at the

An Institute for Women's Policy Research grant supported work on this paper.

bottom of the service, clerical, and manufacturing sectors. They work more hours and harder for lower wages and fewer benefits than any other group of workers, and equal levels of education, professional experience, and job tenure bring fewer rewards (Amott and Matthaei 1991; Foo 1994; Headden 1993; Malveaux 1987; Needleman 1993a; Woody 1992; U.S. Department of Labor 1994).

These women's home situations exacerbate their economic status. More often than not, women of color are the sole, main, or major provider for their families, which tend to be larger, extended, and living in poverty. Their communities are characterized by inferior services, schools, transportation, and resources. Often their poverty forces them to live in the highest crime areas, creating constant anxiety and fear. They cannot afford child care or after-school care. They choose every day between being at home to protect their children and being at work to be able to feed them.

The conditions are even worse for immigrant women. A majority of the immigrants to the United States in the past sixty years have been female; for the past thirty years, they have come primarily from poorer Third World nations: Mexico, Central America, and Pacific Rim countries. Lacking education and unable to speak English, many of these women are forced into menial, low-wage jobs. More than one-third of Chinese and Korean women work in low-wage manufacturing; it is estimated than in San Francisco's Chinatown, for example, half work in the garment industry (Foo 1994; Needleman 1993a).

Because of the contexts of their lives, there is no way to remedy the needs of low-wage women as workers without also addressing their needs as mothers, heads of households, wives, or children. Their needs and problems are inextricably bound up, and they are overwhelming. They cannot subordinate home demands to work demands since they have sole or primary responsibility for both. Language, cultural, and religious traditions, deeply rooted fears of repression or deportation, memories from their homeland or childhood, and threats from employers and government agencies all place barriers in the way of any extracurricular activity in the workplace or outside the home (interviews, Escamilla, Sancho, Shin, Strehlou, and Pefianco-Thomas). Yet these are the workers who most need unions, and unions must find ways to organize them, given the restructuring of work and labor markets. Labor participation rates for women of color are climbing, and their occupations are among those creating the most new positions. They hold a high percentage of the rapidly expanding contingent and minimum-wage jobs and work in the smallest shops (one to nineteen employees), which account for all net job growth in the past decade (Needleman 1993a).

Despite the barriers, hundreds of thousands of immigrant women and women of color take stands against their exploitation, fight employers, convince families and coworkers to support them, and risk all they have to achieve dignity and fair treatment and form a union. The most successful efforts at helping these workers organize have taken into account their status, occupations, and broad needs. Campaigns have centered as much or more in their homes and communities as in their workplaces. They have involved long-term education and leadership development work and have provided structures to address workplace isolation or dispersion and resources to meet language, child-care, and family needs.

An equally important consideration in organizing these women is the current political and economic climate in the country. Changing labor markets and global restructuring have increased job competition and produced a decline in living standards, leading to greater insecurity, fear, and divisions among workers. Anti-immigrant, anti-women, and anti-minority initiatives and biases are on the rise, turning many workers against each other and toward individual rather than collective solutions. Many union workers look to overtime rather than collective bargaining to increase income; they support exclusionary "me-first" policies and fall prey to right-wing appeals on such issues as welfare reform, immigration, and affirmative action. Such an environment is not conducive to union organizing.

Historically, labor has been most successful at organizing during periods when the economy and job market were expanding, when hope and an openness to risk-taking in the workplace were more the norm. Times of despair, fear, and increasing job competition call for a flexible repertoire of tactics and a focus on education and leadership development. Education helps to open unions to the new workforce or minimally to neutralize backward thinking among members. Leadership development helps ensure that the workers entering unions have the skills, confidence, unity, and vision to stand firm.

There are, therefore, both short-term and long-term reasons that cooperation and partnerships between unions and community-based organizations can advance efforts to organize low-wage women workers, including that building such relationships (1) maintains a dual focus at work and in the workers' own communities; (2) addresses workers' family and work-based needs, enabling them to stay in the workforce and participate in self-organization activities; (3) helps these women overcome fears and language, cultural, or legal status barriers; (4) given these women's isolation, high job turnover rates, and temporary job status, builds lasting networks and support systems to sustain unionism across jobs and locations; and (5) lays the foundation for larger organizing campaigns—by occupation or geographical area—down the road.

There are some areas in which unions are extremely successful, in part because of their objectives, size, resources, history, and structures. Unions have the experience and staff to reach large but dispersed workforces; to tackle city, state, and even federal policies or practices that stand as barriers to organization; to connect workers to national and even international networks of support; and to ensure representation is achieved, contracts are signed, and improvements are made in wages and working conditions. Given their community roots, emphasis on one-on-one contact, and long-term perseverance, community-based organizations offer many workers a friendlier, more familiar face, support during individual crises, and training and education over an extended period, at a pace well suited to these workers' overwhelming responsibilities. Through two case studies—the first, CBO led, involving garment workers and the second, union led, focusing on home care—this chapter examines the advantages and the problems in building partnerships, especially among organizations in which the character of the work and the standards for measuring success are very different.

Garment Workers' Campaign

It was "business as usual" the day in May 1992 when twelve Asian immigrant women failed to collect back wages of $15,000 from Lucky Sewing Co., one of many small garment contractors producing high-fashion dresses for manufacturer Jessica McClintock. Among the twelve women, someone knew of a group, the Asian Immigrant Women Advocates (AIWA), that might help them. The penniless garment workers arrived en masse to meet with Young Shin, AIWA's executive director, in an upstairs office in the center of Oakland's Chinatown.

The seamstresses explained that they had been paid with bad checks for more than a year and were owed $15,000 among them. Furthermore, the conditions under which they had worked were intolerable: ten-to-twelve-hour days, six and sometimes seven days a week, without any benefits, in a dim and unventilated shop. There were windows, but they were sealed shut, and signs were posted that said "No going to the bathroom. No loud talking." According to the women, no matter how hard and fast they labored, their piece rate fell below minimum wage. "When you break the money we earn," explained one worker, "it contains blood and sweat, so we use every penny carefully" (Henry 1993:22; Yokota 1994; interview with Shin).

Young Shin had heard similar stories before. She had founded AIWA in 1983 to provide support and referrals for Asian immigrant women; over the first decade of operations, a steady stream of workers had come through her office. What was different about these twelve women, explained Shin, was that they came together and planned to stand together. "They understood injustice in the garment industry. . . . They understood how it works, and they wanted to deal with it." AIWA's approach is rooted in education, leadership development, and self-organization. AIWA, according to Shin, "starts where women are at. Once women start knowing about their rights, then they want to know ways to exercise them."

For a decade Young Shin, AIWA staff, and volunteers worked diligently in the Asian community, handing out leaflets, producing a quarterly newsletter, organizing social events, field trips to Golden Gate Park, English as a second language classes, and leadership training, building community, and encouraging collective activity. Shin reached out for volunteer help in many directions, including to professors and students at the University of California at Berkeley and to other schools, religious, and legal groups, friends, and neighbors. This work, she emphasized, "takes a very, very long time."

AIWA does not see itself as representing workers with employers but rather as an advocacy group that walks with and supports women in what they decide to do for themselves.[1] The first step was to see if the women could persuade the owners of Lucky to make good on their debt. The Oakland contractor, however, had declared bankruptcy, shipped off the remaining inventory, and was already busy setting up shop under a new name. The bankruptcy attorney informed the workers and AIWA that there was no money to be had (Foo, Ho, and Kim 1995).

As Young Shin indicated, these workers understood the garment industry and that contractors are legally liable for wages. It is, however, the major manufacturers, often referred to as "jobbers," who set the poverty-level contract rates and then hide behind the fly-by-night contractors. Lucky sewed garments for several manufacturers; one of the largest and most known was Jessica McClintock, whose $145 million empire sells romance and lacy dresses through high-priced retailers and chic boutiques. Unions and community organizations have been battling to make the manufacturers responsible for the practices of contractors. During the past few years especially, UNITE and many other organizations have worked with the Wage and Hour Division of the Department of Labor to shift accountability in the industry. AIWA seized the chance to target McClintock.

For a graphic lesson in labor economics, the workers paid a visit to one of McClintock's designer shops to examine the finished products and, of course, their price tags. One worker found a green velvet dress she had

1. AIWA is not a traditional advocacy group, however, in that it does not speak *for* clients. Young Shin describes its mission as empowerment, providing women with the skills, confidence, and support they need to stand for themselves. AIWA focuses on developing workers' own agency. Nonetheless, AIWA as well as unions often represent, mediate, and negotiate with or for their constituencies.

worked on; it was selling for $175. Adding up the pieces at their going piece rates, they figured out that she had been paid $5 for sewing the elegant attire. "I felt a pain in my heart," she said, "because we sew for so little and [the dress] was selling so high out there. And even that little amount, we didn't get it."

With the help of AIWA, the women planned a campaign, step by step. They wrote Jessica McClintock directly, asking her to take responsibility for the back wages and to sign an independent contract for two years with these skilled seamstresses. In her reply, she not only refused but disassociated herself from the problem, claiming she "had no control over contractors," that she had paid Lucky, and that she would "continue to do business with independent contractors who act in a responsible manner" (Henry 1993:22).

"Let Them Eat Lace," "Fantasy vs. Reality," and "Jessica McClintock Just Doesn't Get It" headlined a series of ads AIWA placed in the national edition of the *New York Times*. Although costly, the ad campaign put a very human face on the strategy to target the jobbers. Consumers who could not understand the structure of the industry could understand the plight of twelve women: "It's rags to riches for Jessica McClintock. But the women who sew in the sweatshops have still not been paid. You can help." The first ad ran in November 1992, a second in December, and then on and off for two years. McClintock was quoted in one of the ads: "I specialize in the concept of romanticism. . . . You come to me for very romantic clothes." The "very unromantic details" followed: half the wholesale price goes straight into McClintock's pocket; if sold through her string of boutiques, the profit is higher. About $42 goes to the contractor, whose cost is estimated at $15. When paid, only $5 goes to the worker. Each ad asked for donations for the campaign and had a clip-out coupon for the reader to sign and send directly to the designer. The ads paid for themselves and brought national attention to the role of the manufacturer.

McClintock responded with an ad of her own, accusing the immigrant workers of "intimidation and a blatant shakedown." And in an effort to squelch the campaign in its first year, she hired a Chinese-speaking lawyer who convinced five of the twelve women to accept payment in the form of a "charitable contribution." Acceptance of the money required a signature releasing McClintock from any liability for back wages. The other seven women rejected the offer.

The financially powerful McClintock then used her resources against the campaign in other ways, by seeking injunctions to limit picketing and filing unfair labor practice charges with the NLRB, arguing that tiny community-based AIWA was a labor organization. The Asian Law Caucus along with the American Civil Liberties Union provided counsel, won the workers First

Amendment rights to unlimited picketers, and got the NLRB to dismiss all charges.

From the fall of 1992 on, AIWA worked with these and other immigrant garment workers to build a national garment workers justice campaign, picketing McClintock's boutiques and fancy retailers in major cities across the country. "Boycott McClintock" has appeared on T-shirts, banners, and picket signs in New York, Chicago, Atlanta, Seattle, San Jose, Los Angeles, and San Francisco (*AIWA News,* Winter 1995).

A myriad of community-based, union, environmental, and immigrant groups joined the effort. "Support from groups across the nation," explained Young Shin, made the difference; the support "gave courage to the women to stand up and go on." Without their help, understaffed AIWA and a handful of garment workers could never have mounted or funded a national campaign. "The kinds of problems we face in the garment industry," observed Shin, "won't go away unless we're all working on it." She pointed to the massive changes brought about by global restructuring, which require a collective and strategic response.

The McClintock boycott contributed to broader initiatives—a garment workers justice campaign, task forces set up by the Oakland City Council and the Alameda County Board of Supervisors to investigate industry abuses, and a statewide coalition against sweatshops. Union support played a central part. Visible at all pickets and demonstrations were supporters from the International Ladies' Garment Workers Union (ILGWU, now UNITE), the Asian Pacific American Labor Alliance, the Equal Rights Advocates group, central labor councils, an array of area local unions, and health and safety organizations.

AIWA handled campaign decision making to ensure that the women themselves could determine the pace and shape of the struggle. AIWA emphasized empowerment and leadership development. A union would have concentrated on building organization and gaining representation in the shops. CBOs and unions focus on different kinds of campaigns, which has meant that one or the other, depending on the particular situation, has usually taken the lead. Given the differences, this approach sidestepped some of the inevitable tensions that arise in decision making on strategy and tactics. At the same time, this tactic does not allow for long-term cooperative planning, division of labor, and effective pooling of strengths. A true partnership requires a high degree of trust, understanding, and respect among organizations, the development of close relationships that can only emerge through long-term association and practice.

Joint lobbying work by unions and CBOs with the Department of Labor's Wage and Hour Division has been productive and played a decisive role in the McClintock saga. In response to pressure, the department began to publish a "clean clothes" list, highlighting those manufacturers that rely on responsible contractors. Of course, an occasional violator slips through, which is exactly what happened in the winter of 1995–96, when Jessica McClintock's name appeared on the list. AIWA's four-year campaign saw the light of day.

Faced with removal from the list—and worse publicity than AIWA could have generated—Jessica McClintock agreed to negotiate with AIWA and the workers. The fruits of this victory will be widely shared. There will be back wages for the former Lucky garment workers but much more. An education fund for garment workers is to be established as well as a toll-free hotline in English and Cantonese, monitored by the Department of Labor. An outreach campaign to inform workers of their rights will take place, and, most important, a precedent exists for holding corporations responsible for the violations of their contractors. As a result of ongoing negotiations involving UNITE, various advocacy groups, the government, and the manufacturers, a recent agreement promises to put tighter controls on sweatshops and child labor.

Organizing in the Health-Care Industry

As the health-care industry shifts costs to the consumer and care from institutions to homes, the ranks of home-care workers expand. Under provisions of federal social security insurance, poor, elderly, and disabled people can hire a home-care worker paid by the government at minimum wage. In California, there are an estimated 180,000 such workers. They work on a contingent basis, hired for a day, a week, or until the death of the person; the immediate "employer" is the consumer who hires, directs, and can also fire the worker without cause at any time. The workers receive no pensions, no health care, no benefits. The turnover is legendary; out of a group of six thousand workers in Alameda County, six hundred leave or enter every six months. By its very nature, the job isolates these workers from others in their same situation. Three-fourths of the workers are women; the vast majority are members of minority groups—African American or Chicana or non-English-speaking immigrants from Mexico, Central America, the Philippines, and other Pacific Rim nations. If workers provide extra help to the person under their care—grocery shopping, a trip to the pharmacy— not only the time but sometimes the money comes out of their own threadbare pockets (Karwath 1993; Kilborn 1995; interviews, Escamilla and Pefianco-Thomas 1995).

The home-care industry illustrates the importance of union intervention if marginalized and contingent workers are to improve their economic status. To reach these workers, to build networks, and to handle the multiple employers (the elderly or disabled person, the county that does paperwork, and the state that writes the check) requires a large organization with resources and experience. In this case, the SEIU was the union involved.[2]

SEIU formed a statewide Home Care Council, which in the Bay Area includes representatives of three large locals—715, 616, and 250—whose collective membership is in the tens of thousands and whose full-time staff numbers in the dozens. As in the garment industry, the first step toward unionization of the home-care workers involved an analysis of the byzantine system that disguises responsibility and accountability. The international provided support for research and fieldwork.

Working collectively, organizers representing each local developed a strategy that began with the creation of an employer. They organized, publicized, and pressured to get the Board of Supervisors in Alameda County to set up a public authority through which negotiations over wages and working conditions could take place as well as a registry for workers, or a centralized hiring hall. This work was completed at the front end of the campaign.

To get at least one-third of the six thousand home-care workers in the county to sign authorization cards, the union developed an army of organizers to make home visits and phone calls. The SEIU knew such an enormous undertaking would require support from many friends and allies. Gaining help from the AFL-CIO Central Labor Council, a United for Justice coalition, and several advocacy and community based groups, the campaign moved forward, with the SEIU calling the shots. Outreach to the community and to the workers was labor intensive and slow. "Many immigrants," emphasized Myriam Escamilla, a Local 715 staffer, "are so scared. Employers intimidate them. It is hard for them to visualize that they have rights. They feel it is so good to be here and that they should be grateful." Escamilla herself is from Mexico. "We have a labor movement in Mexico," she explained, "but a lot of the people were never in unions. Central Americans," she noted, "think of the union movement in terms of social problems, because in their countries union people got killed or they got laid off."

Reaching the Filipino community was particularly difficult, added 616 organizer Mila Pefianco-Thomas, who is from the Philippines. "Unions are a mystery to many [of us], and Filipino community organizations didn't really give us access to workers." The leaders often are not the workers themselves, and they keep their membership guarded from outsiders, even when they, too, are Filipinos. "Many carry with them other cultural bag-

2. Although I was working at Indiana University at the time of the interviews, I had served earlier as education director for the SEIU. As a result, I have firsthand experience with some of the locals and people involved in this campaign and an insider's understanding of union structures, relationships, and approaches. I have drawn extensively on these experiences.

gage," Pefianco-Thomas emphasized. "For example, in the Philippines, you are in a union, you get shot; unions are trouble."

In each immigrant community, organizers found similar problems. Sandy Strehlou, another home-care organizer, observed: "First you had to establish a relationship with the heads of the community organizations. They had to understand. It takes a long time. . . . They say 'Who are the Filipina workers that you've had contact with? Give me their names and I can go talk to them.' Eventually, they see they can be the bridge to open doors for us." Sometimes, Pefianco-Thomas noted, you need four languages or more to reach the workers, including Farsi, Cantonese, Tagalog, and Spanish. "I go to them to sign a card and they say, 'I'll ask my husband. I'll ask my father, my brother.' You have to organize the whole community."

Efforts to gain support from advocacy groups for the consumers (clients) posed additional problems, according to Sandy Strehlou. The advocacy groups are headed by middle-class whites, not the recipients of home care; these individuals are less cooperative and the organizations are more bureaucratic. Very often, Strehlou noted, "you can't get beyond the leadership." Nonetheless, to restructure the home-care industry, the union had to enlist the support of advocacy groups and their leaders in a coalition. That meant respecting the hierarchy and methods of those organizations. The SEIU organizers worked one-on-one with leaders to identify common ground, so that all parties were convinced that the coalition's goals would be beneficial to all.

Once the registry was established and sufficient cards signed, the union pushed hard for a quick election. Without a workplace, the ballots would go out by mail to thousands of workers, who may or may not have understood the purpose and procedures required by the ballot. "We called two thousand people," explained SEIU organizer Myriam Escamilla.

In July 1994, the home-care workers won their election by a strong majority of those voting, and the SEIU was authorized to represent them. For the union to negotiate better wages, however, it had to obtain another variance; a federal regulation requires special approval to allow up to double the minimum wage to be paid. It took six months to get approval. Now, Myriam Escamilla says, throwing her hands up in exasperation, "the county person says we have to wait. It's very unfair." According to Mila Pefianco-Thomas, the state and county continue to argue over procedural issues, holding up negotiations. As of March 1996, the workers still had no contract.

Because of the high turnover and long delays, sustaining morale and organization is a challenge. "We have a committee of home-care workers who are negotiators, but they are so widespread and the workforce changes so fast, it's difficult to keep groups together," Escamilla observes. "When we have meetings for the registry, we get a response; they get involved and come to meetings. We are building up stewards and creating a network with training. But the workers are so isolated and don't have a chance to interact." When they do, the organizers have observed tensions. Sometimes native workers react to the immigrants in a negative way; the immigrants think native workers, African Americans, for example, rely on welfare unfairly, while the immigrants tend to avoid welfare for reasons of fear and pride. Language barriers are tremendous among the workers. " 'All of us here are workers,' we explain, and we all must stick together."

Without taking the time and doing the education to address racial, national, and cultural biases, the union could not keep the committee together. Even with extensive SEIU work and resources, the union would be hardpressed trying to handle the interconnected problems home-care workers face, from poverty, child care, and spousal abuse to housing and citizenship problems. What does a home-care worker do, for example, if she receives a call that her child is ill and needs to be taken home from school in the middle of the day? What happens to her disabled client?

SEIU has organized six thousand home-care workers in Alameda County, but it wants to put energy into organizing the thirty-two thousand in the region. Although the SEIU is large, the union cannot provide the daily support and community networks so essential to each worker's ability to remain in the workforce. What is more, the union cannot respond to every desperate worker, every isolated low-wage woman with a workplace or home problem.

It is in reaching out to the isolated individuals and small groups of women where they live that community-based organizations play such an essential role. To provide basic support and services to this dispersed population, the SEIU would need community groups like AIWA to provide day-to-day and peer support for new union members. Organizations like AIWA value their own leadership development and organizing work and do not wish to become what they might perceive as service and referral centers for unions.

In the midst of the campaign, a union representative met with Netsy Firestein, director of the Labor Project for Working Families, a nonprofit organization, to discuss the possibility of creating a "service center" for home-care workers. Firestein emphasized that "so many of these workers are on the edge and can so easily fall out of the workforce and get completely overwhelmed by their personal and economic problems." The discussions between the members of the Labor Project and the SEIU led to talks with funders, and the Labor Project was able to obtain funding to work with SEIU Local 616 to conceptualize and develop a center for home-care workers. A second grant has enabled the Labor Project to hire a fulltime organizer, placed with Local 616, to help establish two workers centers in Oakland. Many funding agencies prefer to award grants to partnerships, one clear advantage of unions, nonprofit groups, and CBOs working together.

It is hard for unions to access funding without such partners; it is equally hard for small CBOs and nonprofit organizations to obtain funding if they do not have the structures or resources to implement proposals. In this case, what interested the funder was the blending of the worker-centered organizing and servicing efforts.

The organizations involved established a team made up of several key players, including Netsy Firestein and Mila Pefianco-Thomas. The advisory board includes the executive board members of the new home-care local. Each of the team members understands the connection between effective organizing—whether new organizing or internal organizing—and support services. They also have resisted a common tendency among unionists today to oppose organizing and servicing as contrary approaches. In their view, these two activities can be carried out in ways that involve and empower women or in paternalistic ways that maintain women in subordinate roles.

The workers centers will be run by home-care workers. Designed as neighborhood union centers, they will sponsor social as well as work and union-oriented activities. A job co-op will match workers to jobs at a local level to enhance the referrals of the job registry. A health clinic in east Oakland will provide monthly health screenings at the centers on a voluntary basis. Activities and services will include dances, bingo games, and immigration and legal advice, and one day each week members will be able to meet with a union steward at the center. To take advantage of the co-op or other services, workers will have to volunteer time, for which they will receive points. The idea for this exchange came from the United Farm Workers centers, which required workers to contribute time to receive assistance.

According to Netsy Firestein, all parties come out ahead in this effort: the Labor Project, the SEIU, and the workers. The partnership helped the Labor Project raise more than $100,000, enabling the group to advance its mission to help working families. And Firestein can now commit time to the centers because she has been able to hire interns and staff.

The centers will provide the assistance and networks that will help keep home-care workers on the job and in the union. Workers involved in the centers gain direct benefits that will ease the complications of their lives. They see that unionization brings many results, an important point given the delay in getting a contract (interviews, Firestein and Pefianco-Thomas).

Negotiating Differences, Building Relationships

Unions and community groups have weathered stormy times in developing coalitions and building ongoing relationships. It is not just that they have different approaches; they have also had difficulties because they often lacked a real bridge anchored in personal relationships. The difference in size, decision-making structures, and hierarchies create interface problems. CBOs prefer to work with the same people regularly, people who look like them, speak their language, and have the authority to commit the resources of their organizations. Unions have multiple lines of accountability, not only to their memberships but to the federal government. They maintain centralized decision making in many areas and for good reasons strive for uniformity in policies. Unions and CBOs share long-term goals, but not necessarily short-term ones.

In the past, for example, AIWA staff and the former leadership of the ILGWU spoke different languages. AIWA cared most about the immediate needs of Asian immigrant women; the ILGWU, members and contracts. Following a dramatic strike by Asian and Latina garment workers in New York City in 1983, the ILGWU set out to transform its internal structures and faces to reflect those of the current workforce. Carrying out organizational change in a union, however, is a complicated and long-term process. Unions develop structures, hierarchies, cultures, and traditions as resistant to change as any other organization or institution (Cobble 1993; Milkman 1993; Needleman 1994 and 1993b).

One of the organizers and leaders behind the 1983 walkout, Katie Quan, now heads the northwest region of UNITE. Quan worked for years in New York's garment industry; decades earlier, her grandmothers had worked in the garment industry in San Francisco, where Quan's offices are now located. Her integration into the leadership of the union made it easier for organizations such as the Asian Law Caucus, Equal Rights Advocates, and AIWA to find a common language and build lines of communication. Now the union, too, has set up workers centers, known as Justice Centers, in New York, San Francisco, and Los Angeles, staffed by organizers who speak the languages and know the cultures of the workers. The Justice Centers help organize and assist nonunionized workers and their families and provide associate union membership to those who want it. Although the union's development of workers centers may introduce some turf issues, it mainly reflects a convergence of views on the importance of community-based centers in organizing immigrant and low-wage workers.

The recognition by unions of the value of the CBO approach does not result in an immediate transformation of the union or its leaders, structures, or decision-making procedures. Herein lie the roots of some of the tensions and conflicts in coalitions. CBOs are very patient in their work but less patient with the change process within unions. They wonder why it takes unions so long to learn from their experiences and do things differently. Unions, on their part, applaud the painstaking character of the work of CBOs but grow impatient with their process-centered style. Unions are accountable to their members and their executive boards; they regularly must translate their allocation of resources into numbers. They "dance" to a different rhythm than CBOs. Waiting ten years—as AIWA did—to find a group of women willing to stand up and fight does not fit the time frame for union organizers. Measuring success by numbers rather than through gains in consciousness and leadership makes AIWA uncomfortable.

CBOs express concerns that unions sign up women workers and encourage their participation but do not promote them to leadership. Why do unions walk away from workers who want to organize but lack a majority, CBO activists ask? Is the only help unions want from CBOs a labor gang of service workers and translators? Why do unions come to coalitions with a completed plan and reject alternate ideas? Has their success in organizing been so great that they can stick with what they know?

Union leaders express their own ambivalence and doubts about the ways of CBOs. Union representation and the benefits that come with a contract can enable people to get more involved. Given current laws and antiunion activities, it takes a union's resources and the momentum of a big swift push to overcome obstacles and defeat employer campaigns. Especially given contingent work arrangements, isolated workforces, fear, and diversity, unions have learned that some methods work better than others: strategic targeting, big campaigns, and numbers in the win column. Is it really a virtue, question unionists, to spend years working to help a small handful of workers? If union representation makes the biggest difference in women's economic status, argue union leaders, then the goal should be to move as quickly as possible to unionization.

Each criticism or question reflects genuine problems. To make a breakthrough in organizing low-wage women, work must continue on both fronts: winning union representation among specific groups of workers and developing self-organizing communities open to unionism. Partnerships for the long haul and not just high turnover coalitions can enable labor to move from thousands to millions, from treading water to changing tides.

An analysis of successful and not-so-successful experiences point to several approaches that work in building successful partnerships.

1. *Humanize the link between organizations.* Individual people as well as agendas provide better common ground for the long haul. The partnership between SEIU Local 616 and the Labor Project for Working Families, for example, works because relationships exist and have been cultivated among key people. It takes time to get to know people and organizations, and a rotating set of contact people can destabilize a relationship and greatly extend the learning curve. Equally important, then, is establishing multiple human points of contacts, at different levels of the organization, so that one person's departure does not wipe out an organization's ties. Opening

opportunities at the grassroots level for union and CBO rank and file should be encouraged. CBO activists, for example, could attend the AFL-CIO/ University and College Labor Education Association Leadership Schools for Women Workers. Unions and CBOs could do joint leadership development work in many communities.

2. *Recognize and respect differences and build on the strengths of each partner.* Often organizations assume that they both want the same thing and forget to negotiate and discuss objectives and needs. At the start of a relationship—not in the midst of a campaign—parties should say explicitly what they want, what they can offer, and how they work. All too frequently bridges between organizations are burned over a short-term or tactical difference. Over the long haul, our differences are a rich resource and strength; together, we are smarter than the sum of our parts.

Unions and CBOs tend to approach each other for sporadic help on one or another's current campaign; the rewards of long-term cooperation and partnerships are far greater. Unions can learn new approaches to leadership development, multiculturalism, and relationship building from CBOs. CBOs in turn can learn tactics from unions for turning commitment and activity into organization. Joint or collective work in leadership development, workers centers, research, and lobbying draw on the best of both groups. CBOs and unions could seek funding for joint leadership training programs, for the formation of workers centers, and for issue campaigns and access funds that either one alone might not be able to get. That CBOs are not held to restrictions under the Labor-Management Relations Act also extends the range of available tactics in an organizing campaign.

3. *More efforts should go into publicizing successful partnerships and providing critical evaluations of joint work.* Garment and home-care workers, unions, and CBOs benefited from the collaboration and support in both cases discussed here. In fact, the closer the ties and the more integrated the work, the greater the advantages to the participating groups. It is important, however, in showcasing successful partnerships that we not sweep problems under the rug or speak only of what went well. We learn from an analysis of problems, and collectively done work evaluations would greatly advance our knowledge as well as our understanding among organizations. The most helpful studies provide a balanced analysis of what worked and what did not and explore problems rather than ascribe blame.

In occupations in which low-wage women predominate—light manufacturing, service, health care, temporary and part-time jobs—multiple organizing centers and multiple forms of support can break down the enormous social, political, and economic barriers to organizing. Unions need to find a way to be patient with the labor-intensive, slow process-oriented work of CBOs; unions also need to recognize and respect the

CBOs' accomplishments. CBOs have to acknowledge the significant changes brought to women through unionization, sooner rather than later. They also have to find it in their hearts to be patient with organizational change in unions. The AFL-CIO and many union affiliates have begun a process that is altering the faces and methods of unions, enabling them to work more effectively and democratically at the grass roots.

Chapter 5

Organizing Immigrant Communities: UNITE's Workers Center Strategy

Immanuel Ness

The postindustrial transformation that began in the early 1950s and intensified in the 1970s has significantly compromised the economic power of garment unions in New York City. The shift from a manufacturing to a service orientation has decimated the nucleus of strength organized labor maintained in garment manufacturing among unskilled and semiskilled workers.

Throughout the first half of the century, the manufacturing sector consistently provided dependable and secure jobs for unskilled and semiskilled garment workers, the vast majority of whom were first-generation immigrants (Tyler 1995; Waldinger 1986). As a corollary to the structural decline in garment manufacturing in New York, unions are significantly less able to maintain and increase wages for those workers who remain in the organized sector of the industry. The globalization of production to such areas as East Asia, Latin America, and Eastern Europe, combined with the entry of large numbers of immigrant workers into the U.S. labor market since the 1970s, has resulted in expanded competition and coincided with the disappearance of jobs at adequate wages (Mishel and Voos 1992).

As the number of medium-wage garment manufacturing jobs shrink and competition for the remaining jobs becomes more intense, trade union bargaining power declines. The rise in the use of subcontracting to shops that employ ten to twenty workers has further eroded trade union power in the

The author is grateful to Frances Fox Piven, Robert Pleasure, Lori Minnite, and Michael Farrin for their thoughtful comments on this work. I also thank union leaders and organizers at UNITE—Nick Unger, Rebecca Kessinger, Jeff Hermanson, Dan Yen Feng, and Rodolfo Guzman—for their unflagging support for this project and useful suggestions on this work.

local labor market. The problem is exacerbated because garment manufacturers are able to insulate themselves from the abuses of contractors and
subcontractors operating sweatshops that employ recent immigrants.

The decline of garment and textile unions among low-income workers
who formed the core of the organized labor movement earlier in the century
can be attributed to the inability of these unions to prevent job loss and to
restrain the reintroduction of the sweatshops, which produce apparel at a
fraction of the cost incurred by unionized firms operating in the formal
economy. Compounding the situation, the concentration of production in
midtown Manhattan has been eroding since the early 1960s, when commercial and residential rezoning began to push production industries to the
fringes of Manhattan, to the outer boroughs, and beyond the city limits.
Moreover, the dispersion of standardized garment manufacturing to domestic and foreign locations where wages are lower has diminished the potential
economic strength of the higher-wage garment workers that unions represent (Waldinger 1986; Fernández-Kelly and Sassen 1991).

One creative way in which garment unions have tried to address these
problems is through workers centers. This chapter examines the organizing
strategies undertaken by UNITE through the creation of its Garment Workers Justice Centers (GWJCs).

Transformation of New York's Garment Industry

Although garment manufacturing never dominated in New York in the way
that the automobile industry dominated in Detroit or steel ruled Pittsburgh,
the garment industry has historically provided the most important source
of employment for the city's working poor (Dubofsky 1968). The industry
is made up primarily of small- and medium-sized producers dispersed in
Manhattan's Fashion District and Chinatown and in Brooklyn's Wil-
liamsburg and Sunset Park neighborhoods. Ironically, the small-scale nature
of garment manufacturing in New York City has contributed to the stabilization of the industry since small contractors and even smaller subcontractors tend to be more flexible than large contractors in adjusting to continual
changes in style, particularly in the fashion-influenced outerwear industry
(Waldinger 1986:97).

Although New York City long ago lost such standardized production
lines as blue jeans and undergarments to North Carolina, Texas, and foreign
countries, it has retained control over style-sensitive goods that are subject
to obsolescence and consumer uncertainty (Waldinger 1986:89–91). But
although there are few large firms, the Fashion District supports approximately twenty-five to thirty thousand workers within a twenty-one-square-
block area in midtown Manhattan. New York City producers have also
profited since the early 1970s from a large influx of immigrant workers

from Puerto Rico, the Dominican Republic, Ecuador, Peru, Mexico, and East Asia, a development that has significantly lowered labor costs, and from the emergence of immigrant contractors who can respond rapidly to changes in consumer demand. These trends have been accelerating since the 1980s. Thus, immigration to New York City from low-wage areas in Latin America has continued to swell the number of workers in the industry, forcing greater competition among unionized workers. In the early 1970s, there were fewer than two hundred sweatshops in New York City. By the 1980s, however, the ILGWU estimated that there were three thousand such operations, employing more than sixty thousand workers and home workers (Fernández-Kelly and Sassen 1991). Saskia Sassen calculated that by the early 1990s there were as many undocumented workers in apparel sweatshops in New York City as unionized apparel workers in all of New York State (Fernández-Kelly and Sassen 1991; *New York State 1991–1992 County Profiles*). Since there are so many employers to target, the absence of large-scale industrial facilities has always made organizing workers difficult. This difficulty is only intensified in the current economic environment.

Declining Power of Labor

Wage and work norms in the garment industry are now divided among three sectors of the labor market: (1) the unionized sector, which includes jobs with the highest wages and benefits; (2) a relatively well-paid non-unionized sector; and (3) the rapidly growing nonunionized, undocumented immigrant sector, in which many jobs are part time and seasonal and wages and working conditions are considerably below those of the formal garment industry labor market. This segmentation of the labor market has intensified the decline in industry wage and benefit standards. Employers offer decent-paying jobs to a limited number of union employees without providing similar benefits to increasing majorities of nonunion workers, many of whom are immigrants working in sweatshops. As a result, the working conditions for many garment workers resemble those of laborers working for multinational corporations in Third World countries, where there is a strong incentive to create secondary jobs for nonwhite workers at poverty wages. The relegation of large numbers of entry-level low-wage Latinos and Asians to this contingent backwater of the labor market increases the pressure on trade unions struggling to protect the wages of their unskilled and semiskilled members; it is difficult to organize workers competing fiercely for the same low-wage jobs.

The vulnerability of immigrants to sweatshop employers presents a threat to industrial and service unions representing workers in corresponding industries. Historically, immigrant workers in the United States have been a fertile field for new organizing, particularly among unions that represent poor and unskilled workers. Latino workers who are union members earn 50 percent more than Latino workers who are not ("Hispanic Workers" 1992). Hence, the growing number of nonunionized Latinos has resulted in a dramatic decline in income standards among these workers in New York City. At the same time, increasing employer hostility toward union representation has discouraged many of these workers from improving their positions through unionization. As a result of organized labor's declining influence, wages among immigrant workers in the private sector, and in the garment industry in particular, have failed to keep pace with those of other industrial workers. In 1994, average wages in the apparel industry in New York City were lower than those of all but two of the ten u.s. cities with the largest apparel manufacturing industries (Moore 1995).

The disappearance of apparel jobs from the early 1950s to the mid-1990s has significantly weakened the political clout and bargaining power of trade unions with employers. While union membership in apparel manufacturing remained in the range of 65 to 70 percent during the past twenty-five years, the maintenance of union density has not compensated for a shrinking membership base and increased competition for jobs, which tend to curtail the leverage unions have in larger shops. In 1970, unions representing apparel manufacturers negotiated settlements for 70.2 percent of the 249,000 workers employed in the industry. By 1994, unions still represented nearly 65 percent of the workers in the industry, but garment manufacturing had contracted to fewer than 99,000 workers. These data considerably underestimate the decline of unionized labor in garment manufacturing since sweatshops are not included in official calculations. UNITE officials believe that if sweatshops were included, the garment industry would include equal numbers of unionized and nonunionized workers—70,000 each.

As a result of this decline, the strike threat has become ever less effective, and unions have become ever more timid in invoking it. Trade unions electing to confront management with strikes or walkouts are faced with two primary obstacles that undermine their power. First, high unemployment provides a surplus of replacement workers available for management to counter the threat. Second, the employer threat to close plants and lay off workers is far more intimidating than the strike threat, since striking unionists must be willing to risk being permanently replaced by lower-wage workers. Management's ability to close facilities and relocate to other states and abroad, where substantially lower wages are available, further weakens labor action.

UNITE's Workers Center Strategy

To combat these trends, unions have sometimes merged with other local unions to strengthen their membership base and remain financially viable, as was the case when the ILGWU merged with the Amalgamated Clothing and Textile Workers' Union (ACTWU) to form UNITE in June 1995. This chapter focuses on another innovative effort, begun by the ILGWU and taken up by UNITE, to shore up the declining power of labor unions by establishing workers centers, which provide practical training and ideological education for nonunionized immigrant workers. UNITE's effort has by no means solved all the problems faced by garment workers in New York City. As we shall see, one of the problems it has yet to address fully is the long-term decline in labor's bargaining position in the political economy as a whole. Nevertheless, UNITE's approach is a positive step that warrants further study.

Gary Marks sees unions as reflecting the structure of labor markets, as both defining their potential members and serving as the primary means of improving members' living conditions by bargaining with management over wages and working conditions. He argues that the decentralized structure of the U.S. labor movement promotes great diversity in the political orientation and activity of unions and that this diversity in turn is rooted in the diversity of the labor organizations functioning in distinct industries and occupations. He contends, therefore, that it is inappropriate to study union interests in the aggregate or to treat union movements as similar across an economy. Rather, a comparative approach to union activity helps account for the unique strategies of New York garment unions in responding to the decline of the industry (Marks 1989:3–49).

The dispersed organization of workers in the garment industry, which has occurred as a result of subcontracting, demonstrates the value of community- and industry-based organizing strategies. Specifically, the workers center strategy is an attempt to deal with the reemergence and rapid expansion of sweatshops across the country. UNITE's strategies, therefore, are based on the value of organizing dispersed immigrant workers on a mass scale, an approach that the ILGWU and ACTWU used in the first three decades of this century. Ultimately, unions must initiate similar strategies directed at nonmembers, such as recent immigrants, who may threaten the wage and work standards in union shops. The dramatic decline in union membership in the labor force since the 1960s has prompted several trade unions to initiate such strategies, including the workers center approach, in immigrant communities and in the neighborhoods where they are employed. A majority of the centers have targeted recent immigrants from Latin America and East Asia.

The short-term objective of establishing workers centers is to provide political and ideological support for unionization among disenfranchised low-wage workers; the long-term goal is to engage in union organizing campaigns in their communities. Because of the intense competition from sweatshops, larger unionized contractors have an interest in promoting organization among sweatshop workers. By organizing the workers in these shops and helping to create standardized wage and work norms, garment unions have historically been viewed as a stabilizing vehicle for both responsible employers and workers in both union and nonunion sectors.

Methodology of This Study

This study measures immigrant workers' attitudes toward their working conditions and their interest in participating in collective action. The data are based on an analysis of the activities of workers centers in New York City and a survey of 101 garment workers in the Manhattan Fashion District and in Sunset Park, Brooklyn. The survey questionnaire was translated into Spanish and Chinese and was administered during October and November 1995.

To measure the efficacy of the centers in providing ideological support for unions among immigrant workers, the study (1) analyzes how well the centers are able to create sustainable class-conscious environments among immigrants who are tenuously connected to mainstream sources of union strength by evaluating success in developing the ideological and cultural basis to organize and actively struggle for improved working conditions in the informal sector of the economy; (2) attempts to determine if these centers address the immediate needs of immigrant workers in New York City's garment sector; and (3) measures the efficacy of these centers in promoting support among immigrant workers for organizing collectively and forming trade unions to protect these workers' interests.

To measure the capacity of the workers center approach to affect the political economy in which the centers operate, it is necessary to determine whether this approach can be counted on not only to reduce the most flagrant abuses by private employers but to increase workers' power within the industry as a whole. Can the centers help provide a base for expanding unionization? To do so, they must have the long-term support of established trade unions, which provide financial and organizational resources. But such unions are driven by immediate financial imperatives, which at times may conflict with the center approach.

A sixty-seven-question survey was given to recent Latino and Chinese immigrant garment workers in New York City to help discern the strengths and weaknesses of UNITE's organizing strategy. It is hoped that the analysis may provide some insights into the possibility of organizing low-wage immigrant workers in other industrial and service-sector labor markets and geographic locations. The two main groups answering the questions were a baseline population of garment workers who had not become members of the workers center in the Fashion District in Manhattan and Sunset Park,

Brooklyn and members who had attended the center for at least six months. The questionnaire was given to equal numbers of Latino and Chinese workers in each demographic category, based on immigration status, age, gender, ethnicity, and race, and included questions about their wages and working conditions; employer violations; knowledge of human, legal, and worker rights; concern with job-related issues (job security, wages, benefits, discrimination); support for employee representation and unionization; and willingness to engage in collective action to improve working conditions (support for unions, willingness to take part in organizing campaigns).

Additional data were gained from qualitative semistructured interviews with members of workers centers, nonmembers, center volunteers, union organizers, and union officials to ascertain their perspectives on the efficacy of the workers center strategy. The research also involved observation of the operation of the GWJC in New York City's Fashion District; this included participant observation of workers center actions at local sweatshops employing both documented and undocumented immigrant workers, as well as follow-up interviews with participants in work stoppages.

This study does not focus exclusively on short-term unionization successes. The primary objective is to determine the extent to which workers centers are achieving their goals of educating workers about their rights and creating an atmosphere conducive to collective action. The reseach measures the extent to which this is being achieved by comparing the attitudes of members and nonmembers.

Overview of New York GWJCs

UNITE currently operates workers centers for minority and immigrant garment workers in New York City, Miami, Los Angeles, and San Francisco. Since 1994, these centers have offered unorganized garment workers associate membership in the union, which entitles them to industrial skills training, English as a second language (ESL) classes, human and labor rights education, and access to Union Privilege Benefit Program assistance (Shostak 1991:63–64). In September 1995, UNITE claimed to have organized eighteen hundred to two thousand associate members in the Fashion District and Sunset Park. The organizing success of workers centers is measured not strictly by the increase in the number of unionized members, however, but by the extent to which nonmembers in the local industry are willing to organize to improve their conditions.

One of the advantages of the workers center approach is its inclusion of nonunionized workers. In most unions, membership hinges on continued employment in an organized firm. To become an associate member, however, it is not necessary for an employer to recognize the union as a collective bargaining agent. Individual workers can join as associate members on their own.

Since the early 1990s, UNITE's community-based organizing approach among recent immigrant workers in New York and elsewhere has included three key components: education and training, socializing and solidarity, and industrial organizing.

Education and Training

Members of New York's GWJCs are educated about their basic rights and privileges, including minimum wage laws, the forty-hour workweek, workers' compensation and disability insurance benefits for documented workers, and laws that prohibit discrimination and sexual harassment. They are also informed of their responsibilities to vote and pay taxes and the advantages of becoming active participants in society. ESL classes, with their general education component, give the workers the essential language skills and cultural awareness to survive and become productive members of their communities. Workers in these classes are also educated about the advantages of membership in a democratic union. Workers centers hold annual elections, open to all GWJC participants, to select leadership from among members.

Socializing and Solidarity

Members of GWJCs are encouraged to discuss their wages and working conditions, form friendships, and participate in demonstrations to support changes in unfair government policies and to publicize and protest against flagrant employer violations in selected sweatshops. Many immigrants consider the centers to be safe havens to deliberate openly about common problems, including their low wages, late and irregular payment of wages, and disputes with employers. Members also consider the centers places where they can socialize with fellow garment workers who are dispersed in neighborhoods throughout the New York City area. Members and nonmembers participate in center-sponsored cultural events, theater club performances, dances, and parties.

Industrial Organizing

UNITE does not want workers centers to become service-oriented but hopes they evolve into organizations that promote collective action and unionization. Although the union does not directly represent workers on the shop floor, it attempts to provide immigrants with the knowledge and organizational framework so that they can help themselves in disputes with employers, participate in political campaigns, and create the basis of organizing a union. In more flagrant cases of employer abuse, organizers at UNITE workers centers intervene directly on behalf of workers; for example, they may encourage immigrant workers to halt production if wages are being withheld. The goal is to build and sustain an environment in which the workers can learn how to advocate for their own interests and develop an ongoing organization to defend and expand their rights.

Research Findings

Overall Profile of Members and Nonmembers

All the workers volunteering to complete the survey were Latin American or East Asian in origin and spoke almost no English. Members of the workers centers tended to have resided in the United States longer than nonmembers, more than half of whom indicated they were undocumented; of the members, two in five said they were undocumented. Three-quarters of the workers surveyed were women, and nearly three in five were married. Nonmembers tended to be younger than members and to have fewer children (see table 5.1).

Education and Skills

Members tended to be better educated than nonmembers and to have more years of employment in the garment industry, but members and nonmembers had similar levels of skill; about three-quarters of both groups claimed to be employed as sewers or pattern makers, the higher-skilled jobs in the industry (see table 5.2). About three times as many members as nonmembers said they had worked in business or as professionals before immigrating to the United States. Slightly more nonmembers than members said they had worked in the garment industry in their native countries.

Wages and Workplace Conditions

Qualitative interviews suggest that a large share of the members come to workers centers after receiving assistance from UNITE organizers in strug-

TABLE 5.1. Demographic Characteristics of Respondents to Workers Center Survey

Characteristics	Nonmembers	Members
Foreign-born	100%	100%
English is not native language	100%	100%
Live two or fewer years in New York City	32%	19%
Live five or more years in the United States	28%	46%
Undocumented immigrant status	52%	40%
Female	74%	75%
Younger than 35	57%	35%
Married	59%	56%
Have two or more children	32%	56%

TABLE 5.2. Education, Skills, Wages, and Benefits of Respondents to Workers Center Survey

	Nonmembers	Members
Education and Skills		
Lack a high school diploma	45%	36%
Worked for three or more years in the garment industry	43%	66%
Skilled worker (sewer, pattern maker, or multiple skills)	77%	77%
Worked in the garment industry before coming to the United States	23%	15%
Business or professional worker before coming to the United States	12%	35%
Seeking additional job training in the garment industry	50%	65%
Wages and Benefits		
Do not think the wages they receive are fair	47%	63%
Do not think the piece rates they receive are fair	49%	54%
Currently paid by piecework	79%	83%
Paid minimum wage	27%	41%
Paid more than minimum wage	47%	33%
Employer does not make legal deductions on wages or paycheck	57%	56%
Employer does not provide health insurance	87%	79%
Employer does not pay for sick days	93%	92%
Employer does not pay for holidays off	85%	73%

gles with their employers over wages, piece rates, and other payment issues. One of the more notable findings is that nonmembers appear to be better paid than members, though their employer-sponsored benefits are as poor as those of the members. About three-quarters of both the members and the nonmembers surveyed are paid the minimum wage or higher; however, a larger percentage of nonmembers receive more than the minimum wage. Among members, 26 percent are paid below the minimum wage, 41 percent are at that level, and 33 percent are above it. Among nonmembers, 26 percent are paid below the minimum wage, 27 percent receive the legal minimum, and 47 percent receive more. Members (63 percent) more than nonmembers (51 percent) said they believed there were occupational health and safety hazards on the job. Given that other indicators of poor working conditions were equally distributed among both groups, it appears that the ability to more clearly articulate workplace-related grievances might be related to the decision to join the center.

There appears to be a strong general understanding among the workers surveyed of the possible advantages of union membership as a means of improving wages and working conditions in the garment industry (see table 5.3). Among nonmembers, 79 percent are eager to join the center, and 85 percent said they believed an industrywide union would protect workers' interests; 65 percent were willing to take collective action to build a union. The responses of members were even more affirmative: 90 percent believe that an industrywide garment union would protect workers' interests, and 87 percent are willing to take collective action to build a union, indicating that members of the center are either predisposed to collective action or are energized by their membership in the center. Members (71 percent) tend to be more aware of the advantages of working in a union shop than are nonmembers (57 percent), and a higher percentage of members than nonmembers consider collective action on the shop floor to be beneficial in improving wages and conditions (79 percent versus 57 percent).

Immigrant workers (members and nonmembers) who have been in the United States for a relatively long time, and have thus experienced more of the low-wage stagnation and poor working conditions in the garment indus-

TABLE 5.3. Workplace Conditions, Pro-Union Attitudes, and Knowledge of Benefits of Union among Respondents to Workers Center Survey

	Nonmembers	Members
Workplace Conditions		
25–100 employees at the workplace	48%	67%
Say there are safety and health hazards on the job	51%	63%
Forced to work overtime	47%	49%
Employer has withheld wages or owes employee money	36%	46%
Say employer discriminates based on ethnicity or national origin	79%	77%
Believe employer discriminates based on gender	68%	61%
Pro-Union Attitudes		
Willing to join Workers Center	79%	NA
Believe industrywide garment union would protect rights	85%	90%
Willing to take collective action to help build a union	65%	87%
Knowledge of Benefits of Union		
Know the advantages of a union shop over a nonunion shop	57%	71%
Are unaware of the advantages of a union shop	21%	29%
Believe collective action can improve wages and conditions	57%	79%
Unsure collective action can improve wages and conditions	36%	21%

try here, seem primed for unionization. Those with larger families to support particularly feel the urgency of their condition as low-paid, exploited workers and so are likely to bring the issues into consciousness. This process can be aided by an educational campaign undertaken by the centers to inform workers of their rights to better pay and benefits, safer working conditions, and the advantages of a union shop. In an interview with Rebecca Kessinger, UNITE's assistant director of organization, she noted that "sometimes the union movement ghettoizes us as only educational and cultural, but our long-term goal is clearly to organize members into the union."

A GWJC also influences those who do not participate in it immediately. Many immigrant workers with no direct connection to a center are nonetheless aware of its active role in retrieving unpaid wages and improving conditions at some shops. For example, the center intervened in a dispute that pitted undocumented workers against Goldstitch, a contractor in midtown Manhattan that had not paid wages to some fifty-odd employees in more than four weeks. No worker at this sweatshop was a member of the center, but several had heard about it through word of mouth and through leaflets distributed in the Fashion District. A spontaneous organizing committee, consisting of four Goldstitch workers, appealed to the center to intervene on their behalf. One member of the committee, a forty-five-year-old woman from Mexico, was the lead organizer at Goldstitch. GWJC sent two Spanish-speaking organizers to address the workers and one Korean to speak to the employer.

When the organizing committee and UNITE organizers arrived at the sweatshop at about noon on a bitter-cold day in December 1995, the workers immediately shut down production, demanding to be paid before resuming work. Though vulnerable to job loss and even deportation, they enthusiastically embraced the organizers' appeal. For the first time, workers collectively criticized the manager, who said he would pay them a fraction of what was owed in a few days. His plea to them to resume work fell on deaf ears.

The contractor then called the production manager at the firm that had put out the work. Initially the production manager said that he did not employ the workers, but later he ordered the UNITE organizers not to talk to them and to leave the factory at once. After a standoff, during which the strike leader refused an offer of payment in return for leaving the premises, the production manager agreed to pay all the workers in full on the very next day.

Although the shutdown proved successful in retrieving the unpaid wages, the workers could still not be organized into the union. Most were undocumented and feared that the employer would close the facilities immediately if the union tried to organize them. They knew that other immigrant workers could easily replace them. That is why union officials have suggested organizing a general strike among the workers in the Fashion District, in the tradition of the job actions that occurred from the late 1880s to the early 1930s and that provided the basis for the formation and rapid expansion of the ILGWU and ACTWU (Tyler 1995:32–33).

The strike organizer at Goldstitch had her own history to call on. As a sixteen-year-old seamstress in the late 1960s, she had been involved in an unauthorized work stoppage at Contera Fabrica, a Mexico City shop owned by a New York manufacturer: "After we closed the shop, we got paid everything," she said. "Everybody got together to fight." Today, however, Latin American immigrants working in New York are reluctant to take on these battles. She went on:

> While we would like to work in Mexico, we cannot afford to. Twenty years ago, things were much better. I came here because wages were too low in Mexico. Now it's even worse. The equivalent of one week's work pays thirty dollars in Mexico, while a gallon bottle of cooking oil costs five dollars. But we are treated very poorly here. Many of these contractors try to get as much work out of us without pay, before closing down. That's one reason why we must demand immediate payment of wages.

This sentiment reflects the attitude of most immigrant garment workers. Though many think of themselves as foreigners, they are reconciled to working in the garment industry in New York, which, despite the low wages and poor working conditions, is preferable to the even lower wages in their countries of origin. Hence, absent improved conditions back home, most of these workers will remain in the local garment industry for most of their working lives. While UNITE's workers centers are an unconventional approach to organizing, the strategy is one that recognizes changes in the industry that have eroded union power and the probability that most immigrant workers are here to stay.

According to union officials, the centers have proved more successful in securing back wages for workers than have state and federal authorities (interviews, Unger and Kessinger, 1995). By intervening in cases of gross abuse, workers centers provide an instrument for policing the bottom end of the garment industry labor market. Thus, they serve as brakes on declining labor standards in the industry, where in the last decade and a half the boundaries between union and nonunion work have become more permeable. The centers have proved the value of collaboration in building political and economic power among immigrant workers. The centers provide the troops for mass campaigns. In October 1995, for example, immigrant workers affiliated with the centers were a primary force in organizing the mass demonstrations that followed the AFL-CIO convention in New York; these workers were also central to the campaign to improve conditions at Salvadoran garment plants, contractors for the GAP clothing chain that hired child labor and dismissed workers for any hint of union activity.

Conclusions

Clearly, workers centers engender support for unionization among their members and within communities of immigrant workers. A pivotal question is whether, and at what cost, they motivate these workers to struggle against employers for union recognition. As the survey data indicate, most workers seem to support unions; 87 percent of members and 65 percent of nonmembers were willing to take collective action to help build a union. Yet it is relevant to inquire further into whether they would actively oppose management in a campaign to achieve recognition and collective bargaining. Thus far, UNITE's workers centers have not found a way to prevent manufacturers from insulating themselves from the abuses of contractors and subcontractors operating sweatshops.

Although the centers have successfully intervened in instances of glaring violations against workers, the GWJCs have not yet achieved union recognition for these immigrants. In part, this failure reflects the structure of contract unionism, which does not prevent the exploitation of workers who are not union members. Thus, the centers face the constant threat of dissolution by their sponsors, as unions may choose to discontinue support because these organizations have not produced quickly discernible results along the lines of union recognition and collective bargaining contracts.

Despite these concerns, however, workers centers enjoy, perhaps ironically, a closer and broader relationship with both their members and their nonmembers than do unions with the rank and file. Unions may represent their members in the collective bargaining process and in grievance disputes, but UNITE's centers actively encourage participation through practical and ideological education, cultural events, demonstrations, and political campaigns.

The results of the statistical study reported on here show that the workers centers in New York exert a strong influence in the development of ideological and political consciousness toward unionization. Empirical analysis shows that the centers influence the attitudes and positions of nonmembers and are viewed as agencies that defend workers' interests in disputes with unscrupulous manufacturers and contractors. Workers who are members or former members frequently cross paths with nonmembers; as a result, nonmembers have appealed to the centers to help defend their interests in disputes with management over nonpayment of wages. Thus, the centers should be evaluated not simply on the basis of their ability to recruit members. Nonmembers often hear about the centers by word of mouth and appeal to them to intervene in industrial disputes that often involve work stoppages.

Ultimately, then, the centers cannot be judged solely on the support they generate for employee representation or unionization. The real question is whether that support would be sustained in the face of employer opposition. Pro-union sentiment is thwarted by the decentralized organization of the garment industry, which deprives workers of the ability to form unions. Once a shop is organized, manufacturers can switch production to lower-cost producers. The workers center strategy is a union-building effort that attempts to address this decentralized and undisciplined structure by unifying disparate workers within the community. The program focuses on common problems facing these low-income workers by creating an organizing culture that will allow the union to pressure companies to win improved conditions and organizing victories down the road. Lacking a direct instrument to promote responsible corporate behavior, the model provides a means of defending the most vulnerable workers in the labor market. Simultaneously, political action by members of the centers may eventually restrict manufacturers from shifting production to avoid unionization efforts and induce manufacturers to take greater responsibility for the actions of contractors.

Chapter 6

Helots No More: A Case Study of the Justice for Janitors Campaign in Los Angeles

Roger Waldinger, Chris Erickson, Ruth Milkman,
Daniel J. B. Mitchell, Abel Valenzuela,
Kent Wong, and Maurice Zeitlin

On June 15, 1990, striking janitors and their supporters held a peaceful march and demonstration in the tony Century City district of Los Angeles, where Local 399 of SEIU was seeking a union contract for the workers who clean the huge, glittering office towers that dominate this part of the city. The SEIU's Justice for Janitors (JfJ) campaign had been under way in L.A. for about two years, and this was one of many such demonstrations that had been launched over that period. But, unlike previous demonstrations, this time the L.A. police brutally attacked the marchers, seriously wounding several people and causing a pregnant woman to miscarry.

Although SEIU's organizers initially feared that the police violence might put an end to their effort, the demonstration proved to be a turning point in the campaign to unionize the janitors, most of whom were immigrants from Mexico and Central America. Widespread outrage at the police action, both locally and in SEIU offices around the country, led International Service Systems (ISS), the cleaning contractor for nearly all the buildings in Century City, to sign a union contract soon afterward in the largest private-sector organizing success among Latino immigrants since the United Farm Workers' victories nearly two decades earlier.

Southern California hardly seemed a likely setting for this drama. Never as strong as in the northern part of the state, organized labor had lost legions of well-paid, blue-collar members in the region in the 1970s and 1980s. With the decline of heavy industry, first in the civilian sector and later in defense, union density had declined sharply in this massive manufacturing center. Meanwhile, a new world of labor had emerged—a burgeoning immigrant population employed in low-skilled, low-paying manufacturing and service jobs. For a while it seemed that the advent of this new labor force would still any protest: so long as the newcomers compared a minimum-wage job in the garment center with an unyielding plot of land in Mexico's central plateau, not to mention a visit from El Salvador's death squads, employers could count on their workers being quiescent.

But the tide seems to be turning, as militant union activity among newcomers in a variety of industries suggests that the days of the immigrant helots are over. Emblematic of this shift is the JfJ campaign, which successfully reorganized the building services industry, ultimately bringing more than eight thousand largely immigrant workers under a union contract, in what has become a model for JfJ's national organizing efforts.

This chapter analyzes the recent growth of janitorial unionism in Los Angeles against the background of the previous history of the rise and decline in unionism in the city's building services industry, asking how and why JfJ succeeded in L.A. and whether its success will last.[1]

Origins and Early Growth

JfJ may be a bright new star on the otherwise dim labor firmament, but in many ways organizing janitors today does not differ much from the circumstances under which JfJ's parent organization, then called the Building Service Employees International Union (BSEIU), first emerged in Chicago in 1920. The union's "founding members were drawn from society's poorest ranks. Then, as now, building service workers were disproportionately first- and second-generation Americans and minority workers" (Service Employees International Union 1992:1). Of course, this continuity begs the very question with which this chapter is concerned, namely, how poor immigrant workers built a successful and enduring organization. Historically, the phenomenon of organizing immigrants is not an oddity, but the labor historiography does not usually suggest that an old-line AFL union

---

1. In addition to the sources cited herein, this chapter is based on, among other sources, a Lexis/Nexis search of periodical and other references relevant to the Justice for Janitors campaign and the contract cleaning industry; the public-use microdata samples of the 1980 and 1990 censuses of population; and in-depth interviews conducted with nine union officials, four management spokespersons, and four rank-and-file leaders. Interviews lasted from an hour to the equivalent of an entire day and were recorded both in written notes and, for the important union interviews, on audiotapes that were subsequently transcribed. Unless otherwise noted, interviews are the source for all quotations.

like the Building Service Employees would grow by recruiting "the dregs," as one veteran union official put it (cited in Piore 1994:529).

Whatever the original impetus to organize, the BSEIU took on many of the defining characteristics of the old AFL. Among them were high levels of local autonomy, on the one hand, and a relatively weak, underfinanced, thinly staffed international, on the other. The reversal of these characteristics has created the conditions for organizing janitors today. Locals were autonomous in part because building services was a local industry: the employers were the building owners, most of whom were hometown capitalists, so that the relevant market had relatively narrow geographic bounds.

In the 1930s, the BSEIU spread beyond Chicago, the Depression the catalyst for expansion. New York's janitors organized in 1934; San Francisco's followed suit shortly thereafter. From that bastion of labor radicalism, janitorial unionism was exported to L.A. just after World War II. The newly born Local 399 recruited in-house janitors who cleaned downtown buildings housing the entertainment and financial industries, as well as movie theaters.

Starting in the 1950s, commercial real estate took on a different ownership mix, as local owners were increasingly replaced by national and even international investors. These new owners found it more efficient to purchase cleaning services from a specialized vendor rather than organize a workforce for their diverse and scattered buildings directly.

The advent of contracting initially had an adverse effect on Local 399's membership, but the structure of the industry enabled the union to recoup its losses. As the city grew, the union successfully chased after the employers in each of the newer office centers.

Expansion allowed Local 399 to upgrade conditions significantly, and by the late 1960s, it had upgraded jobs to a full-time basis. The next decade was the union's heyday, and in 1978 membership peaked at about five thousand: "Neither the union leadership nor its militant labor force . . . [was] entirely satisfied with the job conditions that prevailed in 1975. Wages had more than doubled from those available a decade before, but still were only $3.75 an hour. Members also felt that benefits were too low and an eight-hour day too long" (Mines and Avina 1992:436).

Consequently, the local pushed hard to improve conditions and compensation further. Between 1976 and 1983, union wages rose an average of $.50 a year. Union contractors ultimately provided a benefit package that included eleven paid holidays and full medical, dental, vision, and prescription coverage. By 1982, total compensation in the union sector had risen to more than $12.00 an hour, as opposed to $4.00 an hour in the nonunion buildings.

Decline

But then the bottom fell out. By 1985, membership in the janitorial union had fallen to eighteen hundred, a sharp drop from the peak of the late 1970s. The sources of the decline were numerous. First, the local's push to improve conditions and compensation motivated cleaning contractors to explore nonunion options. Cleaning is highly labor intensive, with direct labor making up the single largest part of a company's expenses.

Second, the unionized part of the industry—the larger, more heavily capitalized firms—was under particular cost pressure. The big operators suffer from discontinuous economies of scale. Once a firm meets a certain size/asset threshold (needed to cover large payroll and insurance costs), there are few economies of scale, and none on the labor side, making it hard to pass on wage increases to building owners and resulting in a fiercely competitive industry.

The industry's previous drift away from building owner management had made for increasingly fragile relationships. Since contracts were written so as to permit very short notice of termination, union members could lose work almost overnight if a building owner switched from a union to a nonunion service.

Under these circumstances, motivation and opportunity made for murder. By early 1983, as Richard Mines and Jeffrey Avina recount, "a small group of mid-sized, aggressive firms sensed the union's vulnerability and made their move" (1992:476). Some of the new operators were actually veteran managers who had experience in large, unionized firms. Others were direct or indirect offshoots of a unionized parent, dressed up in nonunion garb. Whatever the provenance, the new, nonunion entities proved to be formidable competitors.

The local tried to fight back with the election route, but to little avail. The last master agreement was signed in 1983; shortly afterward, all increases in wages and benefits were frozen because Los Angeles was going nonunion; the desire to retain members at any price led to a proliferation of concession-ridden side agreements. Only downtown retained a unionized workforce of measurable proportions, and even there, union ranks barely attained 30 percent.

Countywide, the situation was more dismal still—barely one janitor in ten was a member of Local 399. The union had failed to keep up with the city's rapid growth. In the 1980s, downtown L.A.—until then, a collection of old, obsolete structures—underwent an extraordinary building boom, and office construction in the outlying areas grew even faster. But it was not simply that union density fell as the industry grew; the *absolute* number of janitors in Local 399 declined as well. While the local had been recruiting

Kaiser hospital workers during this period, so that its total membership continued to grow, its janitorial membership was hemorrhaging, as employers mounted their counterattack. And with the union all but broken, wages plummeted.

Enter the Immigrants

Scratch a low-paid service worker, find an immigrant. So it goes in the evolving caste society that is late-twentieth-century L.A. But even Southern California once looked different—and not so long ago. In 1970, service work was still largely the province of the region's African American population, which had substantially expanded during the previous twenty-five years. African Americans then made up 33 percent of the region's janitors—yielding overrepresentation by a factor of 4.6—whereas Latino immigrants were a small presence, accounting for barely seven out of every one hundred janitors. Though a menial job, janitorial work was beginning to generate economic dividends for its black incumbents: up until the early 1980s, African Americans comprised half of Local 399's members, and they were both the causes and the beneficiaries of the improvements in compensation that the local delivered during the 1960s and 1970s (Grant, Oliver, and James 1996).

But now immigrants were moving into Southern California, and it was they who would supply the workforce for the emerging nonunion cleaning contractors. Eight percent of the region's population had been foreign born in 1960; thirty years later, the proportion was 27 percent, and the concentration was 10 percentage points higher in the city of L.A., where Local 399 has its employment base. Moreover, the immigration flow accelerated rapidly during the 1980s, precisely when the nonunion sector of the industry began to burgeon (Waldinger and Bozorgmehr 1996).

Like immigrants everywhere, newcomers to L.A. gravitated to the jobs where their kin and hometown friends were employed. By 1970, there was already a significant presence of Latinos among the city's janitors, although the absolute level of employment was still relatively small. But even without initial contacts, the expanding janitorial occupation was an easy port of entry for immigrants with little formal education, in part because of its casual hiring practices. Meanwhile, as wages fell and the union's power waned, blacks left the occupation. Increased turnover accelerated this exodus. "It wasn't that [employers] would actually fire the blacks; [but] with attrition, the replacement pool was Latinos."

"The nonunion firms almost exclusively hired Latinos," explained one union organizer. That the immigrants would work for lower wages was only part of the motivation for employers to recruit among the foreign born: "I think 'cheap' was less of a question as sort of 'cheap' in addition to 'controllable.' "

By virtue of its past history, Local 399 was ill equipped to respond to the influx of the new type of worker. "The union had done a good job of being representative of membership and had black reps. Then the industry switched to Latino workers and disconnected the workforce from the union, because the union couldn't fire its reps the way management could change its workforce."

At the outset, new arrivals from Mexico furnished the bulk of the immigrant recruits streaming into the industry. By the early 1980s, however, events in Central America yielded a new element, as refugees fleeing civil war and violence in El Salvador and Guatemala began converging on L.A. The region's Central American population, which had grown from 43,400 in 1970 to 147,500 in 1980, quadrupled over the next decade. The Central Americans quickly filtered into janitorial work, for all the reasons noted above, plus one: the geographic proximity of the downtown and westside office complexes to the city's Pico-Union neighborhood, which became the principal point of absorption for the newest arrivals to the city.

By 1990, then, the face of janitorial work in L.A. had been utterly transformed. Spurred by the building boom of the 1980s—one-third of L.A.'s office space was built after 1980—the industry burgeoned, employing 28,883 janitors by 1990, more than twice as many as in 1980. Almost all the new jobs went to Latino immigrants, whose share of employment rose from 28 to 61 percent. Among the newcomers, Central Americans had the biggest gain; by 1990, they comprised 26 percent of the workforce, just under the 31 percent share held by foreign-born Mexicans.

The industry's expansion meant that net employment among blacks essentially held steady. But relatively, native-born blacks slipped badly, declining from 31 to 12 percent of the workforce. Native-born whites also lost share, dropping from 24 to 11 percent (calculated from 1990 census of population public-use microdata sample).

The influx of immigrants coincided with a change in the gender composition of the janitorial workforce, presumably also a product of the occupation's dramatically reduced wage rates. "Early on," as one union organizer told us, "the nonunion workforce was more female." In 1980, 60 percent of the Central American janitors were women; the huge gains made over the next ten years left that ratio virtually unchanged. Women comprised 30 percent of Mexican immigrant janitors in 1980; a figure that grew to 43 percent a decade later.

Meanwhile, among those black workers still in the occupation, the proportion of women actually fell, even as earnings for the shrinking pool of black janitors rose. The industry did poorly by all the women it recruited:

between 1980 and 1990, real earnings declined substantially among women of all ethnic groups, yielding a universally large male-female earnings differential (calculated from 1990 census of population public-use microdata sample).

In this situation, union organizing confronted obstacles aplenty. Building services, as with so many other industries that employ high percentages of immigrants, used network recruiting both to mobilize labor and to keep it under control. Front-line supervisors often oversaw the immigrants' relatives. One union activist described a foreman who employed his brother and his cousin and "treated them well."

But regardless of ties to kin and relatives, the ethnic mix often proved combustible, as Central Americans and Mexicans did not always perceive the affinity that labor solidarity would prescribe. "I've been into buildings where the Salvadorans and the Mexicanos don't like each other," explained one experienced, Mexican-born union organizer, "and they hate and they are separate and they eat separate."

Gender differences yielded another complicating factor, though not in the stereotypical way: "Women took the lead in Century City," explained a lead organizer. "Men were the meeting folks; women were the action folks." Still, it was not always easy for women to take action, especially as many worked day jobs as house cleaners.

The influence of machismo and the prevalence of patriarchal family relations provided a further stumbling block. As the same organizer explained, "Sometimes for the Latino women, if they're married, you have to sometimes be sensitive to start talking to the men. Sometimes you have to organize the husband and then the wife comes around."

The immigrant influx coincided with Local 399's troubles, but it would be misleading to suggest a causal link. The building services industry recruited immigrants in virtually any city where they were to be found, but with varying consequences for both wages and union shares. In New York, for example, immigrants comprised 60 percent of the building services workforce, just under the level in L.A.; nonetheless, the immigrants in New York's building services industry earned $7,000 more than their counterparts in L.A. (U.S. Department of Commerce 1990), and New York never experienced the deunionization of janitors that L.A. suffered in the 1980s. Closer to home, San Francisco also experienced an infusion of immigrants, but wages and union density did not take the battering they did in L.A. San Francisco janitors always enjoyed higher wages than their L.A. counterparts, but during the early 1980s janitors' wages in L.A. slipped behind even further.

The Union Returns to Town

While Local 399 was crashing, its parent was taking on new form. SEIU had grown during the 1960s and 1970s, largely through diversification into health-care and public-sector jurisdictions. In the first years of John Sweeney's regime, which began in 1980, these trends continued. But before long, as Michael Piore has recounted, Sweeney "transformed the organization, especially after 1984" (1994:528). He doubled the per-capita tax, historically the lowest in the AFL-CIO, and increased the national staff from twenty to more than two hundred between 1984 and 1988. The new staff members were recruited from the ranks of the not-so-new left; in Piore's view, since few unions were hiring staff during the 1980s, SEIU "had its pick of these 'new' labor militants" (1994:528). These changes were part of the development of a new organizational structure and strategy, one that Piore characterizes as follows:

> The planning process the SEIU has instituted involves considerable staff and leadership training. And another distinguishing characteristic of the SEIU [has] been its willingness to invest in this training. Ironically, and most notably, the union has contracted with the American Management Association to provide it. . . . It is an integrated structure, self-consciously devised and instituted by Sweeney and his staff. The ideas that underlie it were drawn from the business management literature. The staff read widely in the business press and the more scholarly literature as well. Their single most important source was probably the *Harvard Business Review*. (1994:524, 528)

In effect, the institutional changes made SEIU a more sophisticated and more militant union and infused it with at least some of the spirit of the old CIO.

But not until the mid-1980s did SEIU focus its efforts on its home base—building services. Though the founding locals (Chicago, New York, and San Francisco) were still holding fast, the rest of the building services division was in deep trouble, losing ground to nonunionized competitors and getting battered by unionized employers in search of concessions. What is now a codified set of campaign practices under the rubric of Justice for Janitors emerged gradually; a campaign in Denver, where the union raised "enough hell in the downtown area that the industry caved," became the model.

JfJ arrived in Southern California in 1988, but not without trepidation, if only because "it was really huge. . . . Going from little Denver to monstrous L.A. was like, 'Are we ready for this?' " The campaign began in the downtown area, taking responsibility for both representing the remaining union base and organizing the nearby nonunion buildings. The plan involved targeting the nonunion wings of the "double-breasted" companies (firms with both union and nonunion operations under different names) and taking advantage of internal company competition, by letting the unionized companies pick up work at low rates, with the understanding that they would move to union standards once half the market had been organized.

This initial campaign focused on Century Cleaning, a small local player with union and nonunion components and an owner whom the union could "get a handle on." In some respects, this first effort proceeded along traditional lines: contacting workers, making house calls, signing cards, identifying leaders in both the union and nonunion buildings. Otherwise, the game plan was different. Most important, there was no expectation that the drive would eventuate in an election. Part of the thinking on this matter reflected what has since come to be counterconventional wisdom: "Elections are controlled by the bosses and set up for them. It's an alienating process for workers, and takes the concept of power between workers and bosses and separates the union from the workers. The union *is* the workers." But the aversion to traditional procedures was also influenced by considerations specific to the industry, namely, an awareness that the employer was little more than a straw boss and that decision-making power lay in the hands of the property owners, whose interests the board process concealed and protected.

Although this first campaign never ended up reaching the "people who have power in the market," it successfully engaged the company on a variety of fronts. One involved the "in-your-face" protests for which JfJ has since become well known, doing street theater at a popular restaurant that the company's owner frequented or taking a group of workers to the owner's golf club, where they "raised a ruckus, chanting and screaming."

But the union also learned that "it didn't take a contract to redefine the relationship with the company." JfJ pressured employers by activating agencies such as CalOSHA or other state agencies charged with worker protection, which heretofore had turned a blind eye to contractors' lack of compliance with the law.

In the end, the continuing battle took the cleaning contractor "out of the fight," with the union redefining victory as "if the [building] owner would bounce Century Cleaning from the building." This claim was not entirely hollow since some of Century's contracts slipped to union firms.

The next major target, Bradford, the nonunion wing of the national firm American Building Maintenance, proved a formidable enemy—in part because its president was vehemently antiunion, in part because of its larger size. Yet the campaign registered slow but steady progress, and by April 1989, Local 399 had negotiated a master agreement, the first in downtown L.A. since the early 1980s.

Then, in the summer of 1989, the focus of the campaign shifted to Century City, a large westside office complex employing 400 janitors, of whom 250 were employed by a single cleaning contractor, ISS. JfJ marshaled a variety of tactics to put pressure on ISS. As one janitor told a writer for the *Los Angeles Times,* "The strategy is attack, attack, attack" (Nazario 1993). As it had done downtown earlier on, JfJ also staged various in-your-face publicity stunts to draw the attention of Century City building tenants to the janitors' plight; tenants often complained to building managers about JfJ activities, indirectly intensifying the pressure on ISS.

By late spring 1990, the union concluded that employer intransigence left it no alternative but to strike and that it had the strength to take on that challenge. On May 29, 1990, "we pulled the buildings." From that point on, the pace of activity escalated sharply.

The rule was, if you're on strike, you have to come out and do actions. We had daily actions, every morning we walked along the median strip with human billboards, traffic was really tied up. And on some days we had big actions. On the first big one, we stormed through every single building in Century City, every single one. We had a lot of community people, it was about three or four hundred people. We went marching through the buildings, chanting and banging on drums, saying, "What do we want? Justice! When do we want it? Now!" Pretty simple, straightforward things. . . . The LAPD called a citywide tactical alert that day. They just completely freaked out. They were getting panicked calls from every building in Century City, which was the power center of the westside, and in some ways the power center of the city.

This set the stage for the events of June 15, when the L.A. police attacked a peaceful march of JfJ strikers and supporters as they walked from nearby Beverly Hills to Century City. In full view of the media, and recorded on videotape, the police charged the crowd, injuring many, including children and pregnant women. Organizers feared that workers would be intimidated into a retreat, but at a meeting for the strikers shortly after the event, it became clear that the police action had only strengthened the workers' resolve. "It was like, 'Let's go back on Monday. Put the word out, we're going back on Monday, and we're going to be bigger, we're going to be badder! You can't scare us out of Century City.' This was not the organizers' message to the workers, this was the workers' message to the union."

Public outrage at the police attack (which occurred prior to the Rodney King beating) added fuel to the campaign. Then-mayor Tom Bradley came under pressure to act. And in New York, Gus Bevona, the powerful president of SEIU Local 32B-32J, who had previously been unwilling to exert any pressure on ISS, which was unionized in New York, was moved to lend a hand after seeing a video of the L.A. police beating strikers: "Bevona called the president of ISS [headquartered in New York] into his office and, after making him wait in the front office for two and a half hours, threatened that if he did not recognize the L.A. union, all hell would break loose. The contract with ISS was signed that day."

We lack evidence on the motivations that led Bevona to act when and as he did. But bringing ISS to the table undoubtedly involved the expenditure of considerable political capital. As one Local 399 official told us: "People are always calling [Bevona] up saying, 'I can't solve my own problem, you solve it for me.' He's a powerful guy in New York, but there is just so much he can do." In this case, successful mobilization in L.A. created the context in which Bevona was motivated to cash in his chips. And without that mobilization, pressure from afar would not have had much impact: "Gus Bevona could have done this earlier. But if we weren't in a position to hang on to our membership, if the building owners said, 'We don't care what Gus Bevona says, you're out of here,' there's not much that Gus Bevona can do about real estate developers in L.A. Unless we're in a position where we can use that help, it would have been a meaningless gesture on his part." In any case, with ISS brought to its knees, JfJ won the battle for Century City, and this victory in turn paved the way for other successes in L.A. and nationwide.

The Ingredients of Success

In any successful social movement, many factors—some of them unique to the particular moment—combine to produce victory. We can identify three ingredients critical to JfJ's dramatic success in L.A.: centralized union leadership, an industry-specific strategy and tactics, and the presence of a critical mass of class-conscious immigrant workers. The first two elements are typical of JfJ nationwide, and indeed the campaign also succeeded in some cities where immigrants were not present in large numbers; however, JfJ's more spectacular showing in L.A. was due to a special dynamic created by the presence of vast numbers of immigrants from Central America and Mexico in its janitorial labor force.

Centralization

JfJ is widely seen as a bottom-up campaign. That it is, but it also has a crucial top-down component. In part, the importance of centralization comes down to a matter of dollars and cents and the "money thing," as one organizer explained, "is not cheap by any stretch of the imagination." Although SEIU has its origins in AFL unionism of the most traditional, decentralized type, it has evolved a different structure, which effectively redistributes resources from organized to unorganized workers. The *Wall*

Street Journal (Ybarra 1994) reports that 25 percent of SEIU's budget goes to organizing, as opposed to an average of 5 percent for the rest of organized labor, and only passing familiarity with the JfJ campaign indicates why. The campaign is labor intensive, requiring substantial personnel. The local staff includes at least one researcher, from whom there can be no immediate payoff. Further, the campaign involves a substantial legal component, costly in itself. And the high-visibility tactics are also high-risk tactics, especially when the union runs up against owners or developers with particularly deep pockets.

Although only the international would be likely to possess the resources required for such a campaign, a fat treasury is not sufficient. The campaign also requires perseverance. The payoffs are always uncertain; they were surely more so at the early stages when no one could have known how events would unfold. After the first two years of organizing in L.A. (prior to the Century City breakthrough), the yield was not very promising—namely, the addition of janitors from only a handful of buildings to the union fold, at the price of half a million dollars a year.

Moreover, local leadership has been less than enthusiastic; indeed, effective organization has often meant taking matters out of the hands of local leaders. "The leadership in 1987 was old school, conservative," reflected one of the lead JfJ organizers on the mood at the onset of the campaign. "There was concern that they would bail when things got hot." Indeed, the local head of 399's building division was completely cut out of any responsibility for organizing, and JfJ became the downtown building services union, with responsibility for organizing and representation. In early 1989, the L.A. local put a halt to its material support for the campaign, and had the international not intervened, it is unlikely that janitorial unionism in L.A. would have developed as it has.

Nor is L.A. unique in this regard. JfJ has frequently been exported through trusteeships, which were imposed on the San Diego, Atlanta, San Jose, and Santa Clara locals. One seasoned union source with experience in several cities reported that local staff and leaders were frequently resistant to the JfJ model and often threw up roadblocks to organizing. Although local conservatism may reflect economic considerations, other factors are likely to be in play: it is not difficult to imagine that an incumbent leadership will opt for the status quo, especially in light of the political ramifications of a sudden infusion of new, possibly ethnically distinctive members.

Thus, on the one hand, a centralized structure that allowed the international to bypass local decision makers and make direct investments in organizing was a necessary condition of JfJ's success. On the other hand, this structure was not a sufficient condition: the very considerable resources that the international devoted to organizing could have been misspent.

Strategy and Tactics

JfJ's basic strategy is to seek control over all the key players in a local labor market, with the goal of taking labor costs out of competition. "One industry, one union, one contract" is the slogan on a union leaflet. JfJ seeks to compel employers "to fight *on our terms,* not theirs," as Stephen Lerner, former director of building services organizing for SEIU and the architect of the strategy, has described the basic plan (1991:8). If management is not unappreciative of just how much that strategy has changed the rules of the game—"brilliant" was the term used by one informant to describe the union's modus operandi—management understandably describes the strategy in somewhat different terms: "You can't fight the SEIU in the gutter. They are good at that."

JfJ deliberately abandoned the traditional NLRB election approach to organizing, in part because of the peculiar structure of the building services industry. Instead, JfJ developed the idea of a "comprehensive campaign," in the words of a key organizer, "a war against the employers *and* the building owners, waged on all fronts [without] leaving any stone unturned." The war plan had several key elements.

Intelligence. Along with its 1930s-style spirit, JfJ has brought 1990s-style organization and technology to the cause of janitorial unionism; indeed, the union's strategy began with a business-oriented understanding of the industry. From its inception, the L.A. campaign "had a full-time research/ corporate person" functioning exclusively as an "information-gatherer and utilizer." Data supplied by researchers at SEIU headquarters in Washington supplemented information collected at the local level. As one impressed management informant put it, SEIU had the ability to "ferret out the weaknesses" of the ownership/management structure in any particular situation.

Intelligence plays still another role, having to do with activation of the membership base. "Our economists know how to crunch the numbers . . . the real numbers. Someone will get pissed if they learn that it costs the owner one cent to give them a raise." Understanding the industry also becomes a tool in the hands of the workers, allowing them to see how and why they have the potential to change the conditions they endure.

Effective gathering of intelligence requires the appropriate personnel and technology as well as the investment needed to bring these human and capital resources together. Consequently, access to and mobilization of highly skilled, often college-educated organizers and researchers, combined with the ability to command the technological resources that enable them to be effective, were essential to the JfJ's effectiveness.

Guerrilla legal tactics. While abandoning the election route, JfJ found instruments in the NLRA and other legal protections that could be used to gain leverage over employers. JfJ filed complaints with the NLRB over employer violations, such as discrimination against union activists and other "unfair labor practices" prohibited by laws the NLRB is charged with enforcing. "If the company violated Section 7 rights, then we could file Board charges, and we aggressively used the Board for those kinds of things," an organizer explained. This approach also permitted janitors to go on strike under certain conditions with legal protection against being permanently replaced.

Use of such guerrilla tactics served two ends. First, as one management informant told us, they "beat down the contractors economically"; those unprepared to "spend a fortune on lawyers . . . settled pretty quickly." Second, guerrilla tactics transformed the union into the effective, if not the legal, representative of the workers.

The SEIU's proclivity for in-your-face media-oriented events corresponds with management's description of a "fight in the gutter." Such tactics brought public embarrassment to key individuals in the industry while also making life difficult for building tenants. Of course, the ability to carry off such efforts depended heavily on the union's research capacity. While JfJ deliberately cultivated particularly aggressive tactics, it had to do so carefully to avoid being forced by employers into an NLRB election.

In particular, the legal prohibition against secondary boycotts means that in-your-face activities must be handled gingerly. The SEIU has generally been successful in walking the thin line distinguishing acts of free speech protected by the First Amendment from activities that would trigger Board action to protect such "innocent" parties as building owners.[2]

Coalition building. Yet another means of targeting owners involved the political realm. JfJ had the good fortune of beginning in the halcyon days of the 1980s, when investors were falling over themselves to build property in downtown L.A. Since construction could not begin without approval from the city's Community Redevelopment Authority (CRA), the union had a powerful lever on which to lean. During most of the 1980s, the head of the L.A. County AFL-CIO sat on the board of the CRA, as did other potential allies; consequently, no office tower built after 1987 opened up without a unionized cleaning crew.

Most important, the union was able to connect with and move its friends in high places; of particular importance were links to local political leaders. It was not a matter of ending the marriage between L.A.'s political establish-

---

2. We are aware of one case, from the San Francisco area, in which the NLRB specifically addressed JfJ tactics aimed at owners and issued a cease-and-desist order against the union. That case, *Trinity Building Maintenance* (312 NLRB 715 [1993]), now stands as a potential threat to JfJ tactics.

ment and real estate interests but simply altering it so that the deals that political leaders cut with property owners would occasionally yield dividends for someone else. As we have noted, SEIU's allies on the CRA played precisely this role during the late 1980s. In 1990, after the savage police beating at Century City, the union, with help from the county AFL, was able to mobilize then-mayor Bradley, who phoned the principal ownership interest at Century City to voice his concern over the incidents that had arisen in the course of the organizing.

Another important source of strength was support from unions representing janitors in other cities. When janitorial unionism declined in L.A. and other metropolitan areas, it remained strong in such traditional citadels as New York, Chicago, and San Francisco. Most of the key players on the industry side are made up of nationally or internationally operated firms that do business with the union where they must, and such firms are vulnerable to pressure from their unionized employees. But, as we have already noted, SEIU has a tradition of decentralization; and although conditions have changed since the union's early days, negotiations still occur at the local, not the national, level, leaving solidaristic actions subject to local considerations. The story of Gus Bevona's role in securing a contract with ISS after the police beatings in Century City is revealing on this score; only when mobilization had reached a boiling point was he willing to intervene.

Mobilizing the rank and file. Ultimately, the ability to pressure employers derived from the union's success at striking a chord among the rank and file and moving them to action in ways that generated legal charges, caught the attention of the mass media, and forced the hands of other actors, including politicians and such SEIU leaders as Gus Bevona. As one of our informants emphasized: "The reason that L.A. is the shining star of the union is that we've had the highest percentage of workers participation, have the highest worker turnout, and the highest percentage of workers going to jail and getting arrested. At heart and soul, there has to be a mobilized workforce."

This brings us to the third and final ingredient in JfJ's L.A. success: the role of immigrants.

Role of Immigrants

In the period of Local 399's earlier decline, employers used the social structures of immigration to evade the union and to secure a more compliant labor force. But the fact that the workforce was bound by a series of interlocking networks meant that now the same structures could be put to a different purpose. "If you can get into the [hiring] chain, then the chain works both ways." The convergence of ethnicity, residence, and occupational concentration made the union's task easier. An organizer recalled, "I would go to a building in Pico-Union looking for someone from Premier [a cleaning contractor] and someone would say, 'Oh, she's downstairs—with someone else from Premier.' "

Moreover, the peculiar conditions of building services work created a sense of occupational community: working at night, when few others did, the janitors formed a somewhat isolated group. Thus, "even though L.A. is famous for no community, . . . we found a community of janitors." Other common experiences seem to have made that community particularly organizable. One organizer reported a "high level of class consciousness," apparently rooted in the societies from which the immigrants came: "One of the good things about organizing Latino workers is that there is a positive view of unions. They know what they are. There is a saying that is much more common there: *La union hace la fuerza*. Everyone knows it. If you ask, *'Que piensa de la union?'*, they answer, *'La union hace la fuerza*. If the rest of the people want to be in the union, I want to be in it.' "

Among the Central Americans, there was also a sizable component of seasoned activists with a background in left-wing or union activity back home. That experience did more than impart organizing skills or develop a proclivity toward making trouble; it also put the risks entailed in a union drive in a totally different light: "With the Salvadorans, you find different attitudes. Sometimes you found people who fought there. And there, you were in a union, they killed you. Here, you [were in a union] and you lost a job at $4.25."

True, the janitorial workforce included former activists along with their prior enemies—"You find other ones, 'I was the one who killed that trade unionist' "—and erstwhile members of the middle class, as well as peasants and proletarians. But the organizers reported that "no matter what their political background in their country, here they were working class and understood the idea of sticking to your class."

Compared with the situation in the early 1980s, when Local 399 collapsed, by the end of the decade, many immigrant janitors had considerable U.S. experience. For these veterans, the prospects of returning home—a plan that often inhibits organizing—must have seemed increasingly dim. And if one can generalize from the experience of one rank-and-file leader who described herself as having "learned in the university of daily life and gained a diploma in exploitation," settlement in the United States may also have played an embittering, and thereby catalytic, role. As one key rank-and-file leader put it, "We Latino workers are a bomb waiting to explode."

Although there is other evidence to suggest that Latino immigrant workers are demonstrating a militancy and commitment to labor "not seen in many years" (McMahon, Finkel-Shimshon, and Fujimoto 1991), the immigrant presence seems unlikely to have been either a necessary or a sufficient condition of success. Immigrants are certainly capable of spontaneous outbreaks, but the power relations in the building services industry are simply too uneven to imagine that immigrant janitors could have unionized without the extraordinary financial and human investment of the SEIU international and without the strategy the JfJ leadership developed. Nor are immigrants uniquely disposed toward organizing—or else JfJ would succeed only in cities where immigrants are a sizable presence. At the same time, few if any organizing campaigns succeed without mobilizing rank-and-file workers. And in this respect, the JfJ campaign was probably better off with the immigrants than without them, for all the reasons adduced above.

Defeat Snatched from the Jaws of Victory?

In the aftermath of JfJ's successes in the early 1990s, unrest moved from the streets into Local 399 itself. The local union leadership, made up of people highly supportive of the JfJ effort, was turned out of office in the spring of 1995. The international SEIU responded by placing the local in trusteeship. It was not possible for us to determine fully the nature of the dispute, but this turn of events raises the distinct possibility that the future of Local 399 may not be as bright as its recent past.

A pessimistic view would suggest that the union's hold on the industry is very precarious and that the earlier collapse of Local 399 may be recapitulated in the future. Notwithstanding the gains generated by unionization, wages remain very modest, too low to cement attachment to the industry, which means that the workforce will continue to turn over at high rates. Instability is an inherent source of union weakness, requiring the local to continually reorganize the workforce lest the contractors supplant union members with nonunion workers and then go nonunion before anyone is the wiser. Some employers claim that if they pay workers union rates, they can take any given workplace nonunion and that the "union will never know." Although this may be largely bravado, the union's internal preoccupations would suggest that it may be more than an idle threat.

Moreover, there may be less to today's pacific relations with employers than meets the eye: since wage increases in the five-year contract signed in 1995 are back-loaded, employers may grow restive when faced with the thirty-cent-an-hour raise due in 1999. Given that some of the nonunion contractors have not yet been brought to heel, even a marginal decline in Local 399's strength may swing the balance of power back to the nonunion side.

The possibility that employers may turn more obstreperous has much to do with the currently depressed state of the real estate market, and a revival of demand for office space in L.A. may well bode ill for janitorial unionism. Owners differ in their degree of exposure to the pressures that JfJ can apply; since the mid-1980s, it has had the good fortune of confronting institutional investors who find themselves highly vulnerable to the tactics that JfJ deploys. Moreover, bad times make all owners concerned about occupancy: they may be more likely to succumb to union pressure when tenants are scarce and difficult to replace. But if and when good times return to L.A., institutional investors may sell out to more hard-nosed owners who are less concerned with sullying their public image and less fearful of losing tenants who will, in turn, have fewer options.

But there is also an optimistic interpretation of today's internal travails. In this view, the union's current problems are a normal, perhaps even an inevitable, result of such a massive organizing effort. As in other similarly competitive industries, unionized employers have been quick to find virtue in a union that can take wages out of competition; as long as it does so, they may be quite willing to bid nonunion times good-bye. Stable relations are eased by the presence of the large national, even international contractors, who live with unions wherever they must and who have accommodated to the return of janitorial unionism to L.A. While it is true that workers in an industry like building services have to be reorganized continually, this was always true in such labor-intensive, small-establishment industries as restaurants, garment manufacturing, and construction. For much of the twentieth century, these were environments in which unions thrived. And as the pessimist would never have predicted the very considerable success that JfJ has achieved so far, we suspect that one would do better to listen to what the optimist has to say.

Involving Members
and Allies in Organizing

Part III consists of four case studies that focus on strategies to build membership and public support for organizing. In particular, the authors analyze the involvement of rank-and-file union members in the organizing process and the importance of building alliances in the community. Turner considers the importance of involving workers from the unit being organized in the campaign. Nissen looks at efforts to involve current members in external organizing. Sciacchitano reports on important community alliances, while Peters and Merrill focus on the role of sympathetic clergy.

Turner discusses four union drives, two in the United States and two in Germany, in which a common thread was the importance of active rank-and-file participation. Where such participation was present, the drive was successful, whether in Germany or in the United States. Where it was not present, the drive failed to achieve its objective. Although other factors obviously are important in organizing and there are limits to the conclusions that can be drawn from four cases, Turner's work sends a strong and important message about the need for rank-and-file involvement in union organizing efforts.

In an important contribution focusing on two Indiana locals, Nissen examines the role of rank-and-file volunteers in external organizing campaigns. He argues that if the labor movement is to grow in the years ahead, it must encourage union members on a large scale to serve as volunteers in organizing drives to supplement the efforts of paid staff, particularly in the context of scarce resources. Nissen finds that participation by rank-and-file organizers can be decisive in persuading undecided nonunion workers to support the union cause. As more and more local unions start to recruit and train rank-and-file volunteers as organizers, research like Nissen's will prove especially valuable.

Sciacchitano draws lessons from a successful United Electrical Workers

(UE) organizing and first-contract campaign in Milwaukee. The target was Steeltech, a minority-owned business in the inner city with a predominantly African American workforce. Often the most crucial challenge unions must overcome in organizing is the employer's tactic of portraying them as outside "third parties" separate from the workers they seek to organize. UE succeeded by tapping the strength and solidarity of Milwaukee's African American community. The campaign challenged a model of economic development that failed to require that corporations receiving public assistance respect their employees' rights. The publicity generated and the ultimate victory created a more favorable climate for union organizing community-wide and successfully created a link in the public's mind between workers' rights and human and civil rights.

Part III closes with Peters and Merrill's analysis of the role of clergy in union organizing. The authors focus on two recent Illinois cases in which assistance from the local religious community played a crucial role in the success of union organizing and first-contract campaigns. Peters and Merrill remind us that support for workers' rights, including the right to organize, has deep roots in the Judeo-Christian ethical tradition. Support from clergy can strengthen the moral legitimacy of workers' struggles and provide concrete help in overcoming employer opposition. This work clearly demonstrates the potential for religious and labor groups to join together in pursuit of workers' rights to organize.

Chapter 7

Rank-and-File Participation in Organizing at Home and Abroad

Lowell Turner

The dramatic change of leadership at the AFL-CIO in the fall of 1995 occurred in a context of major new efforts aimed at revitalization of the American labor movement. The new leaders and their majority coalition have promised to unleash labor's "social movement" potential by shifting new resources into both union organizing drives and grassroots political campaigns. At the same time, John Sweeney has offered business leaders a "social compact" for economic growth and labor peace if unionism is accepted and labor given a place at the table.[1] Together, these developments offer hopeful signs of new life for organized labor in America.

The rebirth of a long-declining labor movement will not occur overnight, however. It will require patience, persistence, and a fundamental transformation in the attitudes and strategies of many union leaders and activists. Above all, this transformation requires rank-and-file participation.

We know that we need labor law reform.[2] But it is also clear that this is not *all* we need; nor can we expect to achieve legal reform simply by electing Democrats. That strategy did not work in 1978–79 or in 1993–94, and it will not work in the future. In the face of inevitably powerful and well-organized business opposition, even the most well-financed and articulate lobbying campaign for labor law reform can fail. What was missing in 1978–79 and in 1993–94 and is urgently needed now is the pressure of

For help with the research and/or useful comments, the author thanks Lee Adler, Kate Bronfenbrenner, John Delaney, Chris Erickson, James Gibbs, Rick Hurd, Bruce Raynor, Witich Rossmann, Monica Russo, Victor Silverman, and Joe Uehlein.

1. See, for example, Greenhouse 1995.
2. The argument is persuasively made and well documented in Friedman et al. 1994.

a massive social movement, mobilized to transform and democratize the American workplace.

The potential is there for such a movement, fueled by falling real wages, growing income polarization, and a widespread desire for expanded voice in the workplace (Appelbaum and Batt 1994; Commission on the Future of Worker-Management Relations 1994b; Kochan 1995; Levine 1995). But the potential will not be realized unless people are allowed and encouraged to participate fully in the building of their own union organizing drives, union mobilization efforts, including labor-community coalitions, and grassroots political campaigns.

This chapter presents case studies of success and failure in union organizing campaigns in the United States and Germany to support the cross-national—and thus to some extent universal—validity of this argument. Comparative analysis is especially useful in developing and testing causal relationships. If, for example, rank-and-file participation can be shown to have similar effects in organizing efforts in contrasting institutional and cultural contexts, the explanatory power of the hypothesis suggested here may well be significant (thus meriting further and more extensive testing). Germany affords the context of a comparable advanced industrial society but one with very different traditions and institutions of industrial relations (such as codetermination and comprehensive collective bargaining) and historically strong unions facing a parallel need for contemporary revitalization.

The case studies examine parallel organizing drives, two each in the United States and Germany. Although four case studies do not constitute proof, these cases are highly suggestive concerning the impact of and potential that could result from expanding rank-and-file participation in union organizing and contract campaigns. The findings are also consistent with some of the best contemporary U.S.-based research and analysis on union organizing (see, for example, Bronfenbrenner 1993; Johnston 1994; Hurd 1997).

The U.S. Cases

Tultex

Since the late 1970s, the Amalgamated Clothing and Textile Workers Union (ACTWU) had tried on five occasions to organize at Tultex, a large sweatsuit manufacturing plant in Martinsville, Virginia, that in 1994 employed twenty-three hundred employees, 55 percent of them black.[3] After four failed attempts, persistence finally paid off in a two-to-one union certi-

---

3. The Tultex and DuPont case studies presented here are based on interviews conducted with key union organizers active in leadership roles in each campaign.

fication election victory in 1994, followed by the consolidation of an active local (UNITE Local 1994) and the negotiation of a strong first contract in early 1995. The key elements of this important victory were a massive flow of information to educate the workforce about what the union could offer as well as to counter management's antiunion campaign; extensive mobilization of union supporters within the workforce, based on solid groundwork laid during previous organizing campaigns; and focused and strategic use of union resources, including an extensive yet targeted house call campaign, to win over swing voters.

After close union election defeats in 1989 and 1990 (48 percent for the union in 1989 and 46 percent in 1990), ACTWU gave up on Tultex for a few years. Above all, rank-and-file supporters were demoralized and unwilling to carry on after the failure of their major, risk-taking efforts. And the company showed savvy, setting up teams and joint committees to offer workers the promise of voice in lieu of unionization.

After two or three years, however, in response to new cost-cutting pressures, the company forgot its earlier promises and eliminated the joint committees along with pay bonuses and certain shift premiums, thus effectively cutting take-home pay. As anger among the workers mounted, the union sent in probes in April and May 1994, surveying workers to test the "heat." The heat was there, although the continuing demoralization of former workforce activists from the earlier failed campaigns was apparent. Otherwise, conditions were ripe, and in June, the union initiated yet another organizing campaign.

Given the initial demoralization of the workforce, the campaign got off to a slow start, and the union considered abandoning the drive in the first week. But after a strong core of seasoned ACTWU organizers visited the homes of potential rank-and-file leaders, the petition drive began to pick up steam. Critical to the turnaround was a major deployment of ACTWU resources (especially the use of fifteen to twenty union staff members experienced in "reading" the potential for participation on the part of rank and filers), the mobilization of rank-and-file activists to get signatures and subsequently keep the campaign going, and expanded coverage of the organizing drive on local television.

Experts from the union's Comprehensive Campaigns Department came in to help gain media coverage and to counter the company's antiunion message. A local maverick cable station began to cover the campaign, prodded by the union to get the story out. The company also used the cable station to promote its side of the story, and soon the whole town was watching nightly coverage and competing prime-time ads. For the union, such exposure was invaluable, from talk show discussions that included unionized workers from a nearby towel-manufacturing plant to film clips showing the construction of an expensive lakefront vacation home for a Tultex executive juxtaposed with the shacks of employee families facing company cutbacks. Through the medium of local television, the union promoted an active campaign of information and publicity and entered in a powerful way into the conscious life of the community.

The contribution of Comprehensive Campaigns was important in keeping the company at bay and in enabling rank-and-file and staff organizers to push the organizing drive forward. For example, through the media, the union exposed the role of a black consulting firm from North Carolina hired to convince black workers to vote against the union. That checks had been written for black ministers in earlier campaigns was exposed on cable TV; and this time, the union made a major effort to win the support of local ministers. Company efforts to divide black and white workers were effectively countered.

In the course of the petition drive and subsequent election campaign, union staff and rank-and-file activists conducted more than one thousand house calls in which they talked to workers and their families face-to-face, winning people over. Past experience at Tultex was a valuable guide: rather than the blanket house calls that the union had conducted in 1989 and 1990, the visits were well targeted. Visits were focused neither on those who had signed union cards in 1989, 1990, and 1994 (and were thus considered safe union voters) nor on those who had never signed (and were thus considered likely antiunion voters) but on those who had signed once or twice but not all three times—swing voters. In addition, house calls were made to potential rank-and-file leaders and activists to get these folks to carry much of the workload through their own active participation. The strategy worked: the August 1994 NLRB election resulted in an overwhelming 1,321 to 720 union victory.

ACTWU wasted no time in building on the victory, and by early 1995 the new membership had ratified the first union contract at Tultex. In the face of solid rank-and-file support for the union, the company backed down quickly from its adversarial stance and agreed to a particularly strong contract (from the union point of view) that granted ACTWU (now UNITE) representatives unparalleled access in the mill, good communication with management and with the workforce, and the beginnings of a largely cooperative labor-management relationship. And as an important spin-off of this successful effort, the union quickly organized another Tultex plant with six hundred workers, located a forty-minute drive from Martinsville.

The ingredients in this important union victory offer important lessons for other organizing drives: union persistence after earlier defeats, a massive flow of information (including the use of local television as well as extensive house call visits) to support union demands and counter management oppo-

sition, and the mobilization and participation of experienced union organizers and active rank-and-file leadership.

DuPont

As organizers for the United Mine Workers of America (UMWA) put it
these days: "We're coming down out of the coalfields." As the use of auto-
mation has expanded in the coal mining industry, along with alternative
sources of energy generation, UMWA membership numbers have fallen
dramatically with the total number of employed coal miners. Nonetheless,
the industry has experienced continuing union commitment and activism,
resulting in dramatic victories, such as the Pittston strike, under the most
adverse circumstances. That prolonged, militant, and successful strike in
particular once again catapulted the UMWA into prominence within the
labor movement: members in their camouflage suits and with high spirits
have been visible morale boosters at union-led demonstrations (in Washington and elsewhere), while past UMWA president Richard Trumka now
shares governance of the AFL-CIO as secretary-treasurer on the recently
elected Sweeney slate. In part as a spin-off of the long and spirited Pittston
campaign, UMWA organizers have moved "down out of the coalfields" of
Appalachia to play increasingly active roles in other organizing campaigns.

One recent effort took place at a DuPont chemical plant in Martinsville
that employs 550 workers. Facing growing worker dissatisfaction regarding
pay and working conditions, a local, unaffiliated company-oriented union
at the plant approached the UMWA regarding merger talks. Although the
UMWA could have simply accepted the merger, UMWA officials thought it
was important for the workers to vote their union in. The UMWA conducted a card-signing campaign from July to October 1994, resulting in the
collection of signatures by 80 percent of the workforce. Important in the
successful petition campaign was the extensive use of house call visits, a
new tactic for the UMWA.

The company counterattacked, however, and highly effectively. Using the
same cable television channel ACTWU had used during the Tultex campaign, along with in-plant TV monitors, DuPont broadcast a steady stream
of film clips showing past incidents of violence against and by strikers in
the coalfields. Company managers told captive workforce audiences that
this was the kind of thing they could expect in Martinsville if they voted the
UMWA in. Many of the workers who had signed cards got scared; when
elections were held in November 1994, the UMWA lost to a new company-
oriented union by 276 to 218 (with 36 votes for no union at all).

The UMWA credits its strong card-signing effort and its 218 election
votes to the more than eight hundred house calls union organizers and
rank-and-file activists made in the course of the campaign. For the union,

this is clearly the way to go in future campaigns. But obviously, the house calls themselves were not enough.

Why did the UMWA lose this election? First, the union did not want to get involved in a media/television campaign. The Tultex experience suggests that this was probably a mistake. Second, and most important, unlike ACTWU, the UMWA was a new presence in town, a relatively unknown quantity to most of the workforce, with no history of active participation in the plant; it was unable to counter DuPont's campaign on its own turf. When the company showed films of violence in the coalfields, workers had insufficiently close rapport or relations of trust with union organizers to believe the union side of the story. In their house calls and other campaigning, UMWA organizers explained that although it had sometimes been necessary to use aggressive tactics in the past in the face of company violence, UMWA members were not conducting themselves in this way anymore and the union had no intention of bringing such tactics to Martinsville. Although true, this argument did not carry enough weight, given the newness of the UMWA-workforce relationships and the intensity of the company's propaganda campaign.

What is the solution? From this defeat, UMWA organizers have drawn the following lessons: they need to get to know the DuPont workers better, establish an ongoing union presence, build relationships of trust, and engage DuPont workers as active participants in union programs to build the rapport and trust necessary to neutralize the effects of antiunion management tactics in the future. This is exactly what the United Mine Workers have done in the wake of this election defeat: a UMWA local union has been established in Martinsville with a significant number of DuPont workers as members. The new local has offered benefits through the AFL-CIO union privileges program, provided attorneys for compensation cases, sent several workers from the plant to the UMWA's organizing school, and plans to engage in other organizing efforts in the Martinsville area. Hoping to build on past defeats as ACTWU did at Tultex, the UMWA aims to turn defeat into victory by developing trust and encouraging union participation at the DuPont plant, building toward the next certification opportunity in 1998, when the current contract expires.

The German Cases

In the United States, with its growing income polarization, use of aggressive antiunion tactics by corporations, and largely nonunion South, important organizing battles still need to be won in traditional manufacturing industries. By contrast, in Germany, as in much of northern Europe, manufacturing industries are largely organized. Whereas union membership density in the United States has dropped to 15 percent in the 1990s, levels in Germany remain at well over 30 percent, even in the face of job loss and declining union membership rolls. As employment has shifted toward service and white-collar occupations, German unions have maintained membership density not so much by organizing new workers as by deepening membership levels in manufacturing industries, where they were already strong and are now even stronger (Armingeon 1989). There is a limit to this strategy, however. If German unions are to stave off the decline in numbers faced by British, French, and American unions, they must shift their organizing focus to service, white-collar, professional, and technical employees. Thus, efforts by contemporary German unions to do so provide a functional equivalent, or "contextual comparison" (Locke and Thelen 1995), for the American cases presented above.

The two case studies offered below examine union organizing campaigns during the early 1990s at two American computer companies in Germany: DEC, where the metalworkers union succeeded beyond its expectations, and IBM, where union efforts fell short.[4]

The laws, institutions, and practices of industrial relations are, of course, different in important ways in the United States and Germany.[5] The most significant differences are that collective bargaining in Germany typically takes place on a regional/national basis for entire industry sectors, between industrial unions and employers associations (in contrast to union-company bargaining in the United States); and German firms with five or more employees are required to have elected works councils, which have legal rights to information, consultation, and codetermination in specified management decision-making processes, whereas there are no such mandated bodies or employee rights in the United States. In spite of these differences, the cases presented here are unusually comparable: at DEC, the company did not belong to the employers association and thus the union could negotiate only a company-level agreement, while at IBM the company subdivided the firm and pulled much of it out of the employers association so as to pursue its cost-cutting goals; and, in the absence of an initially strong union presence, the works councils at both firms functioned in many ways parallel to the company-oriented union discussed in the DuPont case above.

Digital Equipment Corporation (DEC)

With only a small manufacturing presence in Germany, Digital employs mostly white-collar and highly skilled employees. Most work in software

---

4. I learned of these cases from Witich Rossmann, an IG Metall staff member involved in both the DEC and IBM campaigns, who wrote up these cases for a paper presented at a Cornell conference in October 1994. For more details on these cases as well as an analysis of the broader contemporary German industrial relations context, see Rossmann 1995.

5. For comparisons of industrial relations in Germany and the United States, see Turner 1991 and Wever 1995.

development, technical services, sales and distribution, and administration —many of the modern occupations that German unions must learn to organize. On the heels of a major cost-cutting and downsizing campaign in the early 1990s, the company offered IG Metall (the large metalworkers union that organizes the German auto, steel, machine-tool, shipbuilding, and electronics companies, including DEC and IBM) an opportunity to learn by doing.

In the spring of 1992, Digital announced a wave of layoffs. The union responded by denouncing the company plan (the terms of which would have to be negotiated with the elected works council), calling instead for long-term business planning, no layoffs, downsizing through attrition, re-training, transfers, reduced working time, and work sharing. IG Metall also launched a union membership drive (at DEC-Germany, the union member-ship rate was less than 5 percent, including 10 percent at the main DEC location in Cologne) and called a first brief "warning strike" in Cologne in April 1992.[6]

Although only 10 percent of DEC-Cologne employees belonged to the union, 80 percent participated in that first warning strike. Additional warn-ing strikes and protest actions followed at Cologne and elsewhere in Ger-many between November 1992 and the beginning of a full-fledged strike in June 1993. Management's continued refusal to consider union demands coupled with a major union organizing effort led to a rise in membership levels from 5 to 30 percent nationwide at DEC and from 10 percent to more than 50 percent at the main location in Cologne.

When a strike vote was held in 1993, 92 percent of the union members at DEC participated in the vote, and 85 percent voted for strike authoriza-tion. In typical German fashion, the strike started out small at DEC loca-tions in Berlin, Bremen, Hannover, and Hamburg, spreading after a few days to the main location in Cologne. Only at the end of the first week did management finally agree to negotiate. The settlement that was reached surprisingly quickly at the end of the second week included new job security provisions and an agreement to follow the terms of a typical regional-level IG Metall contract and in general far exceeded the expectations of the DEC workforce.

In poststrike discussion and analysis, IG Metall credited the organizers' grassroots, participatory approach for this first dramatic organizing and strike success in the German computer industry. An open information policy and effective communication structures, both before and during the strike, were particularly important. As IG Metall organizer Witich Rossmann put

---

6. Warning strikes in the German system typically last anywhere from twenty minutes to a full day and are designed to demonstrate union strength in bargaining situations.

it: "Traditional union communication, characterized by a selective and hierarchical information policy, is unsuitable for qualified workforces in the computer industry. Strategic goals must be subject to discussion and alteration at all times" (1995:19). Elected white-collar works councilors (most of whom joined the union) participated actively in both the organizing campaign and the strike, cooperated closely with the union, and subjected their own policies to open rank-and-file discussion and votes. Finally, IG Metall, in a bid to modernize the union's internal structure, gave local organizers and activists not only support but broad autonomy to develop plant- and company-specific policy.

The mobilization of participation (including information, consultation, and codetermination) inside the workforce and union made possible this first upsurge of unionization in the German computer industry. A very different and more traditional approach yielded a much less favorable result at IBM.

IBM Deutschland

Unlike DEC, IBM in Germany did belong to the appropriate employers association. Although unionization levels were low in early 1992, its thirty-one thousand employees were nonetheless covered under the terms of collective agreements. In response to market forces similar to those facing DEC and in a drive to achieve flexibility and cost cutting, IBM launched a restructuring campaign, moving large parts of the company into independent spin-offs and out from under the umbrella of collective bargaining agreements. The explicit intent, articulated in 1992, was to carve out union-free areas of the company and to replace collective agreements with separate plant agreements negotiated with local works councils.

In 1992 and 1993, downsizing was accomplished through voluntary retirements, thus minimizing workforce opposition. The DEC strike in 1993 had a mobilizing effect on the IBM workforce, however, resulting in a campaign to raise union membership (which rose from less than 5 percent to 11 percent by the end of 1993 for IG Metall; a parallel rise occurred in a separate white-collar and competing union, DAG).

Dual unionism proved to be a major obstacle to workforce mobilization at IBM. At most workplaces covered by collective agreements in the metal and electronics industries of Germany, IG Metall is the sole or clearly dominant union. Given the history of weak unionization at IBM, however, the role of the alternative white-collar union—DAG, an independent union unaffiliated with the central labor federation, DGB—took on prominence. DAG was much more willing than IG Metall to sign separate plant agreements, in lieu of existing industry-level collective agreements. Elected works councilors at IBM were divided among IG Metall and DAG members and those belonging to no union. Together, DAG and nonunion works councilors formed a majority, thereby offering management negotiators a more conservative and company-oriented approach.

Given these divisions on the works councils and in the workforce, no unified labor strategy was developed at IBM (as it had been at DEC) in response to company restructuring initiatives. While IG Metall demanded that the company adhere to the industry collective agreements (and was unable to develop company-specific demands), IBM pushed its plans forward through negotiations with works council majorities consisting of DAG members and nonunionists, who together established a collective bargaining committee. Negotiations with the company took place in secret, with no mobilization or involvement of the workforce.

In early 1994, a new company-specific collective agreement was reached to replace existing industry-level (IG Metall) agreements. The new agreement strengthened the hand of the company in its drive toward having separate plant agreements and negotiating with individual employees; at the same time, the agreement included important workforce concessions on salary, bonuses, and working time (weekly working time was increased from thirty-six to thirty-eight hours, thus reversing at IBM IG Metall's largely successful campaign elsewhere in the German metal and electronics industries for the thirty-five-hour week).

The story at IBM is by no means over. IG Metall continues to represent the company's manufacturing workers, while pushing for expanded influence and running candidates in works council elections elsewhere in the company. DAG claims that its broadening of collective bargaining coverage to new areas such as software lays the groundwork for a new and improved industry agreement. But the IBM workforce remains for the most part uninvolved in these events, as, largely unorganized and participating only little in the operations of unions or works councils, workers pursue individual career paths.

Limited workforce involvement, a restricted flow of information, and a top-down union approach to strategy and negotiation (on the part of both IG Metall, which kept to a strict and inflexible union line, and DAG, which held secret negotiations for a company- and concessions-oriented agreement) resulted in a weak and largely ineffectual unionization campaign at IBM in the early 1990s.

Conclusion: No Substitute for Participation

The evidence presented here suggests the importance of informed, hands-on rank-and-file involvement in union organizing campaigns, at home and abroad, in a variety of institutional settings, in traditional and modern industries alike. Broader data on both the United States (Bronfenbrenner 1993; Hurd 1997) and Germany (Armingeon 1989) point in the same direction.

There is a rather extraordinary convergence among contemporary labor movements in various societies toward expanded participation at the workplace and in the union. We see this today in Germany, a society whose comprehensive collective bargaining coverage and workforce codetermination rights have forced companies to take the "high road" (of high-wage, high-productivity production) but where unions are currently under pressure to organize new industries as well as to hold on to past gains in an increasingly open and integrated market. We see it in the United States, where the absence of adequate institutional protection has enabled many companies to take the "low road" (of low-wage, union-free production) and new labor leaders campaign for resurgence and a new social movement unionism based on mass mobilization.

To mention one more inspiring and particularly revealing example, we see it also in South Africa, a new democracy where strong unions have demanded and the African National Congress–led government is implementing German-style codetermination legislation (including mandated company-level works councils), along with a structure of national-, regional-, and local-level tripartite councils, to promote labor-inclusive relations of social partnership. As in the United States and Germany, the mobilization of rank-and-file participation, in the union as in the community and workplace, has become necessary both for the stabilization of democracy in turbulent times and for the expansion of economic citizenship.

Given the long-term decline of the American labor movement, it will be some time before labor here is ready to claim the extent of full social, political, and economic inclusion that South African unions are currently demanding in their transformational society. The key to the South African success lies in a history of active, social movement unionism: largely black unions, with more than 50 percent membership density, mobilized in the battle against apartheid and now in the transformation of society. Unlike business unionism or a servicing model of unionism, social movement unionism is dependent on active rank-and-file participation, a mobilization of involvement that, if encouraged rather than suppressed, can carry over into expanded union, workplace, and political democracy (Johnston 1994). This is true today in South Africa, as it has been in the past and can be in the future, in both Germany and the United States.

The South African context is, of course, very different from that of either Germany or the United States. The point to be emphasized here, however, in cross-national comparative analysis, is that labor movement revitalization and inclusion, based on expanded rank-and-file participation, appear both appropriate and necessary in the contemporary era in a variety of contrasting cross-national contexts.

Case studies of union organizing success and failure at home and abroad suggest that ongoing and extensive rank-and-file participation, rather than a faucet to be turned on and off by employers or unions, is a necessary ingredient for the revitalization of contemporary workplaces, communities, and labor movements.

Chapter 8

Utilizing the Membership to Organize the Unorganized

Bruce Nissen

Unions today face an enormous and daunting organizing task. Demographic changes, global economic changes, technological and industrial shifts, virulent employer opposition to unions, and unfavorable public policy and interpretations of labor laws have forced organized labor to experience a steep decline in membership. The new AFL-CIO leadership is increasing organizing resources, and many national unions are following suit. Nevertheless, the need far exceeds the limited budget.

One partial solution is to use union members as volunteers to supplement paid staff. Unions have always done this, although less frequently in the post-World War II period. Many national unions, among them SEIU, AFSCME, ACTWU (now part of UNITE), CWA, IBT, USWA, and OCAW, have institutional programs to involve the membership in organizing.

Nonetheless, the potential far exceeds the reality. In the vast majority of union locals in this country, no members are involved in external organizing. Yet, for most members, the local is the primary contact with their union, and it is a logical site for member recruitment for such activities. When do union locals undertake programs of member volunteer organizing? What are their successes and failures? What can be learned from their experiences? This chapter addresses these questions by examining the efforts of two union locals to organize unorganized workers.

Scope and Methodology of the Study

I studied two unions in northwest Indiana. Teamsters Local 142, an amalgamated local under new leadership, has been aggressively organizing, using members to supplement paid staff. United Steelworkers Local 1010, representing workers at Inland Steel Company, has involved rank-and-file members in attempts to organize Ryerson Steel, an Inland subsidiary in Chicago. These two locals have done the most in this area. Their experiences should be instructive for other union locals considering a similar approach.

I conducted seventeen interviews of twenty to sixty minutes each with the rank-and-file volunteers, supplemented by close observation of some training and house calls. Important differences between the two cases make some comparisons valuable. Nevertheless, the usual warnings about direct generalizability from case studies to all situations are in order. My results will not fit all situations, but, combined with wider evidence and preexisting knowledge, they can help in constructing general guidelines for "best practice."

Issues Studied

This chapter focuses on four issues: (1) *volunteer motivation* (on what basis are members convinced to volunteer; what is the degree of union commitment by the average volunteer; what erodes or sustains commitment); (2) *volunteer capabilities and training* (what type of training is required; what roles do or do not fit volunteers' abilities; what is the relationship between volunteers and paid union staff); (3) *characteristics of the local* influencing recruitment and use of volunteers (leadership characteristics, internal communications, size, and so on); and (4) *importance and usefulness of volunteers* in organizing success or failure.

Findings are presented in the words of the volunteers themselves, supplemented by my critical comments and evaluations. Thus, this chapter is "from the inside out"—as perceived by those volunteers carrying out the work.

Characteristics of the Two Organizing Efforts

Local 1010

United Steelworkers Local 1010 represents approximately nine thousand working and laid-off workers at the Inland Steel Mill in East Chicago, Indiana. The local has a long active history.

Ryerson Steel is an Inland subsidiary whose main facilities (nine buildings with approximately eight hundred workers) are in Chicago. It is a steel service center where Inland steel products are stored, finished, and shipped out to customers. A few much smaller Ryerson facilities are located in other parts of the country.

The USWA has been trying to unionize Ryerson's Chicago facilities for some time. Following an initial failure in 1983 and a failed partial attempt at only a couple of its buildings in 1989, a full-scale effort was mounted in 1990. Local 1010 members volunteered to do house calling in a close effort that failed by only sixty-three votes. A follow-up attempt in 1992, again with Local 1010 volunteer help, failed badly. A similar effort, in 1993, also failed, by 117 votes, as did a 1994 effort that resulted in numerous charges of unfair labor practices (ULP) by the union.

Thus, the organizing drive that I observed in June 1995 was the fifth attempt in the previous six years. Eleven members of Local 1010, together with twelve volunteers primarily from other unionized Ryerson facilities around the country, received one day's training from national and district staff on a Sunday in early June. The following Monday through Saturday, the volunteers did house calling in teams. A few of the 1010 volunteers had volunteered in previous Ryerson organizing drives, but for the majority this was their first time volunteering.

The program was highly structured. It was confined to a six-day "blitz," although some of the volunteers did a second week some time later. All volunteers were paid lost-time wages for five of the six days. Wages were for eight hours per day, although most volunteers put in twelve- to thirteen-hour days. Each team received information packets containing the addresses of organizing targets, street maps, an evaluation of their attitude in the last drive (if available), ethnic data, age, sex, and so on. All Ryerson workers were numerically categorized 1–4, with 1s being active participants in the drive, 4s antiunion, and 2s and 3s mildly pro- or antiunion.

Efforts were made to match more and less experienced people on the same team. Among the volunteers were one Caucasian woman, five African American men, six Hispanic men, and eleven Caucasian men. Not all of the Hispanic men were fluent in Spanish, although a majority were. The sole woman was fluent in Polish, which is spoken among many Ryerson workers.

A new strategy was in place. Since all contracts with Inland and its subsidiaries would expire in 1996, the union would use Inland's 70 percent union status to force a voluntary card-check recognition in contract negotiations. The union felt that legal and illegal company pressure on workers made a fair NLRB election impossible.

More than 85 percent of Inland and Inland subsidiary bargaining unit employees had signed pledge cards supporting the right of Chicago Ryerson workers to have a union and pledging to assist in that effort. This time, only a majority of the Chicago Ryerson workers needed to sign union cards; the union and the unionized employees would attempt to take care of the rest. The volunteers' task was to get that majority to sign.

Local 142

Teamsters Local 142 is structured very differently from Local 1010, and its volunteer organizing efforts are quite different. The local is an extreme example of amalgamation: it negotiates and services approximately 340 contracts for its six thousand members. Organized employers range from trucking companies to municipalities to laundries to various types of manufacturing operations.

Local 142 was taken over by reformers in 1994 following control for seven decades by a father-son dynasty. The new leadership hired a full-time lead organizer, Larry Regan, and also designated two new business agents as organizers. By early 1996, the local had won twelve campaigns in a row, adding approximately four hundred new members.

In keeping with its more heterogeneous structure and membership, Local 142 has a more varied program of recruitment and arrangement for deploying its volunteers. Through its new stewards council and through recruitment at membership meetings, sixty-eight volunteers have been secured. Of these, seven to ten have turned into "core" volunteers who help on an intense and regular basis. One core volunteer is a woman; two are Hispanic men, and the rest are Caucasian men.

Noncore volunteers help during occasional weekend blitz attempts to reach all workers in two days or attend support rallies or organizing meetings at the union hall with members of the in-plant committee. Even a few unionists from the region who are not Teamsters have helped in some of these efforts.

The local does not pay its volunteers lost-time wages. During the winter, many of the recruits are laid-off construction industry truck drivers. The local will often buy pizza for volunteers, but beyond that it spends little on the program.

Brief training sessions in the union hall are secondary to on-the-job training, which volunteers receive by sitting in on organizing meetings or accompanying experienced organizers on house calls. Volunteers do phone calling, make house calls, and occasionally develop initial organizing leads. The local has recently begun to formalize its training a bit more.

On most weekends, some volunteers are engaged in some organizing activities. The overall program is as unstructured as Local 1010's was structured. Communication between volunteers and paid staff is by telephone or at arranged meetings at the hall, rather than at the beginning and end of each day, as it was during the Ryerson campaign. Volunteers phase in and out of organizing activities depending on their other time commitments; few work intensive twelve-hour days, and duties are rotated periodically to avoid burnout.

The remainder of this chapter relates the volunteers' assessments of their experiences as volunteer organizers. Following that, I draw some conclusions regarding best practice.

Motivation to Volunteer

When asked why they volunteered, fourteen of the seventeen interviewees expressed a strong ideological commitment to unions, unionism, solidarity, and the like. Steelworker Matt Beckman's response was typical: "I'm a firm believer in unions and things that unions stand for. . . . If there's a place out there that is not organized, I feel that it is in the best interests of the worker to be unionized. I don't have a problem with volunteering my time to help someone else reap the benefits that I personally have gotten from being a union member."

Five respondents also mentioned motivations that could be seen as more narrowly instrumental. Three Steelworkers mentioned the prospect of Local 1010 having more leverage over the company if Ryerson were unionized, and two Teamsters mentioned either wiping out nonunion competition or increasing the local's health and welfare or pension funds. Steelworker Dan Rios noted that "I thought that if we organized Ryerson, which is part of Inland Steel Company, that it would help us in our negotiations . . . strengthening our hold on Inland. Negotiation power."

Teamster David Jasin commented: "There's a lot of nonunion truck drivers out there that are getting killed basically, as far as wages, benefits. Instead of going to their level, I think that the need is to bring them up to our level. . . . I don't want to work for less money. . . . And if the competition is on a level playing field, that makes it a lot easier."

Finally, a few respondents mentioned individual motivations, such as curiosity, the opportunity to meet new people, or the chance to get out of the hot mill. Two Steelworkers hoped eventually to get jobs as union organizers; one Teamster had not thought of this initially but had developed such a desire through his volunteer activities.

For the majority of volunteers, the overwhelming motivation was their passionate belief in unions and unionism. As Teamster organizer Larry Regan put it, they are "the staunchest union supporters." This coincides with other descriptions of typical volunteer organizers (Eckstein 1991–92:77–78).

When pressed to state the *personal* or *individual* benefits of volunteering, the most frequent response (eight of seventeen) was learning valuable information on company antiunion tactics, employee fears, and so on that could be useful to a labor activist. The second most frequent response (three of seventeen) mentioned was the benefits to the younger generation or one's children. Both these responses reflect a strong ideological world view, not immediate self-gain. Steelworker Melvin "Skip" Adams said: "How I've benefited? I feel that what I've learned through organizing—I can pass this on to my children because they are the future of our society. If the children don't learn about unionism . . . then we've got a generation of people growing up who will become corporate—I call them corporate slaves."

The Teamsters were proud that they worked on their own time, and the Steelworkers that they worked well beyond the eight hours for which they were paid lost-time wages. When asked if their experiences made them more or less motivated to volunteer again, twelve of seventeen said more, one said less, and four gave ambivalent responses. All four ambivalent responses came from Steelworkers questioning the worth of yet one more go at Ryerson after four to five failures; however, all were *generally* willing to help out.

The most discouraging and the most encouraging experiences occurred because of the volunteers' strong sense of commitment. Seeing evidence of company intimidation and worker fear, running into antiunion workers or cynics, meeting people who thought the campaign hopeless, or losing a campaign were by far the most common causes of discouragement (fifteen out of seventeen). Encouragement predominantly resulted from meeting pro-union workers, persuading reluctant workers, or winning (sixteen out of seventeen).

This portrait makes it clear that the locals are not getting the average or even mildly motivated members to volunteer. Instead, the volunteers are the most devoted members.[1] Steelworker Bill Carey, a Ryerson volunteer who also was coordinating the union's boycott activities against Firestone tires in the area, argues that this situation is appropriate:

> If you're just getting your average member out, you probably want to get them to do something else first. That's why this boycott stuff's been great, because people get good feedback from it. . . . It's only two hours, and . . . there's a good feeling. It's different if you get a car and spend eight hours driving all over Chicago going into places and neighborhoods where you've never been. That's a little more intimidating. I wouldn't recommend that as the first thing I'd try to do to get somebody active in the union.

---

1. Roberta Lynch, of Illinois AFSCME, responded to an earlier version of this essay by arguing that many good volunteer organizers are not typical "union activists." She has found that a *different type* of dedicated union member is often effective—one less involved in internal union political processes (and squabbles) than many conventional activists. This issue is worth further investigation. Research for this chapter unearthed both "typical union activists" and dedicated but less conventionally involved types. In any case, my main point concerns these members' *dedication,* not their degrees or forms of involvement.

Steelworker Fidel Azcona argues that every union member should eventually be involved in organizing, but not as an initial activity. Given the hardships of organizing, "I think it would depend on the individual. The ones that are hesitant, I think I would start out on leafleting, on smaller stuff. Somehow you'd have to be able to determine who was serious and who wasn't."

Volunteers' Training and Abilities

As noted earlier, the Steelworker volunteers received a one-day orientation and training session. Slightly more than half had received some other training for previous campaigns, at a summer school or through the local university labor studies program. An orientation session explaining the organizing history and the new strategy at Ryerson was followed by formal training on house calling. Do's and don'ts were elicited and discussed, a list of tasks for each house visit was covered, an entertaining video on right and wrong ways to approach people was shown, and role plays were enacted for practice and feedback.

The volunteers gave the training relatively high marks, and as a practicing labor educator observing the session, I concur. The limited time available was put to good use. Any differences in opinion were related to differing estimates of how deeply house callers needed to engage in complex discussions. Steelworker Tom Allen, who felt that mill experience and the ability to relate were key to being an effective organizer, evaluated the training quite positively: "We done some role playing back and forth, and they played the devil's advocate, giving us a hard time. They definitely showed us the ropes on how to handle people that would be not real willing to talk. And how to get around the obstacles, and stuff like that. I think overall the training was really decent."

Steelworker Eugene Sufana, who felt that volunteers should be more strategically involved and that house calls required a complex and well-rounded understanding, found the training a bit less adequate: "They went over how to greet people, the points they wanted us to stress, what not to stress, what comments not to make, different things like that. . . . It was all right, but it was vague. . . . To get across the message you really want to point out and how to answer tough questions, I thought they could have dealt with that a little more."

I believe both assessments are correct, depending on the degree to which a local wishes to develop and utilize a core of volunteers. For a one-week blitz, the training was quite good. For longer-term development of core volunteer organizers, as Teamsters Local 142 is attempting, more varied and complex forms of training, both formal and on the job, would be required.

Teamsters Local 142 has run a few short formal training sessions. Lead organizer Larry Regan commented: "I basically go over what their rights are under the National Labor Relations Act. . . . The things that the company can do, and the things that the company can't do. Things that the union can do, and things that the union can't do. . . . Then we go to house calling."

Even after attending these sessions, most Local 142 volunteers emphasized that their main training, their *real* training, had been on the job. Most felt that continuous interaction with and observation of Regan had been their most important training. Teamster Les Lis said: "I got more knowledge on how to talk to people and explain stuff in different ways by just listening to Larry Regan. . . . And you pick up a lot of stuff from that guy."

The differences in training methods and content are instructive. The Teamsters' emphasis on the law is likely related to Local 142's frequent encounters with small employers that are relatively ignorant of NLRA protections of workers' rights to organize. They often crudely fire workers with little or no pretext when a drive starts. Local 142 therefore educates its members thoroughly on legal rights, "inoculates" workers to likely retaliatory tactics, files NLRB charges constantly, and attempts to get work for fired workers while their (often successful) Board cases are pursued. Ryerson, drawing on Inland's professional human resources staff, is much more sophisticated. ULP charges are much harder to prove. Legal rights, while important, are therefore less central to the United Steelworkers' strategy for organizing Ryerson.

The less formal training the Teamsters volunteers receive probably works sufficiently well for Local 142, but its reliance on personal association with a highly admired, effective, accessible, and charismatic lead organizer might make the local's approach to training limited in many situations.

As this brief comparison shows, training must be tailored to exact circumstances. Nonetheless, certain components are crucial for the training to be effective: good listening skills, total honesty and the absence of "hype," "do's and don'ts," answers to the most frequently asked questions or the most frequent objections, and discussion of basic legal rights. And, as virtually all volunteers emphasized, on-the-job training is of course the ultimate learning experience.

Volunteers' self-assessments of the training were all relatively positive. When asked what required task they felt least capable of doing, most could not come up with any (twelve of seventeen). Two mentioned talking in a foreign language (Spanish or Polish), and three mentioned phone calling, answering technical questions, or getting through to hard-core antiunion workers.

Most volunteers felt their ability to relate as peers was their greatest strength. Teamster Marsha Terus said: "I think we make a big difference.

Because people associate with the workers of their own kind. And rather than 'officers,' I think they have a tendency to believe [workers] more." Steelworker James Alexander noted:

> I think I did best in explaining the advantages of being a member of the United Steelworkers, and explaining . . . that local union officers are elected from those people that you're working with right now. . . . I'm an African American myself and . . . I could explain to these people that I was once elected as the grievance committeeman of the department, and then reelected, and that I have served the positions of treasurer and financial secretary, which was all elected positions.

The credibility of the union with African American Ryerson workers was much higher because of volunteers like Alexander.

Most volunteers were also content with their roles and with their relationship with paid union staff. Many Steelworkers complained about what could be called the "disorganization of the organizing campaign": volunteer teams were criss-crossing paths, were being sent to widely dispersed neighborhoods on the same day, and so on. But otherwise, most felt that the professional union staff had utilized them properly. The Teamsters likewise believed they were well served by the paid staff: the homages to the local's lead organizer were universal and strongly stated.

Three or four of the Steelworkers and all of the Teamsters are engaged in ongoing organizing efforts at multiple employers. Under the circumstances, relationships between volunteers and paid staff need to be carefully thought out. In addition to matters concerning ongoing training and deepening of volunteers as organizers, unions need to make decisions about when and how to bring some volunteers onto paid staff, when to pay lost-time wages, what other "perks" are appropriate to reward good and faithful service, and how to avoid burnout among a local's most devoted members.

Neither of the two locals I studied had a fully worked-out plan to address these issues. But comments from volunteers give clues. Teamster John Hesterman believes that a key is drawing more members in to share the burden: "By getting more and more of our members involved in this, we're able to kind of switch off. . . . So I do at times take small breaks. But I do keep them to a minimum."

Steelworker Bill Carey argues for a judicious mix of compensated and uncompensated work, together with a realistic understanding of the demands on members' lives:

> You have some times where you are asked to do things where you're getting paid, some times you're asked to do things where you're not getting

paid. There ought to be some kind of balance on that. . . . But there's a limit to how much people are willing to volunteer; how much time they have. . . . If it's a short stint, or a short campaign, people will volunteer their time. But at a certain point things get built up and they've got to go back and take care of their lives.

Both remarks appear to offer good advice; more detailed and definitive counsel probably awaits more detailed research.

Characteristics of the Locals

Both Steelworkers Local 1010 and Teamsters Local 142 are relatively effective in getting members to volunteer as organizers. I asked volunteers why this is so. The most frequent response was the good leadership (twelve of seventeen). Elements of this leadership that were mentioned included having a broad vision, being knowledgeable, being "doers" as well as "talkers," constantly educating the membership, intense dedication, openness, and a proactive program of actively asking the membership for help. Steelworker Pat Rodriguez answered as follows: "The leadership. When you have people like [Local 1010 president] Mike Mezo, and I'm not praising him, but I've watched this man for a lot of years. He's a doer. He's a motivator. And he's got a good staff behind him. When you see them out there participating, that makes you want to join them too."

Steelworker Tom Allen echoes the sentiment: "We have a very proactive administration . . . .Those people have got the zeal and the desire to really get a labor movement going. They dedicate the resources to do that. And I believe that the administration of 1010 has done that."

A good number of Steelworkers (five of eleven) cited the local's large size, while the monetary ability to pay for lost time came in third (three of eleven). One or two also mentioned such factors as the long history of activism in the local and the local's balanced ethnic mix.

In contrast, the Teamsters compared the present activism with the apathy and alienation under the previous leaders. For these volunteers, the open, democratic, and honest administration was most important. Teamster David Jasin noted: "Our old machine couldn't have done this, because no one liked them. No one trusted them. . . . Before, you couldn't walk in an office in that building. You had to be buzzed in, and it was like going into a prison. . . . Your members have to have some sort of respect for the executives. And I know a lot of unions out there right now that don't have that."

Volunteers from both locals also emphasized the importance of good communications between the leadership and the membership. Steelworkers

Local 1010 members are justly proud of their award-winning newspaper and that there are monthly meetings of all union representatives, departmental meetings, and union leaflets. Steelworker Al Pena emphasized the value of the newspaper: "[We communicate] through our newspaper. We write articles on organizing. . . . And we pass out leaflets in the mill on specific items like the organizing. That's how we keep [the members] informed." Teamsters Local 142 does not yet have a newspaper, although it is working on starting one.

Teamster volunteers emphasize communication through a wide variety of meetings and through a newly created stewards council. With 340 contracts, the local has meetings at the union hall daily, and the new leadership insists that members *from the shops* must now sit in on all negotiating and grievance meetings. This openness, plus the willingness to create democratic structures, such as the stewards council, despite their potential as bases for political opposition, is appreciated by volunteers, who see this openness as the key to the local's success. Teamster Bill Staples, chairman of the stewards council, said:

> For Rick Kenney [the local's secretary-treasurer] and Mitch Sawochka [the local's president] to form the stewards council was a bold step. Because probably we're in contact with the general membership more than they are now. And it would seem like the next platform or men to run against them should come right out of the stewards council. . . . Our council was elected by the general membership, by the stewards themselves. But we weren't hand-picked by Rick Kenney. . . . I think it was bold for them to do this.

This "democratic ethos," dangerous though it may seem to many a conventional labor leader, is the key to this local's success in inspiring commitment among its volunteers. The volunteers from both locals believe that the "union belongs to them," which feeds into the "culture of organizing" crucial to volunteer organizing efforts (Babson 1991–92:66–67).

Importance and Usefulness of Volunteers

The Teamsters and the Steelworkers volunteers believe that their efforts are important for two reasons. First, the union could never afford to undertake as comprehensive an organizing campaign with just full-time paid organizers. There aren't enough resources, and effective organizing requires very labor-intensive methods, including house calling (Bronfenbrenner and Juravich 1995c:3–4) Second, grassroots union members know how to relate to fellow workers. An anecdote by Teamster organizer Larry Regan illustrates this:

We start the house calling. Nobody from the in-plant committee wanted to talk to this one guy. They were deadly scared of him. They said, "He's a maniac; if you go to his house, he'll sic the dog on you if he don't shoot you." Well, one of our volunteers went to his house. He said, "Give me that guy. I'll take him." He takes all of the ones like that. And I'll tell you what: they ended up to become very close personal friends, their wives and families. And the man passed away during the campaign of a heart attack. And when we went to the funeral home, in his coffin, [his wife] pinned a "Union Yes" button on this guy.

The reason that happened is, he told him, "Well, look, partner, I'm not getting paid for this. I'm just doing this because I love my union and I want to see everybody in the union. I'm a union man." That makes a difference. Then he said, "Well, come on in here and talk to me." Before that, he was ordering him off the property. If you're a paid union organizer, sometimes they don't put as much credence in you. The company's campaigns are, "Run them union guys off. Everybody gets a nickel for every signature they get. They just want to take your money."

Summary

The experiences of Steelworkers Local 1010 and Teamsters Local 142 are instructive for others wishing to develop volunteer organizers. In the following section, I will attempt to assess their programs to derive generalizations for best practice in several different areas. These areas are (1) how to motivate members to volunteer; (2) the training that is needed; (3) how to utilize volunteers, based on their capabilities; and (4) internal characteristics and processes that are helpful in furthering this effort.

How to Motivate

If Locals 1010 and 142 are representative, unions should generally look only to their most dedicated, highly motivated members for volunteers. These volunteers will be ideologically motivated to view the union as a *cause*. Other less demanding means should be found to interest and involve lukewarm or disinterested members.

Nevertheless, locals should also appeal to the membership on more narrowly utilitarian grounds. These two locals used the appeal that increasing the membership resulted in more bargaining leverage over the parent company or larger pension and welfare funds as grounds for supporting organizing efforts. Although these narrower aims were *not* the primary motivation that members mentioned for volunteering, *they undoubtedly did help convince the membership at large that the organizing effort was a legitimate use of the local's resources.* So, for political reasons alone, locals should point out the short-term, immediate benefits of putting resources into organizing the unorganized.

Training Needed

These cases demonstrate how training needs to be strategically related to the volunteers' expected roles. Volunteers whose only role is making house calls for a short specified period need only basic training on campaign issues and on interpersonal techniques (the "do's and don'ts") used to draw people out, relate to their concerns, and so on. But more varied roles will require a constant deepening of skills.

As shown by the Teamster local's need to train in legal issues, training needs will vary depending on employer and workforce characteristics. The Teamsters case also shows how much can be achieved by relying primarily on "O-J-T" (on-the-job-training), when volunteers interact extensively with a skilled organizer.

Nevertheless, I am convinced that the relative lack of formal training the Teamsters local gave its volunteers is a weak point, not a strength. Ideally, organizing locals would develop a series of training levels through which volunteers progress as they widen their organizing activities from short-term house calling to longer-term multifaceted tasks. Training needs to be carefully tailored to volunteer utilization and capacities, as addressed in the next section.

How to Utilize Volunteers

In these two cases, the union locals did not have clear long-term or developmental strategies for utilizing their volunteers. But ultimately unions will need to consider several issues in this area. I would recommend the following:

1. *Simple house calling during blitzes is the most manageable and most widespread use of volunteers.* It should be the initial "break-in" activity for almost all volunteers. But unions should also plan for wider roles for those members willing to "graduate" to more varied and complex tasks.

2. *Ideally, unions should set up a relatively clear progression of roles (and training to maintain "quality control") through which volunteers can pass.* An ideal program would progressively widen the tasks as the volunteer continues in it. It would attempt to ensure that at least a portion of the time put in was unpaid, to avoid attracting those with simple careerist motivations. It would ensure that lost-time wages and other perks given to volunteers were evenly applied to all and clearly related to the level of progression within the program, to avoid any appearance (or reality) of cronyism or favoritism. It would build into the progression frequent opportunities to withdraw for a time, to avoid burnout. Finally, if it could be

arranged with the union's higher levels, the progression would end with opportunities to become full-time paid organizers, for those who desire this and who acquire the needed skills.

3. *Unions need to ensure that the volunteers reflect the racial and gender mix of the target population.* For example, Teamsters Local 142 needs to develop more female and African American volunteers, given the work-forces it aims to organize.

4. *Unions should initially rely on the strengths the volunteers already possess: their familiarity with the world of work and their ability to relate well to fellow workers.* As members continue to help out, the on-the-job training should concentrate on developing other strengths required of full-time organizers: the ability to assess campaigns strategically, an understanding of economic and social factors working against unions, and so on.

Some of these recommendations go well beyond the limited evidence for them available in the two cases studied here. They also presuppose that the volunteer program is well developed and has considerable resources. For these reasons, they should be considered the author's "ideal," which most union locals would need to modify under less-than-perfect real-world circumstances.

Useful Union Characteristics and Processes

If these cases are typical, a union will be more successful if (1) it is large and therefore capable of devoting real resources to organizing; (2) there is a highly capable, motivated leadership with vision that extends beyond issues of bargaining and enforcing the next contract; and (3) the local engages in continuous education of the membership and keeps the lines of communication open. Beyond these three characteristics, the Teamsters case in particular illustrates a point that is less frequently emphasized or acted upon: locals must be deeply democratic and exceedingly open to obtain many volunteers, at least volunteers not being paid lost-time wages. An extremely participative ethos has to pervade the union for the members to have the "sense of ownership" of the union that creates a "culture of organizing" (Babson 1991–92:66–67).

Such a deeply participative and democratic method of operating is very hard to create. The average union leader frequently considers such openness too risky, as well as fruitless. Yet the very future of the labor movement may rest on the willingness to take such risks; the members have to believe it is *their* union if they are to volunteer their own time for it.

Concluding Thoughts

The two locals discussed in this chapter are not entirely representative of the labor movement. Other locals that are smaller in size, less overwhelmingly male, or operating in the public sector will exhibit many differences. The lessons drawn above should nevertheless be somewhat useful if adapted intelligently, even to differing circumstances. In particular, most smaller unions will need district or regional union structures to take the lead. Locals still will need the internal culture of organizing, but the greater resources of the district or region or national office can be deployed to draw volunteers out of many locals at once. In a sense this happened in the Ryerson campaign since half the volunteers came from Ryerson locals around the country.

Two points emerge clearly from these two cases. First, the numbers of volunteers are way too small, even in the best cases. Furthermore, most union locals do not fit the best-case category: they have no program of volunteer organizing and have nobody doing it. A major effort from the top to the bottom of U.S. unions will be necessary to turn this situation around. The intense need to put *major* efforts and resources into organizing has to be as well understood by local union leaders as it is by the national leadership of the more forward-looking unions.

Second, there *are* a number of high-quality union members in locals who are motivated and ready to volunteer. The volunteers I interviewed were thoughtful and fully aware of the enormity of the task. They noted that larger changes on many fronts would be necessary for major organizing success. Many steered the conversation toward political activism and change, union public relations and media relations, and the like because they perceived a hostile external environment for organizing. They were thinking broadly and holistically about organizing, not simply about the narrowest questions of technique. Union activists of such a high caliber and commitment are precisely what the labor movement needs to be successful in organizing the unorganized.

Chapter 9

Finding the Community in the Union and the Union in the Community: The First-Contract Campaign at Steeltech

Katherine Sciacchitano

One of the oldest weapons employers use against union organizing is the idea that unions are separate entities from their members and the communities in which they live. Employers paint unions as "outsiders" with no commitment to the success of an enterprise or its workers. If a union overcomes this characterization and wins an election, the employer has a second shot: regardless of the margin of victory, there is "no union" without a contract.

Legal decisions under the National Labor Relations Act reinforce employers' descriptions of unions as outsiders. Paid organizers have no automatic right of access to the employer's property or right of reply to antiunion propaganda. After winning an election, the union is protected from decertification for one year only—unless a contract is negotiated.

Unions themselves contribute to the problem when paid staff "service" members rather than teach them how to do things for themselves, or parachute into town for an organizing campaign and leave immediately after the election. Meanwhile, the media, politicians, and corporations routinely portray unions as "special interests." Even when unions take a broader view and focus on community issues, most are too weak or too isolated to provide answers for the daily struggles—the job flight, deterioration of wages, increases in crime, and decline in public services—that workers face.

As a result, both time and workers' isolation are on the employer's side. Legal challenges to election results can take years, seriously eroding union support before a final order to bargain is issued. Skating the line between good- and bad-faith bargaining can achieve the same end. In either case the union faces the threat of decertification—often without support from the community or other unions.

The campaign for a first contract at Steeltech Manufacturing in Milwaukee, Wisconsin, took place under just such a threat. A newly formed minority defense contractor with a majority African American workforce, Steeltech established itself in Milwaukee's central city with promises of creating needed jobs for residents. The United Electrical, Radio and Machine Workers of America (UE) lost a first election there in 1993. When UE won a second election in late 1994, Steeltech filed election objections and refused to bargain. It also began portraying UE as a threat to its viability and, by extension, to Milwaukee's African American community.

Instead of succumbing to Steeltech's strategy of delay, UE launched an aggressive, multifaceted campaign that combined shop-floor organizing with extensive community support efforts. The result was a highly visible and successful community-based first-contract campaign. The campaign demonstrated the solidarity of Milwaukee's African American community and labor movement. It challenged a model of economic development that channeled public money into private hands without regard for union rights or working conditions. For a time, the campaign also created what one organizer called a "micro-climate" for organizing in Milwaukee, focusing public attention on the justice of workers' struggles and identifying workers' rights as civil rights.

The Steeltech campaign underscores the power of linking workplace organizing with issues of broader community concern. It also demonstrates the broad-based alliances that must be forged between unions and community groups if unions are to overcome workers' isolation and organize effectively in a hostile political climate. Tammy Johnson, an African American community organizer active in the Steeltech campaign, explained how systematic attempts were made in Milwaukee to separate black workers from organized labor, both through arguments that black workers should not "undermine" black entrepreneurs by organizing unions, and through campaigns to convince the black community to support privatization of public services. The Steeltech campaign ultimately succeeded both because the black community refused to be separated from the workers at Steeltech and because UE opened itself to the active involvement of that community in its struggle. It is a lesson for all workers and their unions, a case in point, as Johnson explained, of "why the union must find itself in the community and why the community must find itself in the union."

The Company

Steeltech was hailed as a model of inner-city economic development when it began operations in May 1990. A minority-owned company with a majority African American male workforce, the plant received more than $15 million in public funding and loan guarantees from city, county, state, and federal governments. A consortium of banks provided a special line of credit. Wisconsin corporations contributed another $11.8 million in loans, direct investments, and stock purchases.

Although no legal requirements for job creation or retention were attached to Steeltech's funding, the huge investment of public money and Steeltech's location in Milwaukee's central city created a strong expectation that the community would benefit. News articles proclaimed the creation of 200 to 250 jobs at $6 to $13 an hour. Steeltech promised to hire and train at least 60 percent of its workforce from the central city. Managers and workers were profiled in the local press (Fauber 1991a).

Steeltech's favorable reception by the African American community and city officials is best understood in the context of Milwaukee's economic decline. Once a center of the black industrial working class, Milwaukee was devastated in the 1980s by plant closings and the loss of thousands of union jobs that had provided economic anchors for the black community. In 1993, Milwaukee's unemployment was nearly four times the rate of the rest of the state. For black males, the rate was almost double (Dresser, Rogers, and Whittaker 1996). Thus, although Steeltech promised only a limited number of jobs—one newspaper article (Fauber 1991b) estimated that Milwaukee would have had to create 118 Steeltechs to eliminate unemployment in the city—in the context of black Milwaukee's jobs crisis, this promise seemed a real benefit. Steeltech was a source of pride. Most of all, it was a symbol of economic hope.

Steeltech's presentation as a symbol of hope and economic development was contradicted, however, by its treatment of employees, treatment one African American union leader described as among the worst she had ever seen. Steeltech's claim of minority ownership was also questionable. The brainchild of Fred Luber, a white Republican party kingmaker, chair of a company named Super Steel, and a board member of another called Oshkosh Truck, Steeltech was conceived when Luber needed a minority subcontractor to qualify for a defense contract sought by Oshkosh. Oshkosh's share of the contract was to be $1.5 billion; Steeltech's was $52 million. Steeltech's physical plant and equipment were also narrowly tailored to its subcontractor role. Its primary investment was its $8 million highly specialized "E-Coat" paint line, whose main use was in military projects; Steeltech leased the line from Oshkosh Truck and Super Steel. All but 3 percent of Steeltech's work was for Oshkosh or Super Steel.

If Steeltech were exposed as a front for Super Steel and Oshkosh Truck, its status as a minority contractor would be lost. So would its advantage in obtaining government contracts, as well as the jobs it was to create and millions in public funds (Wilayto and Morgan 1995; Committee for Justice n.d.). Steeltech was a living example of the public funding of private profit.

With millions in public funds at risk and no mechanisms for accountability, the slender thread of hope could well break.

The Union

Midway through the contract campaign, UE summarized Steeltech's strategic vulnerabilities as (1) the huge public investment in Steeltech and the issue of accountability it created; (2) the substantial press coverage that had made events at Steeltech a public issue; (3) Steeltech's need to maintain its minority status with government regulators; (4) the company's heavy debt load and multiple creditors; and (5) the company's need to maintain goodwill to expand its product line (UE n.d.). UE did not, however, target Steeltech on the basis of its corporate research and analysis. Rather, the campaign grew out of UE's choice of Milwaukee as a site for intensive community-based organizing and the worker contacts that resulted from that effort.

In the early 1990s, UE had investigated Milwaukee as one of several potential sites for campaigns targeting inner-city employers with large numbers of women and minorities. UE felt that women and minorities were among those most willing to undertake the strenuous task of organizing. Nevertheless, in UE's view, few groups of workers possessed the strength to win a first contract by themselves. UE therefore wanted to organize in an environment in which it would be possible to mobilize and maintain substantial community support. Milwaukee was chosen because of its long tradition of unionization and UE's own base at the Allen Bradley Corp., where it had represented workers for sixty years. Milwaukee was also chosen because of its community institutions and UE's ties to them. These included the closely knit Milwaukee chapter of the Coalition of Black Trade Unionists (CBTU); the city's activist central labor council; and a fledgling group called Progressive Milwaukee, whose aim was to build a grassroots political movement in the city to form a third party (interview, Muhammad 1996).

Once UE targeted various Milwaukee employers for organizing, it hired local organizers from UE-organized shops, worked to develop a presence in the community, and began building the visibility of its campaigns.[1] In early 1994, UE opened an office on West Burleigh Street and celebrated with a party. Many who attended—community residents, local politicians, members and representatives of local organizations—later played significant roles in the Steeltech campaign.

---

1. UE organizer Carol Lambiase estimated that approximately three out of seven organizers were hired from the community or UE shops.

By the time organizing began at Steeltech, UE had organized several local employers with low-wage African American and Latino female workforces. Worker participation in organizing was high, and a common theme of respect and dignity had emerged among these often abused workers (interview, T. Davis 1996). At Steeltech, with its predominantly black male workforce, the issue of respect had additional resonance. As CBTU stated in a local editorial (1995:1), the struggle for unionization at Steeltech was a struggle not only for justice but "to define black manhood." Workers were subjected to ten-hour shifts, seven-day workweeks, and mandatory overtime. Dangerous equipment and hazardous chemicals were also problems, as were the substandard pay for skilled workers and arbitrary wage rates. Use of racial epithets by supervisors was routine. Workers were often harassed into quitting. Frequent threats of discharge were compounded by predictions that workers, many of whom had been unemployed before being hired, would not be able to find other jobs because "no one else would hire them" (interview, Muhammad 1996).

Management's abuse helped maintain a strong undercurrent of support for the union. It also created a turnover rate of 50 percent each year and intense fear. UE addressed both problems with strategies to build continuous involvement of the rank and file on the shop floor. UE established a representative in-plant committee, estimated at 15 to 20 percent of the 130-person bargaining unit. The union also held frequent solidarity days and lunchtime rallies and started publishing a union newsletter. Just before the second election, UE built a steward structure and began using the newsletter to publicize grievances. Articles were accompanied by speakouts at union meetings, where stewards explained how they found appropriate members of management with whom to discuss grievances and the steps they took to resolve them. Stewards conducted a plantwide survey to elicit negotiating demands. House calling, done in part by volunteer organizers from other UE shops, continued even after UE's victory (interview, Muhammad 1996).

Despite numerous discharges and coercive conduct by the employer, in November 1993, UE lost the first election by only two votes. In September 1994, the NLRB ordered a second election on the grounds that an ethics code promulgated two weeks before the election had interfered with the election by forbidding workers to talk to nonemployees about wages and benefits.[2]

UE increased the public visibility of its second campaign. CBTU was supportive, sending members to rallies, hosting events, and providing im-

2. *Steeltech Manufacturing, Inc. and United Electrical, Radio & Machine Workers of America*, 315 NLRB 213 (1994).

portant assistance. Four days before the second vote, UE held its first press event at the plant: a fifteen-minute rally that included an attempt by Bruce Colburn, the secretary-treasurer of the Milwaukee County Labor Council, and two community organizers to meet with Steeltech management on behalf of the workers. The event was also attended by Spencer Coggs, an African American state representative who was a former AFSCME steward and executive board member as well as a personal friend of Steeltech's CEO, Chuck Wallace. Photographs from the event were used as campaign literature. Three days before the election, Jesse Jackson signed a letter urging Steeltech workers to vote "yes." On November 4, 1994, the union won the election fifty-six to fifty-one.

The Contract Campaign

During an earlier drive in Milwaukee, UE had won a bargaining order after a failed election, only to have the employer—ABQC Corp.—use the appeal process to delay its finality and erode union support. ABQC stood as a ready example for UE supporters of the folly of relying solely on legal strategies. Still hoping that Steeltech would bargain after a union victory, UE girded itself for a stepped-up postelection campaign.

During the month preceding the election, UE began exploring the possibility of creating a more positive organizing environment and greater visibility for the Steeltech workers' struggle (interview, Muhammad 1996). It discussed the possibility of developing an ongoing community support structure with several community organizations; it also talked about arranging a community meeting aimed at holding Steeltech accountable for creating "family-supporting jobs"—a theme often emphasized by Progressive Milwaukee in its own work. At the end of October 1994, with the help of another community organization, UE faxed letters to the Wisconsin congressional delegation and to local African American and progressive politicians asking them for their support (interview, Dempsey 1996).

The campaign shifted into higher gear once Steeltech filed objections to the election. Activities were organized around two principal ideas. First, "accountability" meant including the city and public in thinking about what needed to be done. Second, respect and dignity for workers meant not only the right to negotiate working conditions but, in the words of UE organizer Carol Lambiase, "that a good job is not simply good pay, but the respect you feel in the workplace, how you feel when you go home, and how this reverberates in the community" (interview, 1996).

One of the first activities after the November victory was passage of a resolution by the Milwaukee County Labor Council. The resolution supported Steeltech workers and urged elected officials to ensure that subsidies from the city, county, and state would not be used to interfere with the workers' right to organize. Its import was clear: although not affiliated with the AFL-CIO, UE would not stand alone. The fight of the Steeltech workers would be a fight of the Milwaukee labor movement.

By December, UE's plan for building community support had begun to bear fruit. Publicity from UE's second election campaign had heightened the visibility of the struggle. High turnover in the plant had multiplied the number of community members with a friend or relative who had worked at Steeltech. And African American unionists had mined community networks and contacts to tell people about the need for a union. As a result, on December 4, 1994, a "Community Meeting for Justice at Steeltech" was held at the Amalgamated Transit Union, Local 998, union hall that drew more than fifty individuals and representatives from numerous community groups, local service providers, and unions. Its purpose was to discuss overall strategy and organization for a public campaign.

UE's flyer for the gathering had focused on the millions of tax dollars that had been poured into Steeltech and on Steeltech's use of that money to fight rather than bargain with the union. At the meeting, which was also attended by Spencer Coggs, the state representative, people raised a more immediate and critical concern: high turnover at the plant would accelerate the effects of the employer's delay tactics and increase the need of Steeltech workers for personal support if they were to last through the drive (interview, Cochran 1996). Saladin Muhammad, a UE international organizer, also made a rousing speech about the negative effect on the community of permitting tax dollars to be used to fight the union, and challenged everyone to stand up for justice.

The December meeting resulted in two concrete steps. The first step was the creation of the Committee for Justice at Steeltech, a loosely structured but purposeful formation of individuals, unions, and community groups that was to form the backbone of UE's campaign. The second step was the decision to hold a public hearing in late January to raise the issue of the accountability of Steeltech to the workers and the community.

Organizing for the January event was shared by UE and the Committee for Justice (interview, Cochran 1996). A petition was circulated supporting recognition and calling for the hearing. Leaflets were distributed at Martin Luther King birthday events. Mailings were sent out by UE as well as by the committee's constituent groups. Yard signs appeared on people's lawns publicizing the struggle. The list of contract demands that had been solicited by the in-plant bargaining committee was made public.[3]

---

3. The demands included seniority, regular wage increases and progressions, stewards in all work areas, a grievance system, safety inspections by a workers committee, a union shop and dues checkoff, medical coverage, and the cessation of profanity by supervisors.

A key purpose of the hearing was to build community support for the workers by creating a forum for what was happening inside the plant. Because of Steeltech's minority ownership, however, the hearing also needed to address the community's apprehensions about a union and its desire to protect a minority business and the jobs it could create. Sheila Cochran, head of the Milwaukee Fair Lending Coalition, chaired the meeting. Opening with a heavy swing of her gavel, she directed the distinguished hearing panel—which included city, county, and state officials as well as union and community leaders—to help make a public record by listening and asking questions, not by making speeches or grilling workers.

Testimony began with a statement by UE national secretary-treasurer Bob Clark, whose home local had been the UE's Allen Bradley local. Next came UE organizer Susannah Davis, who had driven from Pittsburgh to present research on Steeltech's ability to support a union contract. Organizer Saladin Muhammad then spoke. Clark, Davis, and Muhammad were followed by several workers. One worker broke down crying as he described the humiliation he went through to support his wife and children. A woman described the toll working at Steeltech had taken on her husband and its effect on their family. Counselors and vocational trainers who had worked with Steeltech workers testified about the disastrous morale in the plant and its effect on production. Community members affected by pollution from the plant came forth. A politician, a minister, and three University of Wisconsin professors, including Paula Voos, a member of the Dunlop commission, spoke. Voos addressed community fears that a union would harm Steeltech and described the positive effects unions can have on enterprises.

The effect of the hearing was electrifying. Organizers had worked hard to ensure that the participants and audience reflected the racial and ethnic mix of the Steeltech workforce and included white as well as black workers, Latinos as well as Anglos. The room was bursting. Workers who testified spoke from their experience but did not sound the part of victims. Every statement ended with resolve not to "take it anymore."

Cochran closed the hearing with a final swing of the gavel and demanded to know why such injustice was occurring in their community and what kind of town people wanted to live in. She concluded with a challenge that galvanized the audience: "If you leave here tonight and do the same thing that you did today, this whole event will have been a failure" (interview, 1996).

The hearing served many purposes. The most important, which Muhammad articulated, was to "surface what was happening in the plant and put it under public scrutiny." The company had access to major media sources to tell its side of the story; the hearing created a legitimate forum for the workers' side of what was happening. It took management's argument to "let the labor board decide" and showed its real purpose was delay and erosion of the union's base (interview, 1996).

The hearing also shifted sentiment away from Steeltech's "minority entre-preneur" image to the needs of the workers. As Robert Wright, head of the University of Wisconsin School for Workers Milwaukee program and a CBTU activist, explained, "The workers had stories to tell, not just as union members but as husbands and wives and brothers and sisters and neighbors" (interview, 1996). Organizers knew these stories needed to be the focus to galvanize public opinion and put pressure on politicians. They also knew a public hearing would make it easier for sympathetic politicians to act.

The hearing was thus a turning point that showed accountability was needed, whoever the employer was. But it was a turning point that marked the beginning rather than the culmination of the struggle. What followed was a multipronged campaign that involved diverse actors with sometimes differing strategies but one unifying theme: the civil rights of the workers at Steeltech. As one black activist put it, "[Steeltech] was a community united for justice" (interview, N. Davis 1996).

Campaign activities were characterized by the acceptance of individual initiatives, multiple approaches, and interrelated objectives. Meetings of the Committee for Justice continued to draw from a handful to one hundred people. A UE organizer usually led the meetings, but interaction was collab-orative and consensual and drew on independent initiatives by constituent groups. Organizations such as the Ad Hoc Coalition of Black Union Leaders and the Committee of 100 Black Men, which was organized to mentor black youths, worked independently, with only loose coordination. Locals of the Amalgamated Transit Union and the United Steelworkers of America played other important roles.

Activities involved the full range of labor and community participants. Community activity was marked as much by the participation of individuals as by that of organizations. For example, two local radio talk-show hosts devoted substantial programming and call-in time to Steeltech, greatly facil-itating community discussion of the issues. A staff member at a local com-munity center gave her personal time to coach workers in public speaking. Neighborhood members took turns on picket lines and came to solidarity events (interview, Wright 1996).

Union participation involved not only officers but stewards and rank-and-file members. Worker-to-worker support, critical to the effort given the vulnerability of the Steeltech workforce, and a major concern of the Committee for Justice, was a strong component of several events. Members of the United Steelworkers hosted a solidarity event where, in addition to providing food and speakers, individuals met with Steeltech workers to share experiences and offer support and advice (interview, Cochran 1996). Nevada Davis, the Milwaukee County United Way labor liaison and president of the Wisconsin chapter of the Coalition of Labor Union Women, hosted a breakfast in her home for the wives and friends of Steeltech employees. In addition to prominent labor and community leaders, she invited a representative from Mary Kay cosmetics, who offered free facials to the women. Davis offered personal assistance to help find resources to deal with medical problems, creditors, landlords, and other family needs (interview, N. Davis 1996).

Campaign activities were aimed at attacking Steeltech's strategic weaknesses and at building solidarity. These included weekly plant-side rallies; marches to city hall; a "road warriors" campaign in which Steeltech workers spoke to church and union groups and appeared on radio talk shows and community access channels; presentations of resolutions to city, county, and state political bodies; demands that the city audit Steeltech's finances; surprise safety inspections by religious and political leaders; a Jobs with Justice pledge campaign; a lobby day in Washington, D.C., to urge oversight of federal subsidies to private companies; writing letters to the editor of local newspapers and working with media; as well as solidarity events and support activities for workers and their families (interview, T. Davis 1996).

Activities targeted at Steeltech's lenders illustrate the synergy of these varied working relationships and approaches. UE had identified Steeltech's dependence on outside funding resources as a strategic vulnerability. Many in the community felt that Steeltech was a fragile company that needed to be protected and preserved. Ultimately, however, people also decided that the union had to make it clear that it could interfere with sources of capital, not to block loans but to raise the issue of whether money was being used to fight the union rather than build the company. Progressive Milwaukee articulated an additional concern that Steeltech's lenders understand they were dealing with an entire community and needed to be responsible to that community.

These interrelated concerns translated into an array of responses. A weekly informational picket was held at Firstar Bank, the lead bank in the consortium of lenders. The leafleting was a community activity, and pickets included members of the coalition groups as well as supportive individuals. Two local unions also threatened to pull pension funds out of Firstar (interview, Wright 1996). A very different tactic involved a direct action at Firstar on February 10, 1995. A Steeltech manager who had been fired for giving a statement to the NLRB gave UE the date and time of a Steeltech meeting with Firstar. UE organizer Saladin Muhammad burst in on the meeting with several community organizers. Before being ejected, Muhammad made a speech about Steeltech's labor practices and their effect on workers and production (interview, Johnson 1996).

This direct action contrasted sharply with the approach of Martha Love, president of the Milwaukee chapter of the CBTU. A longtime friend of Firstar chairman Roger Fitzsimonds, Love did not feel comfortable participating in the kind of action planned by Muhammad. Instead, on March 10, she wrote a letter to Fitzsimonds demanding that Firstar demonstrate its corporate responsibility by conditioning loans to Steeltech on respect for workers' rights to organize. Love followed the letter with a private meeting with Fitzsimonds.

Support from elected representatives also varied. Several state representatives and county board members participated in the public hearing, and half the city council signed a letter supporting Steeltech's workers. But political stakes were high, and other politicians played roles behind the scenes instead (interview, Coggs 1996). State Representative Coggs was one of the most vocal public supporters of Steeltech's workers. A personal friend of Steeltech CEO Chuck Wallace, Coggs nevertheless called for "bringing down the house" if Steeltech did not recognize the union. At the same time, he maintained direct contact with Wallace over the issue of unionization.

UE made strategic use of all these campaign activities, as well as more traditional channels. The union doggedly filed more than fifty unfair labor practice charges. When the NLRB decided in April 1995 to issue a complaint, UE held a public rally at city hall to announce the unfair labor practice hearing, which was to be consolidated with the hearing on Steeltech's election objections.

When Steeltech made it clear that it would still not drop its objections, UE escalated. It prepared a report exposing Steeltech's deteriorating financial condition, corporate irresponsibility, and behind-the-scenes involvement by Oshkosh Truck and Super Steel. A lobby day was planned to present the report to each member of the city council (Committee for Justice n.d.). At the same time, UE sent word through the mayor's office—which had tried throughout the campaign to mediate the dispute—that it would be willing to talk should Steeltech be interested in a settlement. On June 9, 1995, three days before the lobby action was to take place, Steeltech agreed to meet. Within two weeks a contract was signed that included most of the workers' negotiating demands.

Conclusions

Although the Steeltech campaign ended abruptly with the achievement of a contract, hundreds of people who were involved learned that it is possible to organize a low-wage, inner-city workplace. White unionists supported, rather than played a leading role in, the organization of black workers. Union issues were transformed from the narrow confines of the shop floor into a matter of civil rights. Quite literally, the struggle of the workers became the struggle of the community.

What made these successes possible? On the tactical level, the lessons from the campaign are straightforward. UE correctly identified Steeltech's strategic weaknesses and built a campaign to exploit them relentlessly. Organizers used a multiplicity of tactics to involve workers on the shop floor as well as in the community. They also viewed the first-contract campaign as an extension of the basic task of organizing. These lessons are consistent with research showing that unions are more likely to succeed both in organizing and in achieving first contracts when a range of tactics is used to involve members (Bronfenbrenner and Juravich 1995c).

On the strategic level, the lessons are more complex. There was no clear blueprint for success, and no set of tactics or strategies provided the silver bullet. Rather, the Steeltech campaign succeeded because of the depth and degree of community participation it evoked. For a brief time, union issues became community issues and evoked extraordinary degrees of activity and solidarity. The real lesson of Steeltech lies in examining what enabled this high degree of participation to take place.

It would be tempting to conclude that UE was successful in mobilizing such a high degree of support because it was able to identify public issues that were as important to the community as they were to the union. Political and economic issues provided a sympathetic theme and focus for the campaign, and it would have been difficult, if not impossible, to succeed without them. Nevertheless, few participants raised these themes as the reason for their involvement. Rather, what motivated people was a basic sense of justice, personal contacts with Steeltech workers or their families, and solidarity within the black community around the treatment of workers and the need for jobs. What in turn enabled these circumstances to coalesce into a successful campaign was the network of community institutions and contacts on which people relied in their daily lives and through which they came to know and trust each other.

Community participation was anchored in a broad range of organizations and groups. More significant than the array of organizations, however, was the fact that involvement took place as much through the direct participation of individuals as through the organizations themselves. Union members showed the extent to which they were "in their communities" by speaking to friends, relatives, fellow church members, and allies about the Steeltech struggle. Individuals who played key leadership roles in the community lent their personal time, energies, and prestige, whether or not they were also able to mobilize their organizations. Conversely, rank-and-file members of various groups lent direct personal support that went well beyond group demonstrations of solidarity. Without this participation and leadership of the community in the campaign, UE would have been perceived as an outside force and could not have succeeded. Nor could UE have met the critical needs of its African American and Latino members for support.

One reason UE was able to arouse this participation was the role of the Steeltech workers themselves: they spoke at the public hearing, they were interviewed on radio stations, and they addressed community groups, not only as workers and union members but as community members, taxpayers, and consumers. Their presence provided the moral and political foundation for the campaign's force. The work UE spent in supporting and empowering workers to speak for themselves was central to the campaign's success.

UE's community strategy also succeeded because organizers did not attempt simply to mobilize support for predetermined strategies or to appropriate individual ideas. Had the organizers done so, the strategy certainly would have failed. Instead, organizers realized the importance and complexity of the issues that Steeltech raised within the black community, as well as the networks of individuals involved, and decided to permit a degree of creative involvement rarely found in union drives. Most of this involvement took place under UE auspices; monthly coalition meetings chaired by union organizers served a critical coordinating function and helped unify efforts of sometimes disparate groups. But much of the coordination at monthly meetings involved work that was initiated by collaborating groups and individuals outside. This input was vital. As one UE organizer acknowledged, the campaign could not have succeeded if the union had tried to keep a "tight reign" on all activities.

Many participants hoped that these successes and the "organizing environment" that the Steeltech campaign created in Milwaukee would carry over into other campaigns. Yet, to date, Steeltech's success has not been recreated in other drives or community efforts in Milwaukee. One reason is that the Steeltech campaign seems to have succeeded in large part because UE found—stumbled across, as it were—certain networks in Milwaukee's black community that provided specific leadership for this campaign. Another reason is undoubtedly the difficulty of maintaining a labor-community coalition over a single issue or around a single union.

As UE organizer Carol Lambiase emphasized, unions need to form permanent alliances with individuals and community organizations, as well as with other unions. These alliances need to go beyond the single issue of union organizing to matters that touch the community most deeply. And unions need to return the support they receive from these groups by supporting community campaigns as well. Without this mutual involvement and respect, unions are unlikely to evoke the commitment, either from community groups or their members, needed to mobilize the immense resources that enable organizing campaigns to succeed. These are lessons that are likely to become more important as unions engage in broader industry, geographic, and occupationally based campaigns.

Additional comparative research is needed to better understand the problems of building leadership and long-term alliances with community groups during union organizing drives. In the meantime, the Steeltech campaign underscores the importance of approaching organizing from a strategic and critical standpoint. The respect and attention UE paid to the views and long-term interests of community leaders and organizations was as important in developing and adjusting strategy throughout the campaign as UE's own careful analysis of the political and economic issues at stake. Although UE did not create the networks of community leadership on which it relied, it did nurture them. UE supported the working relationships people brought to the campaign and permitted groups and individuals to carry out activities they themselves developed and planned. This in turn enabled an otherwise unachievable degree of participation in campaign activities and sent a clear message to the company—and its workers—that the campaign would continue in whatever form necessary until success was achieved. Although the respect and attention UE showed to the individuals and groups it relied on is not a tactic or a strategy in the normal sense, it was the critical element in winning the first contract at Steeltech.

Chapter 10

Clergy and Religious Persons' Roles in Organizing at O'Hare Airport and St. Joseph Medical Center

Ronald Peters and Theresa Merrill

In 1989, a handful of concession workers at Chicago's O'Hare International Airport sought to form a union in their campaign for higher wages, better working conditions, and the fair treatment of immigrant and minority workers. Three years later, after an antiunion campaign that included discriminatory firings and interrogations of union supporters, 850 O'Hare concession workers won a contract and representation by the Hotel Employees and Restaurant Employees International Union (HERE). In 1993, in the neighboring town of Joliet, six hundred nurses at St. Joseph Medical Center went on a sixty-one-day strike for better working conditions and patient care. The Illinois Nurses Association (INA) won a contract for the St. Joseph nurses, but only after a strike that divided the community.

Clergy and other religious persons played a unique role in both union victories. This chapter describes their contributions to these victories and suggests lessons and strategies for involving religious persons in union campaigns. The chapter first reviews Judeo-Christian doctrine concerning social justice as a context for the analysis that follows.

Labor and the Judeo-Christian Tradition

The Judeo-Christian concept of justice is rooted in the revelation about God in the Hebrew scriptures in which God stands beside the oppressed (Fuechtmann 1989:136). As Christ identified with the poor and victims of injustice, so the Church identifies with and cares for the oppressed.

Christian economic teachings apply principles of social justice in the workplace. Many Catholic and Protestant teachings uphold workers' rights to earn decent wages, organize unions, bargain collectively, and participate in economic decisions of ownership (Fuechtmann 1989:140). From Pope Leo XIII's 1891 encyclical *Rerum novarum* to Pope John Paul II's *Laborem exercens* and his 1991 *Centesimus annus,* the Catholic Church has endorsed the rights of workers to organize and bargain collectively as a means to achieve economic justice.

The 1986 pastoral by U.S. bishops, "Economic Justice for All," is the Catholic Church's modern guide to economic responsibility. It measures the worth of economic institutions by how well they meet the financial and social human needs of all participants (Pawlikowski and Senior 1988:xiv).

The bishops' treatise echoes the social egalitarianism of the Second Vatican Council and the articles of faith in the *Catechism of the Catholic Church.* The primary teachings of the Catholic Church have consistently affirmed worker solidarity and the role of trade unions in securing economic and social justice.

HERE International versus Carson International at O'Hare

Food and beverage concession employees at O'Hare tried to organize for the first time in the early 1980s and again in 1989. Finally, in 1993, the nearly 850 food and beverage workers at O'Hare won a contract. Most were Hispanic; many were from Mexico and Central America. There also were a large number of Filipino and Polish workers. The union believed that Carson International (at the time a subsidiary of Dial-Greyhound), the franchisee of the City of Chicago, had instigated raids by the Immigration and Naturalization Service to harass employees following the unsuccessful 1989 drive (interview, Clifford 1996).

Many of the issues that gave rise to the union campaign focused on the disrespectful treatment of Latino workers. In 1989, Angie Chavez, a Latina concession worker, initiated the campaign by seeking out representation on behalf of workers employed throughout the terminal in restaurants, snack booths, bars, and food-preparation areas. HERE took on the campaign in 1990 and dispatched Paul Clifford as lead organizer. Clifford built committees throughout the airport and began documenting accounts of unfair discipline.

Discriminatory treatment, unfair discipline, and low wages were the primary issues for the O'Hare concession workers. Starting wages began at only $3.30 per hour for servers, $5.40 for snack bar attendants and cashiers, and $6.00 for bartenders. Workers were given a raise every six months at their supervisors' discretion. Spanish-speaking employees were warned by management that they could not speak Spanish at work. Because some of these workers had been undocumented at one time, they were made to feel dispensable, even though they had since become legal immigrants. The workers resented the abusive language used by management and protested unfair suspensions and firings, which were made without any defense on the workers' behalf.

Other complaints included the harassment of union supporters and health and safety issues, such as food spoilage, the lack of first-aid kits, and the inadequate equipment. Tied to these issues of wages and working conditions was the pursuit of worker dignity and respect, which became important rallying points during the campaign.

The Interfaith Committee on Worker Issues

The Chicago-based Interfaith Committee on Worker Issues was founded in 1991 to provide ongoing support for union organizing through a coalition of religious, labor, and community leaders in the Chicago metropolitan area. The committee's involvement in the O'Hare campaign harked back to earlier times when members of the religious community were more closely aligned with workers' struggles and the improvement of the conditions of low-paid workers.[1]

Many O'Hare workers were members of Catholic parishes centered in the largely Hispanic Logan Square and Humboldt Park areas of Chicago, where committee members learned about their struggle. In 1991, the committee contacted Clifford to offer its support, and Clifford readily accepted the clergy's involvement in the concession workers' organizing campaign. Father John Celichowski became the key operative for the Interfaith Committee in expanding involvement by the religious community. Celichowski, a Chicago Catholic Theological Union student at the time, had joined the committee to fulfill a practicum requirement. He had also learned of the workers' campaign through his internship at the Eighth Day Center for Justice and as a resident of Maternity BVM Parish in Humboldt Park.

During the campaign Celichowski worked closely with Clifford, Interfaith Committee director Kim Bobo, and committee member and retired Methodist bishop Jesse DeWitt. The O'Hare campaign soon brought in Michael Rouse, an A.M.E. Zion pastor, and Kurt Olson, an Episcopal pastor whose church was near the airport.

The success of the clergy's involvement in the HERE campaign depended in large measure on Clifford's clear vision and strategies for the clergy's

---

1. Throughout this century Protestant, Catholic, and Jewish groups have worked together on behalf of workers through community organizing and activism, education, and mediation. Interfaith groups, such as the Religion and Labor Council of America, founded in 1932, the Protestant Federal Council of Churches, and the Jewish Labor Committee, headquartered in New York City, are just a few such groups that champion unions and the rights of workers.

involvement. Clifford planned to build broad-based public support and to develop leadership among the rank and file. He sought to establish good, long-lasting relationships between the union and religious persons to achieve these goals. The success of Clifford's plan also depended on the organizing committee's flexibility and willingness to make clergy partners in the union campaign. As Bishop DeWitt related, "Paul kept us informed throughout the campaign: the union made us full partners, and that facilitated our involvement" (interview, DeWitt 1995).

Organizing Community Support

Clifford and Celichowski sought to develop rank-and-file leaders who could talk about the campaign in churches and establish working relationships with pastoral staffs (memo from Celichowski to Eighth Day Center staff, November 1991). Celichowski described his job as building bridges between the labor community and the religious community, which initially was composed of clergy in the Humboldt Park area (interview, Celichowski 1995).

The Interfaith Committee worked with the Ministry of Peace and Justice of the Chicago Catholic archdiocese to locate workers' churches by matching their zip codes with Catholic parishes. Committee members then educated parish pastors and staff about campaign issues and solicited their support (interview, Lund 1995). Catholic and Protestant members of the committee also contacted parish pastors in their constituencies to inform them of the O'Hare campaign. James Lund, archdiocese director of the Ministry of Peace and Justice, in a letter to pastors in the Humboldt Park area, suggested "it may be pastorally appropriate for [them] to consider ways that [they could] bring the Church's teaching on unions to the attention of [their] Spanish-speaking community" (letter to David Belongea, pastor, Maternity BVM, August 1991). Celichowski also wrote periodic memos to area churches and religious persons to update them about the campaign.

Support soon coalesced in the workers' communities. Delegations of workers spoke at churches, including Spanish-speaking churches in the Humboldt Park and Logan Square areas, where they described their campaign to improve working conditions at O'Hare. Clergy and parishioners from many parishes lent their support, including Our Lady of Mercy in Albany Park, Maternity BVM and St. Sylvester in Humboldt Park, and St. Vincent DePaul in Lincoln Park.

Standing beside the Oppressed

Coordinated by Celichowski, in the early months of 1992, clergy and seminarians began appearing in O'Hare food-service areas as "observers" of the working conditions. As they walked through airport terminals dressed in religious garb, these members of the O'Hare Investigative Committee closely monitored management's interactions with workers. According to Bishop DeWitt, "We made commitments to be at O'Hare at least once or twice a week at a given terminal and to personally contact workers. We were present and very evident, and that presence was very important" (interview, DeWitt 1995).

By making their presence known, the clergy and seminarians boosted workers' confidence and lent moral legitimacy to the union's organizing efforts. According to Chavez, who initiated the campaign, "The church's involvement made us feel justified. I never thought we could get that kind of support from our church" (interview, 1995).

Clergy monitored working conditions and provided places within O'Hare for union members to meet. Kurt Olson became assistant chaplain at O'Hare, and Father John Jamnicky made available the terminal's chapel for union meetings, prayer services, and solidarity masses.

Reverend J. Cletus Kiley, rector-president of Niles College of Loyola University, and Father John Clair from Niles College also provided personal support and helped secure the involvement of Joseph Bernardin, archbishop of Chicago. Bernardin's letter in HERE's O'Hare newsletter, published in English, Spanish, Filipino, and Polish, provided a religious and foundational basis for workers to organize and for clergy to support their efforts.

As lead organizer, Clifford cited the central role of clergy in increasing community awareness and legitimacy concerning the issues confronting O'Hare workers, especially the rights of the Latinos. "Because most of the workers were immigrants, the clergy's role reinforced the message of social justice. [The clergy] made the message much deeper and more relevant," said Clifford (interview, 1995). Among its first acts, the Interfaith Committee requested that Carson provide Spanish translations of its employee handbook and other employer communications. Ultimately, Carson provided a Spanish version of the handbook as a contract provision.

Religious leaders and organizations have played a central role in helping successive waves of immigrant labor adjust and improve their conditions in the United States. The experience of Cesar Chavez, of the United Farm Workers, demonstrates the local, national, and international religious support available in helping workers secure civil rights protections and better working conditions (Mooney and Majka 1995:225). Through personal and public support, clergy also played an important role in publicizing and upholding the civil rights of Latino workers at O'Hare.

Mobilizing Public and Political Action

The clergy and HERE worked together to monitor management, facilitate negotiations, and build religious support in workers' communities. As time passed, clergy also staged public and political events that reached a larger audience and helped workers win their campaign. Television news coverage of demonstrations at O'Hare, community petitions, and political lobbying at the Chicago City Council provided some of the most effective means of publicizing the workers' rights and holding management accountable.

According to Clifford, the union was approaching a majority of card signatures when the company made arrangements to lay off twenty-four workers, many of them long term, nearly 80 percent of them Hispanic. Carson claimed the layoffs resulted from business conditions. Clifford publicly questioned Carson's reason given that it had opened new food and beverage areas elsewhere in the terminal.

The Interfaith Committee helped organize worker demonstrations at O'Hare in March 1992, which became the publicity high water mark of the campaign. The demonstrations were meant to "turn [the workers'] fear into anger and to take the offensive" (interview, Clifford 1996). On March 20, 1992, 150 workers demonstrated with HERE organizers and the members of the Interfaith Committee to call upon management to "undo its mistakes" (interview, Clifford 1996). The Reverend Jesse Jackson and Farm Workers leader Cesar Chavez attended and spoke to the concession workers' rights. Their presence attracted widespread media attention to the O'Hare campaign. The public pressure proved effective when Carson general manager William Quirk decided to meet with a small delegation of workers and unionists, including the Reverend Jackson, Chavez, Michael Bruton of the Chicago Federation of Labor, and local clergy. Within weeks, Carson reinstated all twenty-four laid-off workers.

The press attention, combined with the appearance at the March 20 demonstration of such celebrities as Jackson and Chavez, helped boost the workers' morale. The card-signing campaign continued with renewed strength.

Despite the success of the demonstrations, Carson continued its antiunion activities. In November 1990, the NLRB issued a twenty-six-count complaint against Carson, citing numerous violations of law, including disciplinary firings, suspensions, interrogations, and surveillance of union supporters. In July 1991, Carson settled the unfair labor practice complaints through NLRB mediation, pledging neutrality and agreeing in principle to a free and open organizing campaign.[2] In April 1992, the union formally complained about repeated violations of the neutrality agreement, including Carson's complicity in antiunion employee committees.

---

2. A community-wide petition and televised publicity of Carson's health code violations increased the public pressure on management and helped bringing about the neutrality agreement.

Also in 1992, HERE and the Interfaith Committee organized a petition drive to encourage management to recognize HERE once it received a majority of card signatures. A "Justice Delayed Is Justice Denied" petition, signed by area clergy and parishioners, reminded Carson to respect the laws and the rights of the workers and to abide by the 1991 neutrality agreement (memo to Carson from Metro Chicago Religious Community, April 1992). Meanwhile, religious persons continued to monitor workers' conditions at O'Hare and confronted Carson management about labor law violations.

Political lobbying was another way in which religious persons mobilized broad-based community support for the O'Hare workers. In the spring of 1992, when clergy learned of a planned change in the ownership of the concession areas from Carson to Marriott, clergy played a pivotal role in lobbying city council on behalf of the workers. The Interfaith Committee lobbied the fifteen aldermen of the Aviation Committee of the Chicago City Council, who met to approve the sale of the O'Hare concession areas from Carson to Marriott. The committee members were instrumental in prohibiting Marriott, a notoriously difficult bargaining adversary, from engaging in antiunion activities. Once Marriott assumed the contract, the committee members also compelled Marriott to recognize the union "if it was the will of the workers" (interview, Bobo 1996).

In August 1992, an arbitrator confirmed that a majority of the active concession workers supported the union and ordered Carson to begin bargaining. After their three-year struggle, the workers finally joined the ranks of other unionized workers at O'Hare, including flight crews, machinists, and city employees.

During the summer and fall of 1992, Clifford, aided by the clergy, conducted employee surveys and meetings to keep workers informed about the bargaining. The clergy and the Interfaith Committee continued to bolster the workers' spirits and to track complaints of abuses.

By year's end, HERE had negotiated a contract with Marriott, providing the largest wage increase ever for O'Hare employees—17.6 percent over three years for all nontipped employees, which comprised three-fourths of the workforce. The contract, ratified in February 1993, included back-pay awards for workers whose wages had been cut or who had been discharged in February 1992. In addition, there were seniority provisions and a prepaid legal plan ("New Contract" 1993). Marriott also agreed to provide Spanish translations of the employee handbook.

Through Clifford's strategies to involve religious persons in its organizing campaign, to maintain open communication, and to establish a partnership with religious persons, the Interfaith Committee was able to support the workers' representation campaign effectively. The clergy, in effect, helped the concession workers set up a system of self-empowerment. Celichowski compared the role of the clergy in the labor movement to that of President Dwight D. Eisenhower dispatching paratroopers to preserve order as nine African American students attended an all-white high school in Little Rock, Arkansas. In this sense, clergy are neutral and work to build a society in which third-party intervention is no longer needed. According to Celichowski, "We help workers put and keep in place their own system of representation" (interview, 1995).

The Illinois Nurses Association and the St. Joseph Medical Center

The religious community also played a significant role in a successful strike and the resolution of a contract dispute by six hundred nurses at St. Joseph Medical Center, one of only two hospitals in Joliet, Illinois, an industrial city of seventy-five thousand located forty miles south of Chicago. The nurses organized successfully at St. Joseph in 1991 despite the hospital's history of union avoidance. In the mid-1970s, nurses had also tried to organize an independent union, but that time they had been unsuccessful. But in December 1991, despite the hospital's antiunion campaign and retention of the notorious antiunion law firm of Seyfarth, Shaw, the St. Joseph nurses prevailed in winning an NLRB-conducted election. St. Joseph became the first Catholic hospital in Illinois where nurses organized.

Bargaining began in May of the following year. Prominent among the nurses' concerns were the quality of patient care; the inadequate staffing and "pulling" of nurses; the inequitable pay, scheduling, and benefits; and the lack of professional respect and communication. Safety problems arose from the inadequate staffing and the pulling of nurses to areas in which they were not properly trained to work, such as cardiac, emergency, and critical-care areas. Increased workloads, poor equipment, and a reduction in the time allotted to treat patients heightened the job stress. During the strike, the nurses made patient services a central theme in their communications with the public.

Only six months into negotiations, it became apparent that bargaining was stalled. The hospital's salary proposal offered less than the nurses were currently making. Seniority, regardless of service, would be rolled back to zero. In addition, even currently employed nurses would have to serve a probationary period during which they could be fired without cause (Albright, Couturier, and Jones 1993:81). The hospital's extreme position helped galvanize support for the union among previously uncommitted nurses.

On January 18, 1993, after months of stalled bargaining, three hundred out of a total of six hundred nurses went on strike. The hospital immediately brought in replacements from a Colorado-based nurses registry. The Illinois Nurses Association filed a charge with the NLRB that the hospital was paying replacement nurses more than its permanent staff, an issue that would cost the hospital public support (interview, Medow 1995).

The Catholic Church's Response

Judy Steed, then cochair of the St. Joseph's Nurses Association (SJNA), who initiated organizing with fellow nurse Sally Koch, felt that the nurses' demands for representation were based on the human rights of dignity and social justice. For Steed, the union campaign was inspired by the Church's teaching about workers' rights to organize and its concern with social issues (interview, 1995).

Steed and other nurses initially turned to the Franciscan nuns who owned and operated the hospital for consultation about their concerns. But the nuns did not respond to the nurses' requests; the nuns responsible for the hospital's management were unreachable (interview, Steed 1995). According to James Wilson, a Methodist minister who supported the nurses during the strike, the Franciscan nuns sought to thwart the union out of fear that recognition of a nurses union at one hospital would lead to organization at their other three hospitals (interview, 1996).

According to Lutheran minister David Medow, churches of all denominations have an unfavorable reputation with regard to their own labor relations. He said the strike was not about money but about power. His comments provide insight into the conflict: "Economic self-interest often outweighs the church's teaching on workers' rights to organize" (interview, 1995).

The strike posed a particular challenge for the Joliet Catholic diocese and its parishes. Many of the nurses were Catholic, and their families were active in their parishes. Nurses in this largely Roman Catholic city turned to their Catholic parish priests and to Joliet's Roman Catholic bishop, Joseph Imesch, for emotional support and guidance during the labor dispute. Tensions mounted early as the diocese took a nonpublic approach to the nurses and the management of the Catholic hospital. Many priests felt pressured from parishioners, including managers and physicians, to remain uninvolved.

Father Mark Fracaro of St. Jude's, a member of the Joliet Ecumenical Clergy Association (JECA), was openly supportive of St. Joseph's nurses and helped lead ecumenical services for unity and peace. The diocesan newspaper, the *New Catholic Explorer,* carried numerous stories about the nurses' organizing campaign and ran articles challenging the hospital's actions in light of the church's teachings on social justice.

Though Bishop Imesch supported the nurses' right to organize and offered mediation services, he believed that there were two sides to the dispute and insisted on being a neutral, nonpublic party (interview, 1996). He also claimed that his authority in the dispute was limited since the Franciscan nuns were responsible only to their own order.

INA organizer Kay Jones felt that the bishop's lack of public support hampered the involvement of pro-labor churchmen, such as Msgrs. Jack Egan and George Higgins and members of the Chicago Interfaith Committee. "One bishop doesn't go into another bishop's territory," Jones stated (interview, 1995). By contrast, members of JECA praised Imesch's broadminded manner in working with members of other faiths and valued his role in facilitating negotiations behind the scenes. Medow noted that "the 'powers that be' [in the city] returned the bishop's phone calls; they wouldn't ours" (interview, 1995).

The JECA

Nurses who contacted members of the JECA found that many clergy members would give broad-based personal and public support to their campaign. James Wilson, minister of Grace United Methodist Church, became involved when a St. Joseph's nurse who was one of his parishioners asked him for support. Wilson's interest led to the involvement of other JECA members, including Lutheran minister and JECA president David Medow, who also had St. Joseph's nurses in his congregation. Together, Wilson and Medow went on to lead the JECA campaign to end the strike.

The JECA, which included Protestant, Catholic, and Jewish clergy in Joliet, had a record of involvement in community and social justice issues. The JECA felt that the nurses' strike was one in which public pressure and accountability could be brought to bear upon hospital management because managers resided in the workers' communities (interview, Medow 1995).

Limited coverage of the campaign by Joliet's news media made the involvement of the clergy even more significant in generating public awareness of the issues. Joliet's daily newspaper, the *Herald News,* had a reputation for being strongly antiunion and provided very little coverage of the nurses' organizing campaign and subsequent strike. The strike had lasted forty days before the paper ran its first story covering the issues (interview, Jones 1995). Religious persons sought to close the communication gap between the nurses and the Joliet community in an effort to resolve the strike successfully.

Mediation and Moral Support

In their public dealings with management, the JECA maintained a neutral stance—on the side of the community—and sought to facilitate discussion and mobilize the community to end the dispute. Early in the strike, Medow,

Wilson, and other JECA members offered to mediate between the hospital and the nurses since federal mediation had brought little progress. According to Medow, "Mediation is an impulse that comes out of the religious tradition" (interview, 1995). Alvin Abbott, a Presbyterian minister and JECA member who helped settle the 1986 Chicago teachers strike, thought his mediation efforts would also be useful. But hospital administration declined the ministers' offers (interview, Abbott 1995).

Though the JECA's formal role was to remain bipartisan or neutral in a labor dispute, many clergy members provided both public and personal attention to the nurses' campaign. Their support increased as the hospital became more intransigent at the bargaining table. James Wilson and David Medow took a broad-based approach in support of St. Joseph's nurses, which included weekly strategy meetings with members of the INA, community organizing, and support on picket lines. During the winter months of the strike, clergy provided their parish halls for contract negotiations, rallies, and union meetings; held prayer meetings; and gave supportive sermons. Clergy became mentors as well as mediators, standing beside nurses on picket lines and at rallies and providing a steady source of strength.

Many nurses recalled the particular importance of one of Medow's addresses. After five weeks of striking, nurses had gathered at Medow's church to consider whether they should settle short of meeting their primary goals. Medow saw that the nurses were burdened financially and emotionally and offered words of unity, perseverance, and encouragement. He applied biblical lessons to their current dispute with St. Joseph's management. According to Steed, Medow's address strengthened their resolve to continue: "It was Jesus in the marketplace. An official, ordained member of Christianity was telling us we were following Christian doctrine. Even though it was revolutionary, there were times when Jesus was revolutionary, too. He threw the money changers out of the temple. There is justifiable anger when things are wrong" (interview, 1995).

The Interfaith Committee on Worker Issues also provided personal and public support. During the second week of the strike, the committee sponsored an ecumenical mass at St. Jude Catholic Church, one in a series of weekly events to boost the nurses' spirits. The committee also helped distribute tracts and letters outlining the Church's support of workers' rights to organize and bargain collectively. Among the pamphlets was an open letter relating the Catholic patron saint of workers, St. Joseph, to the nurses' struggle. The Interfaith Committee described its role as pro-worker, partisan, and publicly supportive of workers' rights to organize.

During negotiations before the strike, Tom Garlitz, of the Office of Peace and Justice of the Joliet diocese, published a letter highlighting the Catholic Church's teachings on workers' rights and invited the hospital to an open forum at which both sides could tell their stories. The invitation, which was not made publicly, was declined by management. Later, when an invitation was made publicly, management acted differently.

Mobilizing Public Opinion

In early February, the JECA publicly invited St. Joseph's management to debate the nurses about strike issues. Hospital management accepted the JECA's newspaper-advertised offer to save face (interview, Jones 1995). The public forum, which was held on February 16, 1993, galvanized public opinion in support of the nurses and proved to be the turning point in their campaign. The forum, attended by more than three hundred people and televised on local cable channels, received considerable publicity. In addition to discussing primary issues of patient care, staff scheduling, and communication with management, nurses addressed the ULP charges filed against the hospital during the campaign. These issues, including bad-faith bargaining, interference with a bargaining unit by forming a company union, and discriminatory treatment of workers, were brought to the attention of the entire community. Clergy acted as facilitators during the sometimes-heated discussions, asking hospital management and nurse representatives questions gathered from the community.

Union and clergy members credit the open forum with bringing the nurses' issues to the attention of the entire community, shifting public opinion toward the nurses, and helping to bring a successful end to the strike (interview, Wilson 1996). According to Wilson, the largely pro-union city saw that the hospital was denying nurses the right to organize. In the end, according to Bishop Imesch, the hospital was moved by the public pressure to reach a settlement.

After the open forum, the JECA focused public opinion once again on the strike through a petition that more than two thousand community members signed. According to Medow, the petition to "End the Strike" for the sake of the community provided a vehicle for wide-scale involvement of JECA congregations and propelled resolution of the dispute.

The strike ended on March 20, 1993, and the St. Joseph nurses ratified their first contract on March 23. The nurses won seniority provisions, improvements in scheduling, a 9 percent raise over three years, and a grievance procedure with binding arbitration. According to the INA publication *Chart* (April 1993:7), in addition to limiting the practice of "pulling nurses," the contract created a Patient Care Committee to involve staff nurses in management decisions regarding patient care. Jones said that as a result of the nurses' successful campaign, many other workers at St. Joseph organized, including maintenance workers and ancillary staff. In March 1996, nurses successfully completed negotiations on their second contract.

Both St. Joseph's nurses and INA staff consider the involvement of the JECA and the Interfaith Committee on Worker Issues significant in publicizing the nurses' desire to achieve justice and in helping them reach a contract settlement. According to INA lead organizer Kay Jones, INA organizer Michelle Couturier, and SJNA member Vedie Albright, the involvement of religious leaders put the strike in an ethical framework: "The dialogue with the Bishop, the active support of JECA, the wider distribution of tracts on the rights of workers to organize, prayer for resolution of the strike incorporated into Sunday church services—all len[t] legitimacy to the righteous demands of the nurses" (Albright, Couturier, and Jones 1993:90).

INA organizers utilized a broad coalition of clergy as well as labor leaders, politicians, and educators to effectively publicize and champion the workers' rights.

Conclusions

The contributions of religious persons were significant in the two successful campaigns examined in this chapter. Both cases demonstrate the large variety of public and personal roles that religious persons can undertake in union campaigns. The very presence of clergy in religious garb at airport terminals, on picket lines, and at bargaining tables heightened management accountability and improved its behavior toward the workers at O'Hare and at St. Joseph Medical Center. Religious persons also took a more activist approach by helping to create large-scale media events that politicized the workers' issues. As the cases demonstrate, public forums reported on in the media, petitions, and rallies were particularly instrumental in shifting public opinion toward the workers and in helping them win union representation and contracts.

The O'Hare and St. Joseph Medical Center cases provide many lessons for organizers. Some of these lessons, as well as the challenges associated with involvement by the religious community in the labor movement, are summarized below.

1. *Plan and communicate strategies for involving religious persons.* Organizers should have a clear vision and practical plans for involving clergy in workers' campaigns. Organizers should also keep clergy informed of issues and events throughout campaigns. Continual communication creates partnership and greater commitment by these clergy, who can communicate and sustain workers' issues throughout the wider community. Workers should also maintain communication with religious persons to sustain their own long-term goals.

2. *Incorporate varied means to involve those in the religious community.* HERE and the INA utilized the experience and strengths of clergy as educa-

tors, mediators, public speakers, and organizers. Clergy often act in complementary ways, whether neutral or decidedly pro-labor, whether behind the scenes or in the face of management and the press. Campaign strategies to involve clergy, like strategies to involve other members of the community, need to reflect the broad range of contributions that these individuals provide. As leaders in their communities, clergy focus public opinion, attract media coverage of union issues, and provide a natural source of legitimacy and accountability.

3. *Involve seminary students and laypeople of faith.* Seminary students are the future of the church and can provide an excellent source of assistance to unions through internships, as in the case of O'Hare. Union campaigns also provide religious laypeople with opportunities to become involved in issues of social justice.

4. *Build upon workers' religious networks.* As seen in both campaigns, workers' own religious organizations provide a ready source of contacts and support for building public pressure. Facilitating workers' involvement and leadership through grassroots education and public speaking at parishes enhances worker ownership of campaigns.

Challenges

Religious leaders face many challenges in their support of labor. Decreased unionization and increased conservatism nationally have affected religious as well as popular support. The widening personal income gap and limited concern from middle-class congregations pose obstacles to clergy's involvement in unions. As businesses and the middle class move to the suburbs, churches are often the only private institutions left behind to aid inner-city poor, working-class, minority, and immigrant groups.

Clergy's time and resources, however, are increasingly divided by other social demands, such as hunger and homelessness, neighborhood crime, and the demands of maintaining parish schools. In addition, the increased mobility of workers and clergy can make it difficult to sustain clergy and religious persons' involvement in a protracted organizing campaign.

These cases demonstrate the many challenges as well as the opportunities and imperatives for developing cooperation among workers, unions, and religious persons to improve working conditions and increase union representation. Even with their limitations, religious persons and interfaith groups provide accessible and effective partnerships for achieving justice in the workplace.

PART IV

Determinants of Individual Support for Unions

To attract massive numbers of new members, unions must appeal effectively to individual workers. The authors of the chapters in Part 4 examine various influences on the individual decision to support unionization. Cohen and Hurd explore how fear and aversion to conflict affect the attitudes of professional and technical workers. Weikle, Wheeler, and McClendon look at the relative effect of specific employer tactics and worker characteristics on actual votes in NLRB elections. Rundle focuses on the impact of employee-involvement programs on union organizing success. Fiorito and Young study the relationship between human resource management policies and attitudes toward unions. Finally, Cornfield, McCammon, McDaniel, and Eatman investigate the interrelationship between a worker's involvement in the community and his or her interest in unionization.

Although fear of job loss, fear of strikes, and fear of management retaliation have long been recognized for their chilling effects on unionization, conflict as an influence has received less attention. Cohen and Hurd support their thesis that conflict is at least as important as fear in organizing campaigns. They detail how employers introduced the specter of conflict in several cases and, in particular, analyze the CWA campaign at NCR. They conclude that understanding and addressing the issue of conflict is essential for organizing success among professional and technical workers.

Weikle and his coauthors tie organizing success and failure to a theoretical construct based on in-depth interviews with workers. They analyze three union victories and one loss and conclude that workers are more likely to support unions if they feel that they have been deprived of pay or respect and believe that unions can be instrumental in redressing these injustices. Workers who are satisfied with their situations and workplace relationships will be less likely to unionize.

Chapter 13, by Rundle, analyzes union organizing in the era of employee-involvement programs. He finds that where such programs exist, they tend to prevent a union organizing drive from even starting. In the nearly two hundred organizing campaigns Rundle studied, employee-involvement programs were found to be present in one-third of the workplaces, and they substantially lowered union win rates. Rundle concludes that use of rank-and-file-intensive organizing tactics (of the type identified in chapter 1) is especially critical to success where employee-involvement programs exist.

Chapter 14, by Fiorito and Young, which develops and tests a model of union voting intentions, follows more in the tradition of mainstream quantitative industrial relations research. Their findings indicate that compensation cuts, bureaucratic corporate structure, and supportive worker attitudes and norms encourage pro-union voting. Surprisingly, they conclude that the effects of employer human resource policies are minimal, but caution that that may be due to limitations in the data set and their model.

The study by Cornfield and his coauthors includes important new information on the impact of community involvement on workers' attitudes about unionizing. Their findings indicate that an individual's involvement in community organizations lowers the likelihood of a pro-union vote. The authors recommend that unions counteract this tendency by reconstituting themselves as a community. They remind us of early union activities related to worker training, job referrals, and the provision of fringe benefits, as well as nonwork cultural, social, and recreational activities. The authors provide recent examples to demonstrate the effectiveness of the "union-as-community" in membership recruitment.

Chapter 11

Fear, Conflict, and Union Organizing

Larry Cohen and Richard W. Hurd

Workers' fears—of job loss, of strikes, of management retaliation—are well-documented obstacles to successful union organizing. Exploiting these fears is at the heart of employers' union-avoidance strategies (Bronfenbrenner 1994; Freeman 1985; Hurd 1994, Weiler 1983). Unorganized workers are well aware that management opposition creates real and potential risks in organizing. Not so well documented is the effect of conflict generated during the organizing process. Conflict is distinct from fear because the adversarial relationship itself has an impact on undecided workers. Management and their consultants can take actions that polarize the workplace and then transfer blame to "outside" union organizers and inside "troublemakers."

We believe that conflict is at least as important as fear in arousing antiunion sentiments, especially in organizing campaigns among professional, technical, and office workers. Our research indicates that understanding and addressing the issue of conflict is essential for success among these workers. Without more attention to its influence, by default, private-sector organizing may well appeal to only those workers with little to lose.

The role of fear and conflict in employers' union-avoidance campaigns will first be explored with the aid of several cases; we will distinguish between fear and conflict while demonstrating their entanglement. Next, we will explore in detail the campaign by the Communications Workers of America to organize computer technicians employed by AT&T's NCR subsidiary. We will present survey data based on interviews with 320 of these technicians, which enable us to evaluate their attitudes toward unionization. The data along with field experience indicate that aversion to conflict provides a significant explanation for hesitancy to organize among workers who are otherwise favorably disposed toward unions. Finally, we will discuss strategies to overcome fear and conflict and argue that the extent to which workers build their own organizations is directly related to the workers' likely success.

The Specter of Conflict

Employers use a variety of tactics to wage their campaigns of fear and intimidation. Firing union activists, harassing and discriminating against union supporters, threatening plant closings or layoffs, and suggesting the inevitability of strikes are all tactics designed to exploit workers' fears. The intent is to increase dramatically the expected cost of unionization and to convince undecided voters and reserved union supporters that organizing is not worth the risks.

Intertwined with these appeals to fear are efforts to create anxiety about workplace life in a unionized future. In particular, employers attempt to portray union adherents as malcontents committed to a confrontational approach that will translate into a state of perpetual conflict if the organizing campaign succeeds. Typically, this unsavory picture is counterposed with a peaceful and cooperative nonunion future based on promises of improved communication and an increased voice for workers.

For example, when workers at Teksid Aluminum's Dickson, Tennessee, plant attempted to organize with the assistance of the Aluminum, Brick and Glass Workers (ABGW), Teksid's director of human resources referred to ABGW adherents as "union slime." One worker who refused to wear an antiunion button being distributed by the company was ordered to sweep the basement. Another was cursed by his supervisor for wearing a pro-union button at work. A third was fired for theft when he placed an inexpensive file in his back pocket while cleaning his work area. These and a series of similar incidents created an intimidating atmosphere that scared away potential union supporters. After setting this negative tone with its anti-union campaign, Teksid's management complained to its employees that production was suffering because of the "high tension" caused by the organizing campaign. On the eve of the NLRB election, the company's president asked employees to choose cooperation over adversarialism: "You can vote for this union and make me negotiate against you, or you can vote against this union and help me shape Teksid into a team" (Hurd 1994:15–16).

When ACTWU attempted to assist a group of workers interested in forming a union at BMP America in Medina, New York, the company condemned the "name callers" and suggested in a memo that "employees [who] are sick and tired of being hounded and harassed to sign cards . . . [should] tell the union organizer to get lost." Meanwhile, an informal work environment gave way to a crackdown on conversations, especially those involving union supporters. An "Employee-Management Committee" was presented as a peaceful alternative to the union. As described by the ACTWU organizer, "The critical group needed for a majority . . . latched on to the Employee-Management Committee as a way to avoid the need to confront the boss" (Hurd and Uehlein 1994:134–38).

Lundy Packing in Clinton, North Carolina, was more aggressive in its reaction to an organizing campaign initiated by workers with the help of the United Food and Commercial Workers (UFCW). Several captive-audience meetings were supplemented by a series of small-group meetings. Workers were warned of strikes and the likely futility of collective bargaining. Four union supporters were fired, one for wearing a wristwatch on the job (against a seldom enforced policy), even though the watch had been a gift from the company for thirty years of service. The centerpiece of the employer's message was job loss, as summarized by the operations manager in a captive-audience meeting: "The best way to protect your job, your paycheck, is to vote 'no' in this election." Against the backdrop of this intense campaign, a final speech by Lundy's owner undoubtedly rang true: "If we defeat this union, then we can get on with it. If the union wins, well, then as far as I'm concerned, the battle has probably just begun" (Hurd and Uehlein 1994:96–98).

Some employers lay the foundation for union resistance in advance, based on the conflict hyperbole. After facing organizing campaigns in other parts of the country, K-Mart hired a well-known antiunion law firm to help reorganize its human resource management system (e.g., workers were referred to as "associates") and otherwise prepare its Newnan, Georgia, distribution center to retain its union-free status. A year later, the IBT began an organizing campaign, and on cue the company created two committees— the Associate Relations Committee and the Employee Involvement Committee. While these committees went to work addressing employees' concerns (union activists were barred from the meetings), K-Mart implemented a broad-ranging campaign complete with antiunion videos, T-shirts, threats of plant closing, harassment of union supporters, and an attack on "fast-talking home visitors." One flyer directly addressed the issue of perpetual conflict: "The union has already caused a lot of dissension and loss of friendships between our associates so far, how much more are we willing to lose because of the union? AS A TEAM NOT A TEAMSTER, WE CAN RALLY TOGETHER TO PROTECT OUR JOBS, OUR RIGHTS AND OUR FUTURE" (Hurd 1994:50–51).

Our point in reviewing these cases is to show how employers use the specter of conflict to magnify other concerns. Workers are encouraged to think like this: "Even if the union wins the organizing campaign, even if the company stays open and I keep my job, even if the union lets us vote whether or not to strike, the future will be filled with conflict which could flare into war at any time. Who wants to work in an environment like that? Why take the risk?"

HarperCollins and the CWA

Fear and conflict were major components of the management campaign at HarperCollins Publishing in San Francisco.[1] In late 1992, eighty office, marketing, and professional employees attempted to organize a union with help from CWA Local 9410. An experienced organizer met with leaders of the group and conducted inoculation training, portraying a typical employer campaign to fight unionization. Gina Hyams, a rank-and-file leader, described the group's reaction to the training: "Naively we thought, almost all our bosses are liberal Democrats. The company's profits come from publishing tons of progressive self-help books. If we decide to form a union, our management will just recognize that we're trying to help ourselves and they'll be civil and sit down and fairly negotiate a reasonable contract. We were wrong" (Herrera and Marklin 1993:4).

Of the eighty-three mostly college-educated women in the unit, sixty-two signed a CWA election petition. The company responded with a standard antiunion campaign. Top HarperCollins management personnel were involved, in addition to corporate counsel. Four of the most active union leaders were "laid off." Two others were "promoted" out of the unit. CEO George Craig flew in from New York to tell the staff in a captive-audience meeting that he considered organizing "war" and all employees involved in the campaign "disloyal."

Local managers were enlisted to sign a joint letter to employees arguing that unionization "would not serve to promote cooperation and solidarity." These same managers had encouraged the formation of a "nonmanagement group" two years earlier to discuss problems in a collegial manner. In fact, it was the failure to accomplish substantive change after two years of working through informal task forces that had created sufficient frustration to spawn the CWA organizing drive. Although management continued to proclaim its willingness to confer an occasional consulting role on its employees through the nonmanagement group, it would not tolerate an independent organization that could bargain and receive its own support from the CWA. As summarized in a letter sent to every worker at home from Senior Vice President Clayton Carlson: "The current feisty, free and open involvement of the entire staff as part of our working life is ironically what would be

1. For a more detailed account of this case, see Herrera and Marklin 1993:3–8.

most endangered by the success of the CWA petition. . . . To unsettle that dynamic mixture by drawing an artificial line down the middle of our organization is a step backward . . . and endangers most directly those values which we all hold dear (Herrera and Marklin 1993:4).

The CWA lost the election thirty-one to thirty-six, of which four ballots were challenged. Subsequently, the National Labor Relations Board overturned the results, certified the union based on unfair labor practices committed by HarperCollins, and ordered the parties to bargain. Three years later, in March 1996, the U.S. Court of Appeals upheld the NLRB's judgment but reversed the remedy, vacating the certification and bargaining order.

While the use of fear in this campaign was quite obvious, management's use of conflict was more subtle. Its argument was simply that harmony could never be restored, with the proper focus on the editorial function of the office, as long as union activity continued. In other words, management contended that the presence of a union created tension that would only increase with certification. Several swing voters who originally favored the CWA switched to "no" votes when they were convinced that the price for supporting a union would be continuing disruption.

NCR Customer Engineers and the CWA

NCR customer engineers install and repair computer equipment, mostly manufactured by the company. Their average service is twenty years. They are highly educated and receive several months of continuing education each year. Average annual income for the group exceeds $40,000.

Before AT&T's 1991 purchase of the company, NCR had pursued an aggressive union-elimination strategy. As of the mid-1960s, about 60 percent of NCR employees (most in manufacturing) had been represented by unions. According to NCR company documents, management then implemented a containment program to resist further organization, followed by a "Union Free Organization" (UFO) campaign to eliminate collective bargaining in previously organized locations. A management training program conducted in 1987 specified four "losses" from unionization that supervisors were expected to convey to workers: plant closings, strikes, the end of open relationships with supervisors, and discord. The first two appealed directly to fear; the latter two conveyed the specter of conflict. The UFO campaign was successful, and by 1996 less than 2 percent of NCR employees were unionized.

The CWA's support for organizing among NCR's customer engineers began soon after the purchase announcement by AT&T. More than eighty thousand AT&T employees were represented by the CWA, including about twenty-five thousand technicians. Many CWA locals with AT&T technicians as members were willing to "adopt" the NCR technicians in their areas. The unionized workers at AT&T had much better health-care benefits and substantially higher pensions, providing additional encouragement to the customer engineers that union representation could provide material gain as well as a real voice in decision making.

Consistent with its "union-free" strategy, NCR ran an aggressive campaign against the CWA with the assistance of the well-known antiunion law firm of Jackson, Lewis, Schnitzler and Krupman. Shortly after the CWA lost two close elections among NCR's customer engineers in Dayton and Indianapolis in 1992, NCR implemented a union-replacement strategy through company-sponsored organizations known as "Satisfaction Councils." The councils included management personnel, discussed "terms and conditions of employment," and were dominated by the employer, including control of the agenda for the meetings. In several separate decisions, these employee-management committees were ruled violations of section 8(a)2 of the National Labor Relations Act and were ordered "disestablished" by the NLRB.

After the two narrow NLRB election losses in Dayton and Indianapolis, the CWA organizing strategy focused on building a national organization of customer engineers while pressuring for organizing rights through national AT&T bargaining. Of four thousand customer engineers in the United States, about four hundred joined the National Association of NCR Employees (NANE) in twenty different NCR districts. In 1995, the customer engineers renamed their organization the Voice of Informed Customer Engineers (VOICE).

VOICE had been designed by customer engineers, with support from the CWA, to promote their own self-organization. The engineers emphasized that this was their organization; they were not simply joining a union, they were building one of their own with CWA support. Unlike the Satisfaction Councils, they could set their own agendas and launch campaigns on key issues. If majority support was achieved, they could seek recognition through the NLRB and bargain collectively.

During the 1995 round of bargaining at AT&T, organizing rights at NCR were a significant union issue. Union goals included workplace access, neutrality, and card-check recognition. Although agreement was not reached in these areas, the company did agree to a payroll deduction for VOICE membership dues. Payroll deduction without recognition has long been used to sustain employee organizations in the public sector. At least for the CWA, this had never before been attempted in the private sector. Could such an organization be built after thirty years of management antiunion campaigning? Was fear an issue among customer engineers faced with continuing restructuring and cutbacks as well as constantly changing technologies?

Given these concerns, a research project was designed to survey the attitudes of NCR's customer engineers about workplace issues and organizing. Particular attention was paid to barriers to organizing and to what kind of organization the customer engineers would join. The following section reviews the results of the research project, with an emphasis on the effect of fear and conflict on the workers' attitudes.

The NCR Customer Engineer Survey

To evaluate the NANE experience, gather information to help direct the activities of the newly renamed VOICE, and investigate the issues of fear and conflict, a telephone survey was conducted during October 1995. Interviews were limited to nine regions of NCR with active NANE chapters. Of the approximately 1,500 customer engineers in those regions, a representative sample of 500 was contacted and 320 were interviewed. All interviewees were asked twelve questions, which covered job satisfaction, attitudes toward management, the type of workers' organization they preferred (if any), and why customer engineers had not joined NANE.

Answers to the question on the type of organization they preferred are summarized in table 11.1. When those who indicated a preference for a union are combined with those who voiced support for NANE (which was explicitly linked to the CWA in the interview questions), just under 30 percent of the respondents could be considered pro-union. Only a slightly higher share were opposed to any organization, leaving a large group of engineers who were neither enthusiastically pro-union nor decidedly against organization. A large portion of these "organizable" workers would have

TABLE 11.1. Type of Organization Preferred by NCR Computer Technicians

Type of Organization	Number	Percentage
1. Union that negotiates contracts	51	15.9
a. willing to campaign	(24)	(7.5)
b. not willing to support publicly	(27)	(8.4)
2. Voluntary association like NANE	40	12.5
3. Professional association for entire industry	40	12.5
4. Employee-management committee like Satisfaction Councils	48	15.0
5. Unsure	25	7.8
6. Not interested in any organization	111	34.7
7. Refused to answer	5	1.6
Total	320	100.0

to be attracted, however, to attain majority status. In the two formal organizing campaigns conducted in 1992 in Dayton and Indianapolis, the CWA received a combined 45 percent of the vote—close enough to a majority to demonstrate that unionization was a viable possibility for these professional/technical workers if there was an appropriate organizing strategy and the right type of independent organization.

To explore more carefully the concerns of the marginal voters, a second set of twelve questions was posed to workers who showed some interest in an organization but were hesitant to support a union. We defined this *"uncommitted middle"* broadly to include the 180 workers (about 55 percent of the entire sample) who would have liked a union but would not support it publicly, or who chose some type of association short of a union, or who were unsure what type of organization they wanted (categories 1b, 2, 3, 4 and 5 on table 11.1). The additional questions posed to them probed in more detail their attitudes toward unions, their reasons for joining or not joining an employee association, and the types of services that would be of interest.

To put this into the context of a union organizing campaign in which CWA rates workers on a 1 to 3 scale, where 1 represents strong union supporters and 3 represents confirmed opponents, this uncommitted middle represented the 2s.[2] Of course, they were being surveyed after four years of CWA/NANE presence, an antiunion campaign by management, the imposition of Satisfaction Councils, and a successful legal challenge to the Satisfaction Councils. In short, these 2s had been influenced by both labor and management during the organizing campaign.[3]

The most interesting data gleaned from the survey responses relate to the issues of fear and conflict. We asked two questions that were designed to address these issues. By comparing answers to these questions with responses to the rest of the survey, we have been able to develop profiles that help to unravel the influences of fear and conflict. One question specifically asked *all* of those interviewed, "What do you feel is the main reason that some Customer Engineers have not yet chosen to join NANE/CWA?" We offered ten options, including five directly related to fear, three concerned with the activities of NANE/CWA, one on unfamiliarity with the organization, and one concerning antiunion attitudes.

2. Some unions use a five-point scale in which 1 is assigned to organizing committee members, 2 to other union supporters, 3 to fence sitters, 4 to those leaning against, and 5 to opponents. Using this rating system, the uncommitted middle would include all 3s plus some 2s and 4s.

3. The workers in Dayton and Indianapolis experienced the influences of the organizing campaign more directly. Workers from these regions accounted for just under 20 percent of the sample. Their responses were not substantially different from those of other respondents.

TABLE 11.2. Reasons Coworkers Do Not Join NANE, by Type of Organization Preferred (in percent)

Reasons	Union	Voluntary Association (NANE)	Professional Association	Employee-Management (Satisfaction Council)	No Organization	Total
Unfamiliar with NANE	21.6	15.0	20.0	16.7	6.0	14.4
Antiunion	13.7	20.0	20.0	**41.7**	45.7	30.6
NANE mistakes	15.7	20.0	25.0	16.7	22.4	20.4
Fear	**41.1**	42.5	30.0	18.8	12.1	25.3
Unsure	2.0	2.5	5.0	6.3	13.8	9.3
Total	100.0	100.0	100.0	100.0	100.0	100.0

Note: To simplify the table, the answers of those who are unsure what type of organization they would prefer are omitted; however, they are included in the totals.

The responses are summarized in the right-hand column of table 11.2. The relatively even distribution of answers among the four options is less interesting than the breakdown by "type of organization preferred" included in the other columns. The four highlighted cells represent the highest response levels. Those who prefer no organization or those who prefer joint employee-management committees (the two most antiunion categories) disproportionately believe that their coworkers have not joined NANE/CWA because they too are antiunion. Similarly, those in the most pro-union categories (those who prefer a union or a voluntary association) offer assessments that fit *their* biases: they disproportionately believe that fear has kept their coworkers from joining. Looking specifically at the responses of the most pro-union workers, those willing to work on an organizing campaign, 58.3 percent blame fear,[4] three times the share among other workers. In other words, the perceptions of the most activist union supporters about why their coworkers do not join unions are not representative and may be misleading. In the CWA campaign at NCR, the union relied on the organizing committee's strong perception that fear was the key explanation for the reluctance of coworkers to openly support collective action by joining NANE. The survey results indicate that this conclusion needs to be reevaluated and the organizing approach adjusted accordingly.

The second question related to fear and conflict was posed only to those in the uncommitted middle; it asked for "the best reasons not to join any employee organization." Responses are summarized in table 11.3. Given

4. This percentage is not reported in the table, which combines the responses of all those who supported a union whether or not they were willing to work on a campaign.

TABLE 11.3. Best Reason Not to Join Any Employee Organization

Response	Number	Percentage
Dues too high	9	5.0
Make conditions worse	16	8.9
Decrease job security	22	12.2
Decrease possibility of raise	20	11.1
Hurt NCR	36	20.0
Create conflict at work	71	39.4
Loss of individual freedom	50	27.8
Total responding	180[a]	

[a] Only those in the "uncommitted middle" as defined in the text of the chapter were asked this question; thus, the total responding was 180. More than one answer was accepted, however, so the number of responses totals more than 180. Percentages are based on 180.

the centrality of the threat of job loss in the employer's antiunion communications with workers, we expected "decrease job security" to capture fear most directly. The fact that of those interviewed only 12.2 percent selected this option reinforces our conclusion that we overestimated the role of fear. The related option, "hurt NCR," was included to separate out those feeling strong identification with the company; in other words, we used it as an ideological screen. The 20.0 percent of the uncommitted middle who selected this option are also concerned about job loss but are likely to be ideological opponents of unions at any rate.

The most frequently cited "best reason not to join" any employee organization was that such organizations "create conflict at work." Although we understood the role of conflict in employers' antiunion campaigns, we had not anticipated that it would be of such great concern to those in the uncommitted middle. The second most frequent response was "loss of individual freedom," another option we introduced as an ideological screen since those who are concerned about this issue are less likely than others to be attracted to collective action.

Most important for our purposes, 39.4 percent of those in the uncommitted middle selected "create conflict at work"—more than any other option. We will refer to those who selected this option as *"conflict avoiders."* In terms of the type of organization they prefer, these workers are similar to others in the middle. They are a little less likely to be unsure about the type of organization they prefer, a little more likely to support a voluntary association like NANE, and a little less likely to prefer a union. None of these differences is statistically significant, however, so it is safe to say that the conflict avoiders are a reasonably representative group within the uncommitted middle.

Turning to table 11.4, comparisons of the responses of conflict avoiders

TABLE 11.4. Attitudes Associated with Best Reasons for Not Joining Employee Organizations (in percent)

Attitudes	Create Conflict at Work	Hurt NCR	Loss of Individual Freedom	Total Uncommitted Middle
Likely to join NANE	52.1	27.8***(−)	36.0**(−)	49.4
Better off with union	50.7	22.2***(−)	32.0***(−)	48.9
Work-related activities you would support:				
Petitions regarding management policies	23.9	22.2	20.0	23.9
Meet with human resource personnel	46.5	55.6	52.0	46.7
Union organizing	26.8	13.9***(−)	30.0	28.3
None	22.5	27.8	22.0	23.3
What if you joined NANE?				
Better off	16.9	5.6***(−)	12.0	17.2
Worse off	25.4	19.4	20.0	18.9
No difference	42.3***(−)	66.7*(+)	66.0*(+)	55.0
Unsure	15.5**(+)	8.3	2.0***(−)	8.9
More likely to join if management neutral	52.1**(+)	30.6*(−)	38.0	42.8
Reason coworkers don't join:				
Unfamiliar with NANE	16.9	16.7	24.0	18.9
Antiunion	23.9	38.9**(+)	24.0	24.4
NANE mistakes	12.7**(−)	25.0	16.0.	20.0
Fear of management retaliation	42.3***(+)	13.9***(+)	26.0	29.4
Positive view of management	45.0	58.3**(+)	34.0	41.7
Considerations determining job satisfaction:				
Wages and benefits	16.9	22.2	12.0	16.7
Job security	31.0	27.8	40.0	37.2
Working conditions	40.8**(+)	30.6	36.0	30.6
Unsure	11.3	19.4	12.0	15.6

Note: Statistically significant differences from all others in the uncommitted middle are denoted by *** 99% confidence, ** 95% confidence, * 90% confidence; the direction of difference is denoted by (+) or (−); significance levels are based on the Z statistic.

with all others in the uncommitted middle reveal some interesting patterns. For most questions, the answers of the conflict avoiders mirror those of others in the middle. Conflict avoiders are just as likely to join NANE (52.1 percent), to believe they would be better off with a union (50.7 percent), and to have a positive view of management (45.0 percent). They also would support various workplace activities in the same proportion as others in the uncommitted middle.

Given the overall similarity to the norm, the differences are all the more striking:

- The conflict avoiders are significantly less likely to believe that joining NANE would make no difference, significantly more likely to be unsure of the impact, and also more likely to believe that joining would cause problems (25.4 percent compared with 14.7 percent).
- Given this cautiously pessimistic assessment, it is not surprising that the conflict avoiders would be affected significantly more by management neutrality than would others in the middle and would be more likely to join NANE under this scenario.
- When asked why coworkers had not joined NANE, the conflict avoiders were twice as likely as others in the uncommitted middle to select a response related to fear (42.3 percent compared with 21.2 percent). For each "type of organization preferred," the conflict avoiders were more likely to select a response related to fear than were the others preferring that type of organization. This is consistent with the idea that fear and conflict are entangled as influences on potential support for collective action.
- Although job satisfaction for this subgroup (74.6 percent) is essentially the same as for others in the uncommitted middle (75.9 percent), the reasons cited are quite different. For both satisfied and dissatisfied conflict avoiders, the "main reason [they] feel that way" is significantly more likely to relate to noneconomic job conditions and less likely to relate to job security.

The overall picture that emerges, then, is that those concerned about conflict are more pessimistic about the potential benefits of joining NANE, more likely to believe that coworkers do not join out of fear, and more concerned about working conditions/environment than their counterparts. Because they represent about 40 percent of the uncommitted middle, these concerns should be taken seriously. This important and large subgroup of cautious supporters of collective action would be particularly susceptible to management attempts to raise the specter of perpetual conflict during an organizing campaign. At NCR, winning majority status would be virtually impossible without appealing to most of those concerned about potential conflict.

Table 11.4 also reports responses to a range of questions for those who believe that unionization would "hurt NCR" or would lead to "loss of individual freedom." Consistent with the types of organizations they prefer, respondents who answered that unionization would "hurt NCR" are decidedly antiunion. The "individual freedom" respondents are less so. Of particular interest, those who selected "loss of individual freedom" as the "best reason not to join any employee organization" nonetheless are as supportive of union organizing as others in the uncommitted middle and are less likely to have a positive view of management. Perhaps the discontent of these workers could be tapped in an organizing campaign.

Implications

Union organizers have always contended with management-engendered fear. Inoculating workers during organizing by anticipating management's tactics has been standard practice for decades. Mainly the attention has been on fears of firing or management retaliation. This follows a framework established by the NLRB that focuses on illegal discriminatory actions against workers or threats concerning shutdown or conditions of employment. The NCR survey indicates that although fear is an important concern, the closely related issue of conflict may be even more essential in convincing some groups of workers to vote "no" in a representation election.

If concern that unionization will result in conflict is as widespread in other workplaces as it is among NCR customer engineers, it may be appropriate to reevaluate and/or redesign the organizing tactics aimed at dissipating or circumventing appeals to fear. For example, warning workers about management's likely aggressive antiunion campaign may inoculate them against fear, but it may raise their concerns about conflict. Similarly, deploying a team of organizers to sign up workers before management can react may produce short-term gains, but does it also open the union to employer attempts to pin the blame for conflict on outside union agitators? If they are not carefully planned, even efforts to build worker solidarity through demonstrations and actions during the organizing campaign may backfire with the essential group of cautious but organizable workers.

Traditionally, employers have raised the specter of conflict by focusing on the union's use of strikes and job actions. Under this scenario, the union response would include data on the relative infrequency of strikes and violence. But in this era of widespread uncertainty, disruption itself has become a tool for management. The NCR survey data indicate that workers in the uncommitted middle in organizing campaigns are more likely to be affected by the conflict generated during the campaign than they are to be intimidated by perceived management threats of retaliation. For these NCR technicians, disruption and increased tension at work were identified as by-products of any type of union presence.

Obviously, management can create a sense of conflict simply by fighting the union, which it will do in virtually every private-sector organizing campaign. It is almost as if the union is being pressured to assume responsibility for ensuring that worker organization will proceed without continual struggle. Can management, just by being angry or unhappy with the organizing effort, convince employees that the conflict will only grow worse if they support a union? Can union supporters in particular situations such as those at NCR convince their undecided coworkers that they can participate in the organizing effort without signing on to perpetual class warfare? Can unions help workers understand that organization offers them a powerful voice, and *this* is why management intentionally incites conflict as part of the effort to fight the union?

Some lessons from industrial relations and case study research are relevant here. White-collar workers generally and clerical workers specifically are less likely to vote for union representation if they associate unionization with strikes (Maranto and Fiorito 1987; Hurd and McElwain 1988). Clericals also are concerned that they may be ostracized by their coworkers and their supervisors if they support unionization. Because of this reticence, organizing tends to be a very slow process (Hurd 1990). Yet there have been notable successes organizing clerical workers at private-sector universities and professional workers in health care. Furthermore, once they have made the decision to unionize, these workers have displayed incredible tenacity and have moved beyond their initial cautions to use strikes and other militant tactics when necessary.

The key to overcoming reluctance among white-collar workers seems to be organizing around issues of voice using a grassroots approach with a large inside committee. White-collar workers often are confident that they can make a major contribution to their employer and are frustrated when management limits their role in decision making. Once these workers see unions as a vehicle to gain an effective voice, their enthusiasm grows. Both clerical and professional workers react against campaigns that fit the "third-party" image and respond best to a democratic structure that allows them to take control of their own organization and use it to gain influence and respect and to enhance their professionalism (Hurd 1990).

The CWA experience lends further credence to these observations. Recent organizing success among eighteen hundred telephone service representatives in New England can largely be attributed to the voice provided by a local union led by customer service staff. Similarly, CWA Local 9119 has won two representation elections at the University of California for eight thousand technical and professional staff. There has been significant management opposition to the union, featuring "information" designed to increase fear and engender the likelihood of perpetual conflict. But CWA local leadership rests primarily on elected officers with long-term careers at the university, and this committed leadership at each campus has made the difference.

Organizing, then, needs to demonstrate the potential for the union to coexist as an equal with management not only in negotiations and grievance handling but also in solving a wide variety of workplace problems. To demonstrate during the organizing campaign that the potential exists to bargain on a par with the employer, unions must respond to the conflict introduced by management without assuming responsibility for that conflict. Organizers need to be able to assist workers in developing an effective strategy of resisting management when it inevitably becomes necessary, without alienating conflict avoiders and others in the uncommitted middle.

In a successful campaign, workers will realize that genuine voice requires independent organization *and* the ability to resist. Seemingly contradictory, voice and resistance both speak to the concerns not only of union supporters but also of the crucial uncommitted middle. It is this ability to resist that enables workers to have a powerful voice and to challenge management when necessary. Organizers need to be aware of the tension between voice and resistance and make clear that by participating effectively in collective bargaining, labor-management committees, and other forums the union can assure that perpetual conflict is *not* inevitable.

In the CWA's experience, increasing worker ownership and leadership during the organizing campaign makes this dual-track unionism more credible. To win, the union must appeal to those in the uncommitted middle. They are more approachable if they can be convinced that the workers will own and control the future organization. And this ownership is more believable if the organizing committee has the deepest possible reach into the work group. Workers like the NCR customer engineers have tremendous confidence in their ability to understand the technical details of their jobs. They have more faith in their coworkers than they could possibly have in organizers from outside the firm.

The role of the union's organizers is to help build unity but *not* to lead the group. Based on the concerns expressed at NCR by the conflict avoiders, one key to success is for the organizer to convince activist committee members to select tactics with careful attention to the potential effect on uncommitted voters. In particular, when resistance is necessary, it is essential to plan carefully and to maximize the potential for victory. Although the survey does not speak directly to this question, we are convinced that technical workers like the NCR customer engineers are not afraid to fight; they just do not want to be involved in conflict if they are going to lose.

The relevance of our findings to other settings can be assessed fully only by analyzing a wide variety of organizing cases. The NCR customer engineers are, after all, highly skilled and middle income, and they have much to protect. Based on comparisons such as those summarized briefly above, we believe that their situation is representative of professional, technical, and other white-collar workers in the private sector. Similarities and differences in attitudes toward conflict among white-collar workers need to be explored, however, with careful attention to influences of gender, age, and race. We are less confident that our conclusions on conflict apply to manu-facturing, although we suspect that the proliferation of team-based produc-tion systems also may make medium- to high-skilled blue-collar workers susceptible to employer efforts to portray unions as inevitably disruptive. The issue of conflict probably plays a role in most private-sector organizing campaigns, although in some settings (such as low-wage service work), conditions may be so bad that aversion to conflict dissolves. With a repre-sentative committee that is sensitive to the doubts and fears of coworkers, the appropriate emphasis on resistance and voice can be determined. Our ultimate point is that although workers everywhere calculate the risk/re-ward ratio in organizing, different circumstances lead to different solutions.

Chapter 12

A Comparative Case Study of Union Organizing Success and Failure: Implications for Practical Strategy

Roger D. Weikle, Hoyt N. Wheeler, and John A. McClendon

Union growth in the United States depends on winning representation elections. Both parties—labor and management—are very interested in better understanding what makes a campaign successful. Since there is so much interest, it is not surprising that a good deal of research has been done on union organizing in the past twenty years. Much of this research has examined the factors that determine how individuals vote in elections or has tried to isolate overall factors related to who wins or loses.

The research on individual workers has focused on the attitudes and perceptions associated with supporting a union. In an extensive treatment of this literature, Hoyt N. Wheeler and John A. McClendon (1991) classified the variables most commonly used in the individual-level vote studies into one of five categories: attitudes about jobs or unions, the value of union membership, perceptions of social support for membership, and demographic characteristics of those in the unit. Studies of the overall factors affecting outcome have focused on such items as unit characteristics (Crain 1994), procedural variations (e.g., Thomason 1994), and employer and union campaign behavior (e.g., Freeman and Kleiner 1990; Peterson, Lee, and Finnegan 1992).

Although some of the conclusions from both types of studies have been helpful, the research has generally produced inconsistent results and has suffered, according to the critics, from a lack of realism and practicality and a methodology that has made it of limited value to practitioners. One of the major criticisms has been the relative lack of attention paid to the strategies and tactics used by the parties in the elections. Trying to address this weakness, several studies have surveyed union campaign tactics used and organizer preferences, but few have examined the effects of union strategies and tactics. Some more recent programs of research have been designed to further investigate this overall link between the campaign environment, strategic choices, and outcomes.

By interviewing organizers themselves, Richard W. Hurd and Adrienne McElwain (1988), Monty L. Lynn and Jozell Brister (1989), and James Green and Chris Tilly (1987) examined the differences in approaches, using context variables in the campaigns, and considered each campaign an interaction of the strategy choices made by the opponent. After comparing public- and private-sector election results, Kate Bronfenbrenner and Tom Juravich (1995b) concluded that employee tactics are a dominant force in accounting for the results. Bronfenbrenner and Juravich (1995c) also found evidence that personal contact–intensive tactics not only affect certification election win rates but also have an impact on the vitality of the local that results. In the latest offering in this line of research, Bronfenbrenner (1997) reports continuing evidence that union wins are more likely when organizers use the following tactics: intensive person-to-person contact, communications that emphasize the values of democracy and participation, activities that build for first contracts, escalating pressure tactics, and events that highlight workers' dignity, respect, and the like. Consistent with these efforts, this study attempts to incorporate elements of the individual-level studies with the election outcome analysis. This study also includes discussion of the types of organizing tactics and messages used in campaigns.

Purpose of the Study

The purpose of this study is to better understand the union organizing process and to investigate the possible relationships between the Wheeler model of union formation and specific strategies that might be used in organizing campaigns. The model proposes that voting for a union is a two-step process. During the first step, the conditions surrounding a worker provide energy for taking aggressive action. The authors questioned workers in an effort to identify which conditions provide the most energy to mobilize such a group of individuals. During the second step, a set of environmental variables enables the energized group to take collective action. By interviewing workers, we hoped to determine what these variables are.

The workers whom we interviewed for this study were allowed to use their own language rather than forced to provide responses to a few questions. In in-depth interviews, we attempted to capture the feelings of these workers concerning the important variables affecting election outcomes and to judge the extent to which their opinions supported predictions we had made about the relationships among important variables.

Theory *and* Variables

The theoretical basis for this study is *Industrial Conflict: An Integrative Theory* (Wheeler 1985). A two-stage model is used in which the first stage represents a worker's readiness to take some form of aggressive action, and the second stage represents that worker coming together with other individuals as a group and choosing to take collective action. The theory holds that a particular employee usually begins to move toward unionization when he or she experiences feelings of deprivation as to pay, security, or respect. An employee's thought process can be seen as taking the person along one or more possible paths to readiness to take some form of aggressive action—to demonstrate his or her anger—at the employer. Whether such an employee takes the particular action of supporting a union depends on certain conditions. These conditions either encourage or discourage the employee to support a union as his or her choice for collective action.

Deprivation at work occurs when a gap exists between what employees expect from work and what they receive. There are three paths connecting deprivation and readiness to take aggressive action. The first path is "threat" or "attack," which results when the employer takes away or threatens to take away something the workers already have. The second path is frustration and results when workers try to act in their own behalf and this action is blocked or ignored; they have no voice and see no way of achieving effective voice as individuals. Workers take the third path, one not involving anger, as a result of rational calculation whereby they become convinced that the benefits of unionization outweigh its costs.

Even if workers are mobilized along one of the paths, they may not choose unionization but some form of withdrawal or revenge behavior. The conditions that help promote collective action or unionization are love, hope, and saliency. Love in this context is essentially cohesion and solidarity —people caring enough for each other to act together and share good interrelationships. Hope captures the concept that workers believe the union can do what is necessary to bring an end to their deprivations and frustrations. Saliency is the recognition that problems exist and are commonly perceived by the members of the work group. Dramatic events and good leadership contribute to facilitating action.

Along with each of the conditions that promote the union option, inhibiting conditions may also exist. Such conditions may include fear of punishment for supporting the union and the general belief that unions are wrong in principle. Measuring these variables, predicting the combinations necessary for individuals and groups to vote in favor of unionization, and explaining the interactions of the variables is the essence of the program of research of which this study is a part.

Pattern Propositions

From the integrative theory, we derive the following expectations for the relationships that will exist between the variables. These are called pattern propositions because they reflect the patterns of observations that we expect to find.

Individual Readiness

The propositions associated with each individual readiness variable include the following:

DEPRIVATION—individual deprivation as to pay, security, or respect will be positively related to union support.

RECENT DECREASE—Having recently experienced a reduction in pay, security, or respect or the threat of such a reduction will be positively related to union support.

NO VOICE—Having experienced the frustration of being thwarted in prior efforts to remedy conditions of deprivation will be positively related to union support.

CALCULATION—Calculating that the benefits of unionization outweigh the costs will be positively related to union support.

FEAR—Experiencing fear of employer retaliation for union activism will be inversely related to union support.

Collective Action

The propositions associated with each collective action variable include the following:

GENERAL FEAR—A generally held fear of employer retaliation will be inversely related to union support.

UNIONS ARE WRONG—A general feeling that unionization is wrong in principle will be inversely related to union support.

SOLIDARITY/COHESION—Good relationships among workers will be positively related to union support.

INSTRUMENTALITY—A generally held perception concerning the instrumentality of the union conducting the campaign will be positively associated with union support.

DRAMATIC EVENT—The existence of a dramatic event as the theme of the organizing campaign will be positively related to union support.

UNION LEADERSHIP—The existence of good campaign leadership will be positively related to union support.

Method

The results described in this chapter were obtained during a larger research project that is multidimensional both in its method of data collection and its analysis. In the larger effort, data were collected by administering telephone surveys, conducting interviews with workers, conducting interviews with organizers, participating in organizing campaigns, and observing campaigns.[1] The current study uses the data gathered in structured interviews with workers who voted in certification elections. Three of the elections were union wins and one was a loss.

The interviews were analyzed by other readers, not by the authors. By having other readers judge whether or not the data supported the propositions, the tests became both rigorous and systematic.

There were two possible overall outcome conditions for each election—a union win or a union loss—and two possible individual vote conditions—union supporter or union opposer. Included in the analysis were fifty-four interviews representing three of the possible four combinations; that is, workers could be supporters in an election in which the union won, and workers could be either supporters or opposers in an election in which the union lost.

The interview data were collected by the authors in personal interviews with workers at each organizing site. Staff organizers who had worked on the campaigns assisted in identifying candidates for interviews. All responses were recorded and later transcribed. Subjects were aware that their responses were being recorded but were assured anonymity.

The relatively small sample of fifty-four is a cause for some caution when interpreting the results. The way the workers were identified and questioned, however, raises the level of confidence in the findings. Workers were identified as activists by the organizers, who cooperated fully with the authors of the study and had received clearance from their internationals as

1. Six cases—three that resulted in union wins and three that resulted in losses—were included in the larger sample. The units involved ranged from a group of approximately two thousand employees to one that had just more than one hundred. Both units were manufacturing and service oriented. Sample sizes of the units actually surveyed by telephone were 406, 34, 46, 413, 181, and 114. All survey instruments were pilot tested in settings described in the findings. Sampling was done carefully, using random numbers and then alphabetical drawing until a sufficient sample size was achieved. The in-depth interviews of employees and professional organizers followed the administration of the telephone survey. The results of the larger study are reported in Wheeler, McClendon, and Weikle 1994.

well. The interviews were long, and since we knew a great deal about the local conditions, we were able to ask very probing questions about the details of their experiences and the perceptions of others. The interviewees knew and were willing to share what they knew about issues, leadership, and results. They had no agenda and had no idea what we actually expected from the interviews.

Two different types of judges were used. One group of judges was composed of 119 university students in human resource classes. Many researchers are skeptical about using students as judges, but we believe that careful training and standardized instructions lead to useable results. The students were given extensive orientation on the theory on which the research was based and on situations they were likely to encounter.

Each student read the full text of approximately ten interviews. For each interview and each pattern proposition, the judges were asked whether they agreed or disagreed that the interview supported the proposition. Instructions to the student judges were conservative in that they could indicate that an interview supported a pattern proposition only if they could find specific language in the interview text to support their conclusion. It is important to note that the judges were not asked to evaluate the value of any campaign message or worker or campaign characteristic, only the extent to which the answers given and the language used by the workers supported the research questions as to frustration, deprivation, quality of the leadership, and so on. In addition, three expert judges, all experienced arbitrators, were sent interview transcripts, a description of the judging methods, and recording sheets. Two of the experts read interviews and judged whether or not the pattern propositions were supported by the interview content. The third expert was used as a check to confirm the judgments of the first two experts.

The interview data were analyzed two ways. First, we compared the differences from case to case. Second, we compared results against the predictions for each pattern proposition. Chi-square statistical comparisons were also done to evaluate the existence of significant differences in the numbers of judges who said there was or was not support for each proposition in that interview.

Results

The cases that resulted in union wins are identified as Anne, Basil, and Clara. Case David represents the union loss. Cases Anne, Clara, and David were highly contested election campaigns, while Basil was essentially uncontested by the company.

In analyzing the judges' responses, we first consider the individual-level

TABLE 12.1 Summary of Variables by Case

	Union Wins			Union Loss	
	Anne	Basil	Clara	David	
Individual Readiness Variables				Supporters	Opposers
Deprivation					
Pay		P	P		A
Security	P		P		A
Respect	P		P	P	A
Recent decrease in benefits	P		P		A
No voice	P	P	P	P	A
Calculation		P	P	P	A
Fear					
Collective Action Variables					
General fear					
Unions are wrong	A		A		P
Solidarity/cohesion	P	P	P		
Instrumentality of the union	P		P		A
Dramatic event	P		P		A
Union leadership	P	P	P		A

P = Variable present as expected; A = variable absent as expected.

results on a case-by-case basis and then by pattern proposition. In a similar fashion, the results are presented for the collective action variables case by case and then by proposition. The results as summarized in table 12.1 show many of the predicted patterns. Looking down the columns, a "P" indicates that the characteristic the workers mentioned in that campaign was one we expected. An "A" means that the workers did not mention that characteristic but the result is the one we expected in that situation. Tables 12.2 and 12.3 give the results of the statistical tests on which the conclusions in table 12.1 are based. These tables show the frequency with which a judge answered "yes" or "no" to the question of whether a worker mentioned a factor in his or her interview. We considered a factor to have statistical significance if we were confident that the numbers of judges answering "no" and "yes" were sufficiently different for us to make generalizations that a worker did or did not mention a factor in his or her interview.

Individual Readiness: Case-by-Case Results

In the three cases in which the union won the election, the workers we interviewed identified at least three of the characteristics as being present. In case Anne, the workers expressed dissatisfaction with their level of security and respect as well as frustration because something had been taken

TABLE 12.2. Support for Research Propositions, Individual Readiness Level

| | Wins/Supporters | | | | | | Loss/ Supporters | | Loss/ Opposers | |
| | Anne | | Basil | | Clara | | David | | | |
Factor	N	Chi-square	N	Chi-square	N	Chi-square	N	Chi-square	N	Chi-square
Pay deprivation										
Yes	208	1.53	72	30.88[a]	61	38.63[a]	47	2.89[a]	68	39.2[a]
No	234		19		9		65		12	
Security deprivation										
Yes	395	273.99[a]	35	4.84[b]	53	18.51[a]	44	5.14[b]	72	51.2[a]
No	47		56		17		68		8	
Respect deprivation										
Yes	401	293.21[a]	44	.10	62	41.66[a]	94	51.57[a]	72	51.2[a]
No	41		47		8		18		8	
Recent decrease										
Yes	392	264.62[a]	33	6.87[b]	59	32.91[a]	59	.32	65	31.25[a]
No	50		58		11		53		15	
No voice										
Yes	292	45.61[a]	65	16.71[a]	53	18.51[a]	74	11.57[a]	54	9.8[a]
No	150		26		17		38		26	
Calculation										
Yes	237	2.32	78	46.45[a]	51	14.63[a]	96	57.14[a]	49	4.05[a]
No	205		13		19		16		31	
Fear										
Fear	168	25.42[b]	44	.10	22	9.66[b]	71	8.04[a]	1	76.05[b]
No	274		47		48		41		79	

[a] Significant at p>.05; critical value of Chi-square = 3.84.
[b] Significant p>.05 in direction opposite that predicted.

away or they were ignored in some prior effort to be heard by management. In case Basil, worker expectations were not met on pay. They too had been ignored in the past and calculated that the benefits of union membership outweighed its costs. In case Clara, the state of mobilization was high since expectations were not met with regard to pay, security, or respect. In this case the workers expressed anger in response to experiencing recent decreases in pay or benefits and at having no mechanism to get management's attention. These workers were also ready to take aggressive action after calculating the net benefits of unionization.

In the case of the union loss, David, the workers' responses strongly supported our propositions. The supporters felt deprivation because they lacked respect, had been ignored in prior efforts to speak out, and calculated that union membership had benefits. Those voting against the union had experienced no deprivation, no recent decreases in benefits, none of the frustration of being ignored, and had not calculated that the benefits of joining a union outweighed the costs. Although those supporting the union expressed the expected lack of fear of punishment, there was no support for our expectation that those opposing the union would fear reprisals. In fact, the results for the opposers were overwhelmingly in the opposite direction.

Individual Readiness: Proposition Results

The other way to study our results is by focusing on the propositions rather than the cases. Looking proposition by proposition in table 12.1, we find consistent results. Pay deprivation was experienced among union supporters in two campaigns in which the union won but was not experienced among opposers in the campaign that lost. This finding provides reasonably strong support for our proposition on this point—namely, pay deprivation exists among union supporters but not among opposers.

Security deprivation was experienced among supporters in cases Anne and Clara but not among opposers in case David. Respect deprivation was experienced among supporters in cases Anne, Clara, and David and not among opposers in case David. Looking at the whole pattern as to deprivation, we find *some* deprivation among supporters in each case and none among opposers. These findings support the model's overall thesis that experiencing some deprivation facilitates the decision to support a union but that finding all three kinds of deprivation in one particular case should not be expected and is not necessary.

The perception that their benefits had recently been decreased was expressed among supporters in cases Anne and Clara and not among opposers in case David. A calculation favoring the union was found among supporters in cases Basil, Clara, and David and not among opposers in case David.

As to fear of punishment for supporting the union, we find anomalous results, as we have in other settings. That is, we find results opposite the predicted direction among supporters in cases Anne and Clara and among opposers in case David. One possibility is that this response is especially susceptible to a social desirability bias. Opposers may be reluctant to express fear as the motivation for their response. Being averse to the employer may cause employees to believe both that they need the protection of a union and that the employer is bad enough to violate the law and punish them.

Some verbatim quotations from the interviews help personalize the importance of deprivation in pay and respect and the powerful emotions that deprivation can elicit:

> Pay: "Well, I don't think it's right. We doing the same job and they [other workers in the same firm at other locations] getting $8 something an hour and we're doing the same job and getting less, and I don't think it's right."

Respect and lack of effective voice: [If unionized] "we have a voice. They have to stop and listen. They may not listen very good, but they have to stop and recognize us. We have never been recognized."

Respect: [I supported the union] "because I hated to see people dominated and treated like, well, like animals really."

Respect: "I think they are concerned with . . . total control and all the employees being at their mercy."

Anger: "The way [management] was treating everybody. I just got angry. And I just got so I didn't really care."

Anger: [When terminated by a supervisor] "I felt like killing him. I'm sure I would love to. You feel like crying."

Collective Action: Case-by-Case Results

Table 12.1 also summarizes the case-by-case results for the collective action variables considered in the study. When one views the results in the cases at the collective level as set out in table 12.1 and supported statistically by the data in table 12.3, several conclusions are suggested. As to union wins, it appears that in case Basil good relationships existed between workers in a solid, cohesive group. There was also effective leadership, lending saliency and direction to the organizing campaign. Case Clara provides support for our propositions that predict that in wins there will be no belief that unions are wrong, the presence of solidarity among workers, belief in the instrumentality of the union, a dramatic event, and good union leaders. In case Anne, there was support for this same set of propositions.

In the case of the union loss, we find generally strong support for our propositions in the responses of the union opposers but not in those of the union supporters. This may reflect a failure among the supporters to have accurately perceived the general views of the workers.

Collective Action: Proposition Results

Our expectations were confirmed for many of the propositions. Unions were not often seen as wrong when unions won but were so judged by those who voted against them in the losing campaign. Getting along well with each other and seeing themselves as having interests different from those of managers were associated with winning.

In two of the three cases in which the union won, the union was seen as instrumental in solving the workers' problems; this was not the case among the "no" voters in the case in which the union lost. The same exact pattern occurred when there was a dramatic event on which the campaign was based.

TABLE 12.3. Support for Research Propositions, Collective Action Level

							Loss/ Supporters		Loss/ Opposers	
			Wins/Supporters							
	Anne		Basil		Clara		David			
Factor	N	Chi-square	N	Chi-square	N	Chi-square	N	Chi-square	N	Chi-square
General fear										
Yes	149	46.91[a]	39	1.86	13	27.66[a]	54	.14[a]	18	24.2[a]
No	293		52		57		58		62	
Unions are wrong										
Yes	292	45.61[b]	40	1.33	46	6.91[b]	33	18.89[a]	65	31.25[b]
No	150		51		24		79		15	
Solidarity/cohesion										
Yes	272	23.54[b]	60	9.24[b]	53	18.51[b]	50	1.29	27	8.45[a]
No	170		31		17		62		53	
Instrumentality										
Yes	400	289.96[b]	90	87.04[b]	60	35.71[b]	31	23.32[a]	63	26.45[b]
No	42		1		10		81		17	
Dramatic event										
Yes	362	179.92[b]	28	13.46[a]	45	5.71[b]	53	.32	73	54.45[b]
No	80		63		25		59		7	
Union leadership										
Yes	319	86.91[b]	80	52.31[b]	59	32.91[b]	43	6.04[a]	51	6.05[b]
No	123		11		11		69		29	

[a] Significant p>.05 in direction opposite that predicted.
[b] Significant at p>.05; critical value of Chi-square = 3.84.

Our predictions concerning leadership were the most strongly supported. In the three cases in which the union won, those interviewed frequently mentioned the benefit of good leadership in helping the union win the election. In contrast, those voting "no" were not convinced that good leadership had been displayed.

At the collective level, our results as to fear of punishment for supporting the union are, once again, anomalous. They are all in the opposite direction from what we predicted, significantly so for supporters in cases Anne and Clara and for opposers in case David. At the collective action level of study, solidarity was the critical variable held in common by all forms of analysis in the highly contested cases. For the uncontested case, the instrumentality of the union was singularly significant.

Again, some quotations are offered to emphasize the importance of this factor:

Instrumentality: "I believe [unions] are good for employees, the working people, because you need a voice in what you are doing. And that is the only way you get people to come together so the voice is loud enough to be heard. One man walking in alone can't do nothing."

Instrumentality: "I thought we voted for the union . . . because we thought we deserved a little better. Not necessarily that we wasn't doing well, but we could do a little better. I thought the union would help me out a whole lot and give me better working conditions, and maybe higher pay."

Instrumentality (lack of it): "I was against the union because it did cost and [I] couldn't think of any good that could come of my joining, and anyways, what good have unions ever done anybody?" "Kinda sounds like getting married, don't it? Permanent things is hard to accept, especially when hardly any of us has ever been in a union before."

Unions Are Wrong and Instrumentality: "I was against the union mainly because the company was so strong against it. They know what it takes to stay in business, and they said the union was not good for their business. That's enough for me. All the people in town felt the same way; the newspaper, other stores, even the Chamber of Commerce people who know business and what's good for the town were against it."

Conclusions and Strategy Implications

Combining the results reported here with those in the larger research project suggests some broad conclusions. In all union wins, significant levels of deprivation exist among workers in at least one category. In the contested campaigns in which unions won, deprivation was more widespread. In the case in which the union lost, deprivation was not shared by the interviewees. Those who did not express union support did not think they were in a general state of deprivation. This is generally supportive of the predictions that deprivation is associated with increased readiness to take aggressive action. For the organizer, this finding implies that the actual content of the message delivered as part of an organizing campaign does matter. That the chance of winning a campaign improves when messages focus on deprivation in the areas of security, dignity, and respect is supported here and is consistent with the findings of Bronfenbrenner reported earlier.

At the level of individual readiness to take aggressive action, substantial support is found for the proposition that deprivation is associated with voting for the union and actively working on its behalf. There is also fairly substantial support for the hypothesis that maintaining solidarity with supervisors is associated with voting against the union.[2] We find some support

---

2. The full results for the individual-level analysis from the large sample survey are under review elsewhere.

for the hypothesis that anger at the employer makes voting and working for the union more likely and for the hypothesis that a belief that unions are wrong makes these behaviors less likely. The exception is the uncontested case in which, as was predicted, deprivation was less apparent and less of a requirement for readiness. In this case, only calculation of the benefits of voting for the union was required. This finding reinforces the point that good strategy includes intensive personal contact but that there is no "one size fits all" campaign theme, method, or approach. A multidimensional approach, tailored to the local situation, is imperative.

Some of our other findings have more practical and strategic implications for organizers. Looking across the cases, we see some evidence that different variables may be important in different settings. We are struck by the singularity of case Basil as one in which anger at the employer was not associated with working on behalf of the union. This is a rare case in that there were no emotional issues in the group and the employer did not resist the union in an aggressive way. In this case, we appear to have had a nearly pure rational situation in which the primary issue that distinguished union supporters from opposers was one the National Labor Relations Board has traditionally favored—unionization as a reasoned choice by employees. In the other cases, both the wins and the losses, it appears that although employee estimates of instrumentality were important, there was more evidence of the effects of anger. This distinction between situations with volatile issues and those in which the energy for the campaign might have to be provided or focused is one that is well recognized among union organizers but has not received much attention in the scholarly literature.

Organizers have typically been called into shops, and in these cases the campaigns were purely opportunistic. The organizing effort was not always part of a grand strategy aimed at penetrating into a new industry or part of a defensive strategy based on acquisitions, mergers, internationalization of ownership, or other business decisions. If indeed unions are to be more strategic in running targeted campaigns designed to increase union power in emerging industries and involved in changing the character of business organizations, running a tactical campaign that is already "hot" because of the issues is going to be significantly different from running one in which conveying a message of need and instrumentality is the educational responsibility of the organizer. Even workers who are not angry or highly emotional in response to a specific management act can still be organized. The task in such a case is to show by clear and convincing rational arguments that workers, even those who have been frustrated by prior efforts to influence management, can benefit from having a collective action voice in their destiny.

The workplace of the future, and thus the campaign battleground, will bear little resemblance to the traditional union setting. Companies will not have traditional industry identity. Tasks and training will be much different. Traditional craft loyalty may not exist. With so little in common and fewer opportunities to share concerns and problems, organizers must find and use the strategically crafted message of respect and dignity.

Findings from the most compelling campaign we researched (David), in which we questioned both opposers and supporters of the union, indicate that the most clear distinction between the groups was that supporters described themselves as having no voice and made rational calculations concerning the benefits versus the cost of unionization. Those who thought these issues were problems in the workplace voted for the union. When those factors were not part of the workers' description of the issues and beliefs, they voted "no."

Another potentially beneficial conclusion to be drawn from this theory and program of research might be the differences between appropriate strategies for these situations. The volatility and unpredictable nature of individual variables such as fear make them difficult to deal with. It seems that campaigns conducted on such an emotional level have the prospect of backfiring. In cooler situations, more likely encountered in strategic campaigns, capitalizing on emotional variables is not even necessary for union success. Finding more narrowly focused areas of deprivation on which to concentrate and spending time on the positive aspects of solidarity, the calculation of effectiveness, and instrumentality may be more predictable and thus safer with equal effectiveness. Knowing that economic calculation is a path that works and spending some time deciding how much emotional heat is required may pay dividends to the organizer in the long run.

Yet another conclusion of this study is that organizers need to be sure to take advantage of the natural coalitions that exist among the members of the unit. The union should recognize minority demographics, or even subregional differences, biases, or prejudices. Our experiences indicate that management is certainly quick to take advantage of such similarities or differences and to exploit the feelings that might be created to enhance its own campaign themes. This point promises to be more important in organizing the workplace of the future. If unions are targeting "bigger" units with multiple skills—companies, industries, or products—there must be something to promote the commonality of interests that ties members together. If even a small portion of the changes predicted for the workplace of the future are correct, traditional bargaining units may not survive long enough to support successful campaigns. Changing technology and responsibilities may negate any sense of identity and loyalty that are accepted today. The link must be made between the organization and service without the benefit of trade, task, or company. Many of those voting in favor of the union indicated they expected social value from joining others with whom they shared common interests. Those voting against unionization often indicated they felt no solidarity with their coworkers and even that they felt they had more in common with supervisors or company interests.

Another implication of the research may be a caution to those employing the organizing rather than the servicing model of unionism. Although messages about empowerment and self-reliance may be excellent for union members and members of the local's administration, they may not be totally effective with workers during the middle of a campaign or as part of the organizing strategy. The message that the workers *are* the union and that informed workers rather than the professional staff should conduct union affairs may be too much of a departure from the concept of instrumentality. Such a message might be taken as an indication that the union provides no benefit and decrease the likelihood of a successful outcome. It is important to note that the only single variable to show up as expected in every case was frustration with prior efforts to gain effective voice. The workers who supported a union had already tried to organize on their own and were frustrated by management's indifference to their cause. An organizer whose message is "You can do it" is not likely to be embraced. We found differences among union professionals in their approach depending on their positions. Staff representatives, doing many jobs and not exclusively organizing, often conveyed sentiments consistent with the organizing model. Full time-organizers on the campaign rarely used this theme but talked about what the union had done elsewhere and that training in union governance would come after the first contract.

Another of the pragmatic conclusions related to organizing strategy might be that union organizers, on reflection after a loss, should be as attentive to the analysis and opinions expressed by their enemies (opposers) in a campaign as they are to their friends (supporters). In the loss case we studied, the supporters were wrong about the extent to which pro-union perspectives were held throughout the workforce and may have deluded themselves when reflecting on what went wrong in the campaign. Their hopeful recollections may distort the process of deciding what went wrong and actually misguide any follow-up efforts made in the same unit. This is especially true in a long campaign in which, as the election date approaches, the inside organizers close the ranks and surround themselves with only those whom they can count on to share their views. This inward spiraling of the group with whom the professionals circulate might cause them to be fooled about the extent to which opinions are shared concerning the state of union support, acceptance of the themes of the campaign, and alignment with the union agenda.

We suggest that all those involved in a campaign write independent reports and assessments. As was done in this research, those not directly involved in the campaign should be called on to interpret the results and offer their evaluations. A culture tolerant of constructive criticism must become the norm.

Determining effective strategy for a union organizing campaign is a complex issue. The workplace and management tactics are changing rapidly. Our research indicates that workers suffering from a lack of respect and security will often support the formation of a union. This support will likely increase if they have been frustrated in prior efforts to speak out and influence their treatment. Those trying to influence workers should learn to measure these characteristics and design situation-specific messages that appeal to these workers. These personal messages must be delivered through personal interaction and emphasize the value of organizational commitment.

Chapter 13

Winning Hearts and Minds in the Era of Employee-Involvement Programs

James Rundle

The current impact of employee-involvement programs (EIPs) on union organizing has mostly been ignored in the debate over the future of the "company union" prohibition in section 8(a)(2) of the National Labor Relations Act. This portion of the act has been the target of employer organizations and their Republican allies in Congress, who seek to weaken section 8(a)(2) in an attempt to insulate employee-involvement programs from being challenged under the law as forms of company unions.

Whether the Republicans eventually prevail or not, and despite a few high-profile cases in which the NLRB struck down employee-involvement programs, the trend is toward more, not fewer, of these programs. It is important, therefore, that unions assess the extent to which EIPs pose a threat to union organizing and the strategies that organizers might use when they encounter such programs in organizing campaigns. It is these issues that this chapter will address.

Union Organizing and the Ban on Company Unions

The term "employee-involvement program" is used here to encompass a variety of employer-initiated group activities, including quality circles, teams, and the like. They are legally suspect because those that "deal with" issues over which a union would have the right to bargain qualify as "labor

The author thanks Kate Bronfenbrenner for valuable advice and assistance throughout the project, Katie Briggs for excellent research assistance, Vincent O'Brien for use of the AFL-CIO's database on NLRB certification elections, and the Institute for the Study of Labor Organizations, the George Meany Center, AFL-CIO, for funding this work.

organizations" under section 2(5) of the act. Under section 8(a)(2), such organizations are illegal if the employer interferes with, assists, or dominates them. Inasmuch as employee-involvement programs are initiated by employers and usually continue only with the employers' approval and participation, many that would qualify as labor organizations (because of the issues they deal with) are likely to violate the law.

The ban was enacted precisely because of the impact employer-dominated labor organizations, often called "company unions," had on union organizing. After Congress passed the National Industrial Recovery Act (NIRA) in 1933, many employers established "Employee Representation Plans" (ERPs), which, like the current employee-involvement programs, engaged employees in group discussions of workplace issues in a forum controlled by the employer. Section 7(a) of the NIRA gave workers the right to "self-organize," but it was also understood to permit employers to establish ERPs. ERPs proved so effective in thwarting union organizing campaigns that when the National Labor Relations Act was passed two years later, section 8(a)(2), banning all such organizations, was considered the key to enforcing the right to organize (Kohler 1986:530).

Section 8(a)(2) had its intended effect. Even the Steel Workers Organizing Committee, whose successful infiltration of some ERPs is sometimes cited as evidence that such employee committees actually aid organizing, called upon the NLRB to help it get rid of ERPs that it could not take over (Green 1994). Many of the Board's early decisions struck down ERPs, but eventually the number of these cases declined, presumably because most employers had stopped using company unionism as an antiunion tactic.

In recent years, despite the growth of employee-involvement programs and well-publicized concerns about their legal vulnerability, these cases continue to be quite rare (Rundle 1994). From 1972 to 1993, the NLRB disestablished employee committees only fifty-eight times. In 76 percent of these cases, an organizing campaign was in progress when the charges were filed, and in all but one of these cases, the employer was also found guilty of other unfair labor practices. In nearly all the other cases, a union already existed and the employer was refusing to bargain, dealing with employees instead through its own committees. Thus, the function of the law appears to be the same as it was in 1935, except that employee committees have become a minor area of activity. As we shall see, however, using company unionism as an antiunion device is far from a minor employer activity.

Though there has been a long-simmering debate over the legal status of employee-involvement committees, movement toward actually weakening section 8(a)(2) did not begin in earnest until the Clinton administration appointed the Dunlop Commission to review the nation's labor laws. Most of the commissioners, and their legal counsel, were already on record advocating change in section 8(a)(2). In its recommendations (Commission on the Future of Worker-Management Relations 1994b) and its fact-finding report (Commission 1994a), the commission discussed both employee-involvement programs and union organizing. Yet the commission never considered the relationship between the two, focusing instead on the extent of EIPs, their benefits for business, and whether section 8(a)(2) was a threat to EIPs.

This failure was extraordinarily ironic. Not only was section 8(a)(2) written specifically to protect union organizing, not only was *Electromation* (which had brought the 8(a)(2) debate to a head) a modern example of a case in which the law protected union organizing, not only was the commission appointed by a Democratic administration supported by the AFL-CIO, but in the end, the commission concluded that section 8(a)(2) should be weakened in exchange for improvements in organizing rights. It did so without inquiring whether one recommendation might undo the other.

The Impact of EIPs on Organizing

There is considerable evidence that employee-involvement programs inhibit union organizing, both by reducing union win rates in certification elections and by preventing unions from even mounting campaigns. The most elusive effect to measure is prevention. How many potential organizing campaigns never reached the petitioning stage because an EIP provided an effective deterrent? Jack Fiorito, Christopher Lowman, and Forrest D. Nelson (1987) show such an effect indirectly using data from the 1983 Conference Board Survey, which asked "leading U.S. companies" about their human resource policies, including employee involvement, and about union organizing campaigns in their facilities. They found that employee participation and communication policies (but not autonomous work teams) reduced the rate of organizing of new facilities. These factors were also effective in reducing union win rates in certification elections at all facilities.

Fiorito, Lowman, and Nelson (1987) described what they found as "union substitution," as opposed to "union suppression," but Guillermo Grenier showed that this can be a misleading characterization. In a compelling case study, he showed how quality circles were used to identify and harass pro-union employees, pit worker against worker, and "socialize the workforce into accepting the anti-union message" (1987:xviii). Initially a believer in "enlightened" and "innovative" practices, which he had come to the firm to study, Grenier eventually exposed the company's manipulative practices, at some personal risk. He rejected the notion that he had observed an aberration, pointing out that the company—Johnson and Johnson—was a supposed leader in "progressive" personnel practices and that the connections he found between employee involvement and anti-unionism had a long history in industrial practice and in academic research.

Bronfenbrenner (1993) studied the impact of union and employer campaign tactics on certification election outcomes in units of fifty employees or more, based on surveys of union organizers and while controlling for demographic and workplace characteristics. Employee-involvement programs were present in 7 percent of the campaigns. Where they existed, the probability of a union victory was decreased by 22 percent after controlling for other factors. A subsequent study (Bronfenbrenner and Juravich 1995b) found a 26 percent decrease in union win rates due to employee involvement in the public sector. This latter study addressed only programs which had been established prior to the organizing campaign.

My own study extends this aspect of the earlier work through a new survey of union organizers about campaigns for which a certification petition was filed in 1994. It differs from the earlier study in focusing on the employee-involvement programs themselves, as well as the union responses to them. By also including variables that proved to be significant in the previous study, this study controls for the impact of demographic, workplace, and tactical factors.

The study was designed to characterize the kinds of employee involvement union organizers are encountering, to determine whether the proportion of campaigns in which organizers encounter employee involvement programs has increased since 1986, to determine the impact of the presence of employee-involvement programs on the outcome of organizing campaigns, to determine whether the effectiveness of union tactics shown in the earlier study is influenced by the presence or absence of employee involvement, to assess whether unions have used certain tactics in response to employee involvement and, if so, with what success, and to assess whether the ban on company unions in section 8(a)(2) played a role in the campaigns. In addition, by including petitions that were withdrawn, it was possible to examine whether employee-involvement programs had an impact on withdrawals.

Methods

A random sample of 200 union organizing campaigns was drawn from all 1994 NLRB elections in units of fifty or more eligible voters. Also included were 204 campaigns for which a petition had been withdrawn. These units also contained fifty or more eligible voters. The database was compiled by the AFL-CIO from NLRB records.

Surveys were sent to the lead organizers of each campaign and were returned for 135 election campaigns, for a response rate of 68 percent. In addition, thirty of the "withdrawal" campaigns turned out to have had elections and were included in the election data, increasing the total to 165 elections.

Many of the remaining withdrawal campaigns were discarded because the withdrawals occurred for reasons having nothing to do with the campaigns. For example, some turned out to be raids on other unions that were called off by the international. In other cases, the NLRB ruled that the employees were independent contractors. Eliminating such cases left only thirty-two surveys for campaigns that ended in withdrawals because the union concluded that it did not have enough support to win an election. Because of this small sample size, the findings discussed in this chapter are based entirely on the campaigns that went to an election.

The questions covered the type of unit in which the election was being held, the unit's demographics, employer campaign tactics, whether the unit had previously been organized or petitioned for, whether other units of the employer were under union contract, whether the unit in which the election was being held was different from the one for which the union had filed, union campaign tactics, and whether there was "an employee-involvement, quality, or team program in effect." These questions were drawn from Bronfenbrenner's study (1993).

Because the sample was smaller and because of the constraint of including a substantial section on employee-involvement committees, fewer variables were used than in Bronfenbrenner's study. These were selected primarily on the basis of significance in her study. In some cases, the responses were converted into new variables. For example, Bronfenbrenner found that the proportion of women in the unit was not related to union win rates in a direct way. When the unit is predominantly female, however, it is clear that the win rate is higher. Thus, this factor was measured as units having 75 percent or more women. For minorities, however, the relationship with win rates is much more direct, and the variable was simply the proportion of people of color in the unit.

If there was an employee-involvement program, organizers were asked how, if at all, the union responded to the program. They were also asked about the particular characteristics of the program, including which of a list of issues was discussed in meetings, how participants were chosen, the role of management and consultants in the program, and whether the program had gone into effect before or after the union campaign started or before or after expressions of employee discontent. Organizers were also asked to estimate the percentage of the bargaining unit that participated in the program and how much time was spent in meetings.

Organizer questionnaires have not previously been used to characterize employee-involvement programs that coincide with organizing campaigns.

The use of organizer surveys to describe employer anti-union behavior in organizing campaigns, however, is well established in the literature. Supervisor training in anti-union tactics, supervisor one-on-one campaigning, numbers of captive-audience meetings, employer threats and promises, and other tactics, as reported by lead organizers, have all been used to characterize organizing campaigns (Lawler and West 1985; Bronfenbrenner 1993 and 1994; Bronfenbrenner and Juravich 1995b). The information elicited about EIPs was very similar to information reported about anti-union tactics in those previous studies. From discussions with organizers in phone interviews, it was clear that employee-involvement committees, where they existed, were usually monitored closely and discussed regularly by the organizing committee, just as other employer activities were.

Some organizers volunteered more detail than was required by the survey. The results reported here, however, are based only on the survey questions, which asked about "specific actions and behaviors," as John J. Lawler and Robin West advocated as a means of limiting the likelihood of distortion and bias (1985:412). There were slightly more missing data on some of these items than on the other items in the survey, particularly the finer details, such as how employee representatives had been chosen and the amount of time spent in meetings.

Results

Employee-involvement programs were in existence in 32 percent of the union organizing campaigns surveyed. This rate is far higher than it was eight years earlier, when Bronfenbrenner found them in only 7 percent of all campaigns.[1]

Differences between Campaigns When There Are and Are Not EIPs

The difference in the union win rates between campaigns in which employee-involvement programs existed and those in which they did not is striking: the union won in 48 percent of all the elections when there were no EIPs but in only 30 percent of all the elections when there were EIPs. There are many other differences between these two types of campaigns, however, besides the existence of EIPs that are known to have an impact on election outcomes (table 13.1). Most of these differences favor the union in campaigns without EIPs. EIPs are more common in larger units and in blue-collar/production and maintenance units and less common in service

---

1. The frequency of employee-involvement programs in the withdrawal sample was almost identical (31 percent). As noted earlier, however, the sample size was too small to be useful for analysis.

TABLE 13.1. Effect of Presence or Absence of Employee Involvement (EI) on
Election Campaigns

Independent Variable	All Campaigns	Means EI	No EI
Unit Background			
Unit size	182	238	157
Blue collar/production and maintenance	.63	.72	.59
Skilled craft	.04	.04	.05
Professional or professional/technical	.04	.02	.04
Clerical/technical or other white collar	.02	.00	.03
Service and maintenance	.16	.07	.21
Wall-to-wall	.12	.17	.09
Manufacturing (versus service sector)	.72	.83	.67
Previous union election	.30	.35	.27
Other units of employer unionized	.38	.41	.36
Proportion female	.39	.42	.36
Unit more than 75% female	.19	.15	.21
Percentage people of color	.28	.23	.31
Average wage	$8.74	$9.00	$8.54
Average age	33 years	34 years	33 years
Unit changed after petition	.25	.25	.25
Employer Campaign			
Hired management consultant or law firm	.87	.93	.85
Held captive-audience meetings	.93	.98	.91
Number of meetings	10	9	11
Held five or more meetings	.64	.70	.61
Sent five or more letters to workers' homes	.24	.30	.22
Supervisors campaigned one-on-one	.76	.78	.76
Positive changes in management	.38	.38	.39
Unscheduled raises granted	.24	.28	.23
Improved benefits	.28	.25	.28
Discharged union activists	.28	.32	.26
Number discharged	2.7	2.1	3.2
Proportion reinstatement before election	.04	.08	.02
Laid off workers	.11	.07	.13
Used the media to campaign against union	.07	.07	.07
Used bribes or special favors	.42	.48	.39
Held social events with antiunion message	.27	.24	.28
Assisted an employee antiunion committee	.50	.65	.44
Number of employer antiunion tactics	4.7	5.1	4.5
Union Campaign			
Representative rank-and-file committee	.44	.43	.44
House called at least 50% of the unit	.39	.35	.41
Held at least 10 small-group meetings	.39	.41	.38
Held solidarity days (buttons/T-shirts)	.56	.61	.54
Contract survey at least 70% one-on-one	.21	.20	.22
Held rallies	.41	.36	.43
Conducted job actions	.13	.19	.10
Used the media	.12	.09	.13
Involved community or labor solidarity groups	.30	.39	.25
At least 10 volunteers from other units	.17	.22	.14
Number of union tactics	3.3	3.4	3.2
Election Outcomes			
Win rate	.42	.30	.48
Proportion "yes" vote	.48	.44	.50

and maintenance units. Likewise, EIPs are more prevalent in manufacturing units than in service-sector units. Correspondingly, the proportion of units that were predominantly female and the percentage of people of color were lower in campaigns involving EIPs. Campaigns in which there had been a previous election also were more likely to involve EIPs. All of these differences mean that even without any impact of the EIPs themselves, we would expect unions to be less successful in campaigns in which EIPs exist. The only unit background factor favoring the union in campaigns with EIPs was the existence of other unionized units of the same employer.

Employers that used EIPs also ran more aggressive antiunion campaigns. The rhetoric of employee involvement may be about "voice" and "empowerment," but when workers try to organize, the employers who preach such rhetoric are the most likely to use bribes and special favors to win votes, to send barrages of anti-union letters to workers' homes, and to fire union activists. This is consistent with my earlier findings (1994) about EIPs disestablished by the National Labor Relations Board. In nearly every case in which the employer was found to have an illegal employee organization, the employer had also committed other unfair labor practices. This finding is also consistent with Grenier's (1987) view that the intense anti-unionism he observed in the quality circles of an "enlightened" employer was no aberration.

The unions ran remarkably similar campaigns whether EIPs existed or not, at least with respect to the union campaign tactics found by Bronfenbrenner (1993) to have a statistically significant effect on election outcomes. As we shall see, however, the impact of these tactics on union success was very different depending on whether an EIP existed or not. In addition, most unions tried various ways of counteracting or co-opting the EIPs, and the union's approach to the use of these tactics also had an important impact on union success.

Characteristics of the EIPs

Twenty-eight percent of the employee-involvement programs encountered in the organizing campaigns we studied were started after the campaign was begun (table 13.2). When the EIPs predated the campaigns, the union win rate (32 percent) was much higher than in campaigns in which the EIPs were started after the organizing drive was begun (20 percent). Yet this win rate was still much lower than the win rate when there were no EIPs (48 percent). It should be remembered, however, that a screening process had already taken place. As noted in the introduction to this chapter, other evidence shows that the existence of an employee-involvement program can prevent a union organizing campaign from starting. The only preexisting EIPs we evaluate here are those that failed to have this effect.

On average, organizers reported that more than a third of the employees

TABLE 13.2. Characteristics of Employee-Involvement Programs

Variable	Number of Campaigns (out of 54)	Mean	Union Win Rate (Rate When Absent)
Employee-involvement program went into effect:			
before organizing campaign began	37	.24	.32 (−)
after organizing campaign began	15	.69	.20 (−)
either before or after	54	1.00	.30 (.48)
Proportion of unit participating	—	.37	—
50% or more unit employees participated	18	.35	.22 (.33)
Hours per month in meetings during campaign	—	7.3 hours	—
Five or more hours per month spent in meetings	22	.41	.23 (.34)
Consultant used to start and/or run program	31	.57	.26 (.35)
Management participated in meetings	54	1.00	—
Issues discussed in meetings:			
Quality of product or service	27	.51	.30 (.31)
Efficiency of work process/new technology	29	.55	.28 (.33)
Mandatory subjects of bargaining	48	.89	.33 (.00)
Pay	21	.40	.14 (.41)
Union organizing campaign	33	.62	.27 (.35)
Actions management took on issues discussed			
Made important improvements	3	.06	.00 (.32)
Made minor improvements	17	.32	.29 (.31)
Took little or no action	33	.62	.33 (.25)
Employees served as leaders	32	.53	.32 (.28)
Leaders chosen by management	18	.69	.28 (.38)
Management selected from volunteers	5	.19	.60 (.24)
Employer set up elections for leaders	2	.06	0
Employees chose leaders in their own way	1	.03	0
Leaders were mostly pro-union	7	.23	.57 (.26)
Leaders were mixed pro- and antiunion	5	.16	.20 (.31)
Leaders were mostly antiunion	18	.62	.22 (.33)

participated in employee-involvement meetings, but the variation was great, ranging from 5 to 100 percent. Paul Osterman (1994), in his study of the extent of "workplace transformation," used 50 percent participation by "core employees" as a cut-off for "substantial use" of employee-involvement practices. Thirty-five percent of the EIPs in the current study met this criterion, and unions were less successful among those that did.

In many cases, much time was spent in these meetings. Again, the average fails to capture the tremendous variation in meeting time, including two campaigns for which organizers reported that employees spent forty hours per month in such meetings (the union won in both campaigns despite intense employer opposition). Accordingly, a variable was created to represent five or more hours per month, or more than an hour per week. Using this measure, we see that in more than 40 percent of the EIPs employees were in meetings for at least that long and that this variable was associated with a lower union win rate.

Consultants were used to set up and/or to run a majority of the EIPs, and those programs were associated with lower win rates than programs in which no consultant was involved. A variety of questions was asked about the role of these consultants, but no patterns emerged. In any case, that level of analysis probably requires more cases than this sample permits.

Did the EIPs constitute illegal "company unions" under section 8(a)(2)? Organizers consistently said that work-load, hours, grievances, health and safety, and other bargainable issues were discussed. This suggests that the programs would meet the definition of a "labor organization" (section 2(5)), although the Board has tried to carve out a lower threshold for the "dealing with" criterion that might exempt some.[2]

Organizers also reported that managers participated in most of the employee-involvement programs and that when they did, they usually played active roles, including setting agendas and running meetings. This suggests that most of these programs would also be likely to meet the criteria for employer interference or domination under section 8(a)(2).

The various subjects of bargaining discussed in employee-involvement committees for the most part appeared to have no connection with union organizing success, probably because where one topic was not discussed, another one was. Two exceptions emerged, however. When committees discussed pay, the union win rate was substantially lower, and 40 percent did so. When committees discussed the union organizing campaign, as they did in the Grenier case study (1994) and in 62 percent of the cases in our study, the union also lost more frequently.

A majority of EIPs had leaders who were bargaining unit employees. In almost a fifth of these cases, the organizers did not know how the leaders were chosen. From the others, it is clear that democracy does not reign. Even elections run by the employer were extremely rare, and in only one case did the employees choose their own representatives through their own process, as the NLRA requires when the organizations "deal with" mandatory subjects. This is further evidence that the EIPs were dominated by management, in violation of section 8(a)(2). It also suggests that these organizations violated the Labor-Management Reporting and Disclosure Act, which requires, among other things, that the leaders of employee organizations be elected directly by the people they represent. In most of the campaigns, the organizers' responses to questions about the EIPs suggest that the programs might be shown to be illegal if they were challenged.

2. *E.I. DuPont de Nemours*, 311 NLRB 893 (1993).

The organizers reported that the leaders of EIPs were usually against the union. In the rare cases in which the leaders were pro-union, the win rate was very high, but there were only seven such cases. I shall return to this point, as well as the legal issues, when I discuss the union response to employee-involvement programs.

Union Campaign Tactics and Employee Involvement

Do the rank-and-file-intensive campaign tactics shown by Bronfenbrenner to be so critical to union organizing success work just as well when the employer establishes an EIP, or is an altogether different approach required? The most important result of this study is that not only do those tactics work but they are even more important when the employer has an EIP. In table 13.3, campaigns are identified by how many rank-and-file tactics were used. The union win rate is given for each level of tactics, and a comparison is made between campaigns with and without EIPs. When the union uses only a few of the tactics, its chances of winning an election when there is an EIP is vanishingly small. But as the number of tactics increases, the negative impact associated with EIPs is completely overcome.

That EIPs are associated with stronger employer antiunion campaigns means that much of the effect seen in table 13.3 probably reflects the need for stronger union campaigns when employers conduct stronger antiunion campaigns, as Bronfenbrenner (1993) found. That is what unions are up against when they encounter EIPs, but the same tactics that work against other aggressive employer campaigns still work when EIPs are part of the mix. Furthermore, the multivariate analyses that we will examine later (tables 13.5 and 13.7) show that the effectiveness of rank-and-file tactics when there are EIPs hold up even when controlling for employer campaigns and for other factors associated with EIPs.

The response of union organizing campaigns specifically to EIPs shows that win rates also improve when unions respond to EIPs proactively (table 13.4). when union supporters joined employee-involvement committees and

TABLE 13.3. Impact of Rank-and-File Campaign Tactics on Union Win Rates in Presence or Absence of Employee Involvement

Number of Rank-and-File Tactics	Number of Campaigns		Union Win Rate	
	EI	No EI	EI	No EI
Zero or one	5	27	.00	.48
Two or three	26	40	.15	.38
Four or five	15	27	.40	.52
More than five	7	17	.71	.65

TABLE 13.4. Union Campaign Response to Employee Involvement

Union Response	Number of Campaigns Using Response (out of 54)	Union Win Rate (Rate When Not Used)
Ignored the employee-involvement program and stuck to the union's issues	8	.13 (.33)
Promoted the union as a way to engage in employee involvement more effectively or more democratically	34	.35 (.20)
Union supporters joined the committee(s) and used it to promote the union's issues	15	.47 (.23)
Pointed out the undemocratic or manipulative nature of the employee-involvement program	33	.33 (.24)
Said that a union chosen by the employees is the only legitimate representative of the employees	32	.19 (.46)
Explained that the employee-involvement program was illegal (if the union thought it was)	6	.00 (.33)

used them to promote the unions' issues, win rates were more than double the rates when union supporters did not do so.

Some of the effects apparent in table 13.4 result from associations with other factors. Unions that ignored employee-involvement programs and stuck to their own issues also used fewer rank-and-file tactics than average, and unions that got supporters to join the programs also used more rank-and-file tactics than average. When controlling for other factors, the only union response tactic that had a statistically significant impact, positive or negative, was for union supporters to join the EIP and use it to promote their own issues (table 13.5).

Legal Challenges to Employee Involvement

Given that organizers reported employer actions in most of the EIPs that would suggest the programs were illegal, what did the unions (and the NLRB) do about this? The answer is, almost nothing. Unions filed charges against the EIPs in only five campaigns. When organizers were asked why they did not file charges, most thought there were no grounds for a charge or that they could not win a case (table 13.6). The latter may be true. Of the five cases in which the union did file charges, a complaint was issued by the Board in only one case; not a single committee was actually disestablished.

Very few organizers said that they feared that filing a charge would cause a backlash from employees who liked the program. In the five cases in which they did, the union lost anyway.

TABLE 13.5. Impact on Union Win Rate of Union Response to Employee Involvement in Elections Involving EIPs

Independent Variable	Mean or Percentage for Wins (Losses)	Percentage Union Wins (When Absent)	Predicted Impact on Probability of Union Win
Unit size	131 (279)	N.A.	no estimate **
Other units of employer unionized	56 (34)	41 (22)	n.s.
Unit changed after petition	7 (32)	8 (34)	−51% *
Percent people of color	24 (22)	N.A.	n.s.
Unit more than 75% female	18 (13)	38 (28)	+41% *
Average wage	9.25 (8.90)	N.A.	no estimate *
Number of union tactics	4.9 (2.9)	N.A.	+11% for each additional tactic ***
Number of employer antiunion tactics	5.1 (5.2)	N.A.	−6% for each additional tactic **
Employee-involvement program that went into effect after union campaign started	20 (33)	20 (33)	−22% *
Union supporters joined the committee(s) and used it to promote the union's issues	44 (30)	47 (23)	+26% **

* p<0.10, **p<0.05, *** p<0.01.
N.A. = not applicable; n.s. = not significant.

TABLE 13.6. Legal Challenges to Employee Involvement

	Number of Campaigns (out of 54)	Percentage
Union filed charges against EI	5	9
EIP appeared illegal based on responses to questions about issues discussed in programs and management's role	47	87
Regional office (NLRB) issued a complaint	1	2
Reason for not filing a charge against EIP		
Organizer thought there were no grounds or could not win case	22	41
Union feared backlash from employees who liked the program	5	9
Filing a charge might have delayed the election	5	9
No reason to—it wasn't affecting the campaign	7	13

*Impact of Employee Involvement and Union Response Controlling for
Other Factors*

Union win rates were significantly reduced when employee-involvement
programs were put into effect after the union organizing campaigns had
begun, even when controlling for the other factors associated with the programs. The model in table 13.7 estimates that the presence of an EIP reduces
the win rate by 24 percent. Both the union and other employer campaign
tactics, however, are highly significant. On average, each additional rank-
and-file tactic increases the probability of a union victory by 9 percent,
while each additional employer campaign tactic reduces it by an average of
7 percent. Starting the EIP before the organizing drive was begun was also
associated with a lower union win rate, but combining those campaigns
with the ones in which the EIPs were begun after the organizing drives
began rendered the EIP variable nonsignificant.

When the model is applied only to elections in which EIPs existed, EIPs
that went into effect after the organizing drives were begun continued to
show a significant negative impact on union success. When union supporters joined the employee-involvement committee and used it to promote
union issues, however, the probability of a union victory was estimated to

TABLE 13.7. Impact of Employee Involvement on Union Win Rates,
Controlling for Other Factors

Independent Variable	Mean or Percentage for Wins (Losses)	Percentage Union Wins (When Absent)	Predicted Impact on Probability of Union Win
Unit size	143 (188)	N.A.	no estimate *
Other units of employer unionized	41 (35)	46 (39)	n.s.
Unit changed after petition	21 (29)	33 (43)	−15% *
Percentage people of color	31 (26)	N.A.	n.s.
Unit more than 75% female	28 (13)	61 (37)	+19% **
Average wage	8.35 (9.02)	N.A.	n.s.
Number of union tactics	3.8 (3.0)	N.A.	+9% for each additional tactic ***
Number of employer antiunion tactics	4.1 (5.1)	N.A.	−7% for each additional tactic ***
Employee-involvement program that went into effect after union campaign started	19 (32)	20 (33)	−24% *

* $p < 0.10$, ** $p < 0.05$, *** $p < 0.01$.

increase by 24 percent. In addition, the impact of the rank-and-file tactics remained very strong, confirming that what works for organizing generally also works in union campaigns in which EIPs are a factor.

Discussion

The proportion of EIPs found in this study is so much higher than in the Bronfenbrenner study that even if all the unreturned surveys had indicated that there were no such programs, the final proportion would still be three times what it was earlier. Assuming that EIPs prevent some union organizing campaigns from even starting, then the proportion of EIPs would generally have to be higher than it is in the union election campaign sample. Unfortunately, we do not have a reliable measure of the proportion of employment-involvement programs in a comparable population that is not involved in organizing campaigns. The closest we can come to such a figure is probably Osterman's (1994) assessment of the extent of what he called "workplace transformation," which comprised teams, job rotation, employee problem-solving groups, and Total Quality Management (TQM). His study did find a substantially higher rate of employee involvement (meaning all types of transformation except job rotation) than found here (more than two-thirds of the establishments in his sample had at least one type of employee involvement), but it is difficult to assess the comparability of his sample.[3] One of Osterman's findings is suggestive, however. To eliminate establishments in which the workplace transformation might have been only token, Osterman excluded those in which fewer than 50 percent of the employees participated in an EIP. This reduced the proportion of programs by only 20 percent (from approximately 70 percent to 58 percent). In my sample, the same criterion cut the proportion of EIPs in existence during organizing campaigns by 65 percent. In other words, EIPs in organizing campaigns were at the low end of the range of employee participation levels. This, together with the lower win rates found when the EIP participation rate was 50 percent or more, suggests that the workplaces in which unions failed to get a foothold were those that used employee involvement the most extensively.

---

3. Osterman's sample was constructed from the Dun and Bradstreet establishment file, "which purports to be a list of all establishments in the nation" (Osterman 1994). He used only establishments of fifty or more employees; the data are from 1992, and the sizes of firms in which EIPs are most common corresponds to the size range in the organizing sample presented here. Wages and skill level, however, cannot be compared for the two samples. He found that teams existed in 55 percent of all workplaces surveyed and that quality circles existed in 41 percent. TQM was in effect in 34 percent of the establishments. These figures were similar when the sample was restricted to manufacturing, which dominates the union organizing cases. The practices overlap, and the extent of overlap is not defined.

That only an employee-involvement program begun after the organizing drive commences has a statistically significant impact on the election outcome is contrary to the findings of Bronfenbrenner (1993) and of Bronfenbrenner and Juravich (1995b). This finding probably reflects the smaller sample size in the current study. But, in addition, we should expect organizers to petition for a certification election only when they believe they have a reasonable chance of winning. When an EIP is in place before a campaign begins, the organizer has a chance to assess the EIP as a factor in the campaign.

Did it matter whether the employers and employees discussed subjects in EIP meetings that could render the program illegal? Since organizers reported in almost every case that employers used EIPs to discuss mandatory subjects of bargaining (which make the programs legally suspect), we have no way to assess whether doing so hurts union organizing any more than sticking strictly to issues such as quality and efficiency (which do not raise legal issues). That discussing pay was associated with very low union win rates, however, is suggestive. Pay is an obviously illegal subject for an EIP, so that employers who use EIPs to discuss pay may be presenting their programs more aggressively as union substitutes, without regard for the law.

This finding raises the question of why so many organizers did not think they could win a charge when their answers to questions about specific practices would make most of the programs they encountered legally suspect. Are they correct in believing that their cases would be hard to win?[4] It also raises the tactical question of whether a strategy that included a legal challenge to an employee-involvement program might be helpful in certain campaigns. For example, where an employer was using an EIP aggressively, or the program was dominated by employee leaders who were antiunion, using the law, and explaining why, might help discredit an EIP that was a serious threat to the organizing campaign. In any event, it is clear that the successful use of section 8(a)(2) to eliminate illegal employee committees during the organizing of Electromation, Inc., is the exception to the rule.

Does this mean that the law is not important to organizing? The Employee Representation Plans of the 1930s were a target that the National Labor Relations Act was intended to eliminate, and it is likely that the law developed fairly quickly into a strong deterrent. But those were times when the idea of the company union was on the defensive (Brody 1994:41). Such is not the case for employee-involvement programs now. They are widely

---

4. Charles Morris, as a discussant of this paper at the AFL-CIO/Cornell Research Conference on Organizing, argued that these cases are easy to win compared with other unfair labor practice cases.

praised by academics and Democratic politicians, many of whom acquiesce to the idea that section 8(a)(2) is a "problem." In this environment, it would not be surprising if many employers did not take the law seriously.

Nevertheless, there is some evidence that the NLRB decisions in *Electromation* and *DuPont* have had an impact on employer behavior. Management consultants still encourage the use of employee-involvement programs as an antiunion tool, but their advice is full of warnings about the limits of what can be done with them and that being found in violation could backfire in an organizing drive (Cabot 1993; DiMaria 1994). Some organizers I spoke with offered, without solicitation, opinions about the proposed Teamwork for Employees and Managers Act, which would weaken or even nullify section 8(a)(2) for non-union workplaces. They feared that it would encourage employers to use EIPs more aggressively as antiunion devices, and they feared the consequences.

The finding that unions were more successful when they got union supporters on to employee-involvement committees and used them to promote union issues evokes images of the Steelworkers and Communication Workers taking over their Employee Representation Plans. But the limitations of this approach should also be obvious from the data. The ERP takeovers in the 1930s occurred where employers felt compelled to hold elections for employee representatives, opening the door to union takeovers. Now many employees seize hopefully at the chance for "involvement" because they see little hope for anything more substantive. Consequently, very few employers see any reason to allow the election of employee representatives, and they frequently succeed in placing anti-union employee leaders on the committees.

Unions infiltrated the EIPs in fifteen of the fifty-four campaigns in which EIPs existed. The reason other organizers did not do this more may be not that they did not think of it but that other employers did not allow it. Nevertheless, this finding shows that when unions are creative enough to seize an opportunity, they can be very successful, particularly when they use the opportunity to engage the employees themselves in carrying out the actions.

The most powerful result of this study is the effectiveness of rank-and-file campaign tactics. There may be particular union strategies that succeed in the context of certain kinds of EIPs. But when the employer uses an EIP, if the organizer cannot or does not get the employees to develop leadership among themselves—to take risks on behalf of their desire for a union, to take actions that inspire and encourage their coworkers—the union loses almost every time. Either the union creates genuine involvement in the organizing campaign or the employer seizes on the employees' aspirations and fears through its own version of involvement.

Bronfenbrenner (1993) and Bronfenbrenner and Juravich (1995b) demonstrated quantitatively the importance of rank-and-file-intensive tactics to union success in both private-sector and public-sector organizing campaigns. The findings here strengthen the importance and generality of those findings and show that the presence of EIPs intensifies the need for those tactics.

Conclusions

In less than ten years, employee-involvement programs have grown from a blip on the radar screen to a significant new phenomenon facing union organizers. They are now encountered by organizers in one-third of all organizing campaigns. For all the hope that some academics have bestowed on them as vehicles for improving employee "voice" in an increasingly nonunion work world, the EIPs that organizers encounter are far from benign. They are accompanied by aggressive antiunion campaigns and are utterly undemocratic as employee organizations.

EIPs that are started after union organizing campaigns begin significantly reduce the ability of unions to organize. Yet, as the data presented here also show, the best organizing strategies can overcome this impact. Unions that developed leadership among the workers they were organizing and that ran aggressive campaigns won as often when there were EIPs as when there were not. Unions did especially well when pro-union workers were able to get onto employee-involvement committees and raise union issues. Conversely, unions ignored EIPs at their peril, and when the employer was able to create an antiunion employee leadership on the EIPs, the union usually lost.

Having an EIP that predated the start of the organizing campaign was also associated with lower union win rates, but this difference was apparently the result of associations between EIPs and other factors that have a negative impact on organizing. These factors are the aggressiveness of the employer's antiunion campaign and several demographic characteristics. A comparison of the frequency of EIPs with that in another study (Osterman 1994), as well as research by Fiorito, Lowman, and Nelson (1987), suggests that the principal effect of EIPs that are in place before organizing begins is to prevent organizing from beginning.

Union organizing is a struggle by employees to gain power from an employer who does not want to give it up. Our labor law recognizes that: "The inequality of bargaining power between employees who do not possess full freedom of association or actual liberty of contract, and employers who are organized in the corporate or other forms of ownership association substantially burdens and affects the flow of commerce" (NLRA, section 1).

Section 8(a)(2) was enacted not just because real unionism is more democratic than company unionism but because it is more powerful. When employers use employee-involvement programs in organizing campaigns, they so in the hope that a powerless organization will appear to be more than it is and an attractive alternative to the struggle needed to gain a powerful organization. It is a struggle for hearts and minds. When unions can inspire employees to organize themselves and demonstrate organization and power through a representative committee that organizes solidarity days, group meetings, contract surveys, substantial numbers of volunteers from other local unions, house calls, and other actions, organizers can nullify the impact of employee-involvement programs, just as organizers did with the Employee Representation Plans of the past.

Chapter 14

Union Voting Intentions: Human Resource Policies, Organizational Characteristics, and Attitudes

Jack Fiorito and Angela Young

Various explanations for the continuing decline of U.S. unions have been proposed and tested. Among them are that government policies replace union functions ("government substitution"), employers suppress union activity, changes have occurred in workers' attitudes, internal factors within unions are to blame, changes have occurred in the structure of the economy and the workforce, job satisfaction has increased, and employers have instituted more progressive human resource policies ("employer substitution"— in the sense that employer policies provide a substitute for union representation). The merits of these explanations are obviously critical from a union policy perspective. For example, on the one hand, if changes in workers' values are the critical factor, then unions might be well advised to focus their efforts on research on workers' values, broad public relations campaigns to educate workers on the roles of unions, and reforms to make unions more responsive to these new values. On the other hand, if "progressive" human resource (HR) policies are the key, unions need to know more about which policies pose the greatest obstacles to organizing success so that they can target organizing efforts more effectively, determine how best to counter

We wish to thank Bill Anthony, John Delaney, Cynthia Gramm, Paul Jarley, Micki Kacmar, and Pam Perrewé for helpful comments on an earlier draft. John Delaney, Mark Huselid, and David Knoke provided correspondence that aided our use of the NOS data, and Marc Street provided research assistance. We retain sole responsibility for any errors. An earlier version of this essay was presented at a poster session of the Forty-Eighth Annual Meeting of the Industrial Relations Research Association in San Francisco in January 1996 and at the AFL-CIO/ Cornell University Conference on Union Organizing in Washington, D.C., in April 1996.

these policies during organizing drives, and address potential vulnerabilities in employers' HR policies. Although established union-management relationships may be becoming more cooperative, organizing remains a highly adversarial process, and as the old cliché goes, union organizers must "know thy enemy."

As Jack Fiorito and Cheryl L. Maranto (1987) suggest, to explain more definitely the decline of U.S. unions requires additional evidence. They note in particular that one of the more plausible explanations, the "employer-substitution thesis," has been subjected to only limited testing, largely because of data requirements. Ideally, one would need consistent data on employers' human resource policies over time (as well as data on employers' suppression tactics and workers' attitudes) to isolate their effects. Such data simply do not exist. As a practical matter, even if such data did exist, it would be extremely difficult to isolate the employer-substitution effect.

Although ideal data do not exist, a recent innovative data-collection effort, known as the National Organizations Survey (NOS), provides new and potentially better evidence on these issues. Specifically, the NOS provides matched worker and employer responses whereby workers' attitudes toward unions can be linked to employers' human resource policies and other organizational characteristics. In this chapter, we use these data to examine the influences of HR policies and other organizational characteristics on workers' intentions to vote for a union. In doing so, we hope to offer new insight on the employer-substitution thesis, thus allowing union organizers to assess threats to organizing success and to direct funds and efforts to the most critical activities.

Background

Previous empirical studies have sought to establish simply that there *is* an employer-substitution effect—that employers' human resource policies influence unionization outcomes, with some attention to the effect of specific policies. Thomas A. Kochan, Robert B. McKersie, and John Chalykoff (1986) and Fiorito, Lowman, and D. Nelson (1987) analyzed data from Fortune 500-type firms (from a 1983 Conference Board Survey). Fiorito, Lowman, and Nelson offered greater detail on the effects of specific policies on new organizing, whereas Kochan, McKersie, and Chalykoff provided a broader perspective on how progressive HR policies influence various dimensions of unionization, but both studies found an effect. Maranto (1988) found supporting evidence in her analyses for the idea that the financial characteristics of firms—which have been linked to HR policies—influence NLRB representation election outcomes.

A limitation of these studies is that all have examined employer-substitution influences at an aggregate level: the firm or the election unit. No studies have as yet addressed the influence of HR policies on the attitudes of individuals. Thus, from the Kochan, McKersie, and Chalykoff (1986) or Fiorito, Lowman, and Nelson. (1987) studies, for example, we have evidence (from employer reports only) that so-called progressive HR policies are associated with reduced union organizing success. How such policies reduce union success is something of a "black box."

Presumably, the underlying mechanisms involve the psychological concept of dissonance reduction. That is, dissatisfaction resulting from job conditions and employer policies sets in motion processes of dissonance reduction (Wheeler and McClendon 1991:50, 74–77). Workers may see unionization as a means of improving those conditions and changing the policies giving rise to the dissatisfaction (e.g., improving wages or ending policies of favoritism).

As Hoyt N. Wheeler and John A. McClendon note, "At the very heart of the *collective* action of unionization lies the *individual* decision to support it" (1991:47, emphasis in original). In part, our goal here is to identify how specific HR policies and other organizational characteristics might affect worker dissatisfaction, thereby better accounting for the observed relationships. But as Wheeler and McClendon note, individual workers' decisions take place in a broader context and attempts to examine the HR policy effects must therefore consider other influences. Thus, consistent with previous research, we propose a model of the individual's voting intentions that incorporates several factors in addition to HR policies and other organizational characteristics.

Overview of the Model

We propose that there are seven general categories of influence that affect a worker's voting intentions. These include human resource policies, general organizational characteristics, attitudes toward job and employer, attitudes toward unions, worker ideology, worker demographics, and employee involvement. The model is illustrated in figure 14.1.

In the next section, we describe the concepts within each category and discuss their influences on workers' intentions to vote for or against unionization.

Human Resource Policies

There is no "standard" way to conceptualize HR policies. Discussions of employer-substitution effects usually include such terms as "progressive," "enlightened," or "modern," but it is not always clear where particular

Figure 14.1 Model of Union Voting Intentions

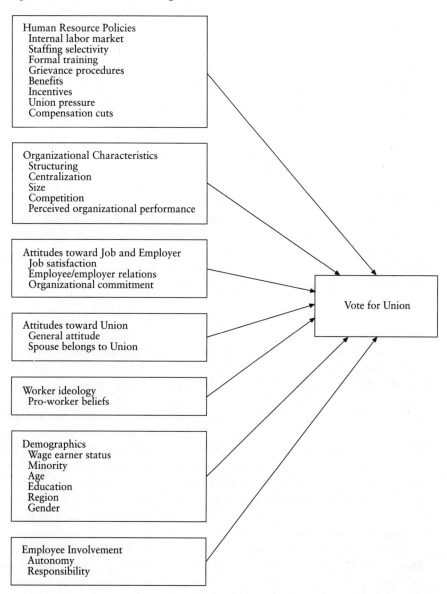

policies fall on the dimensions suggested by these terms. Building on previous work by John T. Delaney and Mark A. Huselid (1996), we identify eight distinct HR policies that may influence workers' attitudes toward unions: (1) the presence of an internal labor market (e.g., promotion from within), (2) selectivity in hiring, (3) emphasis on training, (4) employer-sponsored grievance procedures, (5) benefits, (6) incentive pay, (7) union pressure (e.g., training and wage policies responsive to conditions in union settings), and (8) compensation cuts (e.g., increased deductibles, copayments, or employee contributions, as well as direct cuts in pay and benefits). The existence of the first five policies presents an image of employer "support" and thus is likely to decrease workers' support for unions. Incentive pay has been touted as a means of aligning employers' and workers' interests and thus should reduce support for unions. Union pressure as an influence on company policies could convey to workers what unions can do for them and along with compensation cuts, which threaten living standards, should increase workers' support for unions.

General Organizational Characteristics

Aside from somewhat superficial characteristics (e.g., size of the firm, industry) that are available in NLRB election files, researchers have given little attention to the general characteristics of employing organizations and how they might influence union voting intentions. A notable exception is Maranto's (1988) study focusing on firms' financial characteristics, and Maranto and Fiorito (1987) and Fiorito, Paul Jarley, and Delaney (1995) provide indirect evidence of the importance of such factors in demonstrating that union characteristics influence organizing outcomes.

In addition, there is evidence that certain organizational characteristics, such as decentralized decision making, might influence whether an individual votes for or against unionization. The specific organizational characteristics examined here are (1) bureaucratic structuring, (2) decentralization of decisions, (3) size, (4) competition, and (5) perceived organizational performance. Two of these characteristics—decentralization of decisions and competition—are likely to lower workers' support for unions. In general, it is likely that unions are seen as less instrumental in decentralized organizations, where workers are presented with at least an illusion of control over their environment. Likewise, a lower level of support for unions is likely to be seen in competitive settings, where unions may be less likely to gain economic improvements.

Organizational size has a more complex relationship to union support. Thomas A. Kochan (1980) contends that the personal communications mechanisms used to address problems in small workplaces block unions, while large firms use their extensive resources to engage in effective union substitution. Therefore, we would expect to see less support for unions in extremely large or small firms. Finally, more union support is likely in firms where the perceived organizational performance is high. Good performance may encourage support for a union as a means of sharing in the prosperity.

Attitudes toward Job and Employer

Although human resource policies and general organizational characteristics are the predictors of main interest here, we recognize that workers' attitudes are a well-established influence on union voting intentions. In fact, our arguments concerning organizational-level variables are based on our understanding of the impacts of those characteristics on attitudes. Yet we would not suggest that the characteristics thus far considered fully account for such critical attitudes as job satisfaction. Thus, we control directly for attitudes that are likely to influence voting. Although not the main focus of our hypotheses, the effects of these variables are relatively easy to predict based on previous research. The attitudinal factors of interest are (1) job satisfaction, (2) good relations between management and workers, and (3) organizational commitment. High levels of these attitudinal factors are likely to have a negative impact on union support.

Attitudes toward Unions

Theory and evidence suggest that attitudes play a strong role in predicting behavioral intention toward an object. Numerous studies have verified this premise in the context of union voting (e.g., Deshpande and Fiorito 1989). We use two measures: (1) general attitude toward unions and (2) spouse's union membership. It is likely that both these factors will influence voting intentions positively.

Worker Ideology

The pragmatic nature of U.S. workers' approaches to unions is often emphasized (e.g., Kochan 1980), and perhaps even overemphasized. Recent studies have shown that less pragmatic considerations, such as beliefs about the distribution of profits and altruistic views of unions, also influence whether workers support unionization (e.g., Barling, Fullagar, and Kelleoway 1992; Fiorito 1992). We would expect that worker ideology, as indicated by pro-worker beliefs about profit distribution and class identification, would tend to favor a positive view of unions as vehicles to check management's profit obsession, redistribute profits toward workers, and promote working-/lower-class interests. Thus, we expect pro-worker beliefs to have a positive impact on pro-union voting intentions.

Worker Demographics

Worker "demographics," such as age, education, female gender, minority status, residence in a southern region of the United States, and other characteristics, have been examined in many studies of attitudes toward unions. Evidence suggests that such variables tend to act as surrogates for more relevant attitudinal concepts, and, with the exception of minority status, most show no effect in studies with richer attitudinal measures (Fiorito, Gallagher, and Greer 1986). Our attitudinal measures are less than ideal, however, and thus we will not be greatly surprised if demographic variables add explanatory power to our model. In addition to the relatively "standard" demographic variables, we include a measure for wage and salary earner status. Although self-employment in the usual sense seems to preclude unionization, recent trends have increased the extent to which many persons are self-employed in a "technical" sense. Thus, we include the self-employed in our sample, since such persons may consider unionization relevant, but we distinguish these persons with this measure.

Employee Involvement

James Rundle's (1996) work on employee involvement, presented in chapter 13 of this volume, examined the growing significance of employee-involvement programs in union organizing campaigns. According to Rundle, these programs can reduce support for unions if organizers do not adapt their organizing strategies to deal effectively with the employer-sponsored programs. Following Peter V. Marsden, Arne L. Kalleberg, and Cynthia R. Cook (1996), we proxy employee involvement in the workplace with two variables: (1) autonomy and (2) responsibility. Autonomy measures the extent to which a worker feels decision-making power and control over the work environment and job. Responsibility includes measures for the amount of money controlled by the worker, supervisory duties performed despite a worker's nonsupervisory status, and training duties performed. We would expect to see less support for unions when workers report a high degree of autonomy and responsibility. (We should note that although employee-involvement programs could be considered an HR policy, we have no employer-based measure available from the NOS on EI programs. Thus, we use these proxies for EI effects but treat them as separate from HR policies.)

Data, Measures, and Statistical Methods

As noted earlier, the data are drawn from the National Organizations Survey conducted in 1991. The NOS represents a "hypersampling" strategy, wherein target firms were initially identified as employers of respondents or respondents' spouses in the 1991 General Social Survey (GSS), conducted by the National Opinion Research Center at the University of Chicago, thereby yielding a representative sample of workers and workplaces. Using GSS responses to identify employers, interviews were completed with respondents in 727 firms. Of these, 243 were interviews with spouses' employers and were thus not usable for our purposes. Of the remaining 484 matched GSS/NOS interviews, 101 were with union members or with non-members who did not answer the union voting question and were also not usable for our study, leaving a potential sample of 383 nonunion respondents with a union voting response and matching employer interviews.

Selecting only those cases for which no data were missing for any variable resulted in a final sample of 123 cases. In many instances, however, relatively modest assumptions could result in "reclaiming" substantial numbers of cases. In a situation such as ours in which large numbers of cases were "lost" as a result of a relatively few instances of missing data across a large number of measures, the information gained from a modest investment in "fiction" (mean replacement for missing data) appears large. Thus, we will examine the results for two overlapping samples. The first sample includes the 123 cases in which no missing data replacement was used, and the second includes 383 cases that resulted when there was general replacement of missing values with mean values.

Our measures are summarized in appendix table 14.1, along with descriptive statistics, for the N = 123 sample. A more detailed appendix provides information on all measures, including details on the replacement of missing data, and is available from the authors. The dependent variable, Vote for Union, is a dichotomous variable (1 = would vote for union; 0 = would vote against union). (Although we report ordinary least squares [OLS] results, we also estimated equations using binomial logistic regression and found no substantial discrepancies in the results.)

Before turning to the results, we should emphasize the hypothetical nature of our Vote for Union measure. The question from which the result for this measure was determined was asked of nonunion workers regardless of whether they had or had not experienced an organizing drive and associated union and employer campaigns. Previous studies (e.g., Premack and Hunter 1988) have shown that union voting intentions are very good predictors of actual voting when organizing drives and elections actually occur, but a hypothetical measure of voting intentions is obviously more speculative.

Results

Table 14.1 presents OLS regression results (standardized betas) for the two samples described earlier. For each sample, two equations are estimated. Equations 1a and 2a provide estimates of the influence of each of the independent variables described earlier. Equations 1b and 2b combine into a composite scale (HR composite; $\alpha = .83$) the five HR policies that seem to best fit under the "progressive HR policy" label. Despite the large difference

TABLE 14.1. Standardized Regression Results for Union Voting Intention Study

Measure	Equation 1a	Equation 1b	Equation 2a	Equation 2b
HR Policies				
Internal labor market	−.16*		−.04	
Selectivity in hiring	−.03		−.05	
Training emphasis	.15		.06	
Grievance procedure	.01		−.001	
Fringe benefits	−.01		−.06	
HR composite		.02		−.08
Incentive pay	−.09	−.12*	−.02	−.01
Union pressure	.02	.02	.07*	.07*
Compensation cuts	.20**	.21**	.06	.07*
Organizational Characteristics				
Bureaucratic structuring	.33**	.29**	.09	.10
Decentralized decisions	−.06	−.03	−.01	−.02
Log of total employees	−.72	−.55	.02	.02
Squared log of employees	.35	.21	−.09	−.08
Competitiveness of market	−.10	−.10	−.05	−.05
Perceived performance	.04	−.06	−.04	−.03
Attitudes				
Job satisfaction	.09	.09	−.03	−.03
Good relations	−.11	−.09	−.01	−.01
Organizational commitment	−.04	−.03	−.12**	−.12**
Attitude toward unions	.38***	.41***	.32***	.32***
Spouse belongs to a union	.15*	.14*	.18***	.18***
Pro-worker beliefs	.01	.03	.11**	.11**
Demographics				
Wage or salary worker				
(1 = yes)	.06	.03	.02	.001
Minority race	.13	.10	.07	.07
Age, in years	−.14	−.12	−.06	−.06
Education, in years	−.05	−.07	−.002	−.01
Region of residence				
(1 = South)	.08	.06	.01	.01
Female gender	−.10	−.12	−.02	−.02
Employee Involvement				
Autonomy	.06	.04	−.07	−.07
Responsibility	−.02	−.01	−.03	−.02
Summary Statistics				
Sample size (N)	123	123	383	383
"Explained" variance				
(R-square)	.40	.38	.30	.30
Adjusted R-square	.22	.23	.24	.24
F (overall)	2.26***	2.48***	5.36***	6.24***
Joint F for				
HR policies	1.36	1.76	.77	1.23
Org. characteristics	1.28	1.08	.44	.48
Attitudes	3.95***	4.46***	15.00***	15.25***
Demographics	1.10	.90	.73	.68
EI proxies	.16	.05	1.01	1.10

* $p<.10$, ** $p<.05$, *** $p<.01$ (one-tail tests for coefficients with directional hypotheses specified).

in sample size, the results across the two samples are generally similar for both the individual and composite variable analyses.

Although the overall model is statistically significant (p<.01) in all instances, the results are disappointing in some key respects. For example, we cannot state that human resource policies or, separately, general organizational characteristics have a clear effect on voting intention in either sample. (We could note, however, that the HR composite measure approaches significance, p<.14, in the larger sample.) Similarly, the demographic variables as a group fail to show clear effects. The two measures of employee involvement—autonomy and responsibility—also fail to show clear effects. In contrast, the attitudinal predictors generally show strong influences.

The results for individual measures are significant in several instances. Results from the smaller sample indicate that the presence of an internal labor market and an emphasis on incentive pay reduce workers' interest in unionization, while bureaucratic structuring increases workers' interest in unionization. Results for the larger sample indicate that HR policies shaped by union pressure and a pro-worker ideology increase the likelihood of a pro-union voting intention, while union support is reduced by organizational commitment (commitment to the employer). In both samples, compensation cuts, general attitude toward unions, and spouse's union membership all show positive impacts on union voting intentions. In no instance does either of the employee involvement indicators (autonomy or responsibility) meet the conventional criterion for significance (p<.10), although the autonomy variable shows the expected negative sign and approaches significance (p<.12) in the larger sample.

Discussion

The results speak to a number of questions on union organizing. First, the results confirm previous findings concerning the importance of attitudes toward unions, as indicated by the strong positive and consistent results for the general attitude toward unions measure. Secondary and related support for this finding arises in the consistent positive effect for spouse's union membership. There is also some support for the positive influence of a pro-worker "outlook"—views that managers are obsessed with profits and self-identification as working or lower class—a result not previously noted in a broadly representative sample (but see Barling, Fullagar, and Kelloway 1992).

Second, the results shed some new light on two relatively uncharted territories: the influences of HR policy and of general organizational characteristics. Although numerous instances in labor history associate bursts of union activity with pay cuts (e.g., the Pullman strike), ours is the first broadly based study to show a systematic positive relationship between compensation cuts and union activity. The "downsizing" of recent years and reports of its adverse effect on workers' attitudes toward employers may be a closely related and current example of this relationship. This finding is also notable in light of Wheeler and McClendon's (1991) characterization of pay cuts as a clear influence in spurring workers' interest in unionization.

The result showing that incentive pay systems reduce workers' interest in unionization, although limited to one equation for our smaller sample, is also novel and may have important implications for union organizers. Champions of incentive pay have argued that such systems harmonize workers' and employers' interests by aligning incentives. Our results suggest that this harmonizing influence translates into reduced interest in unionization.

Another novel finding is suggested by the result for the union pressure variable. We suggested that workers perceive such pressure and interpret it as evidence of union instrumentality. The result is consistent with this argument but also suggests an irony: those who shape their policies in response to union pressure, quite possibly as part of a union-avoidance strategy, may succeed in "union substitution" at one level but at the same time enhance perceptions of the instrumentality of unions, which increase union support.

A final novel result arises for the bureaucratic structuring measure in the smaller sample only. Theoretical and impressionistic writings have previously suggested that unions are to some extent a response to bureaucratization in employing organizations (i.e., a "countervailing power"). To our knowledge, our finding represents the first empirical confirmation of this argument, and it suggests the effect may be substantial.

The third general observation concerns the overall results. We considered fourteen individual variables representing HR policies and general organizational characteristics. Of these, five variables had statistical significance with the predicted relationship in at least one of the two samples. Another four variables supported the predicted relationship in both samples but were never statistically significant at conventional levels ($p < .10$), as was the case for the HR composite in equations 1b and 2b. Another five variables were inconsistent and nonsignificant across the two samples, and only one did not support the predicted relationship in either sample. In summary, the results tend to conform to expectations in most instances, although failing to show consistent strong and significant effects. Further, when the combined influence of HR policies or organizational characteristics is considered, we cannot reject the possibility that these effects are simply due to chance. Although the results for some individual variables in these categories are sensible and have practical implications for organizing strategies, overall we are tempted to call the results for HR policies and general organizational characteristics "underwhelming." What does this mean, or why might such results arise?

To begin with, we should acknowledge the possibility that our tests may simply not be sharp enough (low statistical power). Of course, there are other explanations for "no effect," including poor measures and the possibility that we have tested the wrong model (specification error), that we cannot rule out. With regard to the quality of the measures, it is important to remember that our HR policies and general organizational characteristics are based on employers' reports. Although we regard this as a unique virtue of this study, it also entails the possibility that workers and employers view these matters differently. For example, what an employer regards as a formal dispute resolution mechanism, workers may regard as "window dressing."

Two related interpretations stem from the hypothetical nature of our union voting intention measure. First, an employer's campaign against a union will almost certainly call attention to certain current policies and benefits that the employer portrays as jeopardized by the union. This campaign will make these policies more salient to voters in an actual election, and their importance might thus be understated here. Second, despite the law, during actual campaigns employers may introduce, augment, or reinvigorate policies or benefits valued by workers. This would increase the salience of these policies, but it might also imply that the HR policies in effect prior to elections are different than they are otherwise, again leading to possible understatement of HR policy effects. Rundle (1996) noted that 25 percent of EI programs were introduced *after* the union organizing campaigns he studied began. (Also see Hurd [1994] on EI as a union-avoidance technique.)

With regard to specification error, previous researchers (e.g., Delaney and Huselid 1996) have noted the possibility of "synergistic" effects among various HR policies, suggesting that particular policies may be less important than the overall HR policies package. We try to address this concern with our HR composite variable. Similar concerns apply to general organizational characteristics. These are issues deserving further exploration.

Regarding the causal ordering of the variables, it seems fairly safe to assume that a future intention (how one will vote) follows from current organizational characteristics and one's own current attitudes and demographics, but in many instances our arguments suggest possible intervening relationships. For example, the effects of HR policies on union voting may operate primarily through the effects of those policies on organizational commitment rather than directly.

Alternatively, we should consider taking the results at face value. Although exceptions have been noted, the general pattern suggests that we cannot reject the possibility that HR policies and general organizational characteristics simply do not influence workers' union voting intentions. Finding no evidence of an effect is not proving "no effect," of course, but this "spin" on the results raises interesting questions. In particular, how much weight should be assigned to the employer-substitution thesis for union decline in view of evidence suggesting "no effect" exists?

Practical Implications for Organizing

The importance of "progressive" HR policies may be exaggerated. Although previous studies have found effects when relying on employer-based reports of union-avoidance success, our results yield only limited evidence that such policies influence workers' voting intentions. Given the potential problems with our measures and the other cautions noted above, it would be premature to dismiss the employer-substitution argument entirely, but skepticism is warranted. Organizers should be hesitant to assume that the existence of such policies (e.g., worker complaint resolution systems) reduces a site's organizing potential. As Rundle (1996) noted, a union's response to an EI program can play a critical role in an election.

The presence of other HR practices may provide more useful guidance to organizers. As noted, compensation cuts, as history suggests in many instances, become potential rallying points for organizing campaigns. Today these are relatively rare in the form of pay cuts, seemingly replaced by downsizing and shifting benefit costs to workers. Organizers need to consider whether these cuts can provide similar rallying points for organizing efforts. The findings for incentive pay practices may suggest a need to rethink union stances on these issues. Past abuses of discretionary pay systems have contributed to an almost knee-jerk aversion and favoring of pay standardization. But there is no more fairness in equal pay for unequal work than in unequal pay for equal work. Workers appear more receptive to the idea of incentive pay than union policies for pay standardization might indicate. Needless to say, the abuses of discretionary pay systems may remain a hot issue for workers, but the difference between true merit pay and abuse of discretion needs to be recognized. Finally, in this vein, to enhance workers' perceptions of the instrumentality of unions, organizers should continue to point out to prospective members how policies on their job are influenced by unions elsewhere.

There is little indication that general organizational characteristics (e.g., size) are useful in identifying organizing potential. One possible exception that arises here is bureaucratic structuring. In highly structured organizations, emphasizing the union's role in providing a countervailing "voice" may have particular appeal.

Similar to most of the general organizational characteristics considered, our measures of employee involvement did not appear to have an effect on union voting intent. Perhaps a more relevant issue related to employee-involvement programs is how organizers deal with such programs and policies during organizing efforts rather than whether or not such programs and policies exist in a workplace (see Rundle 1996).

Finally, the importance of workers' attitudes, particularly toward unions, is clear and carries critical implications for organizing. The importance of union attitudes implies that organizers need to build a positive image, one would hope with the support of the national union and AFL-CIO efforts and practices. Unfortunately, our understanding of factors shaping attitudes is still fairly limited.

Nevertheless, organizers need to focus on assessing attitudes as well as changing them, and there are obvious practical things organizers can do. To some extent, attitude surveys may be helpful. In general, trying to establish broadly representative organizing committees should help in both assessing and improving workers' attitudes toward unions. Previous studies have demonstrated that the use of large committees and other "organizing model" tactics within the union organizer's control have a positive effect on organizing (Bronfenbrenner and Juravich 1994). In general, it seems likely that the reason such tactics work is that participative tactics are more powerful in changing attitudes.

APPENDIX TABLE 14.1. Variables and Descriptive Statistics for
Union Voting Intentions Study, N = 123

Measure	Mean	Standard Deviation
Dependent Variable		
Vote for Union	0.28	0.45
HR Policies		
Internal labor market prices	0.22	0.89
Selectivity in hiring	0.38	0.93
Training emphasis	0.24	0.93
Formal grievance procedure	0.11	0.97
Fringe benefits offered (checklist)	0.32	0.71
HR composite (combines above five)	1.27	3.16
Incentive pay emphasized	−0.26	0.69
Union pressure influential	0.05	1.06
Compensation cuts	−0.01	0.98
Organizational Characteristics		
Bureaucratic structuring	0.18	0.72
Decentralized decisions	3.64	0.93
Log of total employees	4.46	2.29
Squared log of total employees	25.11	21.29
Competitiveness of primary market	3.42	0.72
Perceived organizational performance	3.10	0.58
Attitudes		
Job satisfaction	3.35	0.74
Good employee-management relations	3.85	0.96
Organizational (employer) commitment	2.88	0.44
General attitude toward unions	0.01	0.79
Spouse belongs to a union (1 = yes, 0 = no)	0.05	0.22
Pro-worker beliefs	−0.05	0.69
Demographics		
Wage or salary worker (1 = yes, 0 = self-employed)	0.93	0.26
Minority race (1 = minority, 0 = white)	0.14	0.35
Age, in years	39.00	12.32
Education, in years	13.94	2.58
Region of residence (1 = South, 0 = other)	0.34	0.48
Female gender (1 = female, 0 = male)	0.51	0.50
Employee Involvement		
Autonomy	.04	3.28
Responsibility	2.20	2.09

Note: Some variables appear in standardized form or are composites based on standardized items.

Chapter 15

In the Community or in the Union?
The Impact of Community Involvement
on Nonunion Worker Attitudes
about Unionizing

Dan Cornfield, Holly McCammon,
Darren McDaniel, and Dean Eatman

By reducing their commitments to workers, corporations, ironically, are providing unions with new opportunities for organizing. As corporations respond to increasing global economic pressures with reorganizations and downsizings, they replace their long-term employment relationships with temporary, part-time, and contingent "just-in-time" employment arrangements. These hollow employment arrangements erode those workplace communities that were associated with long-term organizational careers and employee loyalty to "corporate families" and that have so effectively hindered union organizing drives in the large-corporate sector of the economy for the last quarter of a century (Cobble 1993:14–15; Cornfield 1990).

The effacement of the corporate workplace community provides unions with the opportunity to help working people rebuild their own meaningful communities. Indeed, unions should strengthen themselves as worker communities, especially to increase the effectiveness of organizing drives in the face of employer hostility. As José La Luz, education director of ACTWU, put it: "In the midst of the anti-worker, anti-union climate that prevails in this country, particularly in Right-to-Work states, the fear of losing one's livelihood conditions the behavior and views many workers have about this 'outsider' called the union. We have learned from experience that workers overcome their legitimate fears *only by developing an understanding that the union is not an outside third party* but that they themselves are the union" (1991:63; emphasis added).

As labor movement revitalization occurs through community rebuilding, unions will compete for worker allegiances, not only with employers but with voluntary membership organizations and other organizations that are already entrenched in the community-building "industry." The effectiveness of union organizing, then, may partly depend on how well integrated workers are in their communities. Workers who are actively involved in community institutions may be less likely to unionize, for example, than those who are in search of community.

Little scholarly research has examined how the involvement of individual workers in their communities affects their desire to unionize. Previous research on attitudes toward unionization has generally argued that pro-union and antiunion stances are shaped by workplace factors (Cornfield and Kim 1994). In this chapter, we examine the impact of community involvement outside the workplace on nonunion worker demand for unionization. Given that voluntary membership organizations typically form the context of community involvement and volunteerism in the United States (Wuthnow 1995), we assess, with a 1991 national survey of nonunion workers, the impact of individual participation in these community organizations, as well as social, economic, and workplace factors, on nonunion worker attitudes about unionizing their workplaces. We conclude by discussing the implications of our findings for organizing strategies.

Research on Attitudes toward Unionization

The workplace is the chief context influencing nonunion workers' desires to unionize. Research on attitudes toward unionization has demonstrated that workers weigh the decision to unionize based on rational assessments of their employment and working conditions and the value of unions (Barling, Fullagar, and Kelloway 1992:chap. 3; Cornfield and Kim 1994). The standard statistical model for predicting union attitudes suggests that, given a sufficiently high level of dissatisfaction with his or her working and employment conditions and a strong belief that unions are effective in improving employment conditions, the calculating worker will favor unionization in his or her workplace. Research based on this standard model indicates that pro-union attitudes vary directly with beliefs about union instrumentality, vary inversely with job satisfaction and multiple measures of socioeconomic status, including income, education, occupational prestige, and seniority, and are also linked to specific demographic indicators. These studies, as well as research on the outcomes of certification elections, also indicate that several union and employer actions and characteristics (e.g., employer size, employer and union campaign tactics, campaign duration) influence the formation of workers' attitudes toward unions (Barling, Fulla-gar, and Kelloway 1992:chap. 3; Bronfenbrenner 1994; Comstock and Fox 1994; Cornfield 1991; Cornfield and Kim 1994; Wheeler and McClendon 1991).

Few studies have stepped outside the workplace to examine the im-pact of extra-work factors on workers' desires to unionize. Workers often need a sense of community outside the workplace to unionize, if only because it empowers them in the face of employer hostility and reprisals. We therefore consider the impact of individual participation in nonwork community organizations on workers' desires to unionize. We assume that involvement in community organizations satisfies worker needs for commu-nity that remain unsatisfied by the workplace and thereby preempts union organizing drives. Our working hypothesis is that those workers who are *least* involved in community organizations would be more likely than others to vote pro-union in a union certification election, all else being equal. In the next section, we weigh the effects of community involvement factors against those of the standard model in order to discern whether individ-ual participation in community organizations influences the demand for unionization.

Community, Workplace, and Nonunion Worker Attitudes about Unionizing

We examine the impact of community involvement and standard model factors on nonunion worker desires to unionize using a national social survey of worker attitudes. After describing the data and our analytical methods, we present the findings and assess the implications for organizing strategies.

Data and Method

The data for our study are from the 1991 General Social Survey under-taken by the National Opinion Research Center at the University of Chi-cago. The GSS is a rich database that contains union attitude variables and literally hundreds of background and attitudinal variables, including community involvement indicators, that have not been examined in relation to attitudes toward unionization in past research. We will analyze a nation-ally representative, random subsample of 517 nonunion, nonsupervisory wage earners and salaried employees.[1]

---

1. The actual sample sizes in the statistical analyses vary because some cases were missing. See appendix table 15.1.

Our goal is to "predict" how nonunion workers would vote if a union certification election were held in their workplace. The 1991 GSS asked respondents how they would vote in a hypothetical certification election. Specifically, the survey asked respondents the following question: "If an election were held with secret ballots, would you vote for or against having a union represent you?" Of the 517 respondents in our subsample, 32.5 percent responded that they would vote "for" unionizing. This percentage is similar to that in other national surveys (Cornfield and Kim 1994:525; Freeman and Medoff 1984:29). The remainder said that they would vote "against" unionizing or did not know or answer the question.

We examine the effects of four sets of "predictors" of the odds of a respondent casting a pro-union vote in a hypothetical union certification election. The first three sets of predictors are derived from the standard model for predicting individual votes in union certification elections. The first set of predictors is *work conditions*. These are respondent descriptions and evaluations of their job and employment conditions. We consider the effects of six work conditions: (1) *job satisfaction,* a five-point item ranging from "very dissatisfied" to "very satisfied"; (2) *organizational commitment,* a six-item scale indicating the respondent's commitment to his or her employing organization (alpha = .703)[2]; (3) on-the-job *interpersonal relations,* a two-item scale that measures the quality of coworker and worker-management relations (alpha = .629)[3]; (4) *raises for performance,* the respondent's assessment of whether or not his or her employer gives pay raises to "those workers who work hard and perform well"; (5) *job autonomy,* a three-item scale indicating the amount of on-the-job decision-making autonomy the respondent thinks he or she has (alpha = .764)[4]; and (6) *fringe benefits,* the respondent's count of his or her employer-provided

2. Organizational commitment is the sum of the standardized values of responses indicating degree of agreement with the following statements: "The success of my organization depends a lot on how well I do my job"; "I am willing to work harder than I have to in order to help this organization succeed"; "I would take almost any job to keep working for this organization"; "I find that my values and the organization's values are very similar"; "I am proud to be working for this organization"; and, "I would turn down another job for more pay in order to stay with this organization." Higher values on the scale signify greater respondent commitment to the organization.

3. Interpersonal relations is the sum of the standardized values of responses to these questions: "In general how would you describe relations in your workplace between management and employees?" and "In general how would you describe relations in your workplace between coworkers/colleagues?" Higher scale values signify more positive interpersonal relations.

4. Job autonomy is the sum of the standardized values of responses about the degree of truthfulness in the following statements concerning the respondent's job: "I can work independently"; "I have a lot of say over what happens on my job"; and, "My job allows me to take part in making decisions that affect my work." Higher scale values signify greater job autonomy.

fringe benefits from a total of eleven possible fringe benefits (alpha = .803).[5]

The second set of predictors—*union attitudes*—focuses on the respondent's general beliefs about unions in the United States. We examine the effects of two union attitudes: (1) *union power,* or how strongly the respondent agreed with the statement that "unions in this country have too little power"; and (2) *unions and progress,* or how strongly the respondent disagreed with the statement that "for the most part, unions just stand in the way of economic progress in this country." For each of these attitudes, a higher response indicated a more pro-union belief.

The third set of predictors consists of the respondent's *demographic background and socioeconomic status.* The demographic background characteristics are *South* (southern residence = 1), *Black* (yes = 1), and *Female* (yes = 1).[6] There are four indicators of the respondent's socioeconomic status: (1) *work experience* (in five-year categories), the amount of time since the age of sixteen that the respondent has worked for pay; (2) *education,* the number of years of formal schooling the respondent has had; (3) *family income,* the bracket of 1990 pretax family income from all sources; and (4) *relative family income,* the respondent's assessment of how much larger or smaller than the average his or her family income is "compared with American families in general."

The fourth set of predictors, and those of particular theoretical interest, consists of indicators of the respondent's *community involvement.* Community involvement refers to participation in nonwork community institutions. We measure community involvement in four ways. The first way is by the *number of voluntary membership organizations,* from a total of sixteen possible types of organizations, to which the respondent belongs.[7] The second is whether or not the respondent *belonged specifically to any of six types of popular voluntary membership organizations,* that is, types of orga-

5. The eleven fringe benefits are medical or hospital insurance; dental-care benefits; life insurance; sick leave with full pay; maternity or paternity leave with full reemployment rights; flexible hours, or flextime scheduling; cash or stock bonuses for performance or merit; pension or retirement program; profit-sharing or stock option program; information about child-care services in the community; and assistance with the costs of day care for children.

6. We omit the respondent's age from this analysis because it is highly correlated with work experience and its effect on the likelihood of voting pro-union was statistically insignificant in preliminary analyses. We also omit indicators of ethnicity (i.e., Hispanic, Native American, and Asian American) because their effects on the likelihood of voting pro-union were statistically insignificant.

7. The sixteen types of voluntary membership organizations are fraternal groups; service clubs; veterans groups; political clubs; labor unions; sports groups; youth groups; school service groups; hobby or garden clubs; school fraternities or sororities; nationality groups; farm organizations; literary, art, discussion, or study groups; professional or academic societies; church-affiliated groups; and any other groups.

nizations of which at least 10 percent of the sample said they were members.[8] The third, *religious service attendance,* is the frequency with which the respondent usually attends religious services, ranging from 0 for "never" to 8 for "several times a week." The fourth is the *respondent's religious denomination* (i.e., liberal, moderate, or conservative Protestant, Catholic, other, or none), where "none" denotes a lack of religious affiliation.

The goal of our analysis is to determine how pro-union respondents differ from other respondents in terms of the four sets of predictors. To accomplish this goal, we use logistic regression, a multivariate statistical technique, to predict the odds of a respondent casting a pro-union vote in a hypothetical union certification election from his or her work conditions, union attitudes, demographic characteristics and socioeconomic status, and community involvement.

Findings

The results of our analysis indicate that pro-union respondents differ from other respondents in terms of both the standard model predictors and the community involvement predictors. We first describe the results associated with the standard model, then turn to the results for the community involvement predictors. The statistical findings are presented in appendix table 15.1.

Standard model predictors: The standard model predictors consist of work conditions, union attitudes, and demographic characteristics and socioeconomic status. Of the six indicators of work conditions, two were strong predictors of the odds of a respondent voting pro-union in a hypothetical certification election. These were *job autonomy* and *raises for performance.* The results indicate that a respondent would be more likely to vote pro-union the less autonomy he or she had on the job and if the respondent felt that the employer did not give pay raises to workers who work hard and perform well. As shown in table 15.1, the odds of a respondent with high job autonomy voting pro-union were 9.7 percent lower than those of a respondent with moderately high job autonomy. Also, respondents who perceived that the employer rewarded hard-working employees with pay raises would be 22 percent less likely than other respondents to vote pro-union. The effects of the other indicators of work conditions—job satisfaction, organizational commitment, interpersonal relations, and fringe benefits—on the likelihood of voting pro-union were statistically insignificant ($p \leq .05$, one-tailed test) or negligible and did not sharply distinguish pro- and antiunion voters from one another.

---

8. These six types of organizations are sports groups; school service groups; hobby or garden clubs; literary, art, discussion, or study groups; professional or academic societies; and church-affiliated groups.

TABLE 15.1. Percentage Increase or Decrease in the Odds of Voting Pro-Union in a Certification Election for Respondents with Specific Characteristics Compared with Those without Such Characteristics

Characteristics	Increase or Decrease in Odds (in Percent)
Work Conditions	
Has high job autonomy (versus moderately high autonomy)	−9.7
Perceives that employer gives raises for performance (versus respondent who does not have such perception)	−22.0
Union Attitudes	
Agrees that unions have too little power (versus indifferent respondent)	54.7
Disagrees that unions hinder economic progress (versus indifferent respondent)	132.3
Race	
Black (versus white)	37.7
Socioeconomic Status	
5–9 years' work experience (versus <5 years)	−1.9
Community Involvement	
Has two organizational memberships (versus one membership)	−18.2
Attends religious services monthly (versus several times a year)	−15.0

The likelihood of a respondent voting pro-union in a certification election also depended on his or her general beliefs about U.S. unions. Both union attitudes—*union power* and *unions and progress*—were strong predictors of a pro-union vote. The findings show that a respondent would be more likely to vote pro-union the more he or she agreed that U.S. unions had too little power and the more she or he disagreed that U.S. unions hinder economic progress. Respondents who believed that unions had too little power would be 54.7 percent more likely than indifferent respondents to vote pro-union; and respondents who disagreed that unions hindered economic progress would be 132.3 percent more likely to vote pro-union than indifferent respondents (table 15.1). In other words, respondents who harbored the most pro-union, generalized beliefs about U.S. unions were also those who would be the most likely to vote pro-union in a certification election in their own workplaces.

Finally, pro-union respondents differed from other respondents in their demographic characteristics and socioeconomic status. Blacks would be 37.7 percent more likely than whites to vote pro-union (table 15.1). The impact of the other demographic indicators—South and female—was negligible. Respondents living in different regions of the country did not differ from one another in their union attitudes; nor did men and women differ from one another.

With respect to socioeconomic status, *work experience* was associated with voting pro-union. The more work experience a respondent had, the less likely he or she would be to vote pro-union. Respondents with five to nine years of work experience, for example, would be 1.9 percent less likely to vote pro-union than respondents with less than five years of work experience (table 15.1). The effects of the other socioeconomic indicators —education, family income,[9] and relative family income—were statistically insignificant. Pro- and antiunion respondents differed little in their education levels and relative family incomes.

In sum, the standard model provides insights into the differences between pro- and antiunion respondents. The likelihood of respondents voting pro-union in a hypothetical certification election depended partly on their work conditions, general attitudes about U.S. unions, and demographic characteristics and socioeconomic status.

Community involvement predictors: To the best of our knowledge, this is the first statistical analysis of the impact of community involvement predictors on the likelihood of voting pro-union in a hypothetical certification election. Therefore, to discern the effects of these predictors net of any confounding effects of the standard model predictors, we controlled for the standard model predictors in our statistical calculations. In other words, the results we report for the effects of the community involvement predictors are independent of, and in addition to, any effects of the standard model predictors.

Generally, the findings indicate that *involvement in community organizations lowers the likelihood that workers would vote pro-union in a certification election.* This is suggested by two chief findings. The first such finding pertains to the effect of the *number of organizational memberships:* the greater the number of memberships the respondent had in voluntary membership organizations, the less likely she or he would be to vote pro-union in a certification election.[10] Our calculations indicate, for example, that a respondent who belonged to two voluntary membership organizations would be 18.2 percent less likely to vote pro-union than a respondent who belonged to only one such organization (table 15.1).

Furthermore, the findings suggest that membership in voluntary member-

9. Although the effect of family income was statistically significant and positive (see appendix table 15.1), it was insignificant in an equation, not reported here, that controlled for the percentage of a respondent's household members who were children and whether or not the respondent's spouse was employed. This suggests that once household size and spousal employment status are taken into account, higher family income does not translate into more pro-union attitudes.

10. The analysis of the influence of voluntary organizational memberships is based on a subsample of 292 respondents because the 1991 GSS queried only a random subsample about their organizational memberships.

ship organizations per se, more than the type of organizations to which one belongs, influences the likelihood of voting pro-union in a certification election. In analyses not reported here, we estimated the effects of membership in each of the six types of popular, voluntary membership organizations. Although membership in each type tended to lower the odds of voting pro-union, most of the effects of membership in any one of these organizations were negligible.

The second chief finding concerns the effect of *religious service attendance:* the more frequently a respondent attended religious services, the less likely he or she would be to vote pro-union in a certification election. A respondent who attended religious services monthly, for example, would be 15 percent less likely to vote pro-union than one who attended only several times a year (table 15.1). This finding holds independent of the respondent's religious denomination. Unexpectedly, members of the three Protestant denominations would be more likely to vote pro-union than respondents with no religious affiliation (being a Catholic or a member of another religion had no impact on voting pro-union). This suggests that affiliation per se is less important than active involvement in a religious community in lowering the likelihood that a worker will vote pro-union (and membership in some denominations may actually increase pro-union attitudes).

To summarize, the effect of community involvement, net of the effects of the standard model predictors, is to lower the likelihood of voting pro-union in a certification election. The findings suggest that community involvement effectively competes with unionization for individual allegiances. In addition to the influence of employment and workplace issues on respondents' desires to unionize, involvement in community organizations tends to reduce the desire of respondents to unionize their workplaces.

Implications for Union Organizing

Our findings suggest that worker desire to unionize is driven not only by workplace factors but also by an absence of and desire for community. The study indicates that those workers who are unlikely to support unions, or those who may require the most persuasion by organizers to unionize, are those who are already immersed in community institutions outside the workplace, such as voluntary membership organizations, and that those workers who may be most favorably predisposed at the outset of a union organizing campaign to vote pro-union in a certification election are those who have not achieved such immersion in their communities.

The challenge for unions and union organizers is to help working people achieve community. Unions should reconstitute themselves as worker communities. We say *reconstitute* because contemporary unions can derive inspiration and practical models from early-twentieth-century unions, which performed a larger role in the workplace and the community. These unions performed a wide range of work-related functions in addition to collective bargaining and servicing contracts, such as providing workers with training, job referrals, and fringe benefits, as well as sponsoring nonwork cultural, social, and recreational activities (Cornfield 1990; Cornfield and Hodson 1993). International Typographical Union locals, for example, maintained a wide range of social clubs, lodges, sport clubs, and veterans groups (Lipset, Trow, and Coleman 1956:69); waitress unions functioned as "surrogate families" for their members, establishing sick and death benefits funds and rest and recreational homes, hosting social events, and addressing child-care problems during the first and second decades of the twentieth century (Cobble 1991:131–36); and several unions with immigrant memberships, such as the International Ladies' Garment Workers Union, the Hog Butchers' Union, and the United Furniture Workers of America, published their newspapers and conducted their meetings in multiple languages (Barrett 1987:140–41; Cornfield 1989:69; Siegel and Stansbury 1992:93). By revisiting the activities of the older generation of unions and by modifying those activities for contemporary conditions, unions can enlarge their impact on the lives of individual workers.

To become a community, a local union must become an arena in which workers befriend one another. Assuming that individuals befriend one another as they pursue their common interests, local unions should devote some of their resources to nonwork endeavors—that is, cultural and recreational activities—that interest the members and that will help individuals befriend one another. These activities could include discussion groups, field trips, sporting events and teams, family events, music and drama groups, and community service, as well as parties and other social functions. Furthermore, these activities should occur frequently to maximize contact among union members.

By becoming a community, the local union effectively provides the organizer with a new membership recruitment message for organizing drives. The new message is that the union is not only the fighting organization that improves working and employment conditions and enhances worker dignity but also one that fosters fellowship among its members.

The feasibility of this union-as-community organizing strategy partly rests on the effectiveness of existing union community activities. Whether an organizing drive is conducted by a local union, an international union, or a unit of the federation, organizers must be able to point to successful cases of local union community-building activities in order to deploy this strategy during an organizing drive. Past successes at union community building, when utilized with this organizing strategy, become either the inspiration and model for a new local union in the making or part of the attractiveness for a target workforce of joining an existing local union. An assumption of this strategy, therefore, is that the community activities of existing local unions are part of the union track record that organizers convey to the target workforce in an organizing drive.

The feasibility of this strategy is suggested by recent cases of union community-building activities (Shostak 1991:pt. III). The Bricklayers' program of "study circles," for example, not only succeeded in increasing member awareness of labor history and industry conditions and member participation in the union but may improve organizing efforts (Bensman 1988). The International Ladies' Garment Workers Union's Campaign for Justice organizes workers in their communities and offers such services as classes in English and Spanish literacy, social and sports activities, job referrals, and food-buying coops (Hermanson 1993:55–57). The AFL-CIO California Immigrant Workers Association (CIWA), which offers at-large membership independent of the official union certification process, provides legal assistance, vocational training, and classes that prepare immigrants to become permanent U.S. residents. According to Andy Banks, "Several successful union organizing drives have been developed from CIWA contacts." The Association for Workplace Justice, established by the Communications Workers of America, has organized at-large members by dealing with sexual harassment and sex and race discrimination issues and has helped its members gain union recognition form their employers (Banks 1991–92:26–27).

Reconstituting the union as a community also builds solidarity among union members and strengthens unions. This strategy may not only promote friendships among existing members but attract new members, who are likely to become involved in the union community. Recent research indicates that union members who originally joined the union to make friends were more active in union activities than those who joined for narrow, materialistic, and instrumental reasons (Cornfield and Hodson 1993). This is especially relevant for union organizing drives in right-to-work states, where individual workers in unionized establishments have the option of not joining the union.

The time is opportune for unions to reconstitute themselves as communities. As corporations reduce their commitments to workers by hiring just-in-time workforces, eliminating career ladders, and disavowing seniority rights, they cease to be the powerful workplace communities, or "corporate families" that have preempted union organizing campaigns in the large-corporate sector of the economy during the last quarter-century (Cornfield 1990). Unions can provide community to workers who are witnessing the effacement of their workplace community.

In conclusion, our study suggests that union organizing should assume that the union can play a broad, social, and cultural role in workers' lives. Unions can grow by addressing not only the economic interests of workers but their interest in community. By constituting themselves as communities, unions can provide organizers with an effective means for reaching out to workers and help to strengthen the labor movement.

APPENDIX TABLE 15.1. Logistic Regressions of the Odds of Voting Pro-Union in a Certification Election

Independent Variables	A	B	C
Work Conditions			
Job satisfaction	−.020	−.014	−.007
Organizational commitment	−.031	−.022	.014
Interpersonal relations	−.056	−.035	−.150
Raises for performance	−.248*	−.277*	−.247
Job autonomy	−.102*	−.131*	−.069
Fringe benefits	−.027	−.032	−.004
Union Attitudes			
Union power	.436*	.496*	.659*
Unions and progress	.843*	.854*	.890*
Demographic Background and Socioeconomic Status			
South	.039	.013	.079
Black	.320*	.368*	.181
Female	−.152	−.181	−.054
Work experience	−.019*	−.020	−.014
Education	−.011	.035	.051
Family income	.057*	.058*	.015
Relative family income	−.226	−.222	.017
Community Involvement			
Number of organizational memberships	—	—	−.201*
Religious service attendance	—	−.162*	—
Liberal Protestant	—	.550*	—
Moderate Protestant	—	.643*	—
Conservative Protestant	—	.521*	—
Catholic	—	−.444	—
Other religion	—	.483	—
Constant	−4.008	−2.575	−5.746
−2 log likelihood	443.5	422.4	282.3
Chi-square improvement (df)	126.1*(15)	138.2*(21)	86.1*(16)
g-o-f (df)	440.8(430)	460.8*(418)	315.5*(275)
Percentage correctly predicted	74.0	76.8	75.7
N	446	440	292

* p<.05, one-tailed.

PART V

Organizing Strategies for Changing Industry Environments

Whether analyzing the role of rank-and-file volunteer organizers or assessing the effectiveness of community-based campaigns, the authors of the chapters in earlier parts of this volume tended to focus on union strategies that can be utilized across a diversity of workers and industries. In contrast, the five chapters in this final part detail strategic responses by unions to changing economic and workplace conditions in specific industries and sectors of the economy. These chapters address the critical question of how union organizing strategies need to be tailored and adapted to deal with the specific conditions of the environment in which each union operates.

Juravich and Bronfenbrenner evaluate the ability of public-sector unions to organize and stay organized in a deteriorating public-sector labor climate. Birecree analyzes the structural changes in the bituminous coal industry and the resulting evolution of the United Mine Workers' organizing strategy. Lewis and Mirand and Condit and his coauthors present case studies of IBEW locals in which the Construction Organizing Membership Education Training Program (COMET) has been used to attempt to regain labor market control in their industry. Finally, Murray deals with the very different organizing experiences of two districts of the Canadian Steelworkers as each tries to respond to dramatic restructuring in its industry.

Chapter 16, by Juravich and Bronfenbrenner, is based on their nationwide study of certification, decertification, and multiunion challenge elections in state and local public-sector units. The authors find that in climates of relatively little employer opposition, unions organizing in the public sector have enjoyed win rates averaging well above 85 percent. But just as private-sector unions were ill prepared to deal with the employer onslaught of the 1980s, the current organizing practices and culture of public-sector unions leave them vulnerable to attack in an increasingly hostile public-sector environment. Juravich and Bronfenbrenner also find that the use of the same grassroots rank-and-file-intensive organizing strategies that have been found to be so effective in overcoming employer opposition in the private sector can make significant differences in public-sector organizing efforts.

Chapter 17, by Birecree, presents an in-depth analysis of UMWA organizing in the 1980s and 1990s in the context of the dramatic structural and managerial changes that took place in the bituminous coal industry. As Birecree shows, these industry changes had a devastating impact on UMWA members, as union density dropped from 62 to 34 percent between 1983 and 1992. Birecree chronicles the UMWA's efforts to reverse this decline through the ambitious revamping of its organizing structure, philosophy, and practice. She finds that by 1993, in the aftermath of these union initiatives, UMWA membership in coal mining was increasing for the first time in decades, and the union was also making important gains in organizing workers outside its traditional jurisdiction.

Chapters 18 and 19 focus on recent union organizing initiatives in the building trades. The first, by Lewis and Mirand, examines the organizing program of an IBEW local in Seattle and its efforts to regain its share of the commercial and industrial electrical construction labor market in that city. The second, by Condit, Davis, Grabelsky, and Kotler, analyzes the campaign by IBEW Local 611 to organize a large nonunion electrical contractor in Albuquerque, New Mexico, in the context of the local's broader effort to recapture the New Mexico electrical construction labor market. The case studies show how two very different IBEW locals, operating in different communities and environments, were able to successfully organize previous nonunion strongholds in their industry through a combination of bottom-up rank-and-file strategies and top-down pressure on the employer.

The final chapter, by Gregor Murray, compares the responses of two different Steelworker districts, each faced with the loss of its core membership because of the recession in the industry and restructuring. Murray catalogues how one district successfully adapted to changing conditions and actually increased its membership, while the other district was unable to recoup membership losses through new organizing. Murray finds that the differences can be attributed to the affirmative effort of the successful district to enlarge its membership base through sectoral diversification and integration of smaller bargaining units and the existence of a more autonomous and adaptable local structure and culture. He concludes that the future of industrial unions depends on their ability to move away from bureaucratic structures and practices rooted in a national single-industry bargaining system toward a more flexible, creative, and strategic model of organizing.

Chapter 16

Preparing for the Worst: Organizing and Staying Organized in the Public Sector

Tom Juravich and Kate Bronfenbrenner

The free fall of union membership in the 1970s and 1980s in the U.S. private sector was checked by unionization in the public sector. In many ways the growth of public-sector employment both masked the dramatic decline of private-sector unionization and prevented the wholesale hemorrhaging of the labor movement. Although government workers comprise only 16 percent of the current workforce, workers covered by collective bargaining in the public sector currently make up approximately one-third of the membership of the AFL-CIO.

John F. Kennedy's "Great Society" and Lyndon B. Johnson's "War on Poverty" began an era in which the New Deal ethos of government programs and standards expanded to a whole new range of people and problems. From 1958 to 1978, the number of government employees leapt from 7.8 million to more than 15.7 million. Through a combination of major public-sector strikes (Burton and Thomason 1988) and political pressure on state legislatures and governors (Freeman 1986), this growing number of public employees began to secure the right to organize that had been given to their counterparts in the private sector. Public-sector union density soared from 10.6 percent in 1958 to 38.2 percent in 1977. By 1992, thirty-eight states provided some collective bargaining rights to at least some portion of public employees.

Until very recently, a combination of political and social pressures acted as a restraining mechanism that kept public employers from running the same kinds of aggressive antiunion campaigns as their private-sector counterparts. As a result, the majority of public-sector workers could choose unions and enjoy labor relations in a climate largely free from the threats, intimidation, and coercion that are so commonplace in the private sector.

But a new battleground for labor is erupting in the public sector. In New York, Governor George Pataki is proposing reducing the state workforce by another seventy-four hundred workers after massive cutbacks his first year in office. In New Jersey, Governor Christine Todd Whitman turned twenty-three motor vehicle offices over to private contractors and fought an aggressive battle against striking toll collectors on the New Jersey Turnpike, including offering free passage to travelers over holiday weekends. In Massachusetts, Governor William Weld is proposing the complete elimination of the Department of Motor Vehicles. In New York City, Mayor Rudolph Giuliani has consistently used the threat of privatization and layoffs to force major concessions and work-rule changes from city employee unions. Similar threats were used by Governor John Rowland to extract more than $200 million in concessions from public-sector unions in Connecticut. In other states, such as Oregon, legislatures have directly attacked long-held benefits, such as public employee pensions. Across the country, stories such as these abound, as a kind of open season has been declared on public employees and their unions.

Although many of these attacks started under the Reagan and Bush administrations, they are now for the first time unified under a single ideology and political agenda. With the Republican takeover of Congress and the ascendancy of Newt Gingrich in 1994, the battle cry to stop government intrusion in people's lives and to cut back on big government rang out across the country with resounding fervor. According to Gingrich, government needs to "devolve" as it abandons New Deal activism in favor of the rights and responsibilities of individuals and corporations (1995). As dramatized in the shoot-out at Ruby Ridge and the Oklahoma City bombing, the government has been transmogrified into the new enemy. In a dramatic shift, employees who for more than fifty years have worked in the "public service" are now being blamed for high taxes, municipal insolvency, and the proliferation of unending government regulation and bureaucracy (Troy 1994). As we saw in the 1996 federal government shutdowns, public-sector workers are being sacrificed as part of a larger ideological mission by the Republicans. The passage of the welfare reform bill in the fall of 1996 only further threatened public-sector workers and their unions with its extensive workfare provisions.

Regardless of the precise nature of the attack against public-sector workers and their unions, a rejuvenated and effective organizing program will be required to stem the tide—a program no less intensive than the one currently being proposed for the private sector. Hundreds of thousands of public-sector workers must be organized just to compensate for those lost through layoffs and privatization.[1] Given the current political alignment, it may be increasingly less possible for public-sector unions to use the political arena to effect change or to stave off attacks, as public-sector unions have traditionally been able to do. In the political arena, as well as in new member organizing, public-sector workers and their unions will need to develop a more aggressive grassroots organizing strategy if they are to be effective in meeting the challenges ahead.

Over the past three years, we have conducted three studies of public-sector organizing. These include a national study of all certification, decertification, and challenge elections in 1991–92 in the thirty-eight states that have some form of collective bargaining (Bronfenbrenner and Juravich 1995a) and in-depth studies based on survey data collected from lead organizers from random samples of 195 certification election campaigns (Bronfenbrenner and Juravich 1995b and 1995c) and 164 decertification and challenge election campaigns (Bronfenbrenner and Juravich 1995d).[2] In this chapter, we bring these data together for the first time to evaluate the current state of public-sector organizing. Specifically, we examine organizing in the public sector in light of the new attack on public-sector unions and workers and evaluate the readiness of the American labor movement to rise to meet this challenge. We also evaluate which organizing strategies would be most effective in strengthening and expanding the public-sector labor movement in this more hostile labor relations climate.

Public-Sector Certification Elections and Employer Opposition

Table 16.1 provides an overview of all state and local government elections held in 1991–92. A total of 1,912 public-sector certification elections were held, in which unions won a stunning 85 percent. This compares with a win rate of only 48 percent in the private sector. Unlike the private sector, where win rates vary dramatically by unit and occupation, win rates in the public sector average more than 80 percent in all types of units, whether composed of teachers, police, clerical workers, janitors, or supervisors.

---

1. Not only will public-sector unions have to look to unorganized public-sector workers to fill their ranks but, as current efforts to privatize continue to escalate, the unions will also need to "follow their work" by organizing those workers performing work that has been privatized. Some unions, such as SEIU and AFSCME, currently have several efforts under way to organize workers performing work that was previously done by state and local workers. One example is SEIU's statewide campaign to organize workers in privatized mental health and mental retardation centers in Massachusetts.

2. In the multiunion decertification elections, survey data were collected from the lead organizers of both the incumbent and the challenging union campaigns.

TABLE 16.1. Summary of State and Local Public-Sector Elections Nationwide, 1991–92

Election Type	Number of Elections	Union Win Rate	Votes Received by Winning Union	Average Unit Size	Median Unit Size	Range of Unit Size	Average Delay from Petition to Election (Days)	Turnout	Net Gain
Certifications									
1991	956	.85	83%	58.3	15.0	1–2,788	108.7	86%	44,911
1992	956	.85	84%	55.9	16.0	1–3,922	128.1	85%	45,304
1991–92 Total	1,912	.85	83%	57.1	15.0	1–3,922	118.3	85%	90,215
Voluntary Recognitions, Including Card Checks									
1991 Both	82	1.00	N.A.	27.7	8.0	1–360	62.1	N.A.	2,133
Card checks only	53	1.00	81%				70.9	N.A.	
1992 Both	57	1.00	N.A.	16.8	10.5	2–153	83.9	N.A.	942
Card checks only	30	1.00	93%				99.3	N.A.	
1991–92 Total	139	1.00	NA	23.1	9.0	1–360	71.2	N.A.	3,075
Card checks only	83	1.00	87%				81.1		
Single-Union Decertifications									
1991	85	.46	74%	44.5	19.0	1–474	86.3	87%	–1,754
1992	77	.44	74%	71.0	25.0	1–2,073	101.5	89%	–1,114
1991–92 Total	162	.45	74%	57.1	20.0	1–2,073	93.5	88%	–2,868
MultiUnion Decertifications (Challenge Elections)									
1991	230		73%	218.7	34.0	1–10,759	98.2	85%	–223
65.2% turnover									
1.7% no union									
1992	231		77%	139.7	29.0	1–6,187	112.7	(turnover: 27,057) 85%	–75
68.0% turnover									
1.3% no union									
1991–92 Total	461		75%	179.1	30.0	1–10,759	105.4	(turnover: 18,584) 85%	–298
66.6% turnover									
1.5% no union									
TOTAL	2,674							(turnover: 45,641)	90,124

N.A. = not available.

As shown in table 16.1, unions won these elections with commanding margins, receiving, on average, 85 percent of the votes cast. Election turnouts were also extremely high: well above 85 percent. Despite suggestions that workers are no longer interested in unions (Farber 1987; Freeman and Rogers 1995), workers in the public sector are enthusiastically voting for union representation.

The question that remains is, What accounts for the more than 35 percentage point difference in win rates between the private sector and the public sector? To provide insight into this question, we compared private-sector data from Bronfenbrenner's 1986–87 study of NLRB election campaigns with our data collected on public-sector certification elections (Bronfenbrenner 1993; Bronfenbrenner and Juravich 1995b).

We did find differences between the public and private sectors in election and employer background characteristics and bargaining unit demographics. Yet these differences suggested that win rates would be lower, not higher, in the public sector. For example, the number of days between the filing of a petition and the election was twice as high in the public sector, and workers organizing in the public sector tended to have much higher wages and better benefits than their private-sector counterparts, both characteristics that have been found in the private sector to be associated with significantly lower win rates (Bronfenbrenner 1993). Clearly, then, differences in election background and bargaining unit demographics do not account for the higher win rate in the public sector.

Table 16.2 provides information on employer tactics used in both public- and private-sector union elections. Here we found dramatic differences— namely, private employers are much more likely to oppose union organizing efforts. Whereas in the private sector every employer offered at least some opposition to the union campaign, in the public sector one-quarter of the employers offered no opposition whatsoever and the majority ran very weak campaigns with just a handful of meetings and letters. Private-sector employers were six times more likely to engage in unfair labor practices, including surveillance, discharges for union activity, threats, promises, and illegal wage increases, than public employers. Overall, 38 percent of private-sector employers utilized five or more aggressive antiunion tactics, whereas only 8 percent of public-sector employers ran aggressive antiunion campaigns.

This high level of employer opposition, without sufficient restraints or remedies in labor legislation, has been shown to depress win rates in the private sector significantly (Bronfenbrenner 1993). Until very recently, a different labor relations dynamic existed in the public sector that served as a restraint on the use of this aggressive antiunion behavior. In part, this was because most public employers are elected officials, or beholden to public

TABLE 16.2. Employer Tactics Used in Private- and Public-Sector Certification Elections

	Private Sector			Public Sector		
	Sample Proportion or Mean	Proportion or Mean for Wins	Percent Win Rate[a]	Sample Proportion or Mean	Proportion or Mean for Wins	Percent Win Rate[a]
No employer campaign[b]	.00	.00	0 (.43)	.24	.30	.96 (.68)
Employer discharged workers for union activity	.30	.35	.51 (.39)	.05	.04	.60 (.76)
Complaints issued	.13	.17	.58 (.40)	.02	.02	.75 (.75)
Fired workers not reinstated before the election	.18	.19	.37 (.44)	.04	.02	.43 (.76)
Other ULPs filed	.22	.24	.47 (.41)	.06	.03	.33 (.78)
Complaints issued on other ULPs	.14	.17	.51 (.41)	.02	.01	.33 (.76)
Employer filed election objections	.13	.27	.51 (.41)	.04	.05	.88 (.74)
Employer used consultant	.71	.67	.40 (.50)	.49	.41	.63 (.86)
Employer used layoffs	.15	.18	.53 (.41)	.08	.09	.87 (.74)
Antiunion committee used	.42	.37	.37 (.46)	.24	.17	.52 (.82)
Employer used captive-audience meetings	.82	.82	.43 (.42)	.36	.29	.60 (.83)
Number of captive-audience meetings	5.50	3.97	N.A.	2.21	1.22	N.A.
Employer mailed letters	.80	.79	.42 (.45)	.36	.27	.57 (.85)
Number of employer letters	4.47	3.93	N.A.	1.95	1.42	N.A.
Employer distributed leaflets	.70	.70	.43 (.42)	.24	.17	.54 (.81)
Number of employer leaflets	5.98	5.41	N.A.	1.60	1.51	N.A.
Supervisors did one-on-one meetings	.79	.79	.43 (.42)	.43	.37	.65 (.82)
Employer used media	.10	.13	.52 (.41)	.18	.13	.53 (.80)
Employer gave wage increase	.30	.23	.32 (.47)	.10	.10	.79 (.74)
Employer promoted leaders	.17	.19	.47 (.42)	.07	.08	.79 (.75)
Employer made promises	.56	.44	.34 (.54)	.27	.23	.63 (.79)
Management change after petition	.21	.20	.41 (.54)	.10	.06	.45 (.78)
Employer campaign included more than five tactics[c]	.38	.34	.39 (.45)	.08	.03	.33 (.78)

[a] Number in parentheses is the percent win rate when the characteristic or tactic did not occur.
[b] Employer did none of the following: captive-audience meetings; antiunion committees; antiunion letters; antiunion leaflets; supervisor one-on-ones; unscheduled wage increases during campaign; promises of improvements in wages, benefits, or working conditions; promotion of key union leaders; and media campaigns.
[c] Employer campaign included more than five of the tactics listed above.
Source: Bronfenbrenner and Juravich 1994.

officials, and union avoidance in the public sector had been, until recently, politically unpopular. In the more than thirty states that have collective bargaining rights for at least some state and local workers, the net result was the development of a culture that was significantly more tolerant of unions than the private sector—until the past few years.

This is not to suggest that there was no opposition in public-sector certification elections in 1991–92. Indeed, in some elections, union activists were illegally discharged, threats were made regarding layoff and privatization, and other legal and illegal tactics common in the private sector, such as captive-audience meetings, supervisor one-on-ones, and antiunion committees, were used very effectively to undermine the union campaign. Many of these aggressive campaigns were concentrated in health-care and higher education units. This is not surprising given that public-sector higher education and health-care employers are more insulated from public pressure than other state and local government employers. They are also more closely tied to their private-sector counterparts.

Table 16.2 provides some startling evidence of what happens when public employers choose to aggressively oppose union organizing campaigns. When more than five antiunion tactics are utilized by public-sector employers, the win rate drops to 33 percent, even lower than the rate in the private sector after intensive employer campaigns. Clearly, if public-sector employers choose to oppose unionization, they have the tools to seriously undermine union organizing efforts.

Although it is true that public-sector workers enjoy legal free speech rights and union access rights unheard of in the private sector, most state collective bargaining laws offer no better protection from aggressive employer antiunion behavior than does private-sector law (Bronfenbrenner and Juravich 1995a). In fact, since most public-sector laws are modeled on the National Labor Relations Act, and there has been so little case law developed in public-sector cases, many state labor boards turn to NLRB cases when looking for precedents to decide their public-sector organizing disputes. The data clearly show that if employers in the public sector choose to oppose unions, they have strong weapons at their disposal, and there is little likelihood of significant sanctions or penalties.

These findings are particularly troubling given recent political changes and the changes in the culture of public-sector labor relations. Given the increasingly popular ideology of smaller government, politicians such as Governors Whitman of New Jersey and Pataki of New York have attacked public-sector workers and unions with unprecedented zeal, without the political costs traditionally associated with such antiunionism. Our data indicate that now that these cultural and political restraints are being lifted, the impact on public-sector organizing could be devastating. Particularly given that our data from 1991–92 do not capture these relatively recent changes and may represent "golden years" in public-sector organizing, the impact of employer opposition on public-sector win rates may be even more dramatic.

Union Tactics in the Public Sector

So far, this discussion has assumed current levels of activity and current tactics and strategies by public-sector unions. Yet, as we know from the private sector, union tactics matter more than any other set of factors in organizing, including employer behavior (Bronfenbrenner 1997). In the private sector, where aggressive employer opposition is the norm, union success rates increase by more than 35 percentage points in campaigns in which organizers utilize a comprehensive grassroots union-building strategy that includes a focus on person-to-person contact, rank-and-file leadership development, and escalating internal and external pressure tactics from the very beginning of the campaign. Such a strategy involves a combination of tactics, including establishing an active, representative organizing committee, using small-group meetings and house calls to develop leadership, inoculating against the employer campaign, and building support for the union campaign using solidarity days, community-labor coalitions, and job actions both to develop membership commitment and to pressure the employer, and building for the first contract during the organizing campaign. These tactics, when utilized as part of a comprehensive union-building campaign, have been found in the private sector to be necessary ingredients for unions to successfully overcome intense employer opposition and the fear and intimidation it generates among the rank and file.

The data for the public sector have similar implications, given its changing organizing climate. Compared with unions in the private sector, unions in the public sector are running very low-intensity organizing campaigns. As the figures in table 16.3 show, less than 25 percent of the campaigns used representative committees, only 40 percent used house calling, and fewer used solidarity days or other more aggressive tactics. Like most private-sector organizing campaigns in the 1960s and 1970s, the majority of public-sector campaigns are limited to large- and small-group meetings and a limited number of letters and leaflets.

Because of the relative lack of employer opposition, public-sector unions have still been able to win elections without running very aggressive and rank-and-file-intensive campaigns. Yet, even in this extremely favorable climate, only ninety thousand public-sector workers gain representation each year through new organizing. In fact, half the public-sector campaigns occur in units with fewer than fifteen eligible voters and 80 percent occur in units with fewer than fifty eligible voters. The question then becomes, What kind of campaigns are necessary to organize more workers in much larger units, and, as employer opposition continues to intensify, what kind of tactics would be necessary to win? Given our finding that unions organizing in the public sector lose two-thirds of all elections in which there is intense employer opposition, it is clear that current organizing practice will have to change.

The union tactics data summarized in table 16.3 provide some insight into how union tactics in the public sector must be modified to meet growing employer opposition. Under current practice, the intensity of the union campaign increases only minimally as the intensity of the employer campaign increases. If we compare the 8 percent of the campaigns in which the employer ran aggressive antiunion campaigns with the 46 percent in which the union faced little or no employer opposition, we find that less than one-third of the unions in the sample had an active representative committee, house called the majority of the unit, used solidarity days, elected the bargaining committee before the election, or signed at least 70 percent of the unit on cards before filing the petition. In fact, the primary response to more aggressive employer campaigns was a dramatic increase in the number of leaflets and mass mailings—from an average of 2.68 letters and 3.51 leaflets in campaigns with little or no employer opposition to 18.83 letters and 21.33 leaflets in campaigns with intensive employer opposition.

Overall, the data suggest that unions will need to develop a much more aggressive grassroots response to employer opposition if they are going to have any success in a deteriorating public-sector organizing climate. For example, in medium campaigns in which employers used two to five antiunion tactics, overall win rates averaged only 66 percent. But in those campaigns in which unions had cards signed by at least 70 percent of the unit before the petition was filed, the win rate increased to 87 percent; and in campaigns in which the union had a representative rank-and-file organizing committee, the win rate increased to 76 percent. Win rates were also 10 to 20 percentage points higher in units in which rank-and-file volunteers from already organized units conducted house calls, the union used solidarity days, and the union had at least one organizer on staff for every one hundred eligible voters. These tactics reflect both a more intense union effort and a more grassroots union-building strategy, as opposed to the more traditional public-sector organizing model, in which most of the union response is concentrated in letters and mass meetings.

In the 8 percent of the campaigns with intensive employer opposition, unions in our sample lost all the elections in which they did not use an organizing committee, whereas use of a committee raised the win rate to 33 percent. Committees representative of at least 10 percent of the unit made

TABLE 16.3. Union Tactics Used in Public-Sector Elections

	Overall Sample			No or Weak Employer Campaign[a]		Medium Employer Campaign[a]		Intensive Employer Campaign[a]	
	Sample Proportion or Mean	Proportion or Mean for Wins	Percent Win Rate[b]	Sample Proportion or Mean	Percent Win Rate[b]	Sample Proportion or Mean	Percent Win Rate[b]	Sample Proportion or Mean	Percent Win Rate[b]
OUTCOME									
Election outcome	.75	1.00	.75 (.00)	.90	.90 (.00)	.66	.66 (.00)	.33	.33 (.00)
First-contract outcome	.66	.88	N.A.	.81	N.A.	.58	N.A.	.28	N.A.
Postcontract membership	.70	.72	N.A.	.67	N.A.	.75	N.A.	.76	N.A.
UNION TACTICS									
Percent cards	.60	.63	N.A.	.60	N.A.	.59	N.A.	.59	N.A.
At least 70% cards	.31	.38	.92 (.68)	.36	.97 (.86)	.26	.87 (.59)	.33	.80 (.10)
Organizing committee used	.77	.77	.74 (.77)	.70	.92 (.85)	.81	.67 (.65)	1.00	.33 (.00)
Percent on committee	.07	.07	N.A.	.06	N.A.	.08	N.A.	.08	N.A.
Representative committee	.23	.23	.77 (.75)	.16	.93 (.89)	.29	.76 (.64)	.33	.40 (.30)
Diagrammed workplace	.59	.53	.68 (.84)	.46	.85 (.94)	.66	.66 (.67)	.93	.29 (1.00)
Percent house called	.40	.40	N.A.	.39	N.A.	.42	N.A.	.33	N.A.
50% or more house called	.09	.07	.56 (.77)	.06	.80 (.91)	.11	.60 (.67)	.20	.00 (.42)
Number of mass meetings	4.82	4.37	N.A.	3.74	N.A.	5.14	N.A.	9.67	N.A.
Number of small-group meetings	11.63	10.34	N.A.	6.90	N.A.	12.30	N.A.	36.87	N.A.
Percent surveyed one-on-one	.10	.11	N.A.	.10	N.A.	.11	N.A.	.09	N.A.
Rank-and-file did house calls	.17	.17	.76 (.76)	.08	1.00 (.94)	.23	.83 (.66)	.25	.00 (.33)
Solidarity days used	.17	.19	.82 (.73)	.13	1.00 (.88)	.18	.75 (.64)	.33	.60 (.20)

TABLE 16.3. Union Tactics Used in Public-Sector Elections (*cont.*)

	Overall Sample			No or Weak Employer Campaign [a]		Medium Employer Campaign [a]		Intensive Employer Campaign [a]	
	Sample Proportion or Mean	Proportion or Mean for Wins	Percent Win Rate [b]	Sample Proportion or Mean	Percent Win Rate [b]	Sample Proportion or Mean	Percent Win Rate [b]	Sample Proportion or Mean	Percent Win Rate [b]
UNION TACTICS (*cont.*)									
Number of letters	4.47	3.21	N.A.	2.60	N.A.	3.98	N.A.	18.73	N.A.
Number of leaflets	6.07	4.59	N.A.	3.51	N.A.	6.16	N.A.	21.33	N.A.
Dignity and fairness primary issues	.38	.36	.71 (.78)	.35	.90 (.91)	.40	.63 (.69)	.40	.17 (.44)
Bargaining committee before election	.15	.16	.79 (.74)	.14	1.00 (.88)	.15	.69 (.66)	.20	.33 (.33)
At least one organizer per 100 eligible voters	.09	.11	.89 (.74)	.07	1.00 (.89)	.10	1.00 (.64)	.16	.60 (.46)
Union used five or more rank-and-file tactics [c]									

[a] The employer campaign breakdown was created as follows: "No or Weak Employer Campaign" includes all elections in which the employer ran no campaign or used only one tactic (46% of sample); "Medium Employer Campaign" includes all elections in which the employer used two to five antiunion tactics (46% of sample); "Intensive Employer Campaign" includes all elections in which the employer used more than five tactics (8% of sample). The antiunion tactics include: captive-audience meetings; antiunion committees; antiunion leaflets; supervisor one-on-ones; unscheduled wage increases during the campaign; promises of improvements in wages, benefits, or working conditions; promotion of key union leaders; and media campaigns.

[b] Number in parentheses lists the percent win rate when the characteristic did not occur.

[c] Rank-and-file tactics include the following practices: at least one steward per 30 eligible voters; stewards elected; union conducted orientation; regular membership meetings; regular newsletters; two or more grievances per month; grievance victories and losses publicized; stewards trained to organize around grievances; staff representative frequently visits workplace; internal organizing on meeting agenda; union used one-on-one contract survey; active rank-and-file organizing committee.

an even greater difference; in this case, win rates increased to 40 percent. Similarly, the win rates increased to 80 percent if 70 percent of the bargaining unit signed cards prior to filing the petition. The use of solidarity days increased the win rate to 60 percent, as opposed to 20 percent when they were not used. It is not that any one of these tactics is important individually, but they are all in some ways proxies for a more aggressive organizing campaign involving rank-and-file members in person-to-person contact and a grassroots campaign from the very beginning. In campaigns in which more than five rank-and-file tactics were used, win rates increased by 15 percentage points overall, 11 percentage points in units with moderate employer opposition, and 14 percentage points in units with intense employer opposition. When included in regression and logit equations controlling for the influence of election and unit background and employer tactic variables, the probability of the union winning the election increased by 6 percentage points and the percentage of the votes received by the union increased by 3 percentage points for each additional rank-and-file-intensive tactic used by the union during the organizing campaign (Bronfenbrenner and Juravich 1995c).

Although these data are not as robust as they might be because of the relatively few elections during 1991–92 in which there was intense employer opposition, these findings support research from the private sector on the importance of rank-and-file grassroots strategies (Bronfenbrenner 1993). These data are also reinforced by our examination of first-contract and membership rates in the public sector (Bronfenbrenner and Juravich 1995c). Given the high win rate there, first-contract and membership rates may be the best measures of the effectiveness of organizing campaigns. It is one thing to vote for a union that has a high likelihood of winning; it demonstrates a much greater level of commitment to choose to voluntarily join a union and pay dues.

Table 16.4 provides data on the impact of union tactics on post-first-contract membership rates. Clearly, the use of rank-and-file grassroots tactics leads to significantly higher win rates. For example, representative rank-and-file organizing committees were used in only 3 percent of the campaigns that resulted in post-contract membership rates of less than 60 percent. They were utilized in 34 percent of the campaigns that achieved 60 percent to 90 percent membership, however, and 35 percent in those units that reached more than 90 percent membership. Only 38 percent of the members were house called in elections that yielded less than 60 percent membership, while 40 percent and 44 percent were house called in campaigns that yielded 60 percent to 90 percent membership and more than 90 percent membership, respectively.

Overall, although none of the units that ended up with less than 60

TABLE 16.4. Union Tactics and Post-First-Contract Membership Rates

	Proportion or Mean for All Units with Contracts	Postcontract Membership Rate[a]		
		Proportion or Mean with Less than 60% Membership	Proportion or Mean with 60–90% Membership	Proportion or Mean with 90% or More Membership
UNION TACTICS				
Percent cards	.63	.58	.62	.67
At least 70% cards	.39	.22	.41	.48
Organizing committee used	.77	.78	.74	.80
Percent on committee	.07	.04	.08	.09
Representative committee	.25	.03	.34	.35
Diagrammed workplace	.56	.57	.64	.46
Percent house called	.40	.28	.40	.44
50% or more house called	.07	.03	.10	.07
Number of mass meetings	4.33	4.42	4.50	4.09
Number of small-group meetings	10.13	8.11	14.81	7.57
Percent surveyed one-on-one	.10	.03	.10	.17
Rank-and-file did house calls	.17	.14	.23	.13
Solidarity days used	.19	.19	.21	.17
Number of letters	3.14	4.89	2.05	2.76
Number of leaflets	4.63	5.28	4.88	4.04
Dignity and fairness primary issues	.37	.36	.26	.46
Bargaining committee before election	.15	.03	.24	.15
Number of rank-and-file intensive tactics used[b]	2.32	1.78	2.55	2.59
Union campaign included five or more tactics	.09	.00	.07	.17
At least one organizer per 100 eligible voters	.80	.78	.76	.85

[a] Twenty-nine percent of the elections in the sample had a postcontract membership rate of less than 60%, 34% had a membership rate of between 60% and 90%, and 37% had a membership rate of 90% or more.
[b] Rank-and-file tactics include the following: 70% or more of the unit signed cards before the petition was filed; union had a representative committee; union used small-group meetings; union house called the majority of the unit; union used rank-and-file volunteers to do house calls; dignity, fairness, and service quality primary issues; union used one-on-one contract surveys; and bargaining committee established before the election.

percent membership ran aggressive grassroots campaigns utilizing five or more union tactics, 7 percent of the units with 60 percent to 90 percent membership rates and 17 percent of the units with more than 90 percent membership rates ran more aggressive campaigns. When individual union tactics are combined into a single rank-and-file-intensive variable controlling for the impact of election and unit background and management tactics variables, the probability of the union achieving a postcontract membership rate of at least 60 percent increased by 9 percentage points, and the membership rate increased by 6 percentage points for each additional rank-and-file-intensive tactic the union used (Bronfenbrenner and Juravich 1995c).

Decertification and Challenge Elections in the Public Sector

In addition to low win rates in elections in which public-sector employers choose to oppose the union, another indicator of the vulnerability of public-sector unions in the current political climate is the high level of decertification activity. Returning to table 16.1, a total of 162 single units decertified in 1991–92. In a dramatic departure from certification elections, unions in the public sector won in fewer than half of these elections.

Even more troubling is the large number of challenge elections, in which a union tries to win representation for a unit already represented by another union. In fact, one of every six elections in the public sector is a multiunion challenge election. As reported in table 16.1, incumbent unions fare quite poorly, winning only 33 percent of challenge elections. Although more than ninety thousand workers in state and local government gained union representation in 1991 and 1992, during the same period 2,868 chose to go nonunion, while another 45,641 simply switched from one union to another. Clearly, this is a far-from-ideal organizing situation and one that will need to be changed dramatically if attacks on public-sector unions continue.

The challenge process is also not a mechanism for larger unions to absorb smaller independents. In fact, unions were just as likely to leave the AFL-CIO as to join through challenge elections. One of the findings of this research was that there has been a reemergence of a significant number of independent site-based unions. For all intents and purposes, these unions appeared to be little more than company unions associated with an earlier era in public-sector unionism.

Although the win rates in certification elections look extremely favorable, they hide the fact that most of these elections occur in very small units. When combined with the relatively high level of decertification activity, this makes for a net gain in workers covered under public-sector collective bargaining agreements that is dwarfed by the hundreds of thousands of public-sector workers who lose union representation each year as a result of layoffs and privatization. Further, as shown in table 16.4, a significant number of public-sector unions have not been able to translate their relatively easy organizing victories into lasting union strongholds. Although unions won elections with victory margins that were higher than 85 percent, this translated into average membership rates of only 70 percent once the first contract was negotiated. For too many public-sector units, membership continues to drop in the years following the first agreement, until it reaches a point where a significant minority are ready to sign a decertification petition.

In our intensive look at decertification elections, we examined factors that could possibly explain the high level of decertification activity and the extremely low win rates for incumbent unions. To begin with, we discovered that decertification and challenges are not rooted in worker dissatisfaction with their pay, benefits, or conditions. Nor are employers involved in any significant way in either single-union decertification or challenge elections in the public sector.

Still, the nature of the original organizing campaigns did have a significant impact on the outcomes of decertification and challenge elections. If they won the original organizing campaigns by a large margin, incumbents won only 60 percent of decertifications and challenges. But in units with small margins of victory, the win rates for incumbents rose to 87 percent. What these numbers seem to capture is that to win in the face of aggressive opposition, the unit must coalesce against the employer and in the process build a strong union. When the campaign is easy, there is little opportunity to become a cohesive organization. We are not suggesting that more employer opposition is needed to build stronger unions in the public sector but that, absent an aggressive employer campaign, public-sector unions will need to focus on other avenues of union building to create a union strong enough to withstand future challenges.

As we can see from table 16.5, another major factor in how the incumbent union will fare in decertification and challenge elections is the quality and degree of union representation prior to the decertification petition being filed. For example, win rates for incumbent unions were 5 to 10 percentage points higher in units in which they had at least one steward per thirty eligible voters, conducted orientation for new employees, held regular membership meetings and published newsletters, publicized grievance victories and losses, and trained stewards to organize around grievances. Win rates were much lower in units in which stewards were appointed rather than elected, few grievances were filed, most grievances related to discipline and discharge, and the staff representative never visited the workplace. Bargaining practice mattered as well, so that win rates for incumbent unions were much higher in units in which the union used a one-on-one contract survey and had an active rank-and-file bargaining committee. Overall, incumbents won 68 percent of elections in units in which union practice and structure prior to filing the decertification petition reflected an organizing model, compared with 51 percent in units in which it did not.

Our data also demonstrate that, once faced with a decertification or challenge election, an incumbent union needs to mount an organizing campaign if it is to be successful. One reason that incumbents fare so poorly is that they often match an organizer employed by the challenging union against a servicing representative for the incumbent union. While the servicing staff may be very good at handling grievances, negotiating local agreements, and dealing with management, many servicing representatives have little or no experience with organizing.

TABLE 16.5. Union Structure and Practice Prior to Decertification

	All Decertification and Challenge Elections		
	Mean or Proportion of Sample	Mean or Proportion of Incumbent Wins	Percent Incumbent Win Rate[a]
UNION STRUCTURE			
Ratio of stewards to eligible voters	.05	.05	N.A.
At least one steward per 30 eligible voters	.55	.58	.62 (.54)
Stewards elected	.32	.36	.65 (.55)
Stewards appointed	.29	.23	.46 (.63)
Union conducted orientation for new employees	.36	.40	.65 (.55)
Regular membership meetings	.78	.82	.61 (.48)
Average number of membership meetings per year	5.93	5.67	N.A.
Union had regular newsletter	.42	.46	.64 (.54)
Union filed few grievances	.53	.49	.54 (.63)
Union averaged two or more grievances per month	.16	.17	.59 (.58)
Most grievances related to discipline or discharge	.22	.19	.50 (.61)
Union lost several major arbitrations	.10	.05	.31 (.61)
Grievance victories and losses publicized	.17	.22	.74 (.55)
Stewards trained to organize around grievances	.09	.10	.67 (.57)
Staff rep frequently visited workplace	.55	.54	.58 (.59)
Staff rep never visited workplace	.07	.05	.44 (.59)
Internal organizing campaign conducted	.38	.37	.57 (.59)
Internal organizing on meeting agenda	.27	.28	.61 (.57)
BARGAINING PRACTICE			
Bargaining part of state-, city-, or county-wide negotiation	.10	.10	.62 (.58)

TABLE 16.5. Union Structure and Practice Prior to Decertification (*cont.*)

	All Decertification and Challenge Elections		
	Mean or Proportion of Sample	Mean or Proportion of Incumbent Wins	Percent Incumbent Win Rate[a]
BARGAINING PRACTICE (*cont.*)			
Union used one-on-one contract survey	.50	.56	.66 (.51)
Bargaining conducted primarily by staff and officers	.75	.72	.56 (.65)
Bargaining committee elected	.45	.47	.62 (.55)
Bargaining committee small (less than 5%)	.75	.78	.61 (.50)
Most details of bargaining session remained confidential	.57	.58	.59 (.57)
Active rank-and-file bargaining committee	.34	.36	.62 (.56)
Union used inside pressure tactics	.00	—	—
Union used outside pressure tactics	.13	.10	.47 (.60)
Union reached agreement before last contract expired	.33	.36	.64 (.56)
Last contract never settled	.02	.00	.00 (.59)
Union held strike	.03	.03	.50 (.58)
OVERALL UNION STRUCTURE/PRACTICES			
Union used five or more elements of organizing model scale[b]	.43	.50	.68 (.51)

[a] Number in parentheses lists the percent win rate when the characteristic did not occur.

[b] Scale includes the following practices: at least one steward per 30 eligible voters; stewards elected; union conducted orientation; regular membership meetings; regular newsletters; two or more grievances per month; grievance victories and losses publicized; stewards trained to organize around grievances; staff representative frequently visits workplace; internal organizing on meeting agenda; union used one-on-one contract survey; active rank-and-file organizing committee.

The nature of the incumbent union's organizing campaign matters as well. Just as we found in public- and private-sector certification election campaigns, the use of a grassroots rank-and-file-intensive union-building strategy was found to play a critical role in decertification and challenge election campaigns. As we can see from table 16.6, the use of active, representative organizing committees boosts incumbents' win rates from 50 to 84 percent. The use of solidarity days raises the win rate from 50 to 87 percent. Similar effects are reported for the use of rank-and-file volunteers, one-on-one surveys, and house calling. Overall, win rates for incumbent unions average 68 percent when they run aggressive union-building campaigns incorporating five or more rank-and-file-intensive tactics, compared with 49 percent when they do not.

TABLE 16.6. Incumbent Union Tactics Used during Decertification Campaigns

	All Decertification and Challenge Elections			Single-Union Decertifications		Multiunion Challenge Elections	
	Mean or Proportion of Sample	Mean or Proportion of Incumbent Wins	Percent Incumbent Win Rate[a]	Mean or Proportion of Decerts	Percent Incumbent Win Rate[a]	Mean or Proportion of Challenges	Percent Incumbent Win Rate[a]
Union did not conduct a campaign	.05	.00	.00 (.61)	.03	.00 (.73)	.06	.00 (.58)
Union set up organizing committee	.78	.87	.65 (.34)	.87	.74 (.50)	.78	.62 (.32)
Percent of unit represented on committee	.08	.09	N.A.	.12	N.A.	.07	N.A.
Active representative organizing committee	.23	.33	.84 (.50)	.42	.85 (.61)	.18	.83 (.48)
Union actively used rank-and-file volunteers	.42	.45	.63 (.55)	.48	.80 (.63)	.40	.56 (.53)
Union diagrammed workplace	.63	.73	.67 (.43)	.48	.80 (.63)	.68	.64 (.33)
Union used house calls	.34	.36	.61 (.57)	.48	.67 (.75)	.30	.58 (.53)
Union house called majority of unit	.09	.08	.50 (.59)	.19	.67 (.72)	.06	.33 (.56)
Union held large-group meetings	.61	.56	.54 (.65)	.61	.74 (.67)	.61	.48 (.65)
Number of meetings	5.04	4.10	N.A.	6.58	N.A.	4.53	N.A.
Union held small-group meetings	.61	.71	.67 (.44)	.65	.75 (.64)	.60	.65 (.39)
Number of meetings	17.33	12.10	N.A.	9.15	N.A.	20.15	N.A.
Union used solidarity days	.22	.33	.87 (.50)	.39	.92 (.58)	.18	.83 (.48)
Union used leaflets	.66	.76	.67 (.41)	.65	.70 (.73)	.66	.66 (.31)
Number of leaflets	8.75	9.88	N.A.	6.17	N.A.	9.61	N.A.
Union used letters	.75	.83	.64 (.39)	.87	.70 (.75)	.72	.62 (.34)
Number of letters	4.41	5.02	N.A.	3.68	N.A.	4.72	N.A.

TABLE 16.6. Incumbent Union Tactics Used during Decertification Campaigns (*cont.*)

	All Decertification and Challenge Elections			Single-Union Decertifications		Multiunion Challenge Elections	
	Mean or Proportion of Sample	Mean or Proportion of Incumbent Wins	Percent Incumbent Win Rate[a]	Mean or Proportion of Decerts	Percent Incumbent Win Rate[a]	Mean or Proportion of Challenges	Percent Incumbent Win Rate[a]
Union used one-on-one survey	.13	.18	.78 (.55)	.13	1.00 (.67)	.14	.71 (.52)
Union representatives/officers increased visits	.78	.83	.63 (.43)	.74	.74 (.63)	.79	.59 (.36)
Union offered new benefits, services	.22	.17	.45 (.62)	.16	.60 (.73)	.23	.42 (.58)
Union held rallies	.16	.17	.62 (.58)	.26	.75 (.70)	.13	.54 (.54)
Union provided food or meals	.31	.32	.61 (.57)	.00	—	.40	.61 (.50)
Union organized job actions	.02	.01	.50 (.58)	.03	1.00 (.70)	.01	.00 (.55)
Union held public forums or debates	.13	.12	.53 (.59)	.00	—	.17	.53 (.55)
Union used media	.07	.06	.56 (.58)	.10	.67 (.71)	.06	.50 (.55)
Union used polling	.26	.26	.57 (.59)	.00	—	.34	.57 (.53)
Union involved community-labor groups	.16	.14	.50 (.60)	.19	.67 (.72)	.16	.44 (.56)
Union distributed trinkets	.21	.19	.54 (.59)	.00	—	.27	.54 (.55)
Union distributed items of value	.02	.03	.67 (.58)	.00	—	.03	.67 (.54)
Union used five or more tactics[b]	.49	.58	.68 (.49)	.58	.78 (.62)	.47	.65 (.45)

[a] Number in parentheses equals win rate when characteristic did not occur.

[b] Union tactics include: active representative organizing committee, active rank-and-file volunteers, diagramming workplace, house calls, small-group meetings, solidarity days, leaflets, letters, one-on-one survey, rallies.

Conclusions

In many ways the situation in the public sector is not unlike that in the private sector twenty years ago. Just as private-sector unionists in the early 1970s had many reasons to believe that their membership levels and bargaining power would continue to thrive whether or not they engaged in massive new organizing, many public-sector unionists continue to feel relatively secure about both the employment picture and the labor relations climate.[3] Yet important and significant threats are on the horizon that are beginning to fundamentally alter the situation that public-sector unions have come to know and expect. Just as twenty years ago the private sector began to face the growth of multinational corporations and an unpredicted wave of plant closings and concession contracts, the public sector is facing the devolution of government and massive privatization schemes.

In retrospect, the initial response by private-sector unions to the crisis was woefully inadequate. The commitment and dedication of trade unionists were not the problem, but many continued to see and approach very dramatically changed circumstances with the same attitudes, tools, and practices they had learned and used in the past. Rather than turning to community-labor coalitions, active membership mobilization, or new organizing, most private-sector unions held on to a fairly traditional top-down servicing and bargaining model honed in the 1950s and 1960s. New organizing was one of the first things to flounder as employers became emboldened with a variety of legal and illegal tactics.

This research demonstrates the cost if public-sector workers and unions are similarly unresponsive to the challenges they face. Because of the relative lack of employer opposition in the public sector, a culture and practices have developed that promote and reinforce a traditional top-down model in servicing, bargaining, and new organizing, with a primary emphasis on shoring up union power through lobbying in city halls, state legislatures, and governors' mansions. Although these approaches may have been sufficient in the past, they are clearly inadequate for the future. Given growing employer opposition to organizing, public antipathy toward government workers, and the increasing risk of decertification and challenges, public-sector unions must both strengthen their existing units and build strong and active unions in newly organized units that can withstand these many internal and external challenges.

3. There is also little recognition of the seriousness of the attack on the public sector in the industrial relations community. For example, "Collective Bargaining Outlook for 1995" (Sleemi 1995) doesn't even mention the new threats in the public sector. In fact, one section heading states simply "New Year, Same Issues."

As the findings on the certification, decertification, and challenge process show us, building unions in the public sector will require more commitment to the use of rank-and-file grassroots tactics. The data speak to the importance of rank-and-file activism and of mobilizing public-sector union membership and community support. Given the level of attack, union staff and officers will clearly be unable to solve these problems alone. Although perhaps less dramatic at this point, unions in the public sector, like their counterparts in the private sector, are reaching the limits of service-based unionism.

Particularly given the small size of many of the units being organized and the increasing fractionalization of public-sector employment, it is unlikely that union staff will have the capacity to "service" members in the same way as was done in basic manufacturing or in large geographically specific units in the public sector. More important, only through union building will public-sector unions be able to organize new members in the face of growing employer opposition and to defend their existing members from privatization schemes and political attack.

The stakes are very high. The stability of public-sector unionism in the 1970s and 1980s cushioned the dramatic decline in the private sector and has in important ways provided a base for rebuilding the labor movement. A number of signs, including the new leadership at the AFL-CIO, suggest that this renewal is well under way. Yet, as the painful experience of private-sector unions demonstrates, fortunes can change dramatically. A significant decline in public-sector unionism not only would have a tremendous impact on public-sector workers and their families but could very well threaten the entire labor movement. Given current union density, even a relatively modest downturn could be devastating.

As this research also suggests, a decline in the public sector is not inevitable. Even with growing employer opposition, rank-and-file, grassroots union-building strategies are effective in winning certification elections and first contracts and in achieving high membership rates. As we have seen, these same tactics also inoculate units and unions from both challenge and decertification elections. The message is clear. Public-sector unions today face both great opportunities and great risk. Like their private-sector counterparts twenty years earlier, they can wait until their ranks are decimated and their power severely diminished before they refocus their efforts and vision on new organizing. Or they can learn from the lessons of the past and start strengthening existing units and aggressively and effectively organizing new units before employer opposition and a deteriorating economic and political climate take their toll.

Chapter 17

The Impact of the Changing Structure of the Coal Industry on UMWA Organizing

Adrienne M. Birecree

At the time of the first National Bituminous Coal Wage Agreement between the Bituminous Coal Operators Association (BCOA) and the United Mine Workers of America in 1950, 90 percent of coal miners were UMWA members. By 1992, only 34 percent were. Academics have examined the UMWA's difficulties in organizing the growing number of western surface mines but not its problems in organizing nonunion mines in Appalachia. This chapter examines important changes in the industry's structure and the major operators' market strategies in the 1980s and 1990s that help explain the decline in union coverage, the nature of the problems the UMWA faces in organizing in coal, and the initiatives it has developed to overcome them. It concludes with a discussion of the UMWA's recent organizing success.

The Changing Industrial Landscape

Market Structure

Several important changes have taken place in the structure of the bituminous coal mining industry since 1973.[1] High returns from the energy crisis encouraged major oil, steel, chemical, and metal companies, electric utilities, and independent operators to expand coal mining operations through mergers, acquisitions, joint ventures, and investments in new reserves and mines (Miernyk 1976; Noyes 1978; Spindler 1985; Rodgers 1986; Gordon

---

1. Unless otherwise noted, the factual information in this chapter comes from various issues of the *United Mine Workers Journal* from 1983 to 1996.

1987). These changes caused an increase in the number of western non-union mines so that by the late 1970s only two of the industry's top fifteen firms were coal mining companies, traditional operators produced only 12 percent of output, and oil companies controlled one-third of domestic coal and 40 percent of U.S. reserves (Schnell 1979; Perry 1983; Seltzer 1985; Harvey 1986). Multinational energy and mining conglomerates invested heavily in world coal reserves, production, conversion, transportation, and trade in Colombia, Australia, South Africa, Canada, Chile, and China ("Is Coal the Fuel of the Future" 1986; Moore 1986; Johnson 1992).

During the 1980s, the presence and power of captive steel[2] and of the independent operators declined further as oil companies and utilities dominated western mining and increased their holdings in the East. In 1986, oil and gas companies accounted for almost half of production capacity (Energy Information Administration [EIA] 1987). By 1989, major operators' new mines produced almost 50 percent of the coal output in Appalachia (EIA 1991).

In the 1990s, the low price of coal and scarce finance capital have discouraged new investment ("Experts Debate" 1993). Expansion through mergers and acquisitions has continued, mostly involving properties in Appalachia, and has increased conglomerates' control of production from 14 percent of the total in 1976 to 33 percent in 1991, as well as their presence among industry leaders.

Between 1976 and 1986, the percentage of U.S. coal output controlled by foreign-based multinational mining conglomerates more than quadrupled (EIA 1987). By 1991, foreign producers, which had a 50 percent interest in eight major U.S. operators and controlled 14 percent of total output, led the industry (EIA 1993). Companies in which a foreign investor owned at least 10 percent of the voting securities controlled 24 percent of output. During the 1980s and 1990s, major U.S. operators also invested heavily in Australian, Colombian, Chinese, and Venezuelan coal.

Market Conditions in the 1980s

U.S. coal mining was highly profitable in the late 1970s (Rodgers 1986). Exporters realized even greater profits than did producers that sold coal only domestically (Hershey 1982; Rodgers 1986). Exporters sold Appalachian met coal to foreign steelmakers, especially the Japanese, who were operating at capacity and willingly paid premium prices for coking coal ("What Oils the Market" 1978). European utilities substituted imported steam coal for high-priced oil and entered into long-term contracts with U.S. exporters. Several forces converged during the 1980s to depress domes-

---

2. These were major steel companies that owned mines to obtain coking coal.

tic and international demand and prices for both grades of coal: the growing interest in energy conservation, import competition in autos and steel, and the decline in the industrial North (Seltzer 1985; Harvey 1986); the 1981–82 recession; falling oil prices; record domestic output levels, the consequence of the number of new mines in the industry; and the worldwide recession, weak European steel markets, and large foreign coal stockpiles (Brady 1983; Harvey 1986).

Utilities shifted their purchases from major operators, with which they had had long-term contracts and whose prices were locked in, to the spot market, where prices reflected current market conditions (Morais 1986; "Coal Buying" 1986). Western nonunion surface mines increasingly undercut eastern unionized producers' market shares by offering lower prices that reflected labor compensation absent substantial benefits and higher output per miner. Relative prices became increasingly important in foreign markets as the overvalued dollar and transportation costs of $18 to $20 a ton inflated U.S. coal prices abroad and eroded exporters' market shares. The growing number of alternative mining sites enabled conglomerate operators to take advantage of differences in labor costs, taxes, and environmental regulations abroad; to dominate global energy markets; and to maximize profits (Moore 1986). Unionized Appalachian miners increasingly competed with miners who worked under unsafe conditions for substantially lower wages and no benefits in Third World mines owned by multinational conglomerates. Southern utilities began substituting cheaper imported coal for Appalachian steam coal (Perl 1984).

In 1993, U.S. coal exports reached their lowest level since 1979, while imports, mostly shipments to electric utilities from Colombia, Venezuela, and Indonesia, grew 92 percent between 1992 and 1993 alone (EIA 1994). Intensifying competition in international met coal markets spawned collusion among large consumers, particularly the Japanese, who dominated regional international markets. They agreed on the highest price to be paid for imported coal and purchased it from operators who accepted their terms, depressing international and domestic coal prices (interview, Buckner 1996; Johnson 1992).

Major Operators' Strategic Responses to Market Problems

Unionized operators pursued several strategies to surmount their problems, all of which produced rising unemployment among UMWA miners throughout the 1980s and 1990s. Between 1984 and 1993, employment in mining fell 43 percent in the United States; in Appalachia, it dropped an average of 6.5 percent annually (EIA 1994). Smaller, less efficient mines were closed permanently (EIA 1991), and many major operators upgraded continuous mining systems and/or shifted to longwall technology to improve productivity and reduce costs (Seltzer 1985; Schroeder 1989). Production and employment continued to shift west (EIA 1994). Major operators also used their control of coal reserves to doublebreast operations and/or to subcontract all phases of mining to decrease labor costs. Conglomerates purchased reserves from unionized subsidiaries at prices well below market value and transferred them to newly established operations not subject to union contracts (interview, Buckner 1996). UMWA miners eventually were permanently laid off as reserves at the mines where they worked were reportedly exhausted. Under the auspices of new subsidiaries, nonunion operations then were opened to mine the transferred reserves.[3]

In the past, major Appalachian operators had used small companies to mine reserves that, for geological reasons, they could not mine themselves economically (interview, Buckner 1996). During the 1980s, they increasingly contracted out the mining of their coal reserves and began operating more as coal brokers than producers (interview, Fritz 1996). This activity involved not only U.S. coal but coal imported from South Africa and sold to southern utilities. This strategy enabled the companies to pass contract obligations to union miners on to contractors, to insulate profits from falling coal prices, and to reduce spending on substantial capital investments.

Contractors operated small, independent union and nonunion businesses with their own equipment and workforces; the latter often including laid-off UMWA miners. These contractors were responsible for all financial obligations to the miners, including health care, pensions, and workers' compensation, and for ensuring safe working conditions. Contractors delivered coal to major operators for a fee under contracts that often allowed the operators to reduce agreed-upon prices or to cancel orders unilaterally with little notice. Consequently, unionized contractors often violated contract terms and safety and environmental regulations with little opposition from the miners, who were haunted by the specter of unemployment.

As coal prices fell in the 1980s and 1990s, major operators cut contractors' prices. The majority of contractors went bankrupt, defaulting on their financial obligations to employees. But as quickly as they failed, others replaced them.[4]

The Organizing Challenge

The dramatic decline in union coverage during the 1980s (table 17.1) resulted from the industry's structural and strategic changes described above,

3. In 1984, Consol opened its nonunion Bailey complex in Pennsylvania, currently the largest U.S. underground operation, in this way (Berss 1993). By 1992, 25 percent of Consol's total output came from nonunion mines.

4. A. T. Massey and Island Creek hired more than 725 different contractors in Appalachia between 1980 and 1993.

TABLE 17.1. Employment, Union Membership, and Union Coverage in Coal Mining, 1983–94

Year	Employment	Percentage Change from Previous Year	Total Membership (1,000s)	Percentage Change from Previous Year	Percentage of Miners Unionized	Union Coverage
1983	174,885	—	107,502	—	61.47	62.80
1984	163,566	(6.5)	96,586	(11.3)	59.05	60.40
1985	180,214	10.1	81.601	(15.5)	45.28	46.40
1986	188,680	4.7	80,774	(1.0)	42.81	44.00
1987	161,345	(14.5)	72,541	(10.2)	44.96	46.61
1988	154,222	(4.4)	65,313	(11.1)	42.35	43.30
1989	152,284	(1.3)	60,137	(8.6)	39.49	41.76
1990	159,865	5.0	60,653	.9	37.94	40.27
1991	135,570	(15.2)	47,653	(21.4)	35.15	37.06
1992	116,509	(14.0)	39,450	(17.2)	33.86	33.96
1993	112,817	(3.3)	44,044	11.6	39.04	41.14
1994	117,500	(4.2)	44,500	1.0	38.00	39.90

Source: Barry Hirsch and David MacPherson, Union Membership and Coverage Files from the CPS, 1983–94, Florida State University, 1995.

local labor market conditions, and the characteristics and attitudes of nonunion miners, which, in combination, according to Gary Fritz, deputy director of organizing for the UMWA, has made coal "the ultimate, hardest place to organize" (interview, 1996). Operators engaged in doublebreasting do not simply hire the best-qualified miners; they also carefully screen all applicants at new nonunion mines, especially laid-off UMWA miners. When any union sympathy is displayed, intimidation, discharge, and other aggressive tactics are used to discourage it.

Highly unstable contractors operating small mines employ thousands of nonunion miners, who often work under illegal and dangerous conditions. According to Fritz, employment insecurity keeps most miners silent during organizing drives (interview, 1996). Most often, once a drive begins, contractors shut down operations and move elsewhere. Miners must follow the work. Thus, organizers face constantly moving targets, which makes organizing this industry segment very costly. Because the units are small and substantial resources may have to be committed to lengthy first-contract negotiations, the union may lose money while its membership grows imperceptibly (interview, Fritz 1996).

The problems organizers face in coal support Henry S. Farber's conclusion that "there has been a substantial drop in demand for union representation among nonunion workers that cannot be accounted for by shifts in labor force structure" (1989:166). The characteristics of the average nonunion miner are very different from those of workers now considered most receptive to organizing—urban minorities and women employed in low-wage occupations (Bronfenbrenner 1993). By contrast, miners are predominantly white males, some are college educated, and they earn high wages in rural areas where there are few to no alternative opportunities for employment. Those jobs that are available are in low-paying service industries in which the wages cannot compare with the $14 an hour average paid at nonunion mines. Thus, economic issues alone are not a sufficient focus for organizing drives.

Nonunion miners are not necessarily antiunion but free riders who seek to avoid union dues, though they understand that their earnings depend upon the UMWA's presence (interview, Fritz 1996). Some believe that the union is unnecessary because they are good workers who will be valued under any circumstances. Many are laid-off UMWA miners who often blame the UMWA, rather than operators' market strategies, for their lost job security.

Strategy, Structure, and Success

The organizing program that the UMWA has developed since 1983 to deal with these problems has five noteworthy features: (1) its underlying strategic philosophy, (2) its emphasis on education and training, (3) its institutional structure; (4) its scope, and (5) its favored tactics.

Strategic Philosophy

Beginning in 1983, the UMWA's primary objective became rebuilding the union using an organizing program based on the principle that "every member is an organizer." Rank-and-file members were to be the "front-line troops," teaching nonunion workers about the benefits of unionization. Before this strategy could be pursued, a union culture that had seriously dissipated had to be revived. As Fritz put it: "Our union suffers from the same thing every other union out there suffers from. [Our members] didn't have to work to get the union. It was already there. . . . They know nothing about the union, they know nothing about organized labor, and even if they attend local meetings, it doesn't mean they . . . understand what organized labor is about" (interview, 1996).

In the 1930s and 1940s, all UMWA members were involved in organizing (Duray 1995). Today, virtually no miners are left who participated in these campaigns. Most members entered mines in the 1970s where UMWA locals were well established, and their involvement was limited to paying dues (interview, Fritz 1996). The average member had never participated in an organizing drive and was not able to explain the rationale behind the labor movement or the benefits of unionization. One of the most critical tasks in organizing is convincing workers that "unions can play an effective role in the workplace" (Farber 1989:170). The heart of the UMWA's strategy is the education of its membership, one by one if necessary, about organized labor (interview, Fritz 1996).

The UMWA's leadership is well aware that winning a certification election and/or a first contract does not in itself build a union. The leaders recognize that education and hands-on experience are the best means for rebuilding a union culture. As then vice president Cecil Roberts explained: "When we organize, we are trying to add a new group of trained and active members to our movement for economic and social justice. By the time an organizing campaign is complete, the newly organized workers should be well on their way toward being able to take an active part in the labor movement" ("Every Member an Organizer" 1994:12).

Integral Role of Education and Training

Education and training of the UMWA's staff and of the rank and file have been integral to the organizing program begun in 1983. Intensive programs to provide staff and members with a background in organizing, in the UMWA, and in the labor movement have been developed based on the premise that an organizer's greatest asset is the ability to answer any question a worker might ask (interview, Fritz 1996). Organizers must communicate well, motivate people to work together, and help them learn to represent themselves, handle their grievances, and negotiate contracts. In December 1985, the first in a series of day-long educational seminars for local organizing committees in all districts was held in Pennsylvania to provide an overview of areas important in organizing—corporate investigation, labor law, basic public relations and communication, occupational health and safety laws, and the role of political action.

The UMWA has intensified these efforts in the 1990s (interview, Fritz 1996). In 1995, the Organizing Department held training sessions outside Washington, D.C., for staff organizers and rank-and-file members to increase their knowledge of the organizing challenge, the requirements for a successful campaign, and, thus, their effectiveness in actual drives. There were no prerequisites for participation, so most locals sent officers and members of organizing committees.

In late 1996 and throughout 1997, the union began taking refined sessions of its training directly to the membership, region by region, because many members did not like traveling to the 1995 sessions. To participate in these sessions, miners must be members of organizing committees.

Vast differences in participants' educational backgrounds has made developing program content problematic. All participants are valued equally because general education alone is not considered the best predictor of organizing ability. Thus, programs must be accessible to everyone but engaging enough for those with more ability. The 1995–96 training sessions constitute level one in the UMWA's educational program. Staff and rank-and-file members are familiarized with targeting, the organizing process, and the essentials of making house calls and initial contacts. Details about organized labor and NLRB procedures are imparted through board games that the Organizing Department has developed.

During level two, which began in the fall of 1996, participants develop specific skills more intensively. For example, house calls are so complex that teaching participants how to conduct them requires more than one session. In level one, staff organizers play unorganized workers in simulations of house calls in which they force participants to respond to the workers' fears, doubts, and difficult questions. Staff strongly emphasize that one of the most important tips participants should remember when making house calls is that they should never take a worker's level of knowledge about the UMWA for granted, even if the individual is a long-time union member (interview, Fritz 1996). They must assume initially that every worker they approach has no knowledge. The UMWA plans to provide uniform modular packages of similar training sessions to area organizing councils each month once these councils are formally established.

Institutional Structure

The development of an efficient and effective institutional structure was critical to the UMWA's organizing efforts, and, according to Fritz, the union has been busy "organizing to organize" (interview, 1996). In 1983, newly elected president Richard Trumka and other UMWA leaders reviewed the international's structure to determine the changes necessary to facilitate their strategy. The structure that was developed includes several features of a "high-performance" work system (Appelbaum and Batt 1994) and was expected to be more efficient and effective, a critical objective given the UMWA's declining membership and resource base.

Disciplined teams of well-trained personnel, each composed of a regional coordinator and professional organizers, constitute the structure's center. They develop organizing game plans to be implemented with the active participation of local organizing committees, the cornerstones of the union structure. Early on, all locals were strongly encouraged to establish these committees, and throughout the 1980s the UMWA Journal routinely provided information about how this could be done.

Establishing this structure has been very labor-intensive and time-consuming, and it is still evolving. Currently, the Organizing Department comes under the vice president's office, and the director of organizing is its head. The director works in conjunction with a deputy director, who oversees regional organizing directors. Regional organizing directors are responsible for coordinating the activities of staff/lead organizers, who work directly with local organizing committees.

Recently, some of these features were modified. In 1995, the director and deputy director redefined the team leader's position as one devoted to full-time organizing. G(rowth) O(n) A(ll) L(evels) 2000, the top responsibility, after organizing, of all officers and staff members, was adopted at the 1995 convention. Immediate duties are taken care of first, and any extra time is earmarked for organizing.

Also in 1995, Trumka appointed a special commission, including then vice president Cecil Roberts, international executive board members, district presidents, and rank-and-file members, to determine future institutional changes that would enable the UMWA to organize on a scale greater than ever before (Duray 1995). Then, in 1996, regional directors, whose jobs had been expanded in the past to include all of the region's business, became regional *organizing* directors, giving them their original focus (interview, Fritz 1996).

The UMWA also is establishing a formal network of organizing councils. Some area locals already have informal councils, projects, or committees in place to raise funds and increase public awareness of the UMWA. These are to be transformed into a formal, geographically uniform network of councils to facilitate future rank-and-file education and training specifically.

The UMWA has allocated increasing resources to organizing. At the union's 1990 one hundredth anniversary convention, delegates committed 50 percent of UMWA resources to new growth. In 1994, more than $200,000 of each district's funds were earmarked for organizing.

In July 1995, the international executive board and all district presidents met to formulate a plan to strengthen the organizing program further: $1 million in strike fund monies annually for matching funds for rank-and-file organizing assistance, lower average membership costs, and more financial support for the organizing program overall. These recommendations were presented to rank-and-file delegates in every district in July and August and adopted at the 1995 convention.

Expanding Scope of Activities

The UMWA has expanded the geographic and jurisdictional scope of organizing beyond its traditional boundaries. Since 1985, the Office of Allied Workers (OAW) has coordinated organizing in public- and private-service sectors. These efforts usually occur in regions where the UMWA already is well established. Delegates to the 1990 convention endorsed the establishment of an associate membership program for workers involved in organizing drives, UMWA supporters who worked on unsuccessful drives, UMWA family members, especially women in auxiliaries, and community action groups. In 1991, the UMWA allied itself with the International Brotherhood of DuPont Workers to cooperate in several areas, including organizing.

Recognizing that the relevant workforce is global and that foreign workers are potential allies, the UMWA has developed several international initiatives (Mabry 1992). UMWA leaders realize that to protect members' jobs and take wages out of competition, labor standards abroad must improve. International initiatives were begun in the 1970s when the UMWA spearheaded the U.S. labor movement's Shell boycott campaign during the anti-apartheid struggle in South Africa. The union helped young black South African trade unionists organize major industries and anti-apartheid strikes involving millions of workers. The UMWA also has become more active in the Miners' International Federation (MIF). It has actively cultivated a stronger relationship with the United Mineworkers of Australia (UMA) since it provided critical support during the 1989 Pittston strike. In 1990, the UMWA helped found the International Federation of United Mineworkers, thereby making a formal commitment to cooperative initiatives.

Since 1980, the UMWA also has supported Soviet miners. In the first venture of its kind between a North American union and Soviet workers, as part of a joint project with the AFL-CIO, UMWA representatives traveled to the U.S.S.R. to advise the independent miners union, the NPG, during 1991 unrest. That year, in Geneva, the UMWA and four international mine workers unions representing 1.2 million miners drafted "A Common Approach of International Coal Mining Unions," which recommended that UMWA tactics be adopted to strengthen existing campaigns and increase international union solidarity (Johnson 1992).

In 1992, the president of the German mine workers union, I. G. Bergbau und Energie, met with representatives of the UMWA and South American unions to develop common strategies. In 1994, UMA members attended a UMWA organizing training session in Alabama. Finally, in 1996, the MIF merged with the International Chemical Workers Federation, representing twenty million workers, to coordinate international initiatives formally.

Organizing Strategy and Tactics

The UMWA's organizing strategy includes two basic elements: targeting and the use of less traditional tactics. Highly sophisticated, intense employer resistance requires unions to choose their targets carefully (Chaison and Dhavale 1990). Though targeting is especially time-consuming and problematic when multinational conglomerates are involved, the vast differences in resources available to the union to mount drives compared with those at conglomerates' disposal to resist them in an economic and legal environment highly favorable to employers makes targeting imperative (interview, Fritz 1996).

Information about operators' ability and willingness to respond to unionization through the legal transfer of reserves and/or by moving or subcontracting operations, relationships between major operators and nonunion
contractors, and the potential size of the bargaining unit is essential to
reducing the risk of failure and the waste of precious resources. Staff organizers, organizing committee members, and internal union supporters are
required to collect detailed information necessary to determine the probability of winning an organizing campaign and first contract on a form that
includes more than two hundred questions about the company's financial
condition, ownership, management, customers, sales, profits, new hires,
employee characteristics, and labor relations history, as well as potential
campaign issues, community allies, and UMWA resources available in the
area. The regional organizing director, the director of organizing, and international officers then use this information to decide whether to initiate a
drive. If they decide not to, the information is kept in a centralized database
for future use.

Many organizers prefer to use less time-consuming tactics, such as flyers,
letters, and ads, during campaigns, but the UMWA is committed to what
have become less traditional tactics—house calls and in-house committees
(interview, Fritz 1996). Given conditions in local labor markets and the
characteristics of nonunion miners, one-on-one contact is necessary to educate them about the benefits of unionization beyond purely short-term economic interests. During house calls, organizers explain the union's value,
prepare workers for antiunion campaigns, evaluate individual reactions to
union arguments, and determine the issues of greatest concern to workers.[5]
Organizers also use the opportunity to develop rank-and-file leadership
skills and to get authorization cards signed.[6]

Certification drives and first-contract negotiations are treated in tandem.
The UMWA helps supporters establish in-house bargaining committees long
before a certification election, often with assistance from retirees and family
auxiliaries. Committee members identify issues and goals for first-contract
negotiations, boost morale during lengthy delays before the election and/or
first-contract negotiations, and improve support for the UMWA and its
ability to counter employer resistance.

UMWA organizers have learned that strategic timing increases the proba-

5. The power of house calls was revealed in a case involving the Decker Company's Sheri-
dan mine in the Powder River Basin in Wyoming. After a lengthy strike, UMWA members were
forced to work with permanent replacements hired during the dispute. When an agreement was
not reached during negotiations a few years later, Decker initiated a decertification campaign.
To fend off the threat, local UMWA members had to make house calls on workers who had
crossed picket lines to take their jobs. The UMWA won the election.

6. Election success is greater when members of in-house committees, rather than staff
organizers, collect authorization cards (Bronfenbrenner 1993).

bility of success. They keep a low profile when making house calls and setting up in-house committees. To reduce the time available to employers to resist drives, representation cards are not circulated until house calls have been completed and in-house committees well established.

The UMWA's Organizing Success

Despite its efforts, the UMWA was unable to stop the membership decline exacerbated by the structural and strategic changes occurring in the coal mining industry in the 1980s (table 17.1). Between 1983 and 1994, the union averaged a 42.3 percent success rate in certification elections involving coal miners. In the early 1990s, the rate of success increased to 49.3 percent. The indexes of organizing activity, presented in table 17.2, adapted from Joseph Rose and Gary Chaison's index (1990),[7] indicate the number of total elections and successful elections per one hundred union members. Both increased between 1983 and 1994.[8] Increasing organizing activity and the number of successful elections has not been sufficient, however, to change the industry's union coverage significantly. Even as employment grew in 1985 and 1986 (table 17.1), union membership continued to decline.

Evidence of the impact of the UMWA's program began to appear in the early 1990s. Eleven successful drives brought in twelve hundred new members in 1990. But despite these victories, union membership rose only .9 percent, while industry employment grew 5 percent that year. Faced with unrelenting structural change and opposition from coal operators, the UMWA's efforts made no dent in union coverage between 1990 and 1992. Industry employment declined by 27 percent, union membership by 35 percent.

In 1993, the union won perhaps its most important victory so far, at Zeigler Holding Company's Marrowbone Development Corp.,[9] which spurred the strongest wave of organizing in Appalachia in fifteen years. The union also won six other representation elections at nonunion operations

7. Rose and Chaison measured the intensity of U.S. organizing activity by calculating the number of certification elections per one hundred union members.

8. The indexes understate the intensity of UMWA organizing activity because the membership data available include all union members in the coal industry, not just UMWA members. Since the UMWA still represents at least 90 percent of unionized miners, however, the indexes present a very close estimate of UMWA organizing intensity and the trend in this activity during the period.

9. The Marrowbone complex is the second-largest coal operation in the East. The drive occurred during the UMWA's 1993 selective strike against the BCOA, which included a number of selective strikes at Zeigler's union operations. The Marrowbone victory made it more difficult for Zeigler to pit its nonunion miners against UMWA members called out at its targeted mines.

TABLE 17.2. Indexes of UMWA Organizing Activity in Coal, 1983–94

Year	Certification Elections	Number Won (%)	Union Membership	Index of Activity	Index of Successful Activity
1983	8	4 (50)	107,502	.007	.003
1984	12	7 (58)	96,586	.012	.007
1985	8	3 (38)	81,601	.010	.004
1986	9	2 (22)	80,774	.011	.002
1987	8	3 (38)	72,541	.011	.004
1988	11	4 (36)	65,313	.017	.006
1989	8	4 (50)	60,137	.013	.007
1990	10	3 (30)	60,635	.016	.005
1991	10	4 (40)	47,653	.021	.008
1992	9	4 (44)	39,450	.023	.010
1993	8	7 (88)	44,044	.018	.016
1994	9	4 (44)	44,500	.020	.009

Source: Election data provided by the National Labor Relations Board.

employing some twelve hundred miners, and declining UMWA membership in coal finally ended. That year was unusual because union membership rose by 11.6 percent while industry employment fell by 3.3 percent. Outside coal, the OAW organized more than 450 new members in 1993 and 180 workers in health care and 145 in private and public services in 1994.

In coal, membership increases in 1994 did not keep pace with the previous year. The industry added 4,683 new jobs, but union membership increased by only 456, slightly less than one-tenth of the employment increase. How much of this increase was due to organizing cannot be ascertained from the available data. Clearly, further substantial membership gains will occur only if the UMWA is successful in campaigns at large nonunion operations of traditionally unionized operators first and any remaining resources are used to organize smaller dispersed facilities thereafter. Given the industry's structural and strategic changes, future membership gains will most likely occur only as a result of continued, intensive organizing efforts, not employment growth at union operations, unless the UMWA can win very stringent contract language that will significantly stem the tide of major operators' doublebreasting and subcontracting and U.S. labor law reform is secured.

Conclusions

The UMWA continues to face significant obstacles in organizing major operators' nonunion mines. To its credit, the union, recognizing the impact of the ongoing domestic and international structural changes in the industry, has developed an ambitious long-term organizing program based on a relatively novel strategic philosophy. The program has involved building an institutional structure to support grassroots organizing efforts, expanding the scope of organizing beyond the union's traditional jurisdiction, emphasizing more time-consuming, less popular tactics, and devoting substantial resources to educating and training union staff and members so as to enhance their effective participation in organizing campaigns. Changes in all aspects of this program have been ongoing during its many years of development.

The UMWA has barely begun to reap the fruits of this program. Bringing an end to the declining trend in UMWA membership in coal took ten years. Its numbers there are finally increasing, but at an extremely slow pace. Without the development of its organizing program, the rate of decline most likely would have been worse and might have continued indefinitely. The UMWA also has recorded membership gains outside its traditional jurisdiction.

It could be argued effectively that the UMWA's recent successes are related to the program's underlying philosophy and institutional structure. Its structure exhibits several features of a high-performance work system (Appelbaum and Batt 1994): a relatively flat hierarchy, featuring teams of members from all levels; relatively democratic processes and communication networks that encourage the free flow of information throughout the system; meaningful input from members at all levels in deciding objectives, strategies, and tactics; education and training programs designed to empower all members and increase their organizational responsibilities, thus improving their identification with and participation in pursuing the union's objectives; and a commitment to current and potential members' economic security, no matter the cost.

In the long term, this cooperative work system should improve organizing effectiveness, reduce costs, and provide real improvements in the UMWA's performance and long-term survival. Given the formidable power of multinational conglomerates in domestic and international markets, coordinating the organizing program with hard-line negotiations over doublebreasting and subcontracting (the focus of 1993 negotiations), intensified pressure to reform labor law, and continued efforts to raise labor standards abroad appears to be the path that holds the greatest potential for improving future union coverage in coal.

Chapter 18

Creating an Organizing Culture in Today's Building and Construction Trades: A Case Study of IBEW Local 46

Janet Lewis and Bill Mirand

In the late 1940s, the building and construction trade unions represented more than 80 percent of all construction workers. Building trade unions continued to hold on to this working monopoly of the skilled construction labor supply until the early 1980s, when union representation fell to 20 percent (Erlich 1988). Unfortunately, the construction unions did not respond quickly to the significant decrease in membership or attempt to counter the growing antiunion sentiment pervading the nation. It was not until the late 1980s that they started to initiate new approaches to organizing in an effort to survive and regain their share of the labor market. The International Brotherhood of Electrical Workers was one of the first unions to respond to this crisis. At its 1986 international conference, the rank-and-file delegates issued a mandate to organize, reaffirming the IBEW's original "mission" to represent all construction electricians in the industry (interview, Grostick 1996).

In 1987, the international launched phase 1 of the IBEW's organizing efforts. International representatives, armed with an array of organizing tactics tailored for the construction industry, traveled to local unions to train the business managers and organizers in how to use these new methods. Phase 2, launched in 1988, required local unions to establish attainable organizing goals and appoint progress committees to achieve those goals.

Initially, business managers and local organizers encountered resistance from the rank-and-file members to funding and participating in these attempts at organizing. This resistance led to the creation of the Construction Organizing Membership Education Training Program (COMET) by the IBEW, with the assistance of Cornell University, in 1990.

COMET I is an extensive training program that educates IBEW members about the critical need to organize all unrepresented workers. COMET II trains organizers to engage in "action capsules" or organizing strategy scenarios, specifically designed for the difficult task of organizing in the construction industry.

This chapter examines how IBEW Local Union 46 in Seattle created a successful organizing culture within its electrical construction unit from 1987 to 1995. Since 1987, Local 46 has consistently implemented a comprehensive organizing program blending innovative grassroots ideas with the COMET strategy and tactics. The Local 46 program is based on a whole-market strategy, which requires that the local analyze current and future trends in the local construction market and then change organizing tactics to match the current economy. Our study demonstrates why and how a combination of both "bottom-up" organizing tactics (focusing on employees) and "top-down" organizing tactics (focusing on employers and customers) is essential if local trade unions are to rebuild their memberships. The study also reveals that the Local 46 program is successful because it is a varied, flexible, integrated, and collaborative approach to organizing, ensuring short-term successes evolve into long-term union market strength.

Local 46's organizing campaign, now in its ninth year, has produced a unionization rate of more than 55 percent of all area electricians and 74 percent union density in the commercial/industrial electrical construction market in Seattle in 1995. Local 46 has organized more than fifty-two nonunion shops and taken in more than six hundred unorganized electricians and apprentices since 1987 (IBEW Local 46 1994). Base wages for commercial construction electricians have risen from the low concessionary wage of $17.56 granted in 1984 to $24.31 in 1995. The organizing program was funded initially by a $.25-per-hour assessment of each working member, which provided a budget of $125,000 the first year. This budget has increased to more than $1 million from an assessment of $.40 per hour, voted by the membership in 1994.

Building an Internal Organizing Culture

Recognizing the Nonunion Threat

In 1984, Local 46 lost 100 percent of its share of the residential construction market and controlled only 54 percent of the area commercial/industrial market, down from 94 percent in 1981. A 40 percent loss of the union commercial/industrial market was a wake-up call to members of their tremendous loss of bargaining strength in a major construction market such as Seattle.

With more than 35 percent of its members unemployed, some having abandoned the union, the union leadership was under pressure to stop the wholesale exodus of union employers and members. Thus, in 1983–84, the membership granted a total of $4.50 per hour in wage concessions to its signatory contractors in an attempt to "stop the hemorrhaging and buy time to rethink our future" (interview, Grostick 1996). The wage concession did not create more jobs for union electricians, but it did stop more union contractors from leaving the fold.

Local 46 leaders realized, too late, that trying to make union contractors more competitive through wage concessions and productivity gains had little or no effect on market share. New ways of thinking about how to organize and control the skilled labor pool, as well as other creative ways the union could affect the bottom line of nonunion employers, were needed.

Member Education and Mobilization

Bill Grostick, IBEW's international representative, recalls that the international's overall strategy to regain control of the lost labor pool involved training local labor leaders in new aggressive organizing tactics (interview, 1996). Reluctance to change among the members had been anticipated, but for many local leaders, the depth and breadth of this opposition became an almost insurmountable hurdle.

Exclusionary membership practices had developed within the building trades, causing members to view the nonunion worker as the "enemy." Changing this outmoded and prejudicial thinking about organizing the nonunion workforce became the first order of business. Convincing members that the nonunion worker was not the enemy but was actually the key to the union's survival required an evolutionary shift in members' consciousness and in the union's culture from one of exclusivity to inclusion to guarantee long-term organizing success.

In the late 1980s, then business manager Dave Jordan and organizers Jim Freese and Jim Lukehart created a detailed organizing plan to educate members about the concerted war being waged to break the construction unions and to fight back to preserve their way of life (interview, Freese 1995). The primary goals of the plan included (1) member education and participation; (2) identification of employers and upcoming projects as organizing targets; (3) infiltration and activity from within the nonunion contractors' businesses; (4) bottom-up recruitment of unrepresented workers; (5) better labor relations within the community and with existing union contractors; and (6) the application of economic pressure on nonunion contractors by using corporate campaign tactics to erode their customer base and regulatory oversight to increase their internal operating costs.

Education began in-house with articles in the IBEW's newsletter and special meetings to address the nonunion threat. But many members still felt powerless and unsure of the new aggressive methods needed to stop the nonunion takeover.

Organizing Tactics

The question faced by all building and construction trades in the late 1980s was how to successfully organize a constantly changing, on-the-move workforce employed by numerous local and national employers. The successful campaigns waged by industrial unions offered a model based on organizing a captive workforce employed at a fixed location using the site-specific, single-employer NLRB election strategies. Because of the short-term duration of most construction projects, site-specific union elections often fail because the job is completed and the workforce dispersed before the election can be held. The IBEW began to focus instead on control of the labor pool within a local union jurisdiction, not by organizing employers at specific locations but by organizing employees individually and thereby controlling the availability of the workforce. Employers would then have to seek out the union to fulfill their need for skilled labor or move out of the jurisdiction. "One of the major differences between construction and industrial organizing is that the construction organizer's first concern is to police a geographical trade jurisdiction, i.e., to make sure the work is performed under union standards and to prevent nonsignatory employers from operating there" (IBEW 1994:6). The goal is not to bargain individually with nonunion contractors but to apply economic pressure on them to sign the union's basic construction agreement for the jurisdiction.

The early organizing efforts of Local 46 assumed a confrontational and litigious approach toward nonunion employers. This hard-hitting strategy was adopted in response to the very real threat of extinction faced by the union. The organizers successfully used environmental intervention tactics to stop several nonunion projects by blocking the issuance of permits and to label the developers and contractors as unscrupulous and greedy. Aggressive reporting of workplace safety and prevailing wage violations resulted in fines and adverse publicity for many nonunion contractors, as well as loss of their image-conscious customers. Creating internal costs for nonunion contractors, by forcing their bid prices to increase to levels commensurate with those of union contractors, became a prime focus.

Active recruitment of key nonunion skilled craftspeople into the union, a practice known as stripping, left many employers without adequate manpower. In fact, the union opened its doors to more than 250 individual electricians during the first two years of the campaign. Infiltration, confrontation, and litigation were the strategies of choice used to apply economic pressure on employers to sign union agreements and to eliminate substandard competitors. Trench warfare had begun in earnest against the newly identified enemy, nonunion employers.

Hugh Hafer, attorney for Local 46, offered some insights about the effectiveness of these early organizing strategies (interview, 1996). Too much focus on harassment and litigation against an employer was counterproductive for organizers, who expended huge amounts of time, energy, and money preparing for litigation instead of organizing. According to Hafer, a successful organizing program must include legal tactics as part of the organizer's toolbox but litigation should not be the goal of every campaign. Bringing too many new members into the union without also creating new job opportunities could be detrimental in the long run. A backlash did occur in 1991, when the membership voted to stop funding the organizing campaign. Fearing the entry of large numbers of nonunion workers, the members demanded the formation of a new organizing committee to monitor the spending and activities of the organizers. Hafer credits Bill Mirand, Local 46's current business manager, with guiding the organizing efforts so that they could evolve into a multifaceted whole-market program with an arsenal of legally sound tactics to fit each organizing scenario.

The whole-market approach requires that a local union assess its current bargaining power, its union market share, the strengths and weaknesses of the nonunion sector, the vulnerabilities of owners and developers, the local construction market economy, and the opportunity for support from the community. Local 46 began to examine its unique market conditions in the early 1990s and to identify key market sectors lost to the nonunion sector.

A new way of thinking began to emerge and with it hope for the future. The local union could actually influence, direct, and eventually control some market forces, specifically the hiring process, by using a variety of tactics carefully tailored to fit the local construction economy and each unique employer/employee situation. Local 46 organizers Greg Galusha and John Walsh point out that a successful organizer must use all the tools available and be willing to abandon a tactic when it is not working (interview, Galusha and Walsh 1995). Thorough research into an employer's customers, current high-profile jobs, and the impact of missed deadlines is necessary to orchestrate a successful campaign. Figure 18.1 illustrates the array of tactics available to the construction organizer using the whole-market approach. Some of these tactics are discussed in detail below.

The COMET II program, the official strategic approach for organizing the building and construction trades, advocates this whole-market strategy. By utilizing a combination of tactics, a local union can regain monopoly control of the regional labor pool and at the same time broaden the union contractor base (IBEW 1996b). The whole-market approach embraces both the bottom-up philosophy of organizing individual skilled electricians and the top-down philosophy of signing collective bargaining agreements. The

Figure 18.1 IBEW Local 46's Organizing Tactics

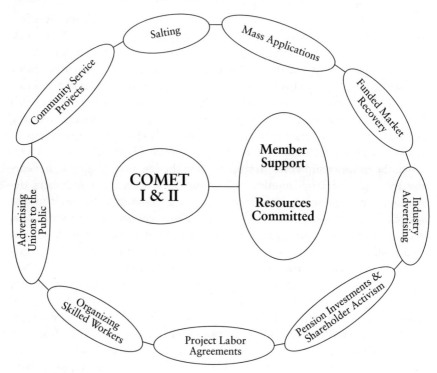

Source: IBEW Local Union 46.

task of organizing electricians cannot take place in a vacuum; the union must also simultaneously organize employers and create new job opportunities. Nonunion employers faced with loss of customers through exposure of their substandard practices and rising costs caused by mounting legal fees may choose to leave the area rather than sign a union contract. This loss is not necessarily detrimental to job growth, however, especially if the exodus opens up more bid opportunities for union contractors, who now can compete on a level playing field.

Bottom-Up Tactics

Education and Outreach

Member education through COMET: COMET I is the internal organizing tool through which IBEW members are educated about the organizing process. This phase of the program serves as the foundation for creating an internal organizing culture (IBEW 1996a).

Member education is divided into three stages. In the first stage, members learn about unionism and the need to organize all nonunion workers to control the labor pool. They also learn that it is essential to overcome the prejudice against nonunion workers, developed from years of restrictive membership practices. The second stage emphasizes that union members can control their destiny and turn losses into gains by actively participating in the union's organizing program. The third stage emphasizes the need for IBEW members to commit both personal and financial resources to a long-term organizing program. COMET I training is a required part of the curriculum for all IBEW apprentices and is mandatory training for new foremen and new nonunion inductees. Local 46 has graduated more than one thousand people from forty-five COMET classes, at a cost of approximately $5.00 per person (IBEW Local 46 1995). COMET classes help energize many members to participate in volunteer organizing activities and help build individual leadership skills and union consciousness.

Entry of nonunion workers: The entry of nonunion workers threatened many union members, who feared more competition for limited jobs and resented the waiver of formal apprenticeship training for nonunion workers accepted into journeyman status. A journeyman placement examination is administered to new recruits; those who do not possess the requisite skill level are placed into apprenticeship training when possible.

Many nonunion recruits become active organizers and make excellent salts because of their knowledge of and past work history in the nonunion sector. Newly organized workers contribute a sense of risk taking, accomplishment, and militancy to the status quo union culture, which helps keep the organizing momentum in forward motion.

Electrician's Digest: Initially, the union undertook the task of educating its membership about the need to organize through articles printed in the local's internal newsletter, *Sparks*. At that time, there was no publication in the Seattle area or in the state directed at unorganized employees. In 1987, Local 46 filled that gap when it developed a regional publication called *Electrician's Digest* for all career electricians. Its primary focus is on education about trade unionism and workers' rights. Today, *Electrician's Digest* is financed by all IBEW construction electrician locals and is circulated to more than fifteen thousand electricians nationwide. It is the most widely read building and construction trade organizing newsletter in the nation. The publication serves as a conduit to inform all electricians of their rights under state and federal law and relays the benefits and protections of unionism. And when the need arises, it serves as well as a means to quickly mobilize thousands of workers to protest antilabor legislation.

Public relations and advertising campaigns: In response to the antiunion messages prevalent in the media, Local 46 funded a comprehensive advertising campaign in 1989–90 to increase awareness of the quality of union work among consumers and the benefits of unionism among workers. Advertisements carrying the messages "Live Better, Work Union" and "Better Built, Union Built" were placed on buses and billboards and in local newspapers. Air time was also purchased on local radio stations to broadcast pro-union messages and to recruit nonunion workers with a 1–800 "Let's Talk Line." Estimated costs for Local 46 for the combined advertising campaign was $50,000 (IBEW Local 46 1990).

A greatly expanded media campaign, funded by the three Puget Sound IBEW locals—46, 191, and 76—and the area chapters of the National Electrical Contractors Association was launched in 1994. An important component of this campaign focuses on educating the customer of construction services about the quality and value of a union-built project. Local 46 was also instrumental in mobilizing the Washington State Labor Council to fund a statewide media campaign entitled "Foundation for Working Families," which emphasizes union values and the importance to working families of receiving living wages.

Salting the Nonunion Contractors' Labor Force

Access to the nonunion workforce: One of the most effective bottom-up tactics the IBEW engages in is called salting. Salting is the practice of sending out union members, individually or in groups, to apply for jobs and gain employment with nonunion contractors. The building trade unions have always forbidden and even fined union members for working for nonunion employers, thereby restricting access to unrepresented workers. More recently, however, many unions have passed salting resolutions that allow their members to work for nonunion employers and also organize while on the job. Union salts or nonunion salts (called peppers) attempt to strip key employees away from nonunion contractors; expose illegal employer practices and substandard working conditions; demand higher wages and better conditions for employees; and document unfair labor practices that may eventually lead to a strike.

Salting and unfair labor practice liability: Discrimination in the hiring process based on union affiliation or nonaffiliation is illegal and is considered an unfair labor practice by the NLRB. An employer found guilty of discrimination will be required to give each union applicant a nondiscriminatory consideration for hire for current and future job openings and may also be required to make all applicants whole with back pay and interest, even if there were more applicants than job openings. The unfair labor practice charge based on refusals to hire union salts has been a very powerful legal weapon and economic tool for local construction unions.

Reinstatement and back-pay awards for numerous refusal-to-hire violations can result in substantial costs for employers. Unfair labor practice cases take an average of one year for the administrative law judge's decision to be handed down and up to two years for a final Board decision when appealed. All the while, back-pay liability continues to accrue, along with mounting attorneys' fees. The economic impact of fighting numerous ULP charges hits small to medium-size contractors the hardest, since these contractors tend to survive on thin profit margins anyway. In an industry in which 85 percent of all employers employ twenty or fewer employees, the threat of ULP liability forces many small contractors to sign union agreements or substantially refrain from bidding on jobs that require additional hiring. Since 1987, Local 46 has filed unfair labor practice charges against approximately twenty-five nonunion contractors for discriminatory refusals to hire and associated illegal actions. Awards from successful complaints approach $500,000, and other large awards are pending NLRB decisions (IBEW Local 46 1996).

Blocking the nonunion hiring process: Local 46 organizers monitor the hiring activity of nonunion contractors through word of mouth, newspaper ads, bid awards, and nonunion employment agency activity. Constant salting of nonunion employers and employment agencies impedes the employers' control over the hiring process. Employers, fearful of hiring union organizers but at the same time fearful of not hiring union applicants because of discrimination, stop hiring altogether. Vigilant salting, combined with stripping away key employees, creates a shortage of skilled manpower. Many nonunion contractors, now unable to obtain adequate labor, either scale back and refrain from bidding future jobs or sign union agreements to gain access to workers.

In 1995, the union purchased a van and hired an additional organizer, Brett Olsen, to conduct the mass salting campaigns. One ongoing campaign is being conducted against the Contractor's Labor Pool, a five-state nonunion construction employment agency. More than one hundred union members answered advertisements for jobs but were rejected because past wages earned (union scale) were higher than the advertised wages. The union filed unfair labor practice charges with Region 19 NLRB, claiming that failure to hire union applicants based solely on past wage history constituted discrimination. The union's salting activity has effectively prevented the Contractor's Labor Pool from hiring electricians until the NLRB makes a decision on this question.

Top-Down Tactics

Regulatory Oversight

Local 46 organizers realized that another effective way to apply economic pressure on nonunion contractors was to force them to comply with the various federal and state labor protection laws, using covert salts to expose abuses. These laws tend to be enforced by labor unions more often against their signatory contractors than by individual nonunion workers against their nonunion employers. By forcing nonunion contractors to comply with labor laws, the burden of the cost of compliance is equalized for the union and the nonunion contractor. More important, the unorganized worker is protected and experiences firsthand the benefits of the collective voice of unionism.

From 1987 to 1989, Local 46 filed or reported more than fifty labor law violations that resulted in fines to employers for safety and licensing violations and more than $200,000 in back-pay awards to employees for prevailing wage violations (IBEW Local 46 1989). All IBEW locals in Washington State now work closely with the state Department of Labor and Industries to ensure that the state consistently enforces its safety, licensing, and inspection laws.

REBOUND

In 1988, in an effort to expand the use of environmental and corporate campaign strategies to other area trade locals, Local 46 provided the primary funding for a coalition called REBOUND. This organization has now assumed the tasks of environmental intervention and labor law compliance activities for all the area building trades. REBOUND maintains an on-line database of pending construction projects and contract awards and a database of the current state legislative agenda affecting labor. Although the Seattle/King County Building and Construction Trades Council currently funds and directs REBOUND's activities, state IBEW local unions contribute the largest share of REBOUND's budget.

Funded Market Recovery

Funded Market Recovery (FMR) is a job-targeting program that Local 46 initiated in 1993. The union offers a wage subsidy to any contractor willing to build its project using union labor. Union contractors that participate are able to bid more competitive wage rates and win jobs in markets dominated by nonunion contractors, such as the large box discount stores. This tactic has been very successful in regaining union density in the light commercial market previously lost to the nonunion sector. The union agrees to subsidize a specific number of labor hours on a project and makes cash payments directly to the contractor. Electricians working on market recovery projects receive full-scale wages, not a reduced concessionary wage package.

Since the inception of FMR, Local 46 has won approximately 150,000 hours of work on forty separate projects. The value of these hours translates into $5 million in real wages and benefits, at a cost of approximately $800,000 in wage subsidies (IBEW Local 46 1996). This is a return to the membership of $6 for every dollar invested from the organizing fund. Other area IBEW locals started market recovery programs several years earlier than Local 46 and claim even greater success rates with their programs. Critics of market recovery point out that it is really only a concessionary tactic and that unless it is used in conjunction with other bottom-up strategies, it will not result in the union regaining its monopoly control of the labor supply.

The Measure of Success

The Local 46 organizing program is successful for several reasons having to do with its structure and its adaptability. First, the approach is varied, because it is both strategic and tactical. The overall strategy of organizing electricians using a whole-market approach, using a variety of tactics, provides the theoretical framework on which a successful program can be built. Second, the program is flexible; able to respond quickly to conditions and challenges in its application and to prevailing market forces. Third, it is integrated, in that it combines a coherent approach with a sound management structure and committed membership participation and financial support. Fourth, and finally, it is collaborative. The program's long-term success depends on networking with other IBEW locals and building trade unions statewide, with state regulatory oversight agencies, with legal counsel, and with the NLRB.

Another measure of the IBEW's organizing success is the positive returns to the membership and to society from the resources expended. By utilizing a combination of tactics, Local 46 has expanded its limited organizing resources to produce an array of benefits and services for its members. Investment in member education produces a more active, committed membership. Engaging the membership in organizing activity develops leadership skills and a sense of empowerment. Salting provides jobs for out-of-work union electricians who return nonunion dollars back to the union workforce. Further, salting uncovers abuses of workers' rights and workplace standards, forcing employers to reallocate resources to cure those abuses. Bottom-up organizing breaks down barriers between union and nonunion workers, creating common ground. Market recovery programs enhance union market share and employ union members.

The success of a long-term organizing program in the building and construction trades cannot be measured solely by the increase or decrease in total union membership. A more accurate way to measure organizing success is by examining both membership and the capture of union market share within the jurisdiction where local organizing has occurred. Local 46 is one of the few locals nationwide that has increased its membership and its contractor base and recaptured 20 percent of its lost market share since 1987. This success story can be attributed to the union's dedicated membership; its creative, focused organizing department; its strong leadership by past and present business managers; and the support it has received from the international. By combining the proven techniques of COMET I and II with local talent, all building and construction trade unions can create their own successful organizing programs and control their futures.

Chapter 19

Construction Organizing:
A Case Study of Success

Brian Condit, Tom Davis, Jeff Grabelsky,
and Fred Kotler

This chapter examines how IBEW Local 611, based in Albuquerque, New Mexico, reversed its decline and between 1988 and 1994 reemerged as a dominant force in its jurisdiction. What the local did, how it did it, and what other building trade unions can learn from 611's success are the central points of the discussion.

IBEW Local 611's experience is instructive for several reasons. Its situation during the 1970s was typical of most crafts unions, and its first response to a crisis that gripped unionized construction in the 1980s was similar to that of many locals within and outside the IBEW: it made concessions and developed market recovery programs. What was remarkable about Local 611 was the way its leadership, at the urging of the international, embraced workforce organizing, developed a dynamic strategy, and mobilized the membership to support and activate it.

Staff organizers analyzed market data and developed this comprehensive strategy by examining the strengths and weaknesses of various players in the market. They creatively used a wide range of tactics, including salting, stripping, market recovery, and legal action, applying different degrees and kinds of pressure, depending on the circumstances, to different contractors. Moreover, they developed broad membership support for the local's organizing program through COMET; once the local had this support, it could identify and mobilize activists, fund full-time organizers, and, quite critically, "open the door" by welcoming new members and revising long-standing internal procedures and practices that were impeding workforce organizing. The local increased its membership by more than four hundred, or about 35 percent, from 1988 to 1995, and organized DKD Electric, the largest open-shop contractor, as well as fifteen other nonunion firms, in its jurisdiction. Further, according to internal documents from 1988 to 1994, the local dramatically diminished the threat from some particularly trouble-some contractors, such as the Gardner-Zemke Company.

Background on Local 611

Local 611's jurisdiction is immense. It covers more than 120,000 square miles—most of the state of New Mexico—and encompasses about 1.7 million people, including approximately twenty-five hundred licensed electricians.

Through the 1960s and 1970s, the local maintained a strong presence in the construction market by relying primarily on large industrial projects that employed large numbers of crafts workers. During the 1970s, the union estimated that its share of the construction market was about 45 percent, on the strength of relatively high levels of unionization in industrial con-struction (internal documents 1988–94).

The demand for skilled electricians during the 1970s exceeded the local's labor supply so that "travelers" from other jurisdictions, as well as non-union "permit workers," were invited to work on the area's mega-projects. When the large industrial jobs began to wind down in the 1980s, Local 611 reacted as did many building trades locals throughout the country: the travelers were sent home and the permit workers were returned to the jurisdiction's nonunion labor pool with new skills in industrial construction and a taste for union wages and conditions but resentful because they had been denied union membership.

Members of Local 611 who had enjoyed many years of uninterrupted em-ployment saw work opportunities dwindle. The local soon reported a decline of almost 50 percent in its "man hours" worked. Many members facing the prospects of prolonged unemployment in the union sector traveled to the few remaining unionized jurisdictions across the United States, left the IBEW tem-porarily (with their "tickets in their shoes"), left permanently to work non-union, or deserted the industry altogether (internal documents 1988–94).

Like the reactions of its counterparts throughout the industry, the early response by Local 611's leadership to the decline in employment was con-cessionary: job targeting and market recovery programs. Ferdie Martinez, Local 611's business manager from 1981 to 1987, negotiated a memoran-dum of understanding with signatory employers that gave him the authority to grant a concessionary wage on targeted projects. This agreement was drawn up with the hope of securing additional work for union contractors and jobs for unemployed members.

Unlike some building trade unions, Local 611 resisted across-the-board concessions in its collective bargaining agreements. But the concessionary wages authorized by the business manager engendered resentment among members employed at lower rates. Between 1986 and 1992, Local 611's market recovery program dispensed cash grants to signatory contractors in excess of $1 million. This enabled the local to keep select union contractors signatory, but it did not lead to signing new contractors or regaining market share. In fact, in many jurisdictions throughout the building trades, absent an effective organizing effort, market recovery plans contributed to a downward spiral in industry standards (Local 611 internal document, 1988–94; interview, T. Davis 1996).

In 1988, almost every major electrical construction project in Local 611's jurisdiction was being done by one of two principal nonunion contractors: DKD Electric or its chief rival, Gardner-Zemke, a former signatory employer that went open shop in 1986 (Local 611 internal documents 1988–94). That same year, Local 611, along with Locals 570, 640, 602, and 583 —all part of the IBEW's southwestern district—participated in an election campaign to organize Gardner-Zemke. Although the IBEW won in Tucson and Phoenix, it lost in Albuquerque, Amarillo, and El Paso. But even in units where majorities were won, negotiations never led to signed agreements.

Local 611 organizer Brian Condit soon recognized the limitation of Board elections in the construction industry, a lesson many building trade unionists still do not understand. Victory in a certification election meant that the union had won the right to bargain, a right it already enjoyed under section 8(f) of the National Labor Relations Act.

Winning the right to bargain is, as typified by the IBEW's post-election experience, hardly equal to winning a contract. For Condit, building the power to win a contract was more important than reaffirming the union's legal right to bargain. As he noted: "The fundamental source of union power in construction is control of the skilled labor supply. We believed that if we organized the workers, the contractors would come. That belief drove our organizing program from the start" (interview, 1996).

Although the immediate outcome of the certification election was disappointing, it represented an important step in union outreach to unrepresented workers and afforded valuable lessons. "We learned how to make contact with nonunion workers," notes Condit, "[and] discovered they were a lot like us. We learned about workers' rights under the Act, but we also learned not to confuse justice with the law" (interview, 1996).

Reaching Out to Unrepresented Workers

Following the election setback, local organizers pursued other approaches. Key among these was salting—sending union members to work for nonunion employers for the express purpose of organizing. An important element of a nonelection strategy, salting revives one of the tactics used by founders of the building trade unions a century ago who supported themselves by working in their trade while they organized their coworkers. Through salting and direct recruitment of unrepresented workers, early organizers built a loose monopoly of an area's skilled labor pool. Contractors signed contracts to gain access to the union-controlled labor supply, and unions enacted internal rules prohibiting members from working for nonsignatory contractors. This strategy provided unions with effective leverage to expand the contractor base and maintain market dominance. Local union bylaws, including those of the IBEW, continued this prohibition long past the time when many locals had high rates of union density. The IBEW recognized and advised that it was therefore necessary for locals to pass special salting resolutions enabling job-site organizing to proceed without compromising the integrity of local bylaws. This was an important policy adaptation at the international level to vastly changed circumstances within the industry.

Local 611's salting resolution, which it passed in 1988, was one of the first internal policy changes aimed at facilitating organizing. Staff organizers provided key leadership by becoming the first salts, and soon rank and filers followed suit. The union's salts were instrumental in identifying the most skilled nonunion electricians and recruiting them into the local, thereby "stripping" open-shop contractors of their most skilled labor.

Recruiting new members into an IBEW local took political courage in 1988. When Brian Condit initiated his first recruit, a former union member and Gardner-Zemke employee named Rick Howe, a near riot erupted at the local union meeting and police had to be called to restore order (interviews, Condit 1996 and Davis 1996). As was the case in virtually every IBEW jurisdiction, the ranks of Local 611 opposed organizing new members because they feared a growing membership would increase unemployment and insecurity. "I just kept organizing," asserts Condit. "I was going to do it or we were going to die." In the long-run, Condit won out. In the short-run, however, his boss, business manager Dub Baker, was voted out of office. Although he retained his position as local president, Condit was subsequently replaced as organizer by Ben Sandoval, who kept the spirit alive. "I felt good about organizing," he remembers. "We continued organizing good hands who couldn't get in when the local was a country club in the late seventies and early eighties" (interviews, Condit 1996 and Sandoval 1996).

The kind of rank-and-file resistance witnessed in Local 611 and throughout the Brotherhood threatened to derail the IBEW's organizing program. The international union implemented COMET, its membership education training program, in 1990 to overcome that problem (Grabelsky 1995). "COMET dramatically changed attitudes," reports Chris Frentzel, Local 611 current business manager.

Before COMET was started, organizing was regarded as a politically volatile issue only a few leaders were willing to support; after only 150 Local 611 members had been "COMETized," organizing new members became a more viable enterprise. Membership support grew, so that by 1992 the rank and file voted for a new assessment to enable the local to hire another full-time organizer and Tom Davis joined the staff in June of that year. "That was not an administration motion," explains Davis. "It came from the heart of the membership." As we shall see, by 1994, the deployment of COMET-trained activists proved to be decisive in successfully organizing DKD Electric (interview, Davis 1996; Grabelsky 1995).

After Tom Davis came on staff, he spent several months collecting data on Local 611's jurisdiction. He found that small and medium-sized nonunion employers were thriving because they had access to an abundant supply of about three hundred electricians who routinely worked for $10 to $12 an hour less than the union wage package. Union employers operating in the same commercial market were struggling to compete with these lower-cost contractors. Davis concluded that if Local 611 could recruit a significant percentage of the unrepresented electricians, he could cripple the ability of nonunion employers to operate open shop while simultaneously enabling signatory contractors with five to ten employees to expand their operations.

Local 611 then began identifying and communicating with unrepresented electricians in a systematic and ongoing way. Given the transient nature of the workforce in construction, this can be a difficult challenge, especially when a local has a vast geographic jurisdiction. But New Mexico's state licensing law facilitated Local 611's efforts to contact nonunion electricians. The local organizers began publishing the *Electrical Workers of N.M. Newsletter,* without revealing the IBEW's direct involvement. The newsletter addressed issues of concern to all working electricians and was distributed to nonunion workers by mail. The response to the newsletter was promising. A typical letter to the editor from 1992 read: "It's about time! . . . Electricians need to be heard in reference to the conditions [under] which we are *forced* to work. Your newsletter is a breath of fresh air to myself (sic) and the others on our crew."

Davis and other organizers often found that open-shop electricians, especially the "best hands," were reluctant to leave their current employers to join a union in which employment prospects were uncertain. This problem was exacerbated by the local's referral procedure, which placed newly organized workers on a lower-priority referral list than current members. So the referral rules were adjusted to allow new members who had worked for any contractor in the jurisdiction for one of the last three years to be included in the top-priority referral category. This represented another significant internal change to support organizing.

Once the referral procedures were altered, Local 611 recruited nonunion electricians more effectively. Each new recruit who passed the local's journey-level examination was inducted into the local and placed in the top priority for future referral to a union contractor, but, in the meantime, he remained with his current employer as a salt to gather information and enlist other electricians.

An improving economic climate aided the local's organizing activities. As construction picked up, union members on Book I were referred out to jobs, and small signatories began to call for additional electricians. On the one hand, many of these calls were for jobs old-time union members shunned: service assignments and projects at targeted market recovery rates of only $14.35 an hour, well below union scale. On the other hand, the newly organized members who had remained with their nonunion employers waiting for the hiring hall to clear were pleased to obtain union employment. The local then began strategically placing these electricians with signatory contractors, who were delighted with the new members' skills and productivity.

As the local replenished its labor pool with newly organized electricians, signatory contractors who had been reluctant to expand their operations became increasingly confident as they successfully bid on work in the expanding commercial market. Their success heightened the demand for union electricians, which in turn facilitated the local's ongoing efforts to recruit more new members.

Through stripping, Local 611 brought in as members about fifty of two hundred to three hundred electricians working in open shops—enough to disrupt nonunion business significantly. Following their basic credo—"Top-down efforts begin after the employer feels our bottom-up pressure"—organizers approached those contractors most severely hurt by the local's stripping activities and persuaded many of them to sign collective bargaining agreements. In doing so, these contractors regained access to a skilled labor pool, which they required to continue operations.

The growing number of newly unionized electricians and newly organized employers produced the perception that employment prospects were more favorable in the unionized sector of the industry. That perception helped generate momentum just as a boom in industrial construction blessed Local 611's jurisdiction. The local's success in constricting the open-shop labor market created a favorable environment to pressure industrial contractors, and IBEW organizers turned their attention to vital targets, including DKD Electric (interview, Davis 1996).

Organizing DKD Electric

DKD Electric opened for business in 1978 and within ten years established itself as one of the key players in electrical construction, earning about $5 million gross annually. On a 1988 DKD project employing sixty electricians, a significant but undetermined number were union members. DKD president Dee Dennis speculates that "some may have been salts. But others were just looking to support their family. . . . The union guys were more qualified than the guys off the street. That was the first place we noticed how poorly trained and skilled the open-shop labor market was." That the local had systematically stripped as much as one-fourth of the most qualified nonunion electricians had clearly affected DKD's plans and capacity to expand (interview, 1996).

DKD retained a relatively stable workforce of about seventy electricians. That number was sufficient until MyCorp Corp.,[1] a computer chip giant, commenced an enormous expansion of its New Mexico operations. As one of the successful bidders, DKD looked forward to doing some of MyCorp's $1.5 billion construction project.

In early 1993, when MyCorp began its new construction, IBEW Local 611 was poised to organize as never before. It had stripped a significant portion of the skilled open-shop labor pool. It had trained several hundred COMET activists. It had acquired the organizational skills and strategic acumen to tackle a major target. The local just needed to get a foothold on the MyCorp site.

Hughes Electric was the only union signatory to be awarded any part of the project. DKD won the lion's share of the electrical work at MyCorp, and other open-shop electrical contractors were assigned smaller portions. When the local sent nearly one hundred members to work for Hughes Electric on the MyCorp project, it instructed them to do two things: perform their work in an exemplary fashion to demonstrate the quality and character of the union labor pool *and* build a good relationship with DKD employees. This second instruction represented a dramatic departure from recent experience on "mixed" job sites in the construction industry, where the relationships between union and nonunion workers have often been acrimonious. The union activists sent to Hughes Electric understood and appreciated their instructions because of the COMET program (interview, Davis 1996).

At the same time that Local 611's activists commenced their "bottom-up" efforts among DKD employees, Ben Sandoval and Tom Davis initiated their "top-down" strategy by visiting DKD's office. Dee Dennis, president of

1. To maintain confidentiality, a fictitious name is used here and throughout.

DKD, remembers the meeting and appreciated their approach. "They were straightforward with us," Dennis recalls, "When they came to us, we knew they had a recruiting plan for DKD. They said, 'We like how you treat your people and manage your business' " (interviews, Davis 1996 and Dennis 1996).

That meeting came at an auspicious time for DKD. The demand for labor on the MyCorp project greatly exceeded the capacity of DKD's eighty-employee workforce and the contractor had gone into a feverish hiring mode, employing a full-time personnel manager to locate and recruit electricians, spending $2,500 a week advertising across the country, and running ads in the local papers every day for almost a year. It was not a pleasant time for Dennis. "We had contractors on the same site competing for the same manpower, and we got into a bidding war," he remembers. "One contractor offered $200 for electricians just to sign up. Wages jumped from $11.50 to $14.50 an hour with full benefits!" Out of necessity, DKD employed lesser-skilled electricians at higher wages than Dennis would have countenanced just a year before. "We lost the advantage that operating open shop gives a contractor who can pay lesser-skilled workers less wages" (interview, 1996).

The new circumstances created turmoil in DKD's ordinarily smoothly run business. DKD crew leaders were confounded by the challenge of meeting production schedules with an underqualified workforce. That was about the time Local 611 organizers came into the picture. Dennis met with Davis and Condit over a period of several months to address how the IBEW could solve DKD's need for skilled labor (interview, Dennis 1996). The extraordinary demand for skilled labor and the impact of Local 611's drive to recruit area electricians combined to make Dennis especially receptive to the union's top-down pitch.

At the same time that IBEW Local 611 was making inroads with DKD, Gardner-Zemke's workforce was gradually reduced from nearly three hundred electricians in 1991 to about fifty journey-level electricians by 1994 through salting, stripping, strikes, and unfair labor practice charges. By contrast, DKD instructed the salts on its payroll to avoid confrontational and disruptive concerted activities so that DKD's steady employees would not be alienated from the union.

As DKD and other newly organized contractors expanded their share of the construction market, the threat of nonunion competition from employers like Gardner-Zemke was dramatically diminished. "Fellow open-shop contractors were being hammered by direct union organizing," concedes Dennis. "We were aware of that." (interview, 1996).

The union's claim of having an available pool of highly qualified workers was reaffirmed by the obvious productivity of the Local 611 members and

IBEW travelers Dennis employed. This led Dennis to believe that it would be "a good business decision . . . [to] arrange an accommodation with the IBEW." On Friday, March 21, 1994, Dennis left the following message for Chris Frentzel, Local 611's business manager: "Tell him to get his ass over here with a pen" (interviews, Dennis 1996 and Davis 1996).

During contract negotiations, Local 611 also had to make certain accommodations to DKD. A six-month trial period was granted before DKD would become signatory to the union's standard agreement. Projects already bid would be "grandfathered" in so that DKD would not be unfairly saddled with higher labor costs on jobs estimated at open-shop rates. Revealing the effectiveness of 611's organizing strategy, when agreement was finally reached, Dennis shook hands with the union's negotiators and asked, "Can you send me five electricians tomorrow?" (interviews, Dennis 1996 and Davis 1996).

The signing of DKD required adjustments in the way the union handled its affairs. One question was how to deal with the sudden influx of workers whose skill levels varied widely. In response, the Joint Apprenticeship and Training Committee (JATC) adjusted its program to meet the needs of organizing. This included developing placement tests, setting up special classes, and training new instructors to deal with the large numbers of new journey-level and apprentice members. DKD had about twenty indentured apprentices who had been enrolled in the state-approved Independent Electrical Contractors' four-year apprenticeship program. Local 611's JATC reviewed these apprentices' records and slotted them into the IBEW's five-year apprenticeship program, asking most to move back a year.

DKD, like other open-shop contractors, also employed unindentured helpers. The use of such semi-skilled workers presents a competitive advantage to nonunion employers, reflects the ways in which electrical construction has been deskilled in the last twenty-five years, and posed another administrative challenge to the local. The JATC agreed to admit ten of DKD's twenty-two best helpers into the local's rigorous apprenticeship training program. Four subsequently dropped out.

Becoming a union signatory has had a dramatic impact on DKD. On the MyCorp project, Dee Dennis gained access to the skilled labor supply his business required. His company now employs more than five hundred union electricians. And according to Dennis, "We wouldn't be a $25 to $30 million contractor and we wouldn't be in markets we're in today without having become a union contractor. The manpower just wasn't there in the open shop." The down side for DKD is that it can no longer compete in markets that are still dominated by open shops. Dennis would welcome unionization of those markets (interview, 1996).

Lessons Learned from 611's Experiences

The circumstances presented and the resources available to IBEW 611 are similar to those of locals throughout the construction industry. The crucial factor in Local 611's success is leadership skill. That skill was exhibited in the following ways:

- The local's leaders retained confidence in the membership to understand and rally behind the goals, strategy, and tactics of workforce organizing.
- Staff organizers provided role models for member-activists by being among the first to salt nonunion jobs.
- Organizers didn't get discouraged but learned and applied valuable lessons from unsuccessful NLRB elections.
- Organizers stayed focused on recapturing control of the skilled labor pool by organizing workers into the union. It was clearly understood that the measure of organizing effectiveness and success is not just signing contractors to collective bargaining agreements but, more important, increasing membership and market share. Membership increased by more than four hundred members, or 35 percent, between 1988 and 1995.
- A market-wide strategy was developed after thoughtful analysis of the strengths and weaknesses of key players within the jurisdiction. The strategy avoided targeting individual contractors in isolation from others and considered the relationships among various players in the market.
- Tactics served that strategy because they were applied dynamically. Although the local used a wide range of tactics, including stripping, salting, work site concerted activities, unfair labor practice charges, and top-down pressure, it never embraced any single tactic inflexibly. It carefully selected the right tools for each target.
- Having significantly dried up the skilled labor supply during leaner times through its solid organizing, the local was able to take full advantage of improved economic circumstances when they arose.

IBEW Local 611's leaders, most fundamentally, understand power: how to build it and how to use it. The ultimate aim for all building trade unions is to achieve sufficient power to determine the terms and conditions of every construction worker in his respective trade and jurisdiction. With such power, unions can negotiate better and better contracts, winning for members growing prosperity, a rising standard of living, a better quality of life, and more democratic control over their work lives. With such power, unions can organize a growing contractor base, expanding employment opportunities and enhancing job security. And with such power, unions can stabilize the industry and tame its most destructive competitive tendencies.

The obstacles to building such power are not insurmountable. With persistence, courage, and a lot of hard work, the leaders and members of IBEW Local 611 have demonstrated how this power can be achieved.

Chapter 20

Steeling for Change: Organization and Organizing in Two USWA Districts in Canada

Gregor Murray

This chapter is about the transformation of industrial unionism in the 1990s. It reports on a comparative study of two Canadian districts of the United Steelworkers of America that provide fascinating insights into recent changes in industrial unionism—District 5 (Quebec and eastern Canada) and District 6 (Ontario). The purpose of this chapter is to chart the evolution of this predominant organizational model of worker representation in postwar Canada, to identify the changing nature of representational forms of unionism as the industrial premises on which they were founded shift significantly in changing labor and product markets, and to consider the servicing-related and structural implications of these changes for union development.

The practical importance of this subject perhaps requires some explanation for U.S. observers. In comparative terms, unions in Canada have demonstrated a high degree of organizing success over the past two decades (OECD 1991). This success can be seen in three areas: the rapid expansion of public-sector unions, the growth of service-sector unions, and, despite the significant job losses that have affected many industries, the ability of

This chapter draws on material that has been gathered over the past several years with the financial support of the Social Science and Humanities Research Council of Canada and the Fonds pour la formation de chercheurs et l'aide à la recherche of Québec. The author wishes to thank the many trade unionists who have assisted in the gathering and interpretation of the data, particularly the staff and activists of the USWA in Canada who participated in this study. He also wishes to acknowledge helpful comments on a previous version of this chapter by current and former USWA staff, discussants at the AFL-CIO/Cornell University organizing conference, and an anonymous reviewer.

some of the major industrial unions to maintain and in some cases even increase their membership levels. It is this latter group that is the focus of this chapter. More specifically, many industrial unions in Canada have maintained membership levels through a new focus on organizing, diversification of their existing membership bases, and structural and strategic adjustments that reflect these new orientations. This chapter is both a case study of the nature of this change and a consideration of the characteristics of the emerging organizational model.

The chapter is divided into five parts. The first part focuses on the defining characteristics of industrial unionism as an organizational form; the second addresses the challenges to this model during the 1980s; the third is a comparative review of the fortunes of the two Steelworker districts under investigation; the fourth is an analysis of the factors that led to the relative success of District 5's strategic renewal; and the fifth, and final part, is a consideration of the larger implications of the transformation of industrial unionism and the emergence of new organizational forms of worker representation and the challenges that this transformation entails for union servicing strategies and structures.

The Legacy of Industrial Unionism

Industrial unionism emerged out of the 1930s and World War II. By the end of the war, there had been a decisive shift in overall union membership toward this new pattern of worker representation, and it would dominate all other organizational models of unionism in postwar North America. Thereafter, not only did industrial unions continue to grow but the old craft unions gravitated to the industrial union model. Indeed, changes in both the organization of production and labor legislation compelled craft unions to open up their ranks to the majority of unskilled or semiskilled workers in industrial units in order to secure monopoly representation rights in these units.

It is important to grasp the way in which this particular model of worker representation emerged out of a legal and production regime. The broad outline of this transformation has been characterized as the emergence of Fordism. This entailed the use of large numbers of semiskilled workers in a normally complex division of labor, such as continuous process or assembly-line production, which made possible considerable economies of scale. Traditional craft models of worker representation did not readily apply to these groups of workers, although there was increasing demand by working people in Fordist industries for some form of representation. Not only did the adoption of the Wagner Act in the United States in 1935 and similar legislation in Canada during World War II (Privy Council Order 1003) compel employers to negotiate with union agents that were representative of their employees as determined by a labor relations board, but it effectively imposed an industrial model in the majority of industries. The general pattern was that there was one monopoly agent for each workplace.

We can identify at least nine organizational characteristics that distinguish the industrial union model (see Murray 1998). It should be emphasized, however, that the reality is much messier, more varied, and more complex than the following portrayal would suggest. What follows is simply an attempt to focus on the most salient characteristics.

First, recruitment for industrial unions was generally concentrated in certain industry jurisdictions or job territories. Although these might span a wide variety of industries, the central focus of recruitment activities was usually limited to several readily identifiable industries or sectors, for example, automobile and agricultural implement production. Moreover, despite many overlaps, a more or less explicit set of understandings developed among the different industrial unions within the larger labor movement about jurisdictional questions.

Second, these unions were generally large, bureaucratic, and fairly centralized organizations. In addition to regional offices involved in direct servicing, they maintained large organizational staffs with specialists located at headquarters in the United States and, increasingly in more recent years, in Canada as well. The legacy of the early CIO organizing was high-profile, specialist organizing campaigns. The hallmark of the rapidly growing industrial unions was the development of specialist and generalist services delivered through a cadre of professional field staff who were employed by the same larger organization and who responded up a vertical chain of command within the larger union bureaucracy.

Third, unlike the craft union model in which locals were often linked in a kind of loose federation, industrial local unions were, to varying degrees, constitutionally subordinate to national or international headquarters. Such differences were in evidence, for instance, in the drafting of union rule books. Dues were generally paid to the national or international union. Some portion of these dues, in conformity with the prevailing constitutional provisions of the organization, were then allocated to the local union. In contrast, under the craft model, the local union generally collected dues directly from the members and paid affiliation fees to the national or international union.

Fourth, local unions depended on the national or international union for servicing, either by permanent staff or by elected officials or by some combination thereof. Local unions most often had part-time presidents, who did not draw their salaries from the union, and the locals were serviced by a cadre of full-time officials employed by the national or international union. Even when local presidents were effectively full time, they would typically receive the equivalent of their salaries (pegged to a particular job grade within the firm) from local dues or directly from the employer and would maintain their employment relationship with their employer. Once again, this departed from the craft union model, under which full-time local staff or "business agents" were more typically employed by the local union, directly accountable to it, and, more often than not, driven by its political imperatives and electoral timetables.[1]

Fifth, the basic structure of these unions was founded on the principle of there being one certification unit per local. This meant that each new certification unit was generally chartered as a new and separate local unless, as was sometimes the case, it was a separate bargaining unit, for example, white-collar employees at the same work site. Locals then participated in the various representative forums of the larger national or international union on the basis of their size.[2] There were, of course, important exceptions to this tradition. For local historical reasons or because of hybrid mergers between craft and industrial unions or because of the small size of the establishments in some industries, many "amalgamated" locals were composed of more than one unit. This was, for example, the case in some of the auto parts industry.

Sixth, local union bargaining activity was generally predicated on what has been labeled "job-control" unionism. Local collective agreements generally conceded large areas of managerial discretion in the organization of work but tightly regulated both work rules governing the definition of jobs and almost all forms of movement of unionized employees within the internal labor markets of firms through the application of the principle of seniority.

Seventh, national bargaining policy was usually premised on some form of pattern bargaining. This meant that general targets were fixed for an industry or a group of workplaces and the union sought to achieve this target successively in the different workplaces in which it negotiated. Coordination was facilitated inasmuch as bargaining was generally conducted by specialist staff working for the same national or international organization,

---

1. The ramifications of these two models for local union democracy are both profound and complex. Although this subject lies outside the scope of this chapter, the models continue to exert a strong influence on the strategic capacity of local unions. Suffice it to emphasize, the political stakes are high when the employment security of local business agents depends entirely on the political fortunes of a particular local "slate."

2. It has been suggested, during the "cold war" period in Canadian union politics at least, that such fragmentation of locals also ensured greater voting clout in multiunion labor congresses in which all locals had the right to at least one delegate and it was deemed to be important to secure as many "sympathetic" delegates as possible.

sometimes even for a multiplicity of units within the same company. Not only were these staff accountable to the same chain of command but units within the same industry often met to establish common targets.

Eighth, the central focuses of organizational activity were contract negotiation and servicing, and the political imperatives of the organization also revolved around these activities. Bargaining expertise was, in particular, a key aspect of the "technostructure" of union bureaucracies, which drove the "line" activities of the field staff. Organizing, by contrast, like education and political action, came to be viewed as a parallel, specialist activity, which was complementary to the central focus. Thus, in many ways, the organizational structure of unions mirrored the corporate "mechanical" bureaucracies with which they dealt and in which there was limited decentralization and an important emphasis on technostructure (bargaining and contract administration) as opposed to ancillary services (organizing, political and community action, and so on).[3] In the case of organizing, most industrial unions relied on a group of specialist organizers who represented a fairly small proportion of the union's total volume of activities. Although some field staff were formally responsible for both contract servicing and organizing, it was readily apparent that contract servicing consumed virtually all of their time and responded, moreover, to the internal political imperatives of most unions.

Ninth, and finally, the model was characterized by a fairly high degree of cultural homogeneity, despite the many ethnic differences that characterized the immigrant populations of so many industries. Thus, members tended to be semiskilled, male, manufacturing workers who had little career mobility, who earned more and enjoyed greater employment security than they would have had they not had union protection, and who depended on the union as a significant, and indeed welcome, regulator of their working lives.

Although this organizational model was undoubtedly more complex and varied in its individual manifestations than this overview suggests, it remained largely intact from the 1940s to the early 1980s. As we shall see, the Steelworkers union, in Canada at least, represented a particularly good manifestation of the model.

Challenges to the Industrial Union Model

The 1980s marked a watershed for industrial unionism as a representational form. In essence, changes in product and labor markets challenged many of the operative assumptions of the industrial union model.

---

3. See, for example, Mintzberg 1979 for a typology of organizational structure and, in particular, of mechanical bureaucracies.

First, significant restructuring in key manufacturing industries led to massive job losses in traditional industries, where industrial unionism was most well ensconced, and to the overall movement of employment into private services, where unions were largely absent. Thus, not only were severe pressures exerted on the employment security of the workers who remained in the traditional industries where industrial unionism had been most prevalent, but many dislocated industrial workers were compelled to take private service-sector jobs, generally for much lower wages. Further, particularly in the United States but to a lesser degree in Canada, many of the new manufacturing establishments in traditional industries were not unionized and it appeared to be a priority for local managements that they remain so. Both job loss and the increasing importance of newer, nonunion establishments translated into dramatic declines in membership in many industrial unions, particularly in the early 1980s. This led to considerable organizational pressure to expand existing union jurisdictions, whether through mergers or by organizing nonunionized workers.

Second, the restructuring of individual firms significantly altered the profile of existing industries. In particular, outsourcing, downsizing, and relocation, both within and beyond national frontiers, led to a decline in average unit size and potential deunionization through the multiplication of smaller subcontracting units.

Third, both the potential exploitation of new technologies and competitive pressures in product markets have led firms to seek greater productivity gains and enhanced control over the quality of outputs. Many firms have thus sought to secure local union agreements on new forms of work organization that entail less tightly specified work rules, greater flexibility in the movement within internal labor markets, and greater employee involvement in the control of quality. These trends tend to result in more decentralized forms of bargaining relationships, both at local levels and in relation to company and industry patterns.

Fourth, the move either to decentralize bargaining and/or to break up existing pattern bargaining challenged operative assumptions about the relationships that should prevail between different levels and different activities within the union structure. Managements sought to eliminate traditional comparisons and to focus on the cost structures of business units or "profit centers." Although this reorientation fostered wage and productivity competition among units and establishments within the same firm, it was argued that only in this way could jobs be safeguarded. Similarly, there were challenges to the presumption that secondary labor market bargaining was to follow patterns set in primary labor markets, which, in turn, led to questions about the organizational emphasis to be placed on primary labor market bargaining rounds by industrial unions. Furthermore, servicing requirements were much more varied, as, for example, in the case of work reorganization involving more flexible work rules and teamwork at local levels.

Fifth, the loss of existing core jobs and their replacement, where possible, by secondary labor market jobs led to severe cost, servicing, and structural pressures on industrial unions, which were obliged to organize and service more and smaller certification units, as opposed to the large units that had characterized union structure in the past. This raised new questions about the ability to organize workers into unions in these new secondary labor market and service-sector areas. The degree to which smaller units could be integrated into existing larger union structures on a viable basis also needed to be addressed.

Sixth, the shift or potential shift in membership composition raised important cultural questions as industrial unions were obliged to move away from their fairly narrow and sometimes homogeneous base—semiskilled, male manufacturing workers, often in primary labor markets—to a much more culturally diverse constituency. In particular, the massive entry of women into the labor market raised important questions about equity. The greater diversity of demands placed on workers in their workplaces and the relative decline of centralized bargaining and, in some cases at least, the move to greater worker participation in their workplaces changed workers' expectations of their union organizations as well. For some unions, it meant that they needed to play a new servicing role that took account of workers' more diverse needs. For others, the workplace changes that were occurring raised more worrying questions about whether there was even a need for the traditional links between decentralized units and centralized union structures.

These challenges raise key questions concerning the industrial union model. It should be emphasized, however, that, in comparison to Canada, the prevalence of antiunion managerial strategies and the latitude afforded to management by existing labor legislation has compounded the adjustment problems of industrial unions in the United States. To explore in greater detail the adaptability of the industrial model and the strategic options available to industrial unions, we turn now to a case study of the two major United Steelworkers of America districts in Canada during the 1980s.

Comparing the Fortunes of Two USWA Districts

The United Steelworkers of America is the prototype of the North American industrial union. Few unions, moreover, were more severely affected by the recession of the early 1980s and the industrial restructuring of the last decade. Districts 5 and 6 provide particularly good illustrations of how industrial unions have been shaken to the core by the transformations in industrial structure that occurred during the 1980s. Drawing on documentary evidence, participant observation, and a considerable number of interviews with district and local officers and activists in each of the two districts, this section focuses on how these districts developed and implemented strategies to deal with such tremendous change. The following section points to a number of factors that appear to contribute to the greater initial success of District 5 in its attempt to enlarge its membership base through sectoral diversification and increasing integration of smaller certification units. Before considering these explanations, let us briefly compare the fortunes of these two districts over the decade of the 1980s.

In 1969, District 5 in Quebec represented 45,429 workers in 249 different certification units or collective agreements (see table 20.1).[4] The average unit size was 182 dues payers per agreement, and there were approximately 1.02 collective agreements per local (table 20.2). Roughly 4.0 percent of the district's members were women. In other words, District 5 exhibited many of the characteristics of the industrial union model identified above: its units were fairly large (mainly in the primary and secondary sectors) and overwhelmingly male, and the organizational model was based on there being one agreement per local.

By 1979, just before the recession of the early 1980s, this portrait remained much the same. District 5 represented 55,105 workers, of which just 3.8 percent were women, in 347 certification units. Although membership and the number of agreements negotiated had grown over the first half

TABLE 20.1. Union Membership and Number of Collective Agreements in Districts 5 and 6

	District 5 (Quebec)			District 6 (Ontario)		
Year	Total Members	Women Members	Number of Collective Agreements	Total Members	Women Members	Number of Collective Agreements
1969	45,429	4.0%	249	92,543	5.2%	412
1979	55,105	3.8%	347	102,469	9.0%	638
1982	39,413	6.7%	415	82,926	8.8%	664
1989	57,081	15.6%	682	82,412	12.8%	714

Note: Calculated from data provided by Statistics Canada.

4. District 5 of the USWA in fact covers all of eastern Canada. In 1990, 86.7 percent of its 57,801 members were located in Quebec province; the other 13.3 percent were in the four other maritime provinces. Unless specific reference is made to Quebec, all membership data refer to the entire district.

TABLE 20.2. Locals, Members per Collective Agreement, and Number of Collective Agreements per Local in Districts 5 and 6

	District 5 (Quebec)			District 6 (Ontario)		
Year	Number of Locals	Members per Agreement	Agreements per Local	Number of Locals	Members per Agreement	Agreements per Local
1969	244	182	1.02	378	225	1.09
1979	261	157	1.33	451	161	1.41
1982	248	95	1.67	465	125	1.43
1989	206	85	3.31	395	115	1.81

Note: Calculated from data provided by Statistics Canada.

of the 1970s, these figures had been either stable or in decline over the latter half of the decade and average unit size had continued to decline, falling to 157 dues payers per agreement in 1979. The number of collective agreements per local had risen slightly, from 1.02 to 1.33. These members were concentrated, as can be seen in table 20.3, in the primary (31.4 percent) and manufacturing sectors (61.9 percent); only a small percentage of members were in services (6.7 percent).

District 6 in Ontario followed a roughly similar pattern. Its membership rose from 92,543 in 412 units in 1969 to 102,469 in 638 units in 1979 (table 20.1). The number of members per agreement declined over this period, from 225 to 161, while the number of agreements per local rose slightly, from 1.09 to 1.41 (table 20.2). As in District 5, District 6's membership was overwhelmingly in the primary and manufacturing sectors (22.0 percent and 74.6 percent, respectively), as opposed to services (3.4 percent) (table 20.3). Indeed, District 6 was really in a holding pattern through the latter half of the 1970s as many key indicators—membership, number of certification units, number of members per unit, number of units per local —were all highly stable.

In other words, both districts were fairly traditional representations of industrial unionism: the jurisdictional focus was on certain industries, the units were fairly large in size (though more so in Ontario, where there was a small number of locals that were very large), there was roughly one certification unit or collective agreement per local, the membership was overwhelmingly concentrated in the primary sector and manufacturing, and the profile was characterized by a high degree of stability through the latter half of the 1970s.

As can be seen in tables 20.1 and 20.2, the 1981–82 recession had a very dramatic impact on the Steelworkers in Canada, as it did on most other industrial unions in North America. District 5's membership fell precipi-

TABLE 20.3. Percentage Distribution of Membership by Sector in Districts 5 and 6

	District 5 (Quebec)			District 6 (Ontario)		
Sector	1979	1990	Variation in number of members	1979	1990	Variation in number of members
Primary	31.4	22.8	− 5.133	22.0	16.8	− 6,726
Manufacturing	61.9	61.0	− 1,473	74.6	76.9	− 4,380
Services	6.7	16.1	+ 4,923	3.4	6.3	+ 2,379

Note: Calculated from internal data, United Steelworkers of America.

tously—32 percent—over a six-month period in 1981–82 as a result of restructuring, closings, and layoffs. District 6 was similarly affected, losing 16.1 percent of its membership during this period.

The central focus of this analysis is what happened during the rest of the decade, as the trajectories of the two districts varied quite sharply. By the end of the 1980s, District 5 had actually increased its membership to 57,081 members in 682 units, giving it an average unit size of 85. During this period, the number of women members increased by 341 percent, the number of certification units virtually doubled, and most of the increase in membership was accounted for by new service-sector members (+ 133 percent). An average of 3.3 collective agreements were signed per local. This membership growth was in fact concentrated in Quebec: whereas membership in the maritime provinces declined by 32.1 percent during the 1979–89 period, it increased in Quebec by 16.3 percent.[5]

By contrast, District 6 never fully recovered from its membership losses. By the end of the decade, it represented only 80.4 percent of its 1979 membership (82,412 members), an excellent performance compared with most other USWA districts but nowhere near the real increase in membership registered by District 5. During this period, the number of women members in District 6 increased by 16.4 percent; the number of certification units increased by seventy-six (11.9 percent), the average unit size decreased from 161 to 115, and the average number of collective agreements per local increased from 1.4 to 1.8.

Thus, although both District 5 (Quebec) and District 6 (Ontario) underwent considerable and similar transformations—increases in the number of

---

5. The contrast developed here between the varying fortunes of Districts 5 and 6 is therefore more marked than the summary data suggest because of the inclusion of the semiautonomous subdistrict of the maritime provinces. The organizational profile and fortunes of the USWA in the four maritime provinces was in fact much closer to that of District 6 (Ontario) than District 5 (Quebec).

certification units but declines in average unit size, increases in service-sector members and women, and increases in the number of agreements per local —District 5 appeared to adjust more rapidly, actually increasing its membership over a decade when all other USWA districts actually lost members and dramatically increasing the number of units it organized, its female membership, and its presence in the service sector.

District 6's "performance" was, of course, much better than that of many of the other USWA districts south of the border, where the extent of restructuring had an even more enduring impact on the union. Thus, whereas USWA membership was more than a million members in the mid-1970s and estimated to be 767,600 in 1980, it was 481,000 in 1989 (62.7 percent of its 1980 membership), and that figure has declined further (see Gifford 1994:68).

Explanations for District 5's Success

The case of District 5 is notable because the results stand out in such sharp contrast to those of many other industrial unions in declining sectors. How do we account for this success?

District 5's performance represented a conscious organizing and servicing strategy in Quebec designed to better meet the needs of new membership groups in both the service sector and small manufacturing units. Indeed, District 5 aimed to create union locals that were better able to adjust to the small size of the new units typically being organized during this period. District 5 also sought to achieve a viable servicing strategy based on reducing the relative costs of reaching a multiplicity of small units and providing access to basic services, sometimes assured by using newly trained full-time lay representatives rather than professional business agents or servicing staff. This strategy was linked to an educational program that involved considerable modification of staff culture and an expansion of local autonomy.

Since there is limited scope for a longer narrative here, I will simply attempt to identify some of the key factors associated with the relative success of District 5 in pursuing its successful strategy of membership diversification, new organizing, and structural adjustment. The focus of the discussion will be on eight indicators that contributed to its turnaround.

Strategy Making and Strategy Implementation

The capacity to make a timely and appropriate assessment of the best strategy given the circumstances as well as the possibility to pursue it were certainly key dimensions of District 5's success. District 5's leadership came to an early conclusion that circumstances had changed for good and that different approaches were required. Moreover, the leadership had already begun to develop a strategy to deal with the decreasing size of its units, which, although initially intended for the manufacturing sector, contributed greatly to the district's precocious development in the service sector. Moreover, District 5's leadership clearly demonstrated an interest in experimenting with new avenues of development.

By contrast, and for a variety of reasons, the strategic response of District 6 was more traditional: await the upturn after the recession and then pursue recruitment, an activity that was largely complementary to the central tasks of negotiating and servicing. Indeed, this more traditional stance was evident through much of the 1980s, before the district began to pursue a different strategy more closely aligned with that of District 5, toward the end of the decade and into the 1990s.

Staff Culture and Renewal

One of the areas in which District 5's leadership engaged in the most experimentation was staff management. The membership loss at the beginning of the 1980s shook the union to the core. The transformation was quite dramatic. The number of staff decreased from fifty-four in 1980 to forty in 1984 but rose to fifty-two by 1989. District leaders encouraged laid-off staffers to engage in new organizing, holding out the promise that they might eventually get their jobs back if they could organize new members. All staffers, including district leaders, were directly involved in organizing, and a premium was placed on this skill in new recruitment to staff positions. In other words, organizing became a key dimension of staff performance. Indeed, in one organizing campaign, that of taxi drivers in Montreal, all union staffers, including support staff, were involved in the campaign. This represented a real shift in organizing culture. As one staffer put it, "We used to get a kick out of negotiating a 15 percent wage increase for industrial workers in well-paid industries; now we get our kicks out of getting minimum-wage workers a little respect and a 50-cent-an-hour increase."

The change in District 5's strategy entailed both a reorganization of the internal division of labor among staff and a significant shift in its organizing culture. There would eventually be some backlash by staffers against the move to "generalist" organizing and in favor of a return to regionally based specialist organizers. That debate was indicative, however, of the degree to which conscious organizing had reentered the vocabulary of all staffers.

In District 6, staff numbers decreased from 101 to 80 in 1984 and remained fairly stable thereafter, rising to 83 in 1989. Successive early-retirement packages created some opportunities to renew staff, but the pattern of recruitment remained fairly traditional—that is, individuals with a male, manufacturing focus and a degree of political loyalty to the new leadership. Again, it was only in the early 1990s that District 6 began to innovate in this respect.

Structural Reform

One of the most important factors that contributed to District 5's capacity to pursue an aggressive organizing strategy was the modification of its local structures. By the mid-1970s, District 5 leadership had concluded that its local structures were increasingly an impediment to organizing in the manufacturing sector. Not only was it too expensive to service the small units characteristic of Quebec's relatively weak manufacturing sector, but these units were often too small to offer local financial viability in terms of basic contract servicing, for example, the cost to the local of going to arbitration. The early development of composite or amalgamated locals was a strategic effort to organize new groups of workers into viable structures, to devolve some basic servicing to the local level, and to achieve new coordinating mechanisms among workers in the service sector. Although much of the real structural reform took place after the recession, the union did considerable work, particularly on the educational side, during the early 1980s toward developing these structures. This proved particularly important when the district later sought to diversify its membership base by organizing in the service sector.

The reform of its local structures was a particularly important component of the district's greater emphasis on organizing. District 5 organized 697 new units between 1978 and 1990. The average size of these units was forty-three members, but almost half the new units (48.5 percent) had fewer than twenty members. Such new organizing could clearly not be sustained without a move to some form of composite or amalgamated local.

Political Rivalries

The absence of organized, internal political opposition was another significant difference between the two districts. In District 5, there was little visible opposition to the leadership in place. The previous director had retired after fifteen years in his position, and the new director was extremely popular and recognized as the person most qualified to succeed him. There was also a high degree of continuity, since the two leaders continued to work closely together.

District 5's experience stands out in sharp contrast to that of District 6, which was divided throughout the first half of the 1980s by bitter political rivalries. In 1981, a nationalist slate was elected to the leadership of the district, and the entire tenure was characterized by overt and underlying tensions between the national and international offices and the district leadership and within the district among staff members. These tensions, particularly those between staff and district leaders, were undoubtedly an important impediment to the development and implementation of renewal strategies.

Bargaining Unit Mix

The lesser importance of large bargaining units and of primary labor market bargaining rounds also appears to have been significant in the development of District 5's new strategies. District 5's membership was much more evenly distributed in a large number of small locals. This had both economic and political consequences. Perhaps because of its location in a weaker industrial sector, its leadership may have been more sensitive to the nature of the economic changes taking place and the need to rethink certain strategies. District 5's mix contrasted markedly with the composition of District 6, especially in southern Ontario, whose firms led in the development of product and technological innovations in their respective sectors. In political terms, the comparative absence of very large locals also meant that District 5's leaders had more discretion to pursue new strategies—strategies that perhaps had greater intuitive appeal to smaller, as opposed to larger, existing locals in district conference debates.

By contrast, in District 6, the political agenda was often set by the leadership of the three largest locals in the steel and mining industries, whose combined membership represented at least one-third of the district's total membership and whose strategic inclinations revolved around their traditional priorities. It was not so much that the large locals in District 6 were against new strategic initiatives as that their leaders thought that these initiatives did not really concern them.

Also of significance was the relative importance of the pattern bargaining driving major bargaining rounds. Centralized bargaining initiative and preparation consumed a considerable amount of resources in District 6 as opposed to District 5, where central office staff were more concerned with development strategies than with direct servicing strategies. In other words, there was greater scope in District 5 to move away from the traditional focus on contract servicing that so characterized life in the industrial union model.

District Autonomy

The degree of autonomy of the district relative to the union's international and national offices appears to have been another significant factor in District 5's success. District 5 enjoyed a greater degree of autonomy from national and international offices because of linguistic and cultural differences that had allowed the space to develop and pursue appropriate local strategies. For example, District 5's leaders developed their own supplementary fund to enhance union support for members on strike. District leadership was also able to maintain deficit financing, because the district's expenditures were higher than its revenue.

Again, this experience contrasts sharply with the conflicts that characterized the relations between District 6's leadership in the early 1980s and the international headquarters of the USWA. The new leadership elected in 1981 in District 6 sought to gain greater autonomy from the international. This issue was a source of bitter internal divisions within the district, to which the international office was not indifferent at the time of budgetary allocations.

Education as a Strategic Variable

The importance of the USWA's educational program and its adaptability and integration into the overall strategic direction of District 5 also appeared to be important to its success. District 5 pioneered several educational initiatives that were to prove important in the development of the union. Aware of the weaknesses of traditional union education, in the 1970s it recruited a specialist in adult education whose formative experience was with community groups and in Third World education. The district also placed a high priority on member education, so much so that the organizational structure ended up reflecting it in its division of labor: the director was seconded by an assistant director on the operational side (overseeing regular servicing) and an assistant director on the development side (overseeing education, research, and a variety of other functions). In this sense, it can be argued that the educational and developmental aspects of union work outgrew the more marginal role they were given in the traditional model.

Educational activities were also important in District 6, where the national leadership backed a highly successful "back-to-the-locals" campaign through the early 1980s. Educational activities were more typically part of a broader range of servicing activities, however, and were less tied up with new efforts to organize new members and modify local structures. Further, they were affected, in part at least, by the aforementioned political tensions.

Cultural Diversity

The diversification of District 5's membership presented many problems that eventually were to prove fairly important politically. The new membership groups, such as women in the hotel and catering industries, taxi drivers, and security guards, represented a marked departure from the cultural traditions of the industrial union model. The union leadership worked to break down at least some of the barriers that separated these traditions and to try to limit the backlash. The latter was primarily in evidence in servicing concerns and the bargaining profile of the union. There was indeed a real transfer of resources taking place from direct servicing to organizing, and it was necessary to subsidize many of the new units.

Concern also arose that insufficient resources were being allocated to primary bargaining-round activities. Many existing locals were quite naturally very wary of the possibility that their local autonomy might be compromised in the interests of structural reform. District 5's leadership was fairly successful in dealing with some of these internal "cultural" tensions. Successive changes in leadership at the end of the decade provided further opportunity for manifestation of these tensions, however, and, ultimately, a reaffirmation of some of these more traditional concerns.

Two further clarifications are required here to round out the picture of these two districts with respect to the events that have taken place since the initial field research was conducted and that therefore alter our understanding of the case.

Not all of District 5's initiatives were successful. The union attempted a major raid on a rival union in a traditional sector (aluminum manufacturing) that failed. It also invested considerable resources into an organizing campaign of taxi drivers in Montreal that ran into insurmountable legal obstacles regarding the right of a significant proportion of these workers to belong to a union.[6]

Since the study, it would appear that a more traditional approach to organizing has, to some degree at least, made a comeback. Some of District 5's initial gains in the service sector, particularly in catering, now appear to be somewhat fragile. Although composite locals constitute an important structural reform, they have not proved to be a panacea for the many problems encountered in the development of unionism in small units in the private service sector. District 5 has, however, continued to expand its presence in the service sector.

District 6 has since pursued many of the same kinds of strategies first developed in District 5. It has engaged in considerable new organizing in the service sector, particularly among security guards, taxi drivers, and hotel workers, all groups that District 5 had targeted earlier. Moreover, the USWA in Canada was also involved in a merger with the Canadian section of the Retail, Wholesale & Department Store Union, further enhancing District 6's efforts to develop a profile in the service sector. District 6 has also invested heavily in innovative adjustment strategies, such as the USWA's

6. It was ruled that most of the taxi drivers who sought union certification did not have access to the representation rights afforded by the Québec Labour Code because they were deemed to be independent contractors rather than salaried employees.

joint sectoral training strategies, in its traditional areas of strength through the development of the Canadian Steel Trade and Employment Congress.

Wider Implications

What are the implications of this transformation of industrial unionism to new organizational forms of worker representation, and what are the challenges for union servicing strategies and structures?[7]

First, financial pressures on the union have everywhere pushed toward the rationalization of servicing. Increasing decentralization and the changing composition of union membership, particularly because of the lower dues revenues coming from the low-wage and contingent members in the new service sector, contribute to a growing pressure on the traditional model because of the limited supply and the virtually limitless demand for services by union members. This results in a continuing tension between the forces of decentralization and coordination.

The widespread movement toward decentralization of bargaining has important implications for the industrial union model. Industrial unions are obliged to devolve general services, for both practical and financial reasons, closer to local units. At the same time, new forms of coordination—education, training, recruitment, and corporate campaigns—can also entail increased resources at the center, at least prior to the development of local expertise. Increased employee participation, for example, entails the development of specialized services, such as research and training, that are not easily organized at the local level.

Thus, there are increasing and contradictory pressures concerning roles in the delivery of services. Activists are likely to be more involved in such issues as contract administration, health and safety, pay equity, and even recruitment; hence, the considerable demand for activist training. As was explored in the case of District 5, this shift in roles marks a departure from the traditional industrial union model. Full-time union staff can thus play a more consultative or advisory role, limiting their involvement in some routine activities.

There is also pressure to increase the range and quality of specialist services available to local units from central union offices on such issues as work reorganization, financial analysis, work study, and ergonomics. This change is readily apparent in the shifting role played by the national office of the Steelworkers in Canada. There is also tremendous pressure to develop local experts on these issues; hence, the importance of new educational

7. These observations draw on the conclusions of a larger comparative study of changes in union strategies and structures. See Murray 1995.

resources and initiatives. The emergence of new organizational models in industrial unions thus entails the development of new relationships between activists and staff, between local and centralized specialists, between conceptions of activism and consumerism in union servicing. Many of these issues are still being worked out and were highly visible in the case studies discussed in this chapter.

The second and related challenge concerns the emergence of new local structures. The key structural question is, of course, how to sustain small units in both the service and other sectors in a viable organizational model. District 5 is not alone in its movement to embrace composite or amalgamated locals to deal with this challenge. The fundamental problem remains, however, how to make these new (and not so new) local structures work effectively. The most enduring challenge is how to promote worker participation and "ownership" of local union structures.

Apart from the economies of scale derived from pattern bargaining, the real strength of the industrial union model lay in the virtual identity between local structure and certification unit. This real proximity meant that the local union usually directly expressed the concerns of its members. The prevailing organizational model at the local level in the service sector has too often been that of "cash box" or dues-collection unionism in which union members are only minimally involved and have little sense of ownership of their local structures. Much experimentation and educational work is required to make these new local structures both organizationally efficient and democratic. Composite or amalgamated locals are by no means a panacea. Yet the great majority of nonunionized workers in Canada are in small units. Their access to union representation depends on the emergence of appropriate local structures that are able to meet this dual challenge.

Third, current political and economic changes lead to a reconfiguring of economic and political action. The "economism" that typified "bread-and-butter" unionism of the postwar years has, of course, been greatly weakened. Yet it is also difficult to sustain unionism with a macro-political focus on Keynesian demand management. This creates a double opening.

Unions are liable to play a much enlarged role in the democratization of the workplace. Their ability to pursue successfully this broader workplace agenda also depends on the success of their larger social project. The latter, in turn, is contingent on how well unions can forge new community and social alliances that enhance the unions' capacity to mobilize and that increase the efficacy of their political interventions.

In comparison with the fortunes of the U.S. labor movement, part of the success of Canadian labor over the past two decades can certainly be attributed to its greater institutional leverage. Such is the challenge for what has been labeled "social unionism." Both Districts 5 and 6 have had some success in this approach: District 5 maintained a high degree of visibility on broader social questions throughout its expansion into the service sector; District 6 somewhat later sought to modify the image of the union and to enhance its presence on a broad range of social issues, be it in terms of workplace discrimination, humanitarian and human rights concerns in developing countries, or policing issues in multiethnic, metropolitan centers such as Toronto.

Fourth, there are increasing tensions between different projects that seek to respond to changing values and identities at work: narrower solidarities based on new forms of work reorganization and/or new occupational identities, on the one hand, and larger labor market solidarities, on the other. The interplay between these possible trajectories is extremely important. If the organizational principle adopted is too narrow, exacerbating enterprise-based or corporatist identities, then the introduction of larger labor market solidarities is extremely difficult. If the organizational principle is too extensive or inclusive, then membership commitment might be weakened. Thus, there is a need to find the right synergy between these two principles. This has proved to be a particularly delicate problem in District 5: as it expanded its membership into new sectors and expounded the virtues of wider labor market solidarities, tensions certainly arose in those who felt that their particular, and perhaps narrower, labor market identities were being ignored.

To conclude, unions are entering a period of considerable experimentation in the search for organizational models conducive to new forms of representation and workplace citizenship. There is unlikely to be a single organizational response, a "one best way," to take account of the considerable challenges outlined above. The movement is certainly away from the kinds of vertical, bureaucratic structures that characterized the industrial union model in the past toward new forms of organization. Union structures and practices are the result of activists' creativity as they attempt to solve the daily problems of union action in highly varied contexts. It appears particularly important to avoid the standardization of these structures and practices so as to foster the emergence of new structures and services.

Union organizations need to provide their activists, members, local officers, and staff with the necessary space for innovation and adjustment. They can then learn from their continuing experiments in the search to respond better to workers' needs for protection and voice in their workplaces and also in their communities and their societies.

References

AFL-CIO. 1991. *Rules Governing AFL-CIO Central Bodies*. Washington, D.C.
————. n.d. *Handbook for Central Labor Councils*. Washington, D.C.
AFL-CIO Department of Economic Research. 1996. *America Needs a Raise*. Washington, D.C.
Albright, Vedie, Michelle Couturier, and Kay Jones. 1993. "Making Pigs Fly: Nurses Beat Hospital with Internal Organizing, Broad and Deep Community Support." *Labor Research Review* 21 (Fall-Winter): 81–88.
Amott, Teresa L., and Julie A. Matthaei. 1991. *Race, Gender, and Work: A Multicultural Economic History of Women in the United States*. Boston: South End Press.
Appelbaum, Eileen, and Rosemary Batt. 1994. *The New American Workplace: Transforming Work Systems in the United States*. Ithaca, N.Y.: ILR Press.
Armingeon, Klaus. 1989. "Trade Unions under Changing Conditions: The West German Experience, 1950–1985." *European Sociological Review* 5 (May): 1–23.
Ashenfelter, Orley, and John Pencavel. 1969. "American Trade Union Growth: 1900–1960." *Quarterly Journal of Economics* 83:434–48.
Babson, Steve. 1991–92. " 'Come Join Us': Volunteer Organizing from a Local-Union Base." *Labor Research Review* 18 (Fall-Winter): 61–71.
Bain, George Sayers, and Farouk Elsheikh. 1976. *Union Growth and the Business Cycle: An Econometric Analysis*. Oxford: Blackwell.
Banks, Andy. 1991–92. "The Power and Promise of Community Unionism." *Labor Research Review* 10 (Fall-Winter): 17–31.
Banks, Andy, and Jack Metzgar. 1989. "Participating in Management: Union Organizing on a New Terrain." *Labor Research Review* 14 (Fall): 1–55.
Barbash, Jack. 1956. *The Practice of Unionism*. New York: Harper and Brothers.
Barling, Julian, Clive Fullagar, and E. Kevin Kelloway. 1992. *The Union and Its Members: A Psychological Approach*. New York: Oxford University Press.
Barrett, James. 1987. *Work and Community in the Jungle: Chicago's Packinghouse Workers, 1894–1922*. Urbana: University of Illinois Press.
Bensman, David. 1988. "BAC's Comeback: The Bricklayers' Renewal Program." *Labor Research Review* 7 (Fall): 59–69.
Berss, Marcia. 1993. "Against the Wall." *Forbes,* July 5, 43.
Block, Richard N., and Steven L. Premack. 1983. "The Unionization Process: A Review of the Literature." In *Advances in Industrial and Labor Relations,* edited by David B. Lipsky and Joel M. Douglas, 1:31–70. Greenwich, Conn.: JAI Press.

Bok, Derek C., and John T. Dunlop. 1970. *Labor and the American Community.* New York: Simon and Schuster.

Brady, Rosemary. 1983. "Up in Smoke." *Forbes,* June 20, 88.

Brody, David. 1994. "Section 8(a)(2) and the Origins of the Wagner Act." In *Restoring the Promise of American Labor Law,* edited by Sheldon Friedman et al., 29–44. Ithaca, N.Y.: ILR Press.

Bronfenbrenner, Kate. 1993. "Seeds of Resurgence: Successful Union Strategies for Winning Certification Elections and First Contracts in the 1980s and Beyond." Ph.D. diss., Cornell University.

———. 1994. "Employer Behavior in Certification Elections and First-Contract Campaigns: Implications for Labor Law Reform." In *Restoring the Promise of American Labor Law,* edited by Sheldon Friedman et al., 75–89. Ithaca, N.Y.: ILR Press.

———. 1997a. *Final Report: The Effects of Plant Closing or Threat of Plant Closing on the Right of Workers to Organize.* Dallas: Secretariat of the Commission for Labor Cooperation.

———. 1997b. "The Role of Union Strategies in NLRB Certification Elections." *Industrial and Labor Relations Review* 50:195–212.

Bronfenbrenner, Kate, and Tom Juravich. 1994. "The Promise of Union Organizing in the Public and Private Sectors." Working paper, Institute for the Study of Labor Organizations, George Meany Center for Labor Studies, Silver Spring, Md.

———. 1995a. *Union Organizing in the Public Sector: An Analysis of State and Local Elections.* Ithaca, N.Y.: ILR Press.

———. 1995b. "The Impact of Employer Opposition on Union Certification Win Rates: A Private/Public Sector Comparison," Working paper no. 113, Economic Policy Institute, Washington, D.C.

———. 1995c. "Union Tactics Matter: The Impact of Union Tactics on Certification Elections, First Contracts, and Membership Rates." Working paper, Institute for the Study of Labor Organizations, George Meany Center for Labor Studies, Silver Spring, Md.

———. 1995d. *Staying Union: The Dynamics of Union Success in Public Sector Decertification Campaigns.* Washington, D.C.: AFL-CIO.

Burke, William M. 1968. *History and Functions of Central Labor Unions.* New York: AMS Press.

Burton, John, and Terry Thomason. 1988. "The Extent of Collective Bargaining in the Public Sector." In *Public Sector Bargaining,* edited by Benjamin Aaron, Joyce M. Majiata, and James J. Stenes. Washington, D.C.: Bureau of National Affairs.

Cabot, Stephen J. 1993. "Scary New Union Activism . . . How to Fight It and Win." *Boardroom Reports* 22:5–6.

Catechism of the Catholic Church. 1994. Collegeville, Minn.: Liturgical Press.

Chaison, Gary N., and D. G. Dhavale. 1990. "A Note on the Severity of the Decline in Union Organizing Activity." *Industrial and Labor Relations Review* 43:366.

Chaison, Gary N., and Joseph B. Rose. 1991. "The Macrodeterminants of Union Growth and Decline." In *The State of the Unions,* edited by George Strauss, Daniel Gallagher, and Jack Fiorito, 3–46. Madison, Wisc.: Industrial Relations Research Association.

"Coal Buying: The Old Boy Network Is June." 1986. *Electrical World,* April, 85–86.

Coalition of Black Trade Unionists (CBTU). 1995. "Employees at Steeltech Define Black Manhood." *Milwaukee Courier,* Feb. 11, 1.

Cobble, Dorothy Sue. 1991. *Dishing It Out: Waitresses and Their Unions in the Twentieth Century.* Urbana: University of Illinois Press.

———. 1993. "Introduction: Remaking Unions for the New Majority." In *Women and Unions: Forging a Partnership,* edited by Dorothy Sue Cobble, 3–23. Ithaca, N.Y.: ILR Press.

Commission on the Future of Worker-Management Relations. 1994a. *Fact Finding Report.* Washington, D.C.: Bureau of National Affairs.

———. 1994b. *Report and Recommendations.* Washington, D.C.: U.S. Department of Labor.

Committee for Justice at Steeltech. n.d. "Private Greed and the Betrayal of the Public Interest at Steeltech." Unpublished report.

Comstock, Phil, and Maier Fox. 1994. "Employer Tactics and Labor Law Reform." In *Restoring the Promise of American Labor Law,* edited by Sheldon Friedman et al., 90–109. Ithaca, N.Y.: ILR Press.

Conrow, Teresa. 1991. "Contract Servicing from an Organizing Model." *Labor Research Review* 17 (Spring): 45–59.

Cook, Stephen L., and Miles C. Stanley. 1970. *Making It Go: A Handbook for Local Central Bodies . . . Their Functions and Activities.* Information Series no. 8. Morgantown: Institute for Labor Studies, West Virginia University.

Cooke, William N. 1983. "Determinants of the Outcomes of Union Certification Elections." *Industrial and Labor Relations Review* 36:402–13.

———. 1985. *Organizing and Public Policy: Failure to Secure First Contracts.* Kalamazoo, Mich.: W. E. Upjohn Institute for Employment Research.

Cornfield, Daniel. 1989. *Becoming a Mighty Voice: Conflict and Change in the United Furniture Workers of America.* New York: Russell Sage Foundation.

———. 1990. "Labor Unions, Corporations, and Families: Institutional Competition in the Provision of Social Welfare." *Marriage and Family Review* 15 (3–4): 37–57.

———. 1991. "The U.S. Labor Movement: Its Development and Impact on Social Inequality and Politics." *Annual Review of Sociology* 17: 27–49.

Cornfield, Daniel, and Randy Hodson. 1993. "Labor Activism and Community: Causes and Consequences of Social Integration in Labor Unions." *Social Science Quarterly* 74 (Sept.): 590–602.

Cornfield, Daniel, and Hyunhee Kim. 1994. "Socioeconomic Status and Unionization Attitudes in the United States." *Social Forces* 73 (Dec.): 521–32.

Craft, James A., and Marian M. Extejt. 1983. "New Strategies in Union Organizing." *Journal of Labor Research* 4:1–32.

Crain, Marion. 1994. "Gender and Union Organizing." *Industrial and Labor Relations Review* 47:227–49.

Cunningham, Donald J. 1988. "Complexities of the Grape Boycott." *Christian Century,* Oct. 5, 150.

Delaney, John T., and Mark A. Huselid. Forthcoming. "The Impact of Human Resource Management Practices on Perceptions of Organizational Performance." *Academy of Management Journal* 33:949–69.

Deshpande, Satish P., and Jack Fiorito. 1989. "Specific and General Beliefs in Union Voting Models." *Academy of Management Journal* 32:883–97.

Diamond, Virginia. 1988. *Numbers That Count: A Manual on Internal Organizing.* Washington, D.C.: AFL-CIO.

Dickens, William T. 1983. "The Effect of Company Campaigns on Certification Elections: Law and Reality Once Again." *Industrial Relations* 36:323–34.

Dickens, William T., and Jonathan S. Leonard. 1985. "Accounting for the Decline in Union Membership: 1950–1980." *Industrial and Labor Relations Review* 38:323–34.

DiMaria, Alfred T. 1994. "The Risks of Establishing or Maintaining an Unlawful EPC." *Management Report,* April, 3–4.

Dresser, Laura, Joel Rogers, and Julie Whittaker. 1996. *The State of Working Wisconsin.* Madison: Center on Wisconsin Strategy.

Dubofsky, Melvyn. 1968. *When Workers Organize.* Amherst: University of Massachusetts Press.

Duray, John. 1995. "Delegates Prepare for Convention." *United Mine Workers Journal,* July-Aug., 5–6.

Eccles, Robert, and Nitin Nohria, eds. 1992. *Networks and Organizations.* Boston: Harvard Business School Press.

Eckstein, Enid. 1991–92. "Using People Power: A Successful Member Organizing Program Builds New Unions, Strengthens Your Own." *Labor Research Review* 10 (Fall-Winter): 73–81.

Energy Information Administration. 1987. *The Changing Structure of the U.S. Coal Industry, 1976–1986.* Washington, D.C.: U.S. Department of Energy.

———. 1991. *Coal Production 1990.* Washington, D.C.: U.S. Department of Energy.

———. 1993. *The Changing Structure of the U.S. Coal Industry: An Update.* Washington, D.C.: U.S. Department of Energy.

———. 1994. *Coal Industry Annual 1993.* Washington, D.C.: U.S. Department of Energy.

Erlich, Mark. 1988. "Who Will Build the Future?" *Labor Research Review* 12 (Fall): 1–19.

"Experts Debate Best Way to Sell Coal Assets." 1993. *Coal Outlook Supplement,* April 5, 1.

Fantasia, Rick. 1988. *Cultures of Solidarity: Consciousness, Action, and Contemporary American Workers.* Berkeley: University of California Press.

Farber, Henry S. 1983. "Worker Preferences for Union Representation." In *Research in Labor Economics,* edited by Joseph D. Reid, Jr., Suppl. 2, 171–205. Greenwich, Conn.: JAI Press.

———. 1987. "The Recent Decline of Unionization in the United States." *Science,* Nov., 915–20.

———. 1989. "Trends in Worker Demand for Union Representation." *AEA Papers and Proceedings* 29 (May): 166.

Fauber, John. 1991a. "Steeltech Unveils Plans for Hiring and Training."*Milwaukee Journal,* Jan. 6.

———. 1991b. "Can Success of Steeltech Be Repeated?" *Milwaukee Journal,* Dec. 15.

Fernández-Kelly, Maria P., and Saskia Sassen. 1991. *A Collaborative Study of Hispanic Women in Garment and Electronics Industries.* New York: New York University Center for Latin American and Caribbean Studies.

Fetonte, Danny, and Larry Braden. 1990. "Showdown at Nacogdoches: The CWA in Texas." *Labor Research Review* 15 (Spring): 24–35.

Fiorito, Jack. 1992. "Unionism and Altruism." *Labor Studies Journal* 17 (Fall): 19–34.

Fiorito, Jack, Daniel G. Gallagher, and Charles R. Greer. 1986. "Determinants of Unionism: A Review of the Literature." In *Research in Personnel and Human Resources Management,* edited by Kendrith M. Rowland and Gerald R. Ferris, 269–306. Greenwich, Conn.: JAI Press.

Fiorito, Jack, and Charles Greer. 1982. "Determinants of U.S. Unionism: Past Research and Future Needs." *Industrial Relations* 21:1–32.

Fiorito, Jack, Paul Jarley, and John T. Delaney. 1995. "National Union Effectiveness in Organizing: Measurement and Influences." *Industrial and Labor Relations Review* 48 (July):613–35.

Fiorito, Jack, Christopher Lowman, and Forrest D. Nelson. 1987. "The Impact of Human Resource Policies on Union Organizing." *Industrial Relations* 26:113–27.

Fiorito, Jack, and Cheryl L. Maranto. 1987. "The Contemporary Decline of Union Strength." *Contemporary Policy Issues* 5 (Oct.): 12–27.

Foner, Philip S. 1974. "A Labor Voice for Black Equality: The *Boston Daily Evening Voice,* 1864–1867." *Science and Society* 38 (Fall): 304–28.

Foo, Laura Jo. 1994. "The Vulnerable and Exploitable Immigrant Workforce and the Need for Strengthening Worker Protective Legislation." *Yale Law Journal* 103:2179–212.

Foo, Laura Jo, Laura Ho, and Thomas M. Kim. 1995. "Worker Protection Compromised: The Fair Labor Standards Act Meets the Bankruptcy Code." Unpublished manuscript.

Freeman, Richard B. 1985. "Why Are Unions Faring Poorly in NLRB Representation Elections?" In *Challenges and Choices Facing American Labor,* edited by Thomas A. Kochan, 45–64. Cambridge: MIT Press.

———. 1986. "Unionism Comes to the Public Sector." *Journal of Economic Literature* 24 (1): 41–86.

———.1992. "Is Declining Unionization of the U.S. Good, Bad or Irrelevant?" In *Unions and Economic Competitiveness,* ed. Lawrence Mishel and Paula B. Voos, 143–68. New York: M. E. Sharpe.

Freeman, Richard B., and Morris M. Kleiner. 1990. "Employer Behavior in the Face of Union Organizing Drives." *Industrial and Labor Relations Review* 43:351–65.

Freeman, Richard B., and James Medoff. 1984. *What Do Unions Do?* New York: Basic Books.

Freeman, Richard B., and Marcus E. Rebick. 1989. "Crumbling Pillar? Declining Union Density in Japan." Working paper no. 2963, National Bureau of Economic Research, Cambridge.

Freeman, Richard B., and Joel Rogers. 1994. "Worker Participation and Representation Survey: Report on the Findings." Typescript.

Friedman, Sheldon, et al., eds. 1994. *Restoring the Promise of Labor Law.* Ithaca, N.Y.: ILR Press.

Fuechtmann, Thomas G. 1989. *Steeples and Stacks: Religion and Crisis in Youngstown.* New York: Cambridge University Press.

Gallup Organization. 1988. *Synopsis of the 1988 Gallup Study of Public Knowledge and Opinion concerning the Labor Movement.* New York.

Gerlach, Luther. 1983. "Movements of Revolutionary Change: Some Structural Characteristics." In *Social Movements of the Sixties and Seventies,* edited by Jo Freeman, 133–47. New York: Longman.

Getman, Julius G., Stephen B. Goldberg, and Jeanne B. Herman. 1976. *Union Representation Elections: Law and Reality.* New York: Russell Sage Foundation.

Gifford, Courtney D. 1994. *Directory of U.S. Labor Organizations, 1994–95 Edition.* Washington, D.C.: Bureau of National Affairs.

Gingrich, Newt. 1995. *Renewal for America.* New York: HarperCollins.

Golper, John, and Higdon C. Roberts, Jr. 1973. *Local Central Labor Bodies: The Community Link of the AFL-CIO.* Reprint series no. 2. Birmingham: Center for Labor Education and Research, University of Alabama.

Gordon, Richard L. 1987. *World Coal: Economics, Policies and Prospects.* London: Cambridge University Press.

Grabelsky, Jeffrey. 1995. "Lighting the Spark." *Labor Studies Journal* 20 (Summer): 4–21.

Grabelsky, Jeff, and Richard Hurd. 1994. "Reinventing an Organizing Union: Strategies for Change." In *Proceedings of the Forty Sixth Annual Meeting of the Industrial Relations Research Association,* edited by Paula S. Voos, 95–104. Madison, Wisc.: Industrial Relations Research Association.

Grant, David, Melvin Oliver, and Angela James. 1996. "African-Americans: Social and Economic Bifurcation." In *Ethnic Los Angeles,* edited by Roger Waldinger and Mehdi Bozorgmehr, 379–411. New York: Russell Sage Foundation.

Green, James, and Chris Tilly. 1987. "Service Unionism. Directions for Organizing." *Labor Law Journal* 38 (Aug.): 486–95.

Greenhouse, Steven. 1995. "Labor Chief Asks Business for a New 'Social Compact.' " *New York Times,* Dec. 7.

Grenier, Guillermo. 1987. *Inhuman Relations: Quality Circles and Anti Unionism in American Industry.* Philadelphia: Temple University Press.

Harris, Howell John. 1982. *The Right to Manage: Industrial Relations Policies of American Business in the 1940s.* Madison: University of Wisconsin Press.

Hart Associates, Peter D., and the Mellman Group. 1996. "Summary of Opinion Research on Living Standards." Report to AFL-CIO Executive Council.

Hartmire, Wayne C. 1965. "The Plight of Seasonal Farm Workers." *Christianity and Crisis,* Oct. 4, 203–5.

Harvey, Curtis E. 1986. *Coal in Appalachia: An Economic Analysis.* Lexington: University of Kentucky Press.

Headden, Susan. 1993. "Made in the U.S.A." *U.S. News & World Report,* Nov. 11, 48–55.

Henry, Sarah. 1993. "Labor and Lace: Can an Upstart Women's Group Press a New Wrinkle into the Rag Trade Wars?" *Los Angeles Times Magazine,* Aug. 1, 38.

Hermanson, Jeff. 1993. "Organizing for Justice: ILGWU Returns to Social Unionism to Organize Immigrant Workers." *Labor Research Review* 12 (Spring-Summer): 53–61.

Herrera, Yvette, and Anne Marie Marklin. 1993. *Heroines and Hurdles: A Look at Women's Struggle for a Voice in the Workplace through Unionization.* Washington, D.C.: Communications Workers of America.

Hoxie, Robert F. 1923. *Trade Unionism in the United States.* New York: Appleton and Company.

Hurd, Richard W. 1989. "Learning from Clerical Unions: Two Cases of Organizing Success." *Labor Studies Journal* 14:30–51.

———. 1990. "Organizing Clerical Workers." In *Meeting the Challenges of Change,* edited by Pamela Wilson, 5–11. Washington, D.C.: AFL-CIO Department of Professional Employees.

———. 1994. *Assault on Workers' Rights.* Washington, D.C.: AFL-CIO Industrial Union Department.

———. 1996. "Union Free Bargaining Strategies and First Contract Failures." In *Proceedings of the Forty-Eighth Annual Meetings of the Industrial Relations Research Association,* edited by Paula S. Voos, 145–52. Madison, Wisc.: Industrial Relations Research Association.

———. 1997. "Contesting the Dinosaur Image: The Labor Movement's Search for a Future." Working paper, New York State School of Industrial and Labor Relations, Cornell University, Ithaca, N.Y.

Hurd, Richard W., and Adrienne McElwain. 1988. "Organizing Clerical Workers: Determinants of Success." *Industrial and Labor Relations Review* 41:350–73.

Hurd, Richard W., and Joseph Uehlein. 1994. *The Employer Assault on the Legal Right to Organize.* Washington, D.C.: AFL-CIO Industrial Union Department.

International Brotherhood of Electrical Workers. 1990. "COMET Trainer's Manual: COMET Survey, 1994." Typescript.

———. 1994. "Union Organization in the Building Construction Industry." IBEW Special Projects Department, Washington, D.C. Typescript.

———. 1996a. "COMET I, Construction Organizing Membership Education Training. Trainer's Manual." IBEW International Education Department, Washington, D.C. Typescript.

———. 1996b. "COMET II, Worksite Organizing with COMET Activists. Trainer's Manual." IBEW International Education Department, Washington, D.C. Typescript.

International Brotherhood of Electrical Workers, Local 46. 1989. "Internal Organizing Summary Report."

———. 1990. "Internal Organizing Summary Report."

———. 1994. "Internal Organizing Summary Report."

———. 1995. "Internal Organizing Summary Report."

———. 1996. "Internal Organizing Summary Report."

Jarley, Paul, and Jack Fiorito. 1991. "Unionism and Changing Employee Views toward Work." *Journal of Labor Research* 12 (3): 223–29.

Johnson, Tom. 1992. "The Dollar Knows No Borders: The High Costs of Low-Priced Coal." *United Mine Workers Journal,* March-April, 6–8.

Johnston, Paul. 1994. *Success While Others Fail: Social Movement Unionism and the Public Workplace.* Ithaca, N.Y.: ILR Press.

Jost, Kenneth. 1996. "Labor Movement's Future." *Congressional Quarterly,* June 28, 1996, 557.

Karwath, Rob. 1993. "Low Pay Standing in the Way of More Home Care." *Chicago Tribune,* Sept. 14.

Kenney, Martin, and Richard Florida. 1988. "Beyond Mass Production: Production and the Labor Process in Japan." *Politics and Society* 16 (1): 121–58.

Kilborn, Peter T. 1995. "Strategies Changing for Union: Home Care Aides Are Fresh Target." *New York Times,* Nov. 22.

Kochan, Thomas A. 1979. "How American Workers View Labor Unions." *Monthly Labor Review,* April, 23–31.

———. 1980. *Collective Bargaining and Industrial Relations*. Homewood, Ill.: Richard D. Irwin.

———. 1995. "Using the Dunlop Report to Achieve Mutual Gains." *Industrial Relations* 34 (July): 350–66.

Kochan, Thomas A., Robert B. McKersie, and John Chalykoff. 1986. "The Effects of Corporate Strategy and Workplace Innovations on Union Representation." *Industrial and Labor Relations Review* 39: 487–501.

Kohler, Thomas C. 1986. "Models of Worker Participation: The Uncertain Significance of Section 8(a)(2)." *Boston College Law Review* 27:499–551.

Kwong, Peter. 1994. "Chinese Staff and Workers' Association: A Model for Organizing in the Changing Economy?" *Social Policy* 25 (Winter): 30–38.

Labor Council for Latin American Advancement. 1992. *Hispanic Workers: Underutilized National Resource*. AFL-CIO Reviews the Issues 64. Washington, D.C.: AFL-CIO.

La Luz, Jose. 1991. "Creating a Culture of Organizing: ACTWU's Education for Empowerment." *Labor Research Review* 10 (Spring): 61–67.

Lawler, John J. 1984. "The Influence of Management Consultants on the Outcome of Union Certification Elections." *Industrial and Labor Relations Review* 38:38–51.

———. 1990. *Unionization and Deunionization*. Columbia: University of South Carolina Press.

Lawler, John J., and Robin West. 1985. "Impact of Union-Avoidance Strategy in Representation Elections." *Industrial Relations* 24: 406–20.

Lazo, Robert. 1990. "Latinos and the AFL-CIO: The California Immigrant Workers Association as an Important New Development." Working paper, Stanford Law School, Stanford, Calif.

LeLouarn, Jean-Yves. 1980. "Predicting Union Vote from Worker Attitudes and Perceptions." In *Proceedings of the Thirty-Second Annual Winter Meeting of the Industrial Relations Research Association,* edited by Barbara D. Dennis, 72–82. Madison, Wisc.: Industrial Relations Research Association.

Lerner, Stephen. 1991. "Let's Get Moving." *Labor Research Review* 18 (Fall): 1–15.

Levine, David L. 1995. *Reinventing the Workplace: How Business and Employees Can Both Win*. Washington, D.C.: Brookings Institution.

Lipset, Seymour M. 1986. "Labor Unions in the Public Mind." In *Unions in Transition,* edited by Seymour M. Lipset, 287–322. San Francisco: Institute for Contemporary Studies.

Lipset, Seymour, Martin Trow, and James Coleman. 1956. *Union Democracy*. New York: Free Press.

Locke, Richard L., and Kathleen Thelen. 1995. "Apples and Oranges Revisited." *Politics and Society* 23:337–67.

Lynn, Monty L., and Jozell Brister. 1989. "Trends in Union Organizing: Issues and Tactics." *Industrial Relations* 28:104–13.

Mabry, Marcus. 1992. "New Hope for Old Unions? Organized Labor Looks for Ways to Reverse Its Slide." *Newsweek,* Feb. 24, 39.

Malveaux, Julianne. 1987. "The Political Economy of Black Women." In *The Year Left,* edited by Mike Davis et al., 2:53–73. Stony Brook, N.Y.: Verso Press.

Maranto, Cheryl L. 1988. "Corporate Characteristics and Union Organizing." *Industrial Relations* 27:352–70.

Maranto, Cheryl L., and Jack Fiorito. 1987. "The Effect of Union Characteristics on the Outcome of NLRB Certification Elections." *Industrial and Labor Relations Review* 40:225–40.

Marks, Gary. 1989. *Unions in Politics.* Princeton, N.J.: Princeton University Press.

Marsden, Peter V., Arne L. Kalleberg, and Cynthia R. Cook. 1996. "Gender Differences and Organizational Commitment." In *Organizations in America,* edited by Arne L. Kalleberg et al., 302–23. Thousand Oaks, Calif.: Sage.

McMahon, June, Amy Finkel-Shimshon, and Miki Fujimoto. 1991. "Organizing Latino Workers in Southern California." Working paper, UCLA Center for Labor Research and Education, Institute of Industrial Relations, Los Angeles.

Metzgar, Jack. 1991. "Reviews of *Labor at the Ballot Box, Building Bridges, Robust Unionism,* and *A Troublemakers Handbook.*" *Labor Research Review* 17 (Spring): 91–97.

Mezo, Mike. 1995. "To Survive We Must Organize." *Local 1010 Steelworker,* May, 20.

Miernyk, William K. 1976. "Regional Economic Consequences of High Energy Prices in the United States." *Journal of Energy and Development* 1:213–39.

Miles, Raymond. 1989. "Adapting to Technology and Competition: A New Industrial Relations System for the Twenty-First Century." *California Management Review* 31 (Winter): 3–28.

Milkman, Ruth. 1992. "Union Responses to Workforce Feminization in the U.S." In *The Challenge of Restructuring: North American Labor Movements Respond,* edited by Jane Jensen and Rianne Mahon. Philadelphia: Temple University Press.

———. 1993. "Organizing Immigrant Women in New York's Chinatown: An Interview with Katie Quan." In *Women and Unions: Forging a Partnership,* edited by Dorothy Sue Cobble, 281–98. Ithaca, N.Y.: ILR Press.

Mines, Richard, and Jeffrey Avina. 1992. "Immigrants and Labor Standards: The Case of California Janitors." In *U.S.-Mexico Relations: Labor Market Interdependence,* edited by Jorge A. Bustamante, Clark Reynolds, and Raul Hinojosa Ojeda, 429–48. Stanford, Calif.: Stanford University Press.

Mintzberg, Henry. 1979. *The Structuring of Organizations.* Englewood Cliffs, N.J.: Prentice-Hall.

Mishel, Laurence, and Paula B. Voos, eds. 1992. *Unions and Economic Competitiveness.* Armonk, N.Y.: M. E. Sharpe.

Mooney, Patrick H., and Theo J. Majka. 1995. *Farmers' and Farm Workers' Movements.* New York: Twayne.

Moore, Lila. 1995. "Top Ten Apparel Manufacturing Areas." *Apparel Industry Magazine,* Sept., 38–54.

Moore, Marat. 1986. "Energy Multinationals: Importing Coal, Exporting Jobs." *United Mine Workers Journal,* June, 14–16.

Morais, Richard. 1986. "Coal: Whatever Happened to the Energy Crisis? Whatever Happened to the Utilities? Whatever Happened to the Steel Business?" *Forbes,* Jan. 13, 109–10.

Muehlenkamp, Robert. "Organizing Never Stops." *Labor Research Review* 17 (Spring): 1–5.

Murray, Gregor. 1995. "Retooling Unions: Comparative Union Adjustment in the Canadian Labour Movement." *Policy Options* 16 (8): 39–42.

————. 1997. "The Political Economy of Trade Unionism: Restructuring and Adjustment in Industrial Trade Unions." In *Critical Political Economy and Industrial Relations,* edited by A. Giles and Gregor Murray. Unpublished manuscript.

Nazario, Sonia. 1993. "For This Union, It's War." *Los Angeles Times,* Aug. 19.

Needleman, Ruth. 1993a. *Raising Visibility, Reducing Marginality: A Labor Law Reform Agenda for Working Women of Color.* Washington, D.C.: U.S. Department of Labor, Women's Bureau.

————. 1993b. "Space and Opportunities: Developing New Leaders to Meet Labor's Future." *Labor Research Review* 20 (Spring-Summer): 5–20.

————. 1994. "Building an Organizing Culture of Unionism." In *Proceedings of the Forty-Fifth Annual Meetings of the Industrial Relations Research Association,* edited by John F. Burton, Jr., 358–66. Madison, Wisc.: Industrial Relations Research Association.

"New Contract . . . and a New Owner . . . at Chicago O'Hare." 1993. *Catering Industry Employee,* Sept.-Oct., 7–8.

New York State Bureau of Economic and Demographic Information. 1991–92. *County Profiles 1993.* Albany, N.Y.

Northrup, Herbert. 1989. "Construction Doublebreasted Operations and Pre-Hire Agreements: Assessing the Issues." *Journal of Labor Research* 10 (Spring): 215–38.

Noyes, Robert, ed. 1978. *Coal Resources: Characteristics and Ownership in the U.S.A.* Noyes Data Corporation.

OECD. 1991. "Trends in Trade Union Membership." *Employment Outlook,* July, 97–134.

Osterman, Paul. 1994. "How Common Is Workplace Transformation and Who Adopts It?" *Industrial and Labor Relations Review* 47:173–88.

Pavy, Gordon, and Brett Smith. 1996. "A Question of Fairness: Employer Opposition to Negotiating First Collective Bargaining Agreements." Paper presented at the Forty-Eighth Annual Meetings of the Industrial Relations Research Association, San Francisco, January.

Pawlikowski, John, and Donald Senior. 1988. *Economic Justice: CTU's Pastoral Commentary on the Bishops' Letter on the Economy.* Washington, D.C.: Pastoral Press.

Perl, Peter. 1984. "UMW Pact Is Personal Victory for Trumka." *Washington Post,* Sept. 29.

Perry, Harry. 1983. "Coal in the United States: A Status Report." *Science,* Oct. 28, 377–84.

Peterson, Richard B., Thomas Lee, and Barbara Finnegan. 1992. "Strategies and Tactics in Union Organizing Campaigns." *Industrial Relations* 31 (2): 370–81.

Piore, Michael J. 1994. "Unions: A Reorientation to Survive." In *Labor Economics and Industrial Relations,* edited by Clark Kerr and Paul D. Staudohar, 512–41. Cambridge: Harvard University Press.

Powell, Walter W. 1987. "Hybrid Organizational Arrangements: New Form or Transitional Development?" *California Management Review* 30 (Fall): 67–87.

Premack, Steven L., and John E. Hunter. 1988. "Individual Unionization Decisions." *Psychological Bulletin* 103:223–34.

President's Council of Economic Advisors. 1995. *Economic Report of the President.* Washington, D.C.

————. 1996. *Economic Report of the President.* Washington, D.C.

Rathke, Wade, and Joel Rogers. 1996. "Everything That Moves: Leverage, Critical Mass, Union Organizing in Political Space." Paper presented at AFL-CIO/Cornell University Research Conference on Union Organizing, Washington, D.C., April.

Reed, Thomas F. 1989. "Do Organizers Matter? Individual Characteristics and Representation Election Outcomes." *Industrial and Labor Relations Review* 43:103–19.

————. 1992. "Incidence and Patterns of Representation Campaign Tactics: A Comparison of Manufacturing and Service Unions." *Industrial Relations—Quebec* 47:203–17.

Reich, Robert B. 1991. *The Work of Nations.* New York: Knopf.

Richardson, Doug. 1995. "Chicago-Cook County Co-operative Organizing Committee." Typescript, AFL-CIO.

Rodgers, Kathryn S. 1986. *U.S. Coal Goes Abroad: A Social Action Perspective on Interorganizational Networks.* New York: Praeger Special Studies.

Rose, Joseph, and Gary Chaison. 1990. "New Measures of Union Organizing Effectiveness." *Industrial Relations* 29:457–68.

Rosier, Sharolyn A. 1996. "Energized Central Labor Councils Explore New Roles." *AFL-CIO News,* Aug. 5, 5.

Rossmann, Witich. 1995. "The Transformation of Industrial Relations in the German Computer Industry: IG Metall Battles at DEC and IBM." Typescript.

Rundle, James R. 1994. "The Debate over the Ban on Employer-Dominated Labor Organizations: What Is the Evidence?" In *Restoring the Promise of American Labor Law,* edited by Sheldon Friedman et al., 161–76. Ithaca, N.Y.: ILR Press.

Sabel, Charles F. 1982. *Work and Politics: The Division of Labor in Industry.* Cambridge: Cambridge University Press.

————. 1993. "Can the End of the Social Democratic Trade Unions Be the Beginning of a New Kind of Social Democratic Politics?" In *Economic Restructuring and Emerging Patterns of Industrial Relations,* edited by Stephen Sleigh, 137–65. Kalamazoo, Mich.: W. E. Upjohn Institute for Employment Research.

Schnell, John F. 1979. "The Impact on Collective Bargaining of Oil Company Ownership of Bituminous Coal Properties." *Labor Studies Journal* 3 (Winter): 201–27.

Schriesheim, Chester A. 1978. "Job Satisfaction, Attitudes toward Unions, and Voting in a Union Representation Election." *Journal of Applied Psychology* 63:548–52.

Seeber, Ronald L. 1983. "Union Organizing in Manufacturing: 1973–1976." In *Advances in Industrial and Labor Relations,* edited by David B. Lipsky and Joel M. Douglas, 1:1–30. Greenwich, Conn.: JAI Press.

"Seems Like Old Times." 1989. *Economist,* July 1.

Seltzer, Curtis. 1985. *Fire in the Hole: Miners and Managers in the American Coal Industry.* Lexington: University Press of Kentucky.

Service Employees International Union. 1992. "Twentieth International Convention. Report to the Building Service Division." Washington, D.C.

Shostak, Arthur. 1991. *Robust Unionism: Innovations in the Labor Movement.* Ithaca, N.Y.: ILR Press.

Siegel, Lou, and Jeff Stansbury. 1992. "Beyond English: The Labor Press in a Multicultural Environment." In *The New Labor Press: Journalism for a Changing*

Union Movement, edited by Sam Pizzigati and Fred Solowey, 86–105. Ithaca, N.Y.: ILR Press.

Sleemi, Fehmida. 1995. "Collective Bargaining Outlook for 1995." *Compensation and Working Conditions* 47 (Jan.): 19–22.

Spalter-Roth, Roberta, Heidi Hartmann, and Nancy Collins. 1994. "What Do Unions Do for Women?" In *Restoring the Promise of American Labor Law,* ed. Sheldon Friedman et al., 193–206. Ithaca, N.Y.: ILR Press.

Spindler, G. R. 1985. "The Unfulfilled Promise of Energy Independence: Effects on the U.S. Coal Industry." *Vital Speeches of the Day,* March 20.

Streeck, Wolfgang. 1992. *Social Institutions and Economic Performance: Studies of Industrial Relations in Advanced Capitalist Economies.* London: Sage.

Sweeney, John, Richard Trumka, and Linda Chavez-Thompson. 1995. *A New Voice for American Workers: Rebuilding the American Movement—A Summary of Proposals from the Unions Supporting John J. Sweeney, Richard Trumka, and Linda Chavez-Thompson.* Washington, D.C.: New Voice for American Workers.

Tarrow, Sidney. 1994. *Power in Movement.* Cambridge: Cambridge University Press.

Tasini, Jonathan. 1995. *The Edifice Complex.* New York: Labor Research Association.

Thomason, Terry. 1994. "The Effect of Accelerated Procedures on Union Organizing Success in Ontario." *Industrial and Labor Relations Review* 47:207–26.

Tomlins, Christopher L. 1979. "AFL Unions in the 1930s: Their Performance in Historical Perspective." *Journal of American History* 65 (March): 1021–42.

Troy, Leo. 1994. *The New Unionism in the New Society: Public Sector Unions in the Redistributive State.* Fairfax, Va.: George Mason University Press.

Turner, Lowell. 1991. *Democracy at Work: Changing World Markets and the Future of Labor Unions.* Ithaca, N.Y.: Cornell University Press.

———. 1993. "Prospects for Worker Participation in Management in the Single Market." In *Labor and Integrated Europe,* edited by Lloyd Ulman, Barry Eichengreen, and William T. Dickens, 45–79. Washington, D.C.: Brookings Institution.

Tyler, Gus. 1995. *Look for the Union Label: A History of the International Ladies Garment Workers' Union.* Armonk, N.Y.: M. E. Sharpe.

Ulman, Lloyd. 1966. *The Rise of the National Trade Union.* Cambridge: Harvard University Press.

Ulman, Lloyd, Barry Eichengreen, and William T. Dickens, eds. 1993. *Labor and an Integrated Europe.* Washington, D.C.: Brookings Institution.

United Electrical, Radio and Machine Workers of America. n.d. "Justice for Steeltech Workers: Vote Union Yes." Pittsburgh. Unpublished document.

U.S. Department of Commerce. Bureau of the Census. 1990. *Census of Population. Public Use Microdata Sample.* Washington, D.C.: Government Printing Office.

———. 1995. *Current Population Survey.* Washington, D.C.: Government Printing Office.

U.S. Department of Labor. Women's Bureau. 1994. *1993 Handbook on Women Workers: Trends and Issues.* Washington D.C.: Government Printing Office.

Waldinger, Roger D. 1986. *Through the Eye of the Needle: Immigrants and Enterprise in New York's Garment Trades.* New York: New York University Press.

Waldinger, Roger D., and Mehdi Bozorgmehr. 1996. "Introduction." In *Ethnic Los Angeles,* edited by Roger D. Waldinger and Mehdi Bozorgmehr, 3–37. New York: Russell Sage Foundation.

Weiler, Paul C. 1983. "Promises to Keep: Securing Workers' Rights to Self-Organization under the NLRA." *Harvard Law Review* 96:1769–1827.

Wever, Kirsten S. 1995. *Negotiating Competitiveness: Employment Relations and Organizational Innovation in Germany and the United States.* Boston: Harvard Business School Press.

"What Ails the Market for Metallurgical Coal?" 1978. *Business Week,* Aug. 21, 27.

Wheeler, Hoyt N. 1985. *Industrial Conflict: An Integrative Theory.* Columbia: University of South Carolina Press.

Wheeler, Hoyt N., and John A. McClendon. 1991. "The Individual Decision to Unionize." In *The State of the Unions,* edited by George Strauss, Daniel Gallagher, and Jack Fiorito, 47–84. Madison, Wisc.: Industrial Relations Research Association.

Wheeler, Hoyt N., John A. McClendon, and Roger D. Weikle. 1994. "Toward a Test of Wheeler's 'Integrative Theory' in Six Union Election Cases." *Relations Industrielles* 49 (Summer): 465–81.

Wilayto, Phil, and John-David Morgan. 1995. "Prying the Lid off Steeltech: Can Black Solidarity Crack the Shell Game?" *Shepherd Express,* Feb. 2–9.

Wong, Kent. 1993. "Asian Pacific Workers Organizing for a Change." Typescript.

Woody, Betty. 1992. *Black Women in the Workplace: Impacts of Structural Change in the Economy.* New York: Greenwood Press.

Wuthnow, Robert. 1995. *Learning to Care: Elementary Kindness in an Age of Indifference.* New York: Oxford University Press.

Ybarra, Michael J. "Waxing Dramatic: Janitors' Union Uses Pressure and Theatrics to Expand Its Ranks." *Wall Street Journal,* March 21.

Yokota, Ryan. 1994. "McClintock Boycott Continues." *Pacific Ties,* May.

Interviews

Abbott, Alvin, interview by Ronald Peters and Theresa Merrill, December 1995.

Adams, Melvin "Skip," interview by Bruce Nissen, January 1996.

Alexander, James, interview by Bruce Nissen, September 1995.

Allen, Tom, interview by Bruce Nissen, January 1996.

Azcona, Fidel, interview by Bruce Nissen, October 1995.

Beckman, Matt, interview by Bruce Nissen, January 1996.

Bobo, Kim, interviews by Ronald Peters and Theresa Merrill, October 1995, February 1996, and March 1996.

Bravo, Ellen, interviews by Ruth Needleman, April 1995 and March 1996.

Buckner, Michael, interview by Adrienne Birecree, January 1996.

Carey, Bill, interview by Bruce Nissen, September 1995.

Celichowski, John, interviews by Ronald Peters and Theresa Merrill, September 1995, October 1995, and March 1996.

Chavez, Angie, interview by Ronald Peters and Theresa Merrill, September 1996.

Clifford, Paul, interviews by Ronald Peters and Theresa Merrill, September 1995, January 1996, February 1996, and March 1996.

Cochran, Sheila, interview by Katherine Sciacchitano, October 1996.

Coggs, Spencer, interview by Katherine Sciacchitano, March 1996.

Colburn, Bruce, interview by Katherine Sciacchitano, March 1996.

Condit, Brian, interviews by Tom Davis, Jeff Grabelsky, and Fred Kotler, February 1996.

Couturier, Michelle, interview by Ronald Peters and Theresa Merrill, March 1996.

Davis, Nevada, interview by Katherine Sciacchitano, February 1996.

Davis, Susannah, interview by Katherine Sciacchitano, February 1996.

Davis, Terry, interview by Katherine Sciacchitano, February 1996.

Davis, Tom, interviews by Brian Condit, Jeff Grabelsky, and Fred Kotler, January 1996 and February 1996.

Dempsey, Bill, interview by Katherine Sciacchitano, February 1996.

Dennis, Dee, interview by Brian Condit, Tom Davis, Jeff Grabelsky, and Fred Kotler, February 1996.

DeWitt, Jesse, interviews by Ronald Peters and Theresa Merrill, October 1995 and March 1996.

Echaveste, Maria, interview by Ruth Needleman, February 1995.

Eisenberg, Julie, interview by Katherine Sciacchitano, March 1996.

Escamilla, Myriam, interview by Ruth Needleman, March 1995.

Firestein, Netsy, interview by Ruth Needleman, February 1996.

Florey, Mike, interview by Bruce Nissen, January 1996.

Foo, Laura Jo, interview by Ruth Needleman, February 1995.

Freese, Jim, interview by Janet Lewis and Bill Mirand, November 1995.

Frentzel, Chris, interview by Brian Condit, Tom Davis, Jeff Grabelsky, and Fred Kotler, February 1996.

Fritz, Gary, interview by Adrienne Birecree, January 1996.

Galusha, Greg, and Tom Walsh, interview by Janet Lewis and Bill Mirand, October 1995.

Garlitz, Thomas L., interview by Ronald Peters and Theresa Merrill, October 1995.

Grostick, Bill, interview by Janet Lewis and Bill Mirand, January 1996.

Hafer, Hugh, interview by Janet Lewis and Bill Mirand, February 1996.

Hesterman, John, interview by Bruce Nissen, February 1996.

Ho, Laura L., interview by Ruth Needleman, March 1995.

Imesch, Joseph, interview by Ronald Peters and Theresa Merrill, December 1995.

Jasin, David, interview by Bruce Nissen, February 1996.

Johnson, Tammy, interview by Katherine Sciacchitano, February 1996.

Jones, Kay, interviews by Ronald Peters and Theresa Merrill, September 1995 and March 1996.

King, Charlotte, interview by Katherine Sciacchitano, February 1996.

Kingsley, Robert, interview by Katherine Sciacchitano, March 1996.

Lambiase, Carol, interview by Katherine Sciacchitano, February 1996.

Lis, Les, interview by Bruce Nissen, February 1996.

Love, Martha, interview by Katherine Sciacchitano, February 1996.

Lukehart, Jim, interview by Janet Lewis and Bill Mirand, November 1995.

Lund, James, interview by Ronald Peters and Theresa Merrill, September 1995.

Mangan, Martin, interview by Ronald Peters and Theresa Merrill, October 1995.

McCullough, Judith, interviews by Ruth Needleman, April 1995 and February 1996.

Medow, David, interviews by Ronald Peters and Theresa Merrill, October 1995 and December 1995.

Muhammad, Saladin, interview by Katherine Sciacchitano, February 1996.

Olson, Kurt, interview by Ronald Peters and Theresa Merrill, September 1995.

Pefianco-Thomas, Mila, interviews by Ruth Needleman, March 1995 and March 1996.

Pena, Al, interview by Bruce Nissen, January 1996.

Quigley, Michael, interview by Ronald Peters and Theresa Merrill, February 1996.

Regan, Larry, interview by Bruce Nissen, February 1996.

Rios, Dan, interview by Bruce Nissen, February 1996.

Robbins, Pamela, interview by Ronald Peters and Theresa Merrill, October 1995.

Rodriguez, Pat, interview by Bruce Nissen, September 1995.

Rouse, Michael, interview by Ronald Peters and Theresa Merrill, October 1996.

Sancho, Raquel, interview by Ruth Needleman, March 1995.

Sandoval, Ben, interview by Brian Condit, Tom Davis, Jeff Grabelsky, and Fred Kotler, February 1996.

Shin, Young, interview by Ruth Needleman, March 1995.

Staples, Bill, interview by Bruce Nissen, February 1996.

Steed, Judy, interview by Ronald Peters and Theresa Merrill, October 1995.

Strehlou, Sandy, interview by Ruth Needleman, March 1995.

Sufana, Eugene, interview by Bruce Nissen, September 1995.

Terus, Marsha, interview by Bruce Nissen, February 1996.

Volpp, Leti, interview by Ruth Needleman, March 1995.

Wilson, James, interview by Ronald Peters and Theresa Merrill, March 1996.

Wright, Robert, interview by Katherine Sciacchitano, February 1996.

Contributors

ADRIENNE M. BIRECREE is a professor of economics at Radford University. Birecree, who holds a Ph.D. in labor economics from the University of Notre Dame, has presented several papers on the importance of industrial restructuring to labor relations in the bituminous coal industry in the 1980s and 1990s and currently is working on a book about the evolution of the United Mine Workers during this period. Her publications include case studies on the effects of corporate restructuring on labor relations at the International Paper Company in the 1980s. Birecree's most current research concerns the nature and implications of restructuring in the Virginia system of higher education.

KATE BRONFENBRENNER is director of labor education research at the New York State School of Industrial and Labor Relations at Cornell University. Before assuming this position, she was an assistant professor at the Pennsylvania State University and worked as a union representative for the United Woodcutters Association and for the SEIU. Bronfenbrenner, who completed her Ph.D. at Cornell in 1993, is the author of several articles on union strategies in organizing and first-contract campaigns and on unions and the contingent workforce. She is the author, with Tom Juravich, of the book *Union Organizing in the Public Sector* and is currently completing a book with him on the history of the Steelworkers' victory at Ravenswood Aluminum.

LARRY COHEN is assistant to the president and director of organization for the Communications Workers of America. Cohen was also a founder of and has been actively involved in Jobs with Justice, a national workers rights coalition of labor and community organizations.

BRIAN CONDIT is a full-time organizer with the International Brotherhood of Electrical Workers, Local 611, in Albuquerque, New Mexico, a position he has held since 1993. He also served in this capacity from 1987 to 1990. A journeyman wireman and a twenty-two-year member of the local, Condit was president of Local 611 from 1987 to 1993, has served on the local's executive board, and is currently the president of the New Mexico Building Trades Council.

DAN CORNFIELD is a professor of sociology at Vanderbilt University and the editor of *Work and Occupations,* a sociological quarterly on work, employment, and labor. He received his Ph.D. in 1980 from the University of Chicago. Among his publications are "The U.S. Labor Movement: Its Development and Impact on

Social Inequality and Politics," in the *Annual Review of Sociology*, and "Socioeconomic Status and Unionization Attitudes in the United States," in *Social Forces*. He is currently chair of the Section on Organizations, Occupations, and Work of the American Sociological Association.

TOM DAVIS is a full-time organizer with the International Brotherhood of Electrical Workers, Local 611, in Albuquerque, New Mexico. After serving for four years in the U.S. Coast Guard, Davis completed a four-year apprenticeship with the IBEW Joint Apprenticeship and Training Committee and became a journeyman wireman in 1987. An activist in the local union, he has worked on the legislative committee and as a volunteer organizer.

DEAN EATMAN is a doctoral student in the sociology program at Vanderbilt University, where he received his M.A. degree in 1994. He has presented his research on religion and union activism, cultural consumption, and interfaith marriage at meetings of the Society for the Scientific Study of Religion, the Association for the Study of Religion, and the Southern Sociological Society.

CHRISTOPHER L. ERICKSON is an associate professor in the Human Resources and Organizational Behavior Area of the Anderson Graduate School of Management at the University of California at Los Angeles. He holds a Ph.D. in economics from MIT. Erickson's areas of specialty include labor relations in the U.S. aerospace industry and the labor market implications of economic integration. Currently, he is working on an analytical study of the relationship between labor standards and free trade agreements and on a comparative study of industrial relations system change.

JACK FIORITO is a professor of management at Florida State University. His research focuses primarily on the causes, consequences, and functioning of unions. Fiorito, who received his formal education in the Department of Economics and the Institute of Labor and Industrial Relations at the University of Illinois, has conducted several studies on workers' attitudes toward unions and on unions as organizations. He has published more than forty articles and chapters on these and other topics and coedited the 1991 Industrial Relations Research Association research annual, *The State of the Unions*.

BILL FLETCHER, JR., is director of the AFL-CIO's Education Department. Before taking this position in September 1996, he was the assistant to the president for the east and the south for the Service Employees International Union. He has also served as organizational secretary and administrative director of the National Postal Mail Handlers Union and as an organizer for District 65 of the United Automobile Workers. Fletcher got his start in the labor movement as a member of the Industrial Union of Marine and Shipbuilding Workers of America. He is the author of numerous articles and coauthor of *The Indispensable Ally: Black Workers and the Formation of the Congress of Industrial Organizations, 1934–41*.

SHELDON FRIEDMAN is an economist for the AFL-CIO. Before starting this position in 1991, he served for ten years as director of the UAW Research Department in Detroit. He began his labor movement career as a research associate for the UAW in 1975, after studying economics and industrial relations at MIT. Friedman coedited *Restoring the Promise of American Labor Law* and has published numerous articles in the fields of economics and industrial relations, including most recently, "First Contract Arbitration: The Canadian Experience." He has served on the executive board of the Industrial Relations Research Association.

FERNANDO GAPASIN is a faculty member at the University of California at Los Angeles at the Center for Labor Research and Education. He received his Ph.D. from the University of California at Santa Barbara. A member of the Amalgamated Transit Union, he has been a trade union activist for twenty-eight years and has served in a wide variety of union offices. His publications focus on issues of race, class, leadership, and education.

JEFF GRABELSKY is the director of Cornell University's Construction Industry Program. He received his M.A. from Syracuse University and his M.I.L.R. from Cornell University. Grabelsky worked as an IBEW construction electrician for fifteen years and is the author of the *COMET Trainers Manual.* He has also published numerous articles on construction unions, including "Lighting the Spark: COMET Program Mobilizes the Ranks of Construction Organizing" and "Steward Training in the Construction Industry: The UBCJA Faces the Challenge" Grabelsky served as co-editor of a *Labor Research Review* special issue, "Up Against the Open Shop—New Initiatives in the Building Trades."

RICHARD HURD is a professor and the director of labor studies at the New York State School of Industrial and Labor Relations at Cornell University. Since earning his Ph.D. in economics from Vanderbilt University, he has published numerous articles on issues related to union strategy, including organizing, political action, and alternatives to the strike. Hurd is the author of *The Assault on Workers' Rights,* "Reinventing an Organizing Union," and "Contesting the Dinosaur Image: The Labor Movement's Search for a Future," and a co-editor of *Restoring the Promise of American Labor Law.*

TOM JURAVICH is an associate professor and the director of the Labor Relations and Research Center at the University of Massachusetts at Amherst. He is the author of *Chaos on the Shop Floor: A Worker's View of Quality, Productivity and Management* and the coauthor of *Union Organizing in the Public Sector* and *Commonwealth of Toil: Chapters in the History of Massachusetts Workers and Their Unions* as well as numerous articles about union organizing, worker culture, employee involvement, and political action. Juravich, who holds a Ph.D. in sociology from the University of Massachusetts at Amherst, is completing a book with Kate Bronfenbrenner on the Steelworkers victory over the Ravenswood Aluminum Company. He is also a well-known singer and songwriter who has recorded several albums of labor and contemporary folk music.

Fred Kotler is the associate director of Cornell University's Construction Industry Program. He received a J.D. from the University of San Francisco in 1980. Before coming to Cornell, Kotler was the director of the Labor Education Program at Northern Michigan University and, before that, worked as a business agent and organizer. He is co-author of *COMET II—Worksite Organizing with COMET Activists* and frequently conducts training sessions on construction organizing and labor law.

JANET LEWIS received her J.D. from the University of Washington in 1996, specializing in labor and employment law. The first woman to successfully complete the four-year Puget Sound Electrical Apprentice Training Program for construction electricians, in 1978, Lewis owned and operated a unionized electrical contracting firm in Seattle from 1983 to 1993, after working as a construction electrician. She recently completed a six-month legal internship for the National Labor Relations Board, Region 19, in Seattle.

HOLLY J. MCCAMMON is an associate professor of sociology at Vanderbilt University. She received her Ph.D. from Indiana University in 1990 and has written a number of articles on the U.S. labor movement and labor law, including "Disorganizing and Reorganizing Conflict: Outcomes of the State's Legal Regulation of the Strike since the Wagner Act," in *Social Forces* and " 'Government by Injunction': The Role of the U.S. Judiciary in Managing Labor Militancy in the Late 19th and Early 20th Centuries," in *Work and Occupations*.

JOHN MCCLENDON is an associate professor of human resource administration in the School of Business and Management at Temple University. He received his Ph.D. from the University of South Carolina in 1989. His primary research interests include union organizing, individual members' strike behavior, pay systems, and union restructuring. His research articles have recently appeared in *Industrial and Labor Relations Review,* the *Journal of Labor Research,* and *Personnel Psychology.*

DARREN C. MCDANIEL is a doctoral student in the sociology program at Vanderbilt University. McDaniel, who received an M.A. in southern studies from the University of Mississippi in 1994, includes among his varied interests the social and cultural dimensions of the lives of southern working people, identity formation among professional musicians, ethnographic studies, and film documentaries.

THERESA MERRILL earned an M.A. degree in labor and industrial relations at the University of Illinois at Urbana-Champaign in 1996. She is now attending law school at the State University of New York at Buffalo and plans to pursue a career in labor law. During her two years at the institute of Labor and Industrial Relations at the University of Illinois, she conducted research on labor law and social topics for the Labor Education Program.

RUTH MILKMAN is a professor of sociology and women's studies at the University of California at Los Angeles. She holds a Ph.D. from the University of California at Berkeley. Her books include *Women, Work and Protest: A Century of U.S. Women's Labor History; Gender at Work: The Dynamics of Job Segregation by Sex during World War II; Japan's California Factories: Labor Relations and Economic Globalization;* and, most recently, *Farewell to the Factory: Auto Workers in the Late Twentieth Century.*

BILL MIRAND has served as the business manager and financial secretary of IBEW, Local 46, in Seattle since 1993. He earned an M.S.W. degree, with a focus on social welfare research and planning, from the State University of New York at Buffalo in 1978. Mirand is the appointed labor representative on the Washington State Apprenticeship and Training Council and currently serves as a labor trustee on the IBEW Pacific Coast Pension Fund. He is also the international IBEW delegate to the AFL-CIO Metal Trades Council and is a journey level inside wireman.

DANIEL J. B. MITCHELL is a professor at the Anderson Graduate School of Management at the University of California at Los Angeles, where he also holds a joint appointment with the School of Public Policy and Social Research. From 1979 to 1990, Dr. Mitchell was the director of UCLA's Institute of Industrial Relations. He is co-author of *Human Resource Management: An Economic Approach* and co-editor of *The Human Resource Handbook*.

GREGOR MURRAY is an associate professor in the Industrial Relations Department at Université Laval in Quebec City, Canada. He works with unions on structural and strategic questions and, in collaboration with one of the larger Quebec trade union centrals, is currently completing a two-phase study of local union presidents and their members. Murray, who holds a Ph.D. in industrial relations from Warwick University, is the author or editor of books and articles on various aspects of trade unionism, labor law, and industrial relations in Canada.

RUTH NEEDLEMAN is an associate professor of labor studies at Indiana University. Needleman, who received her Ph.D. from Harvard University, has worked for several unions, including for two years as SEIU's education director. She is currently coordinating a special college program for adult workers, Swingshift College. Her publications focus on race and gender issues in organizing and leadership development and include *Raising Visibility, Reducing Marginality: Labor Law Reform for Working Women of Color;* "Building an Organizing Culture of Unionism"; and "Women Workers: A Force for Rebuilding Unionism."

IMMANUEL NESS is an assistant professor of political science at Brooklyn College and at the Brooklyn College Graduate Center for Worker Education of the City University of New York. Ness, who received his Ph.D. from CUNY Graduate Center in political science, has written articles on trade union responses to unemployment, immigrants, and low-wage workers and is the author of *Trade Unions and the Unemployed: Organizing Strategies, Conflict and Control* and the coauthor of *The Book of World City Ranking: The Quality of Life and Work in Over 100 Urban Centers*. As a trade union organizer, Ness has successfully managed recognition, collective bargaining, and political action campaigns.

BRUCE NISSEN is program director at the Center for Labor Research and Studies at Florida International University in Miami. He has been a labor educator for sixteen years. He is the author of *Fighting for Jobs: Case Studies of Labor-Community Coalitions Confronting Plant Closings* and is co-editor of *Grand Designs: the Impact of Corporate Strategies on Workers, Unions, and Communities*.

RUDY OSWALD is an economist in residence at the George Meany Center for Labor Studies. A former director of economic research for the AFL-CIO, a position he held for twenty years, he has also served as research director for SEIU and for the International Association of Fire Fighters and on a number of government advisory committees. He is a past president of the Industrial Relations Research Association.

RONALD PETERS is a professor and the head of the labor education program at the Institute of Labor and Industrial Relations at the University of Illinois at Urbana-Champaign. He has conducted labor education programs throughout Illinois for the past twenty years and during that time has closely followed collective bargaining and union organizing struggles in the state.

JAMES RUNDLE is a labor educator at Cornell University. He has taught labor studies courses on contemporary labor issues, labor law, and labor history and has led workshops and seminars for union members in a variety of topics, including unions and employee-involvement programs, building solidarity in the local union, contract campaigns, civil rights in the workplace, and the North American Free Trade Agreement. He testified before the Senate Small Business Committee in a hearing on the TEAM Act in 1996. The following year Rundle served as a fellow with the Senate Labor and Human Resources Committee staff of Senator Edward M. Kennedy.

KATHERINE SCIACCHITANO is an assistant professor at the School for Workers of the University of Wisconsin. She has served as an attorney with the National Labor Relations Board, as a staff representative for the American Federation of State, County, and Municipal Employees, and as deputy director of the United Mine Workers Organizing Department. She received her J.D. from the Catholic University of America.

RONALD L. SEEBER is an associate professor and the associate dean of the New York State School of Industrial and Labor Relations at Cornell University. Seeber's research activities have covered a wide range of topics, including the impact of technological change on labor relations in the arts and entertainment industry, drug testing in the workplace, and union organizing strategies. The author or editor of six books, he has also been published extensively in academic journals and in the proceedings of the Industrial Relations Research Association. Seeber received his Ph.D. from the University of Illinois.

LOWELL TURNER is an associate professor in the New York State School of Industrial and Labor Relations at Cornell University. He is the author of *Democracy at Work: Changing World Markets and the Future of Labor Unions* as well as numerous articles and book chapters on European, German, and American industrial relations. Before pursuing an academic career, Turner served as shop steward, chief steward, and branch editor for the National Association of Letter Carriers, Branch 214, in San Francisco. Turner received his Ph.D. from the University of California at Berkeley.

ABEL VALENZUELA, JR., is an assistant professor in the Cesar Chavez Center and the Department of Urban Planning in the School of Public Policy and Social Research at the University of California at Los Angeles. Valenzuela's research focuses on the misfortunes of urban minority groups in labor markets and impoverished communities. He teaches courses on immigration and U.S. society, urban poverty and public policy, and urban labor markets. He is currently investigating the labor market processes of day laborers in Los Angeles who congregate at street corners to solicit temporary work. He earned his M.C.P. and Ph.D. from MIT in urban and regional studies.

ROGER WALDINGER is a professor of sociology and the director of the Lewis Center for Regional Policy Studies at the University of California at Los Angeles. He received his Ph.D. from Harvard University. He is the author of more than fifty articles or book chapters on immigration, ethnic entrepreneurship, and urban change as well as four books, most recently, *Still the Promised City? New Immigrants and African-Americans in Post-Industrial New York,* and *Ethnic Los Angeles* (edited with Mehdi Bozorgmehr), winner of the 1997 Thomas and Zhaniecki Award for the best book in the field of international migration.

ROGER D. WEIKLE is a professor of industrial relations and the dean of the College of Business Administration at Winthrop University, where he teaches labor relations, employment law, and general human resource management courses. He holds an M.B.A. from Marshall University and a Ph.D. from the University of South Carolina. His research focuses on legal issues, negotiations, adjustment to technological change, and organizing. He serves on the South Carolina Department of Labor Arbitration Panel and is associated with the Expedited Arbitration Panel for the United Steelworkers and the canning industry.

HOYT N. WHEELER is a professor and Distinguished Foundation Fellow in the College of Business Administration at the University of South Carolina. The author of books on industrial conflict and workplace justice, he has also practiced law and is a member of the National Academy of Arbitrators. Wheeler holds a J.D. from the University of Virginia and a Ph.D. in industrial relations from the University of Wisconsin. He was the 1996 national president of the Industrial Relations Research Association.

HOWARD WIAL is an assistant professor of labor studies and industrial relations at the Pennsylvania State University. He holds a Ph.D. in economics from MIT and a J.D. from Yale Law School. Wial is the author or coauthor of several articles on industrial relations, labor law, and labor markets, including "The Emerging Organizational Structure of Unionism in Low-Wage Services," in *Rutgers Law Review,* and "Is Job Stability Declining in the U.S. Economy?" in *Industrial and Labor Relations Review.*

KENT WONG is director of the Center for Labor Research and Education at the School of Public Policy and Social Research at the University of California at Los Angeles, where he teaches labor studies and ethnic studies. He also directs UCLA's labor studies program. Before joining UCLA, Wong worked as staff attorney for SEIU and as staff attorney for the Asian Pacific American Legal Center of Southern California. Wong is founder and national president of the Asian Pacific American Labor Alliance, AFL-CIO, the first national organization of Asian American unionists. Wong received his J.D. from the People's College of Law in Los Angeles.

ANGELA YOUNG is an assistant professor of business at California State University at Los Angeles. She holds a Ph.D. from Florida State University and an M.B.A. from California State University at Sacramento. Before pursuing the Ph.D., Young provided computer training to workers at Sacramento-area companies. Her current research interests include mentoring, organizational relationships, and the perceptions of equity in the workplace.

MAURICE ZEITLIN is a professor of sociology at the University of California at Los Angeles. He received his Ph.D. from the University of California at Berkeley. His books include *Revolutionary Politics and the Cuban Working Class, Insurgent Workers: Studies of the Orgins of Industrial Unionism in the U.S., The Large Corporation and Contemporary Classes,* and (with J. Stepan Norris) *Talking Union.*

Index